CASES IN
CORPORATE FINANCE

CASES IN
CORPORATE FINANCE

by

Elroy DIMSON
and
Paul MARSH

London Business School

JOHN WILEY & SONS
Chichester · New York · Brisbane · Toronto · Singapore

Library of Congress Cataloging-in-Publication Data:

Dimson, Elroy, 1947—
  Cases in corporate finance.

  Includes index.
  1. Corporations-Finance-Case studies.
I. Marsh, Paul (Paul R.) II. Title
HG4015.5.D56 1988   658.1′5   87-6299

ISBN 0 471 91764 8
ISBN 0 471 91596 3 (pbk.)

British Library Cataloguing in Publication Data:

Dimson, Elroy
  Cases in corporate finance.
  1. Corporations—Finace—Case studies
  I. Title   II. Marsh, Paul
  658.1′5′0722   HG4015.5

ISBN 0 471 91764 8
ISBN 0 471 91596 3 (pbk.)

Typeset by Quadra Associates Ltd, Oxford
Printed and bound in Great Britain by
Courier International Ltd, Tipree, Essex

Contents

Topic Index

To identify suitable cases on a particular topic, use the index below. For each topic, the most strongly recommended cases are shown in bold, others are shown in lighter type while the more peripheral cases are shown in italics. Cases are identified by their case numbers (see **Contents**). For additional information, read the **Case Abstracts** (pp. xvi–xxiv) and the suggested **Case Questions** (pp. 399–412).

This book is dedicated to our wives, Helen and Steff.

Introduction

In recent years, the jobs of the finance director and corporate treasurer have undergone radical and far-reaching changes. Companies have had to make complicated decisions about where and how to invest, and where and how to fund the firm's activities. In doing this, they have had to choose between the vast array of new financial instruments and techniques which have evolved over the last 10 years or so. At the same time, organizations have become increasingly aware of the broader contribution of financial policy to their profitability. The greater sophistication of financial markets, the growth of share ownership and the threat of acquisition have all concentrated the minds of senior executives and board members on the need for effective financial decision-making within their firms.

An understanding of the principles of finance has also become particularly important for the general manager and non-financial specialist. These are the people who make the key decisions that ultimately create corporate wealth, and increasingly they are being called upon to communicate in the language of finance. Consequently, business people have a far greater desire than ever before to be familiar with the principles of investment decision-making and financial planning. A good manager can no longer afford to plead ignorance about finance.

The growth in the importance of the finance function has coincided with related developments within the academic world. During this period, the field of finance has grown from a backwater of economics into a major subject in its own right. Over 200 scholarly journals have emerged to disseminate the work of researchers in finance, and they have been joined by a similar number of publishing houses. Rapidly, new theory and evidence has come to offer a cohesive and coherent view of how capital markets operate, and of how company finances should best be managed. This body of knowledge has been, and is being, communicated to a wide audience through courses taught at business schools throughout North America, Europe and elsewhere.

Finance has, in fact, become the favoured discipline in many of the world's leading business schools. Up to half the MBA graduates of many schools take jobs in the finance function. Leading financial institutions compete to offer lucrative jobs to PhD graduates in finance. And more executives seek to extend their skills in financial management than in any other functional area. Finance has a major, and a still increasing, impact on both practice and practitioners.

Cases in finance

The interest of managers and students in finance is not surprising. Financial economics provides a rich body of theory and supporting empirical work, with important implications for the way company finances should be managed. The subject is taught at hundreds of business schools, universities and colleges with the object of training students to use a knowledge of finance in a business environment.

However, it often seems as though the simplifications of financial theory are inconsistent with the complexities of the real world. A wealth of analysis is therefore difficult to apply, and even more difficult to implement. Thus there is a danger that students will complete a course well trained in techniques, but not capable of applying their knowledge to real financial decision-making.

Our view is that improved financial practice will always tend to emerge from the juxtaposition of good theory and the grounded analysis of real world financial problems. New and better theory can only be developed by observing the conflict between current theory and current practice. Theory and practice are thus complementary: we cannot fully understand either without studying the other.

This is where case studies have a crucial role to play, for they help us to focus on applying and testing the theory of finance in real decision situations. Yet in spite of this, there is a paucity of good cases focusing on financial issues, especially in a European context. This is a need which we have tried to meet with the collection of cases presented here.

Orientation of the cases

Each of our case studies reports on a business situation and its background. Usually the case is left open at a critical point when an important decision is to be taken within the organization. The available options are influenced by the product and capital market contexts, by the internal organizational context, and by earlier decisions which were taken by the organization; where relevant, these are all described.

The cases are not exercises; they have not been devised in order to illustrate a technique; they cannot be solved by plugging in a formula. Instead, they provide information which was available at the time to decision-makers within an organization. The information is sometimes hard, numerical, explicit, and relatively unambiguous; but at other times it is soft, qualitative, implicit, and subject to interpretation. In all cases, however, sufficient evidence is available for the reader to analyse alternatives and reach a conclusion.

Because the cases represent real problems, only rarely are they confined to applications of finance. Usually they involve other disciplines and functions. Several case studies require a comprehension of financial accounting, management accounting or control; others deal with relationships with government, with legal or regulatory issues, with marketing strategy or broader questions of business policy. And since they involve issues of implementation, many cases raise questions related to individual behaviour, organizational design and the management of change. Finally, once a case 'solution' has been developed, articulating the analysis will require skills of presentation, advocacy and, sometimes, negotiation.

Yet despite their breadth, these case studies are quite definitely focused on issues in corporate finance. They deal with topics such as capital budgeting; the cost of capital; performance measurement; project and company valuation; new issues; mergers, acquisitions and divestment; financing decisions; dividend policy; capital structure; bank lending; leasing; convertible, warrant and bond valuation; international finance; and short-term and long-term financial planning. The topics covered are varied and comprehensive.

Our cases do have a common attribute, however, in that like most other 'true' case studies in this and other subject areas, they have no single correct solution. There may, of course, be many incorrect solutions! Indeed, one important role of cases and case teachers is to help students learn to spot flawed arguments, eliminate some 'wrong' answers, and devote effort to choosing between alternative worthwhile courses of action.

Intended readership

Most of the cases were originally written for use by MBA and executive students at the London Business School. Our MBA students typically have between 3 and 15 years business experience before starting the programme. The executive programme participants are either taking a general management course or a specialist course in corporate finance, and thus generally have even greater relevant experience.

We have therefore had substantial opportunities to teach the cases to students who have experience in management, but who often have only a rudimentary prior knowledge of finance. Equally, we have taught students who are finance specialists, and who are working either in financial institutions or within manufacturing or service organizations. These two groups constitute the primary target audience for this book.

In addition, many of the cases may be read enjoyably (and instructively) as documents which are of interest in their own right. The cases provide an insight into how financial decisions are made in a variety of organizational settings. These settings include the public as well as the private sector; small enterprises as well as large organizations; both successful and failing firms; both manufacturing and service industries; and both high and low technology businesses. Specific situations of particular interest to the general reader include a record of how a major rationalization was achieved in the country's largest health authority; an acquisition which was the biggest to date in the United Kingdom; the first flotation on the Unlisted Securities Market (USM); a valuation exercise which rocked the Irish parliament; the first issue of sterling zero-coupon bonds; Europe's largest-ever privatization; the start-up of England's smallest international airline; a warrant issue which dominated the London warrant market; the legal case against a nationalized industry's monopoly pricing; and the most celebrated rights offering in history.

Design of the book

We have divided the book into eight parts. The parts have been structured to correspond to the topics covered in the leading MBA-level textbooks in corporate finance. Any such grouping is necessarily subjective, however, and since every case has many facets it is likely that many instructors will pick a selection that is unique to their course.

The case studies in Part A focus on the area of investment appraisal. This section starts with a relatively straightforward capital budgeting decision, and progresses through more complex problems in project evaluation. Successive cases rely increasingly on judgemental considerations in addition to quantitative analysis; and the final study deals with the complex process of capital expenditure planning in the public sector.

Part B turns to determination of the cost of capital. Cases here deal with required rates of return for risky investment, as well as for divisional performance measurement. The first case deals with setting target rates for new projects and for existing divisions; the second deals with the use of inflation-adjusted accounts for allocating funds and for forward planning in general; and the last deals with allowable rates of return for regulated (nationalized) industries, and how these targets relate to pricing policy.

Part C contains three problems in company valuation. The first case is a classic in which a fair price is to be established for an Irish lead/zinc mine. Each of the two other cases involves valuing a new business which is to be floated before having achieved a track record. In addition to the financial projections, extensive market research and ancillary data are presented.

More complex valuation problems are encountered in Part D, which focuses on acquisition and divestment decisions. These decisions include a merger, a contested acquisition and a divisional sell-off, and the companies vary in size from a purely domestic operation to major multinationals. Despite the wealth of data available about these well-established companies, valuation is difficult and acquisition/defence strategies are problematic.

In Part E we move from investment to financing decisions. This section consists of three very different cases. One deals with the timing, terms and procedures used in a celebrated rights offering of equity; the next focuses on the capital structure chosen for a public utility which was being prepared for privatization; and the final case deals with bank financing of a business which was the subject of a management buyout.

Every financing decision raises questions about how the ensuing corporate liabilities are to be valued. Part F concentrates on the valuation of a number of financial instruments. The initial case, which is overtly about an issue of zero-coupon bonds, puts the choice of financing method in the context of treasury management, financial strategy and debt policy. Other cases focus on setting the terms of financial leases; on the valuation of a (government) loan guarantee; and on the pricing of warrants, executive options and other contracts.

Part G is on international finance. In the first case, an exporting company, which is exposed to foreign exchange risk, has to decide on whether and how to hedge. The second case is more complex in that it deals with a company whose economic exposure must be determined before it can decide on methods of currency protection. The last case deals with the financing strategy of a multinational during a period when the company emphasized overseas growth, currency protection and offshore financing.

The book is concluded in Part H with three cases on corporate financial planning. Short-term financial management is emphasized in a case study about a distressed company acquired by a turnaround specialist. The next case deals with a successful company that needs to reassess its cash flow position after a period of difficult trading. The final case examines the long-term financial strategy followed by a company whose unceasing quest for growth eventually led to corporate collapse: an underlying question is whether bad luck or poor financial planning was to blame.

Using the casebook

It must be obvious that many of our case studies could, in fact, be reallocated to another part of the book. We encourage users of the collection to regard our grouping as no more than an imperfect attempt to make the choice of case easier. However, our personal judgements cannot take the place of careful case selection by an informed instructor. Our guidance on using this casebook is, therefore, addressed first to the finance teacher who may use this volume.

To help the reader select the most appropriate cases, we have included in the book three sets of reference material. First, the **Case Abstracts** provide a one-paragraph overview of each case study. Each abstract briefly summarizes the events experienced within the organization and the situations in which management finds itself. The abstract also indicates some of the issues which need to be resolved. Where appropriate, the existence of a follow-up case is identified for those who are interested in subsequent events.

Second, the **Case Questions** at the end of the book provide an additional pointer to the issues raised in the case studies. The questions focus on various aspects of each case, though they are far from exhaustive. Purists who prefer to read each case unfettered by a list of questions should ignore this section. Conversely, some teachers may wish to provide more detailed guidance to students than is contained within our list of questions. When a more detailed assignment is to be formulated, the Instructor's Guide (see below) may be helpful.

Third, the **Topic Index** is provided as a means of identifying the topics raised within each case. For each topic, we list the cases which are most strongly recommended (in bold face) as well as others which also incorporate significant coverage of the topic (in lighter type). More peripheral cases are also listed (in italic). The Index may be used to ensure that, regardless of the particular course, cases are selected which cover most or all of the syllabus. In the Topic Index, cases are referred to by their chapter number, as in the Case Abstracts and Case Questions.

We also have some observations which might be helpful for the student user of this book. Our cases have been developed to extend students' analytical and diagnostic skills beyond what may be learned from textbooks and lecturers. Cases include only such information as was available to managers at the time; yet there is enough data within each case to develop proposals which are supported by analysis and reasoned argument. Though they do not necessarily contain every relevant fact, often more material is assembled within the case than was readily available in a structured and orderly format to the decision-maker. Consequently, demands for 'more information' will rarely receive a sympathetic hearing from the instructor. Similarly, an objection that a story is 'incomplete' will not usually be received with warmth: complete 'case histories', which follow a situation through to its final outcome, are often of limited use in a case-teaching context.

The cases in this book expose students to an extremely wide range of financial problems. The benefit from discussing them will depend on how thoroughly they have been prepared and on each student's willingness to contribute actively to class discussion. In analysing a case, students should read and reread the document carefully; it will not be possible to dig deeply into the case unless it has been fully absorbed. Readers should continually look for problems and alternative responses to them. They should not accept at face value opinions expressed in the case, but instead question the views, analyses and decisions described there. If there is a need to use an unfamiliar technique to analyse the case, it will be necessary to refer to the relevant textbook. Once a student moves on to developing a preferred option, it is essential for him or her to keep in mind that cases demand practical, implementable and well-defined solutions. Waffle, generalities and abstractions are to be avoided.

During class discussion, each student should be prepared to contribute a terse but fluent record of his or her recommendations and of their rationale. They should listen to and build on the suggestions made by other participants; but each student must also seek to convince the rest of the class of his or her point of view, despite the fact that others will have different, though equally well-researched, suggestions. The instructor may guide the discussion and put right errors and omissions, but the detailed nature and content of the class session will often be determined by students. When appropriate, the instructor may conclude the session by highlighting what the class has learned from the case. If he or she also indicates what subsequently happened, the student should not take this too seriously, for the task was not to predict the future but to analyse the situation given in the case.

Finally, for teachers only, an **Instructor's Guide** is available on written request to the authors. The guide contains teaching notes, specimen case analyses, follow-up case studies and other material which may be helpful to the instructor. It is not available to students or other readers of this case book.

ACKNOWLEDGEMENTS

The cases in this collection have been taught by us and our co-authors at London Business School and at leading business schools and universities in Europe and North America. We are grateful to the many colleagues who have given valuable comments to us on the cases, and we warmly encourage other users to provide us with further feedback.

Case-writing is a time-consuming and difficult task, and we wish to express particular appreciation to those who have contributed cases to this volume or who have co-authored case studies with us. They are Dick Brealey, Julie Fedorko, Stewart Hodges, Evi Kaplanis, Ewan Labrom, Antonio Mello, Anthony Neuberger, Pamela Pocock, Stuart Slatter, Jennifer Smerdon and Mike Staunton. Others who have assisted us or who have helped with earlier drafts of the cases include Paul Arwas, Patrick Barwise, Ian Cooper, Julian Franks, Robert Porter, Cecilia Reyes, Nicholas Walker and Robin Wensley. Each of these individuals is also acknowledged on the front page of the appropriate case.

In addition to thanking our colleagues at London Business School for encouraging us in the development of this collection, we are especially grateful to the organizations and individuals who are the subjects of our cases. All financial data have been reproduced with the kind permission of the companies concerned, although we remain responsible for any errors. Readers should note that our cases describe the companies at a particular point in time, and that there will, of course, have been subsequent changes in both the companies' activities and policies.

Finally, we want to record our appreciation to our secretaries, Gaye Gresham and Anitra Hume-Wright, for their painstaking effort and dedication in typing numerous drafts of each case.

Case Abstracts

PART A: INVESTMENT APPRAISAL

1. United Metal

This case is loosely based on a make-versus-buy decision faced by Standard Telephones and Cables (STC) Components Group (alias United Metal). Switching over from manufacturing to purchasing a particular component will affect costs, have personnel implications, free up a recently purchased machine, require some additional capital expenditure, and alter the amount of stock held, and hence the space required. Internally, there is a debate between the purchasing and production managers about the importance and relevance of these various issues. Judgements are needed on which manager is correct, and what decision United Metal should take.

2. Lee Valley Water Company

In 1981, Lee Valley Water Company (LVWC) gave customers the choice of installing a meter and being charged directly for water (and sewerage services) used, rather than continuing to charge according to the rateable value of the property. This case provides data on LVWC's area of supply, household water usage, the alternative charging systems, and the capital costs of meter installation. The key issue for customers is the economics of installing a meter. For LVWC, the question is how many customers will install meters, and how this impacts on LVWC's revenues. The wider policy issue for the water industry is the merits of alternative charging methods.

3. Dane Carter International

A French subsidiary within Dane Carter packaging division has put up a proposal to produce containers for the Egyptian pharmaceutical market. The containers would be made by using capacity on existing injection blow-moulding machines, although capital expenditure is required for new moulds. The project is thus typical of many others in this division. Jonathan Long, a head office financial analyst, has to decide whether to sanction this project. He is concerned, however, about the subsidiary's low profitability and disappointing returns from past projects. On investigating matters further, he is wondering whether changes are required in the way projects of this kind are evaluated.

4. Guinness Hop Farms

Guinness Hop Farms grows hops for use in beer-making. One of their farms is afflicted by a hop-killing disease, wilt, although so far, some of their hop gardens are only slightly infected. Diseased areas can be replanted with new, higher yielding, wilt-tolerant hops, but only after 2 years 'grassing down'. A series of replacement decisions has to be made about when each garden should be replanted. These in turn depend upon the extent of infection, the speed it is spreading, the relative yields of the old and new varieties, hop prices, the lives of the gardens, and the cost of replanting.

5. Bloomsbury Health Authority

The Bloomsbury Health Authority is considering proposals to combine the obstetrics units of University College (UCH) and Middlesex Hospitals into a single unit at UCH. While capital spending will be required, the rationalization frees up much needed space at the Middlesex, and brings operating cost savings. These in turn could 'finance' equipment and ward accommodation quality improvements, although there is a potential tradeoff here with the size of the new unit, which has implications for the catchment area served, and teaching requirements. This case describes the alternatives, the tradeoffs, the analysis, the assumptions, and the qualitative factors involved. It outlines the positions taken by the various parties, the criteria employed, and the way the decision-making process evolved over time.

PART B: COST OF CAPITAL AND PERFORMANCE MEASUREMENT

6. Norcros

This case describes the history of Norcros, a diversified holding company, and the activities of its various divisions and businesses, which operate in the construction, consumer products, engineering, and printing and packaging industries. The case outlines the company's corporate financial strategy and techniques, and its method of charging divisions for the use of assets. The principal focus is on senior management's concern over how to set hurdle rates for new capital projects, how to set rate of return targets for their different businesses, and how to ensure consistency between these rates and targets, and their existing method of charging for the use of assets.

7. Chandler Group

This large diversified engineering company (identity disguised), currently produces inflation-adjusted (current cost) accounts for external reporting purposes. The Finance Director is now suggesting extending their usage to divisional performance measurement, to forecasting and forward planning, and for use in allocating capital between divisions. This case outlines Chandler's current system for making inflation adjustments according to accounting standard SSAP16, their proposed model for extending this for use in forward planning, and the objections raised to this by senior divisional managers and the Chief Executive. The dilemma facing the Finance Director is how to respond to the criticisms, and whether to implement the new system.

8. British Airports Authority

In 1981, 19 airlines using Heathrow airport started High Court proceedings against the British Airports Authority (BAA), claiming that following recent price increases, airport user charges were excessive. They alleged that BAA was abusing its monopoly position, and earning an excessive rate of return at Heathrow. This case outlines the airlines' arguments and case against BAA, and BAA's defence and response. A key issue is how financial and operating targets, and required rates of return are (and should be) set for nationalized industries such as BAA, and how these targets relate to pricing policy. This case lends itself to a debate and/or to a prosecution-versus-defence role-play.

PART C: COMPANY VALUATION

9. Bula Mines (A)

Bula, a privately owned company, was set up to exploit a deposit of zinc and lead ore in the Republic of Ireland. The Irish government arranged to purchase part of the equity, and set up an arbitration panel to value the shares. This case describes the background to Bula, and the Irish government's involvement. It provides technical data on estimated ore reserves, metal prices, and the capital and operating costs involved in mining. The key issue is to evaluate Bula, and establish a fair price for its shares. *Bula Mines (B)* (available in the Instructor's Guide) describes the approaches adopted, and the valuations obtained by the various expert advisers to both Bula and the Irish government.

10. London European Airways (LEA)

LEA was set up by two entrepreneurs to offer scheduled services between Luton airport and major European cities. LEA obtained a licence for Luton–Amsterdam, and was planning to sell shares on the over-the-counter market to raise the necessary finance to begin operations. The case provides information on the proposed service and aircraft; the airport; LEA's market research; the competition and pricing; the background of the LEA directors; LEA's operating plans and financial projections; and the company's overall strategy and future plans. The immediate question facing the directors is how many new shares to issue, and at what price.

11. Hesketh Motorcycles

By mid-1980, Lord Hesketh's company, Hesketh Motorcycles (HM) had developed a new high performance, high capacity motorcycle ('superbike'). HM needed further finance to launch the superbike, and a venture capitalist had suggested selling shares to the public, thus making HM the first company to be offered on the Stock Exchange's new Unlisted Securities Market. This case describes the company and its background; its management; the planned product range; the market for superbikes; the competition; HM's market research; its production, marketing, pricing, and distribution plans; and HM's balance sheet and financial projections. Based on this information, the terms of the issue now have to be finalized.

PART D: ACQUISITION AND DIVESTMENT

12. Thorn-EMI (A)

In October 1979, Thorn Electrical Industries, an engineering, electrical and TV rental company, made a bid for the troubled music, electronics and leisure company, EMI. This case describes the history and business of each company, together with the reasons for EMI's demise. It outlines Thorn's strategy after Sir Richard Cave took over as Chairman, and how this led to the search for a suitable acquisition. EMI was a potential target, and Thorn's interest was brought to a head when EMI put its defence electronics business up for sale. Thorn reassessed the commercial logic of acquiring EMI, decided to bid, and settled on the price. The case ends with the bid announcement. Judgements are needed, from both Thorn and EMI's perspectives on the logic of the bid, the bid price, and future tactics and strategy. *Thorn-EMI (B)* (available in the Instructor's Guide) describes EMI's and the market's reaction to the bid, and the events which took place before the merger was finally consummated; *Thorn-EMI (C)* (also in the Instructor's Guide) documents the post-acquisition history up to Sir Richard Cave's retirement in 1984.

13. Hanson Trust

In 1985, Hanson Trust, an industrial conglomerate, announced a £1.9 billion bid for Imperial Group, making this the UK's largest acquisition offer to date.

Only 4 days before, Imperial Group, a cigarette, food, brewing and leisure company, had itself announced an agreed bid for biscuit manufacturer, United Biscuits. This case describes the three players, Hanson Trust, Imperial Group and United Biscuits, and their businesses and strategies. It also describes the initial two bids, the stated rationales, their subsequent progress, and the details of a subsequent counterbid for Imperial Group made by United Biscuits. Judgements are required about the synergy and commercial logic of each bid, the prices offered, and the acquisition (and defence) strategies and tactics of the three players and their advisers.

14. Anglian Canners

Anglian Canners is a small manufacturer of canned food products which are distributed throughout the United Kingdom. It is owned by Amalgamated Manufacturing, a large US multinational, which was considering divesting Anglian, since it was a misfit within their structure. This case describes Anglian's manufacturing facilities, employees and management, product lines and markets, competition, marketing policies, past financial performance and future plans. It also presents a set of future financial projections which Anglian have prepared at the request of Amalgamated. The principal question for Amalgamated is whether to divest, and if so, what price they can expect to obtain.

PART E: FINANCING DECISIONS

15. Commercial Union Assurance

In the depths of the 1974 bear market, Commercial Union (CU) surprised the financial community by announcing a large equity rights issue, thus flying in the face of conventional wisdom. This case outlines the background to, and reasons for, the issue, and describes the reception it received in the market-place and press. The obvious issues raised are whether this reception was justified; the wisdom of CU's decision versus possible alternative options; and the importance of timing, issue terms and underwriting in this situation, and in rights issues generally.

16. British Telecom (BT)

BT's privatization in 1984 was the largest share offering ever made. This case describes the background to, reasons for, and steps taken to prepare BT for privatization. The focus is on the debate between BT and the Government on what BT's capital structure should be. This, in turn, was influenced by a parallel debate on regulation and competition policy, by BT's massive capital spending programme, and by dividend policy considerations. The case concludes in April 1984 just prior to the final decision on capital structure. Although the flotation was still 7 months away, the case inevitably raises questions about dividend policy and the pricing and marketing of the shares, as well as about capital structure.

17. Williams (Hot Stampers) (A)

Williams Hot Stampers (A), a subsidiary of Caversham Holdings, manufactures brass stampings and associated non-ferrous products. In 1980–81, its market collapsed, and although savings were achieved through redundancies, and through rationalizing manufacturing onto a single site, the situation remained serious. Caversham therefore decided to sell Williams, and suggested a management buyout to David White, its Managing Director. This case describes the company's business, the background to the buyout, and the proposed terms. For David White, the key issue is to obtain suitable financing for the company. He has therefore approached two banks, armed with financial projections and information on business prospects. *Williams (Hot Stampers) (B)* (available in the Instructor's Guide) traces the subsequent history of the company up to a subsequent refinancing operation.

PART F: VALUATION OF CORPORATE LIABILITIES

18. Redland

In 1985, Redland, a building materials and roofing tile company, made an innovative financing move by issuing a zero coupon Eurosterling bond. This case outlines the background to, and rationale for, the issue, and sets this in the context of treasury management, financial strategy and borrowing policy within Redland. There is a detailed description of how the issue terms were set, and the case ends at the point where only the price has yet to be finalized. Apart from the obvious valuation problem, the case raises interesting questions about the costs of alternative sources of finance to Redland, and about Redland's gearing and debt policy.

19. Oasis Lines

Two fictitious shipping companies, of which Oasis Lines is one, are attempting to negotiate leasing arrangements for a small fleet of ships. They have approached three potential lessors, who have been asked to respond with sealed tenders stating their terms. This case is designed to be conducted as a role-playing financial negotiating exercise, although it can also be used as a straightforward lease evaluation case.

20. ICL

In March 1981, the government announced that it would assist the troubled British computer manufacturer, ICL, by guaranteeing £200 million of new borrowing for 2 years. This case describes the background to ICL's financially distressed state, the reasons why the government acted, the rationale for intervening through a loan guarantee, and the terms of the guarantee. It documents commentators' views on the government's action and the value of the loan guarantee, including one suggestion that the guarantee could explicitly be valued using option theory. In addition to this valuation question, the case raises broader issues about the merits and appropriate form of government intervention in key sectors.

21. National Westminster Bank

By the late 1970s, National Westminster Bank's financing policies and share issues had produced an interesting and instructive balance sheet which provided examples of most of the important methods used by listed companies for raising finance. This case focuses on three of the Bank's more interesting and 'option-like' issues, namely loan stock with warrants attached; a savings-related, employee-share option scheme; and an underwritten rights issue of equity. These particular issues all pose interesting valuation problems. More generally, however, the case raises questions about the types of companies and circumstances which might favour the use of option-like instruments of this kind.

PART G: INTERNATIONAL FINANCE

22. Svenska Neuhaus

This Swedish high technology company (identity and country disguised) has won a bid to install a control system for a UK chemical plant. A payment of £4 million is due in 3 months' time. Svenska's senior management are concerned about exchange risk, and are discussing with their bankers whether to hedge their exposure. Hedging could be achieved using the forward market, the money market, or via the Deutschmark. In the latter case, they could hedge using currency futures or options. This case provides data on interest rates, spot and forward exchange rates, and currency option and futures prices. Svenska need to decide whether to hedge, and if so, how.

23. Hallgarten Wines

This is a prominent UK wine importer, specializing in German and French wines. Wine is purchased for forward delivery, as well as in the spot market. Transactions are denominated in Deutschmarks or francs, and payment made when the wine clears the bonded warehouse, where it can remain for up to a year. Hallgarten promotes its wines through an extensive, illustrated price list, reprinted annually. Once the price list is fixed, Hallgarten is exposed to adverse wine price fluctuations. Exchange rate variability is a particular concern here. Hallgarten are looking at alternative methods of managing and hedging their exposure, perhaps using currency options and futures. But first they need to decide just how exposed they are.

24. Cadbury Schweppes

In March 1985, Cadbury Schweppes (CS) announced an $80 million convertible Eurobond issue. This was the culmination of a series of major financing decisions, including the rights issue in 1981, the launch of its US commercial paper programme in 1983, the American listing and American Depository Receipt issue in 1984, and the series of swap transactions used to restructure its debt. This case describes these various decisions, focusing particularly on the reasons for and negotiations surrounding the convertible Eurobond issue. Detailed information is provided on Cadbury Schweppes' business and financial strategy, and on the key but changing role of treasury management, during a period when CS placed great emphasis on overseas growth, currency exposure management, and the use of overseas and international financial markets.

PART H: FINANCIAL PLANNING

25. Precision Engineering (A)

Precision Engineering (PE) is a small company undertaking medium/heavy precision engineering subcontract work for the metal processing industries. In April 1982, after two years of losses, PE was acquired by new owners, who specialized in turnarounds. Despite considerable progress, PE faced a cash flow problem in November 1982, and was seeking £250 000 from the Industrial and Commercial Finance Corporation (ICFC). This case describes the company, its activities and product lines; its markets and competition; its directors, management and organization; its recent performance; and the proposal to ICFC outlining future plans and expected financial performance. An assessment is required of PE's short (and longer) term financial projections, prospects, and financing requirements. *Precision Engineering (B)* (available in the Instructor's Guide) outlines the subsequent history of the company.

26. Wallis Fashion Group

Wallis Fashion Group (WFG) is a vertically integrated women's wear manufacturing and retailing business. It grew rapidly during the 1970s, opening many new outlets, and in 1978, was one of the Stock Market's star performers. In July 1979, WFG had to decide on the year's final dividend. They had previously indicated there would be a dividend increase, and yet business had recently turned down. There had been unseasonably bad weather, serious misjudgements about fashions, and an increase in Value Added Tax which squeezed margins. A decision was required on the dividend, which in turn required an assessment of the company's cash flow position.

27. Burmah Oil

In December 1974, Burmah Oil faced serious cash flow problems, and was in default on one of its loans. This necessitated a major and highly controversial rescue by the Bank of England. This case outlines Burmah's history, particularly since the 1962 strategy review, which heralded a decade of expansion into specialty oils, refining, retailing, industrial products, engineering, tankers, terminals, and exploration. It documents the fall in Burmah's fortunes in 1973–74, and the Bank of England's rescue. The case raises a wide range of issues in corporate financial management, including gearing, dividend policy, strategic investment decisions, vertical integration, acquisitions, the link between strategic and long-term financial planning, financing policy, financial distress, company valuation, and stock market efficiency. An underlying question is whether Burmah was just unlucky, or was poor financial planning to blame?

PART A

INVESTMENT APPRAISAL

1. United Metal

Just over a year ago, United Metal purchased new machinery for £45 000 for use in the manufacture of a particular component. The total direct manufacturing costs for these components are £50 000 per year with raw materials costing a further £40 000. The current level of output is some 100 000 items per year. United expect to continue making the final product in which these components are incorporated for another 8 years.

Amalgamated Components, one of United Metal's regular suppliers, has developed a new method of producing the component in question and has offered to supply United's entire needs under a renewable one-year contract at a cost of 83p per piece.

United Metal's Purchasing Manager believes this offer to be most attractive. With the cost of own manufacture running at 95p per piece (including the capital cost of the machine), he argues that the savings will total £96 000 over 8 years. He is therefore suggesting that United should axe this particular manufacturing operation, sell their recently purchased machinery and accept Amalgamated's offer.

The Production Manager, however, who was responsible for the original decision to install the new machinery, is claiming that problems of quality control and security of supply aside, there is still no economic case for purchasing rather than manufacturing. The machinery, though virtually new and having a useful remaining life of some 8 years, has few alternative uses and could be sold for only some £5000. Since its current book value is £40 000, this would result in a loss of £35 000. The Production Manager, proud of his recently acquired grasp of discounting techniques, pointed out that this initial loss of £35 000 followed by annual savings of some £7000 for 8 years gave a return on the 'buy rather than make' idea of only some 12 per cent, while the company's current cutoff rate was 20 per cent.

He pointed out that even this, however, was a highly conservative analysis, since it ignored three other serious problems. First, the components produced

This case was written by Paul Marsh for the purposes of class discussion. While inspired by a real-life incident, the case is not intended to illustrate either effective or ineffective handling of an administrative situation.

Copyright © 1987 Elroy Dimson and Paul Marsh, London Business School.

by Amalgamated's new process could vary in diameter by up to 2 mm. While this in no way detracted from the quality of the final product in which these components were incorporated, it did mean that United would have to fit a variable dimension sensor to one of the machines used in subassembly, and this would cost £8000. It was true that United would obtain tax allowances on the new machine (capital allowances at this time were 25 per cent per annum on a declining balance basis on plant and machinery, and 4 per cent per annum on a straight line basis for industrial buildings; the corporation tax rate was 35 per cent). Nevertheless, the production manager argued that even on an after-tax basis, the variable dimension sensor represented a significant, and in his view, unnecessary expenditure.

Second, while Amalgamated's delivery service was good, they would not deliver batches of less than 30 000 items, and this implied an average stockholding of 15 000 items throughout the year. This was a substantial increase over the 2 weeks' supply of both raw materials and components currently held in stock, and would occupy an additional 10 per cent of the total warehouse space. Finally, the only alternative job which the Production Manager could offer his chief operator was one currently being advertised at £7000 per year in another department. Because of the chief operator's contract with the company, he would have to be transferred at his present salary of £8000.

The Purchasing Manager felt the problem with the chief operator was trivial and that the inventory question was a 'red herring'. The warehouse was only 60 per cent utilized, and on the basis of current plans, no additional space would be required for another 4 years when an extension costing £50 000 was planned. Since the use of this capacity involved no cash outlays, the Purchasing Manager argued that the cost of inventory could be ignored. As far as he could see, spending £8000 to save £96 000 looked a pretty good deal.

At this stage, it was becoming clear that someone would need to act as arbiter in this dispute. A judgement was needed on which issues were important, which manager was correct, and what decision United Metal should take.

2. Lee Valley Water Company

The Lee Valley Water Company has given notice to consumers that they now have the option to be charged for water used. Previously they were obliged to pay a tariff which is related to the rateable value of their property. By metering domestic as well as commercial water usage, the company hope to enhance the efficiency with which water is used. As in the case of electricity, gas or telephone, metered consumers will be able to make more informed choices about the volume of service they receive. The current volume of service provided to domestic consumers is indicated in Exhibit 1.

In aggregate, there are one million individuals and 18 000 firms in the Lee Valley area of supply. They are provided with nearly 60 million gallons (270 million litres) of water per day, and the maximum daily supply has risen to as high as 77 million gallons (350 million litres) (on 18 May 1981). The area of supply is shown in Exhibit 2.

Exhibit 1: *Average household water use within the Lee Valley area*

Nature of usage	Quantity consumed
Cooking, drinking, washing-up, personal hygiene (excluding items below)	9 gallons (41 litres) per person per day
Toilet flushing	2 gallons (9 litres) per flush
Bath	20 gallons (91 litres) per bath
Shower	6 gallons (27 litres) per shower
Washing machines	17–30 gallons (77–136 litres) per cycle
Hosepipe or sprinkler	2 gallons (9 litres) per minute
Average three-person household	30 000 gallons (136 350 litres) per year

This case was written by Elroy Dimson as a basis for class discussion rather than to illustrate either effective or ineffective handling of an administrative situation.

Exhibit 2: *Lee Valley Water Company's statutory area of supply*

The 860 square mile (2200 km^2) area of supply includes the following local authority areas supplied in whole or in part:

LONDON BOROUGHS:
Barnet, Enfield, Haringey
COUNTY OF HERTFORDSHIRE:
Districts of Dacorum, East Hertfordshire, Hertsmere, North Hertfordshire, St Albans, Stevenage, Welwyn, Hatfield
COUNTY OF ESSEX:
Districts of Brentwood, Epping Forest, Harlow, Uttlesford
COUNTY OF BEDFORDSHIRE:
Districts of Luton, South Bedfordshire

Domestic metering choice

Until 1982, domestic consumers could not select the basis on which they were charged for water. They had to remain on an annual standing charge plus annual rate. The annual rate is proportional to the rateable value of their property, and the valuation list is maintained by local councils as a basis for raising local rates. In the Lee Valley area, rates are mainly in the range £100–600, with a few thousand homes outside these extremes (see Exhibit 3).

After studies by the National Water Council in the 1970s, four water companies and three water authorities made optional metering available to households in 1980–81. This was rapidly followed by the Lee Valley Water Company's scheme. Like the other schemes, this involved substituting a meter reading fee plus consumption based charge for the annual rate. For consumers with low water usage but high rateable values, there could be sufficient financial advantage to domestic metering to induce them to install a meter at a cost of around £50. The approximate costs incurred by the householder (for installation) and by the water company (for meter provision and reading) are detailed in Exhibit 4.

The charges set by the Lee Valley Water Company are specified in Exhibit 5. It will be seen that the company also bills consumers for sewerage disposal. This is undertaken on behalf of the Thames and Anglian Water Authorities, who are responsible for these environmental services.

Implications for the company and its consumers

Officials within the Lee Valley Water Company clearly wished to estimate the likely impact of their new charging scheme. In particular, they were attempting

Exhibit 3: *Range of domestic rateable values within Lee Valley area*

Rateable value	Number of properties
0–100	4 622
101–250	183 059
251–400	129 326
401–450	11 503
451–500	7 037
501–600	6 862
601–700	2 481
701–1000	2 185
1001–1500	496
1501 and above	221
All Lee Valley domestic properties	347 792

Source: Lee Valley Water Company, March 1982

Exhibit 4: *Estimated costs of installing domestic metering*

Cost item	Amount
Once-off costs to be met by the householder	
Average installation costs (range £20–80)	£50.00
Annual costs incurred and recovered by water company	
Meter provision and replacement	£4.00
Inspection	£2.00
Reading (once), billing (twice), etc.	£3.00
Gross annual cost of metering	£9.00
Less: Cost of rate-based billing, approximately	£1.50
Incremental annual cost of metering	£7.50

Note
Metered tariffs will usually include a standing charge for other system costs which are not sensitive to usage.
Source: National Water Council, October 1980

Exhibit 5: *Lee Valley Water Company charges for water services*

Basis for charge	Rateable value based charges		Domestic metering based charges	
	Water	Sewerage	Water	Sewerage
Standing charge, per annum	£8.00	£8.00	£8.00	£16.00
Meter reading fee, per annum	—	—	£12.00	—
Annual rate, per £ of rateable value of the property	7.7p	5.4p	—	—
Consumption charge, per 1000 gallons (4545 litres)	—	—	78.0p	56.5p
Additional annual charge if hand-held hosepipe is used	£4.50	—	—	—
Additional annual charge if sprinkler is used	£12.50	—	—	—
Additional annual charge for swimming pool	£12.00	—	—	—

Source: Lee Valley Water Company, October 1981

to estimate how many customers would benefit from switching to domestic metering, and what guidelines should be given to consumers contemplating making such a change. For long-term planning purposes, they also wanted to estimate what proportion of households might have taken this option in, say, 20 years' time, and what impact this would have on the company's revenues.

More generally, Lee Valley Water Company were wondering what other policy options they could pursue for water charges. Should they, and the water industry, for example, be considering any compulsory changes in the methods used for charging for water?

3. Dane Carter International

Financial analyst Jonathan Long was considering a capital expenditure proposal which had been submitted to Dane Carter International's head office in London. Dane Carter is a highly diversified manufacturing company with major interests in the leisure, fashion, engineering and packaging industries. This particular submission had been received from one of the firms in Dane Carter's packaging division, a medium-sized company in France. The proposal involved the tooling of moulds and the commitment of manufacturing capacity in order to produce containers for the Egyptian pharmaceutical market.

Like a number of similar companies in the packaging division, the French firm had been producing injection blow-moulded containers for many years. Mr Long observed that, as in most previous proposals he had evaluated, the French subsidiary was expecting to utilize spare capacity on existing machines in order to produce the containers.

The current proposal

The proposal, which had recently been received, was for the manufacture of a 10 ml bottle, cap and plug. These were to be sold direct to a client in Egypt. It was forecast that 6.5 million units would be sold in the first year (this was already contracted for), and an estimate had been made of 10 million further units spread over the following 2 years. These estimates had been agreed by Dane Carter's commercial representative in Egypt.

For the study, it had been assumed that 5 million units would be sold in years 2 and 3 respectively. The selling price would be Ffr. 198 per thousand in year 1, from which 2 per cent and 5 per cent would successively be deducted as sales commissions. This left a net price of Ffr. 184 per thousand. Price inflation was estimated at the rate of 12 per cent for each of the following 2 years.

This case was written by Elroy Dimson and Paul Marsh as a basis for class discussion rather than to illustrate either effective or ineffective handling of an administrative situation.

The bottle was to be manufactured on a Sidel IBM (injection blow mould) machine from the existing range of machines. The plugs and caps were to be made on an F40 press, again part of the existing range of machines. These machines were expected to be available for working on a 3 × 8 hour shift basis under normal conditions. The expected percentage of the machines' total capacity that was to be utilized for the order was 39 per cent (falling to 30 per

Exhibit 1: *Attributable fixed costs for the project*

(a) Machine costs

	Year 1	Year 2	Year 3	Total
	F fr.	F fr.	F fr.	F fr.
Sidel IBM machine:				
Annual cost	97 000	97 000	97 000	97 000
Utilization (per cent)	39	30	30	99
F40 press:				
Annual cost	24 700	24 700	24 700	24 700
Utilization (per cent)	50	38	38	126
Total cost	50 180	38 400	38 400	126 980

These fixed costs are based on the average purchase cost of existing Sidel and F40 machines (respectively, Ffr. 970 000 and Ffr. 247 000) depreciated to a zero residual value over a 10 year life. Utilization rates are approximate.

(b) Tooling costs

Mould	Total cost F fr.	Cost per year F fr.
Bottle mould	185 000	62 000
Manufacturing block	30 000	10 000
Cap mould	175 000	58 000
Plug mould	165 000	55 000
Total cost	555 000	185 000

These fixed costs have been spread equally over 3 years.

(c) Total attributable costs

	Year 1	Year 2	Year 3	Total
	F fr.	F fr.	F fr.	F fr.
Machine costs	50 180	38 400	38 400	126 980
Tooling costs	185 000	185 000	185 000	555 000
Total cost	235 180	223 400	223 400	681 980

cent) for the Sidel, and 50 per cent (falling to approximately 38 per cent) for the F40. Accordingly, the attributable costs for machine utilization were computed as in panel (a) of Exhibit 1. In total, the cost of the machines' capacity was estimated at Ffr. 126 980.

Exhibit 2: *Profits and cash flows for the project*

(a) Operating profit and tax calculations

	Year 1	Year 2	Year 3
Sales revenue	*Ffr.*	*Ffr.*	*Ffr.*
Output quantity	6 500 000	5 000 000	5 000 000
Net selling price	184.34	206.46	231.24
(per thousand)			
Gross income	1 198 210	1 032 300	1 156 150
*Production costs**			
Raw materials	204 020	172 630	189 860
Labour costs	60 900	53 870	61 975
Direct selling costs	15 340	12 980	14 280
Indirect selling costs	131 425	114 880	130 760
Total costs	411 685	354 360	396 875
Profit and taxation			
Operating profit	786 525	677 940	759 275 = 2223740
Capital allowances†	235 000	223 400	223 400
Taxable profit	551 525	454 540	535 875 = 1541940
Tax payable	275 763	227 270	267 938

Annual rates of price inflation have been assumed as follows: 12 per cent for sales revenue, 10 per cent for raw materials, 15 per cent for direct labour, and 10 per cent for direct selling costs

(b) Cash flow summary

	Year 0	Year 1	Year 2	Year 3	Year 4
	Ffr.	*Ffr.*	*Ffr.*	*Ffr.*	*Ffr.*
Fixed assets	−681 980				
Working capital		−284 215	39 355	−29 380	274 240
Operating profit		786 525	677 940	759 275	
Corporation tax		−275 763	−227 270	−267 938	
Net total	−681 980	226 547	490 025	461 957	274 240
Cumulative total	−681 980	−455 433	34 592	496 549	770 789

*Production costs include an allocation for heating, lighting, power, supervision, maintenance, fringe benefits and rent; indirect selling costs consist largely of distribution costs to Egypt.
†Injection moulding machines are written off over 10 years on a straight line basis for tax purposes; moulds and tools are written off over the life of the particular project (3 years in this case).

The investment requirements for the project amounted to Ffr. 555 000 for tooling costs. These are detailed in panel (b) of Exhibit 1. For capital budgeting purposes, however, the Ffr. 126 980 cost of utilizing the existing machines was included. The evaluation was therefore based on an assumed initial investment of Ffr. 681 980.

Exhibit 2 shows the cash flow calculations which were proposed for the Egyptian pharmaceutical container project. On the basis of these figures, the company was seeking authorization for an expenditure of Ffr. 555 000 plus incremental working capital amounting to Ffr. 284 215. On these figures, the project had a payback period of 2 years and an internal rate of return of 37 per cent. At the company's required rate of return of 15 per cent, the net present value amounted to Ffr. 346 000 with a profitability index of 1.51.

The wider issues

Mr Long was sympathetic to the French concern's desire to accept the order, and felt that this proposal looked as attractive as recent requests he had approved. However, he was wary about the discrepancy between the high promised returns on such projects and the modest profits they typically provided to the parent company.

This discrepancy was stressed in a recent report by a firm of management consultants who had been brought in to investigate the French subsidiary. They noted that the ratio of contribution to sales, averaged over all product lines, was 52 per cent. On the other hand, the average profit margin was a meagre 5 per cent. The difference reflected, in the main, unallocated overhead expenditure, as well as a smaller element which included depreciation and other non-cash charges. While some of the overheads were general indirect costs, Mr Long suspected that these overheads included a substantial amount for unallocated equipment costs.

On investigating this issue further, it emerged that of the subsidiary's 90 machines, some 60 had been purchased in the last 10 years. These machines had an average age of 5½ years, and in recent years had involved capital expenditures of some £500 000 per annum on presses and moulds. Existing equipment experienced a utilization rate of some 50–60 per cent, with considerable variation both over time and from machine to machine. There were several reasons for this. First, there was inevitably an uneven pattern of demand for the different machines leading to both busy and idle periods. Second, the machines operated 'hot', so that time was unavoidably lost in start-up, as well as in set-up, and in retooling and switching between operations. Finally, there were several older or specialized machines which were used only occasionally. Since the old machines had low scrap values, there was little incentive to dispose of them as long as floor space remained available.

A possible explanation for the underperformance of the companies within the packaging division was that sales forecasts tended to be overoptimistic. However, a check on some relatively recent capital expenditure proposals did not support this view; projected orders for years 2 and 3 were about as likely to be underestimates as overestimates. Nor did the new material costings or price assumptions appear to be wildly out.

One pattern, however, was apparent in the proposals which Mr Long reviewed. There was a tendency for orders that required new moulds to have capital expenditure requests that utilized existing machine capacity. This was accompanied by a tendency for new machines to be justified either on the basis of cost savings or in order to manufacture products utilizing fully-depreciated moulds from past projects. Yet Mr Long could not see how this, in itself, would necessarily create a situation in which projects as a whole failed to live up to their promise.

With these matters as yet unresolved, Mr Long started to review the figures. His task was to decide whether to sanction the Egyptian pharmaceutical container project. At the back of his mind, however, he was also worried about the wider issues which this proposal raised.

4. Guinness Hop Farms

In 1985, the principal activity of Arthur Guinness and Sons was the brewing and marketing of beers, principally draught and bottled Guinness, a stout with a characteristic rich dark colouring. Guinness' Dublin brewery was one of the largest in Europe. The company was also heavily involved in lager, having created Harp, and in addition, had interests in retailing, publishing and health. Guinness was marketed in 140 countries, but the principal markets were Ireland, Great Britain, Nigeria and Malaysia.

Beer enthusiasts regard Guinness as a very good, high quality beer. Indeed, one of the famous catch phrases used in advertising the product has been 'Guinness is good for you'. The goodness of Guinness, so the senior brewers argue, lies at least partly in the quality of the hops.

Brewing and hops

The brewing of beer is a centuries-old tradition which can be traced back to 4000 BC in Mesopotamia and to pre-Christian times in England. Beer-making begins with the conversion of barley into malt. The malted barley is then taken to a brewery where it is ground to a powder and mashed with hot water. The resultant sweet liquid is then boiled with hops before being filtered off, cooled, and run into fermentation vessels.

Until the 14th century, British ale was brewed without hops. Hops were introduced to Britain by Dutch brewers, and are now used in all British-brewed beers. Hops are a climbing plant, with names (varieties) such as Bullion, Goldings, Fuggles and Northern Brewer. The ingredient in the hops known as alpha acid gives beer its bitterness, and acts as a preservative. Hops are picked in the autumn, when the cones are separated from the leaves and stalks. They are then taken to oast houses, where they are dried.

This case was written by Paul Marsh from information provided by, and with the assistance of, Robert Porter. It has been prepared as a basis for class discussion rather than to illustrate either effective or ineffective handling of an administrative situation.

Guinness Hop Farms

Guinness Hop Farms Limited (GHF) is a wholly owned subsidiary which operates two farms, one in Kent, Teynham Farm near Sittingbourne, and one in Worcestershire, Braces Leigh Farm near Malvern. Each farm is divided into 20–30 hop gardens, typically of some 2–6 hectares each. The two farms cover a total hop area of some 180 hectares.

Teynham is the larger of the two, and in 1984–85, it will produce just over 60 per cent of the total production of alpha (20 900 kg, compared with 13 400 kg for Braces Leigh, and total GHF production of 34 300 kg).

In 1984–85, GHF anticipates pre-tax operating profits of £4000 on sales of £728 000 (Exhibit 1). This is very considerably below 1983–84, when operating profits were £410 000 on sales of £1.2 million. The fall in profits is entirely attributable to the sharp fall in the price of hops. The collapse in price was due to reduced demand as tastes had moved towards less bitter beers, and increased supply due to replanting with higher yielding varieties.

Exhibit 1: *Guinness Hop Farms profit and loss account and funds flow statement*

Revenues, expenses and flows (£'000)	1983–84 Actual	1984–85 Latest Estimate	
Sales volume (kg of alpha)	34 100	34 300	
Sales revenue	1 169	728	
Variable costs	370	371	
Fixed operating costs	286	256	Profit
Engineering costs	27	17	and
Administration	76	80	loss account
Operating profit	410	4	
Other income	60	134	
Profit before tax	470	138	
Add back depreciation	84	83	
Funds generated from operations	554	221	Funds
(Additions) to fixed assets	(69)	(9)	flow
Disposals of fixed assets	16	63	statement
Net change in fixed assets	(53)	54	
Net operating funds flow (before 'balance sheet' items)	501	275	

The problem of wilt

Hops are perennials which have a productive life of about 20 years. There is a disease known as wilt which has spread through Kent, and which kills the older varieties of hops which are sensitive to it. However, varieties have been bred which can tolerate the wilt fungus. These newer, tolerant varieties are also higher yielding.

The planting of tolerant varieties is controlled by Act of Parliament in the Wilt Prevention Order. In order to be able to plant a tolerant, wilt must have struck the old garden, and the land must be cleared of hops and a substantial area grassed down for 2 years before planting the tolerant. The reason for this is that the Ministry of Agriculture Fisheries and Foods is concerned that unless the land is largely cleared of the fungus by planting a non-host, namely grass, the tolerant could host the fungus, and act as a carrier and source of infection which could spread to other farms.

If wilt is diagnosed in a plant, that plant together with 54 adjacent plants have to be removed and the square area grassed down. A wilted garden therefore looks like a grass/hop patchwork. To replant with tolerants, a substantial area (at least 1 hectare) has to be grassed down for 2 years and planted as a block. This requirement of 2 years applies to the grass squares which may have been under grass for some time, so in practice some parts of the farm have an interval of more than 2 years from removal of the old sensitives to planting of the new tolerants.

Teynham Farm

GHF's Teynham Farm suffers from wilt. It has 57 hectares of high-yielding tolerants and 47 hectares of wilt-sensitive varieties. Currently, about 7 hectares of the farm are under grass. Each year, another 2 hectares of sensitives have to be grubbed (dug out and cleared away) due to wilt. Of the 12 hop gardens still planted with sensitives, all are affected by wilt to varying degrees (see Exhibit 2 for details of the gardens, varieties planted, yields and wilt damage).

There are benefits to be gained from grubbing the remaining sensitives and replacing them with tolerants. First, this controls the wilt. Second, the tolerants have a higher yield. Third, this would mean that the grassed-down areas would be returned to hops. However, there is a 4 year gap between grubbing out sensitives and taking a full crop from the new plants, because of the 2 year grassing-down period, and the time it takes for new plants to reach maturity. For example, if the old plants are grubbed in October 1985, the area must be left under grass for 2 years. Replanting with tolerants in October 1987 will yield a crop from the first-year 'baby' plants in September 1988, but the first full crop will not be harvested until September 1989.

Exhibit 2: *Teynham farm gardens planted with sensitives*

Garden	Variety of hops	Date planted	Yield in kg alpha per hectare of hops	Area of Hops (hectares)	Area of Wilt (hectares)	Total area of garden (hectares)
Tank	Northern Brewer	1970	117	2.82	.74	3.56
Rushett	Challenger	1976	217	.69	.42	1.11
Lowes South	Challenger	1976	217	2.93	.79	3.72
Plough	Bullion	1959	171	1.43	.07	1.50
Norton West	B. Gold	1972	165	1.93	.52	2.45
Whinbourne	Bullion	1956	171	6.33	.72	7.05
Lowes North	B. Gold	1970	165	2.66	.18	2.84
Salmon	B. Gold	1956	165	10.94	1.16	12.10
Lower Barn	Bullion	1968	171	3.45	.17	3.62
Silo	Bullion	1967	171	6.22	.50	6.72
Selby	B. Gold	1977	180	2.35	.20	2.55
Upper Tickham	Northern Brewer	1981	190	5.41	.29	5.70

Bob Porter, Managing Director of GHF, recognized that there was a number of key variables which had to be considered in the timing of any replanting programme. These included:
(a) the starting proportion of the garden lost to wilt;
(b) the rate of loss of the garden to wilt;
(c) the relative yields of the old varieties and the tolerants;
(d) the capital costs of replanting;
(e) the assumed life of the new gardens;
(f) the price of hops.

Costs, prices and yields

The variable costs of growing hops (whether sensitives or tolerants) is £2075 per hectare, at current prices (£'1985). Predicted hop prices, expressed in £/kg of alpha, are given in Exhibit 3. The expected yields of alpha from each of the gardens planted with sensitives are given in Exhibit 2.

Studies of recent rates of wilting suggest that gardens planted with the Challenger variety (see Exhibit 2) will suffer a loss from wilting of 11 per cent (of hop area) per annum, while for all other varieties, the rate of loss is 3 per cent per annum. Once gardens reach a high level of wilt (say 20 per cent or more) this begins to impose a number of real, but difficult to quantify costs. First, gardens with this level of wilt become a threat to other gardens. Second, high levels of

Exhibit 3: *Hop price forecasts*

Year	Prices in nominal terms	Prices in real terms (£'1985)	
1984	34.5	36.2 ⎱	actual
1985	21.0	21.0 ⎰	prices
1986	23.2	22.1 ⎫	
1987	27.5	24.9 ⎪	
1988	31.7	27.4 ⎬	forecast
1989	33.9	27.9 ⎪	prices
1990	36.0	28.2 ⎪	
Beyond 1990	—	25.0 ⎭	

Notes
1. Prices are in £/kg of alpha.
2. The nominal prices for 1986–90 crops are based on a recent forward quotation from the Hop Marketing Board.
3. Prices expressed in real terms assume a 5 per cent rate of inflation.
4. The Manager Hops has advised that the price assumed beyond 1990 should be £25 per kg (£'1985), which is less than the prices for 1988–90.

wilt lead to operating difficulties, and hence higher costs in terms of poorer labour utilization, and wastage of fertilizers and sprays.

Grubbing and grass seed costs are £222 and £41 (£'1985) per hectare respectively. If a significant area were grassed down, there would also be an incremental saving of one farm labourer, worth £8000 per annum, since Teynham is presently one under establishment.

Replanting with tolerants involves the planting of bedded sets. The capital cost of planting is estimated at 74p (£'1986) per set for hill peg, labour and plant, and 2690 sets are required per hectare. Capital allowances for hop plants are 8.33 per cent per annum, straight line. The corporation tax rate (from April 1986) will be 35 per cent.

It is anticipated that a crop of 70 kg of alpha per hectare will be taken in the first year, that is from the 'babies'. Growing costs for 'babies' are assumed to be £1725/hectare (£'1985), which is 83 per cent of the costs for mature plants. This is based on the assumption that reduced chemical sprays and nitrogen (67 per cent of normal) will be required. First year 'mature' tolerants are expected to yield 200 kg of alpha per hectare, while the yield for fully mature plants will be 220 kg per hectare. The best guess of the life of a replanted garden is 20 years. This could change, however, if there were a major technological innovation, or a new disease which afflicted the tolerants.

The replanting decision

Bob Porter recognized that the problem they faced at Teynham Farm was not whether they should replant the gardens hit by wilt, but when. In reaching his decision on the replanting programme, he felt that it was important to be guided both by longer-term financial analysis, and also, shorter-term profit and cash flow considerations.

Within Guinness, the financial appraisal of capital projects was generally based on discounted cash flow (DCF) analysis, using a real discount rate of 15 per cent, after corporation tax. In addition to a DCF appraisal, however, Bob Porter also naturally wanted to consider the impact on his P and L account and on his funding requirements. It would be convenient if the replanting programme could be financed internally, at least over the next couple of years.

5. Bloomsbury Health Authority

Reorganization of the National Health Service in 1982 (see Appendix, p. 38) brought together two large London teaching hospitals, University College and Middlesex, under one management — the Bloomsbury Health Authority. This presented health service managers with possibilities for rationalizing services and with the opportunity for revenue savings. Medical staff from the obstetrics departments of both hospitals therefore met together in early 1982 — shortly after the Secretary of State had announced the creation of Bloomsbury Health Authority but before the Authority had been established — to form a working party to consider the future of the two departments.

It had long been felt that the Middlesex department could and should be rationalized. Obstetrics was a relatively discrete area, and the Middlesex unit was below the accepted minimum size (generally regarded as 1500 births per year) for a separate obstetric department. Because of this, the working party quickly submitted a paper to the district management team recommending the amalgamation of the two departments into one, physically located at University College Hospital (UCH).

The Health Authority was keen to pursue this recommendation and incorporate it as an early element in its strategy. There were two reasons for this: first, it would allow the establishment of a Bloomsbury obstetrics unit with the facilities and standards of care demanded by modern practice; and, second, it would allow space currently occupied by the Middlesex department to be used by the displaced Royal National Orthopaedic Hospital (RNOH). The RNOH was then housed in Great Portland Street but the lease on the building was due to expire in July 1984. The cost of renewing the lease would be £350 000 per annum, or the building could be purchased outright for £3.5 million.

This case was written by Pam Pocock under the direction of Paul Marsh and Elroy Dimson as a basis for class discussion rather than to illustrate either effective or ineffective handling of an administrative situation.

Background

In 1982 there was an obstetric department at the Middlesex Hospital and another at UCH. The Middlesex had 38 beds and ten special care baby cots; UCH had 76 beds and also housed the regional neonatal intensive care unit, which had 38 special care baby cots (20 of which were recent additions and not yet fully commissioned). Statistical details of the services and use of the two units are given in Exhibit 1.

The fabric of the two departments was not in bad condition and the District Works Officer felt that they were among the district's better pieces of estate. He estimated that if the two departments remained separate, capital expenditure of £131 000 was required immediately for backlog maintenance, and a further £275 000 would be required for maintenance over the next 10 years. However, both departments were planned over 50 years before and had not had any major upgrading since. The amenities were below the standard required of a modern obstetrics department and would fall further behind unless action was taken.

The main problems were poor provisions in the antenatal clinics, inadequate waiting space and education facilities, substandard operating theatre and delivery accommodation, the need to transfer patients between first stage and delivery rooms, lack of privacy, poor day accommodation, inadequate laundry and beverage-making facilities, insufficient and inadequate sanitary provision, no waiting space for fathers, inadequate office accommodation, and at UCH, a lack of full ultrasound services.

The rationalization of the two departments would generate savings in running costs, which would, in turn, provide an opportunity to upgrade the facilities and accommodation to modern standards. Indeed, in the current climate, it was felt extremely unlikely that the regional health authority (RHA) would provide the capital required for this unless there were substantial revenue savings (see Appendix). Not surprisingly, therefore, the project was immediately attractive to Bloomsbury, since it brought improvements for patients, as well as economic benefits. However, since this was the first proposal of its kind to be considered by the new Authority, they felt it especially important that planning should be thorough.

A number of alternative locations were considered for the combined department. The most suitable was the UCH obstetric hospital, which was on a separate site from the main hospital. The UCH department could be extended by using the nearby Nixon Ward and the second to fifth floors of the adjacent Darbyshire Nurses Home. The basement, ground and the first floors of the Nurses Home were already part of the obstetric department. Other users of the Nurses Home, including the nurses, would have to be rehoused. Consultants were engaged to prepare a feasibility study and estimates of capital costs. At that time, October 1982, preliminary guesses suggested that the capital cost of the scheme would be something over £1 million. While part of this was required to

Exhibit 1: *Obstetric service statistics for the University College and Middlesex Hospitals*

Service measure	1976	1977	1978	1979	1980	1981	1982
UNIVERSITY COLLEGE HOSPITAL							
Obstetrics: in-patients							
Average available beds	77.5	77.7	76.8	76.4	76.2	74.4	77.1*
Occupancy rate (per cent)	82.2	83.4	84.2	84.7	79.0	76.6	74.4
Discharges (including deaths)	2701	2951	3053	3077	3182	3279	3350
Live births as per cent of discharges	72.6	72.6	72.8	73.7	72.3	69.7	68.4
Average length of stay (days)	8.6	8.0	7.7	7.8	6.9	6.4	6.3
Special baby care/neonatal unit							
Available cots	18.8	18.9	18.5	17.9	18.1	18.3	18.4
Discharges (including deaths)	444	451	369	429	378	245	151
Out-patient services							
Total clinics (antenatal and postnatal)	300	299	301	338	381	397	284
Total attendances (thousands)	20.0	21.0	20.8	19.4	17.8	18.8	18.5
Average attendances per patient	9.0	9.0	8.7	8.8	7.9	8.6	8.3
Average number patients per clinic	66.7	70.2	69.2	57.4	46.7	47.3	65.3
MIDDLESEX HOSPITAL							
Obstetrics: in-patients							
Average available beds	34.3	38.0	37.4	38.2	38.0	38.1	39.7*
Occupancy rate (per cent)	61.5	67.4	74.1	80.1	77.4	75.3	69.7
Discharges (including deaths)	927	1022	1120	1190	1254	1347	1289
Live births as per cent of discharges	78.6	76.8	68.5	76.9	73.0	67.4	77.3
Average length of stay (days)	8.3	7.8	9.0	9.4	8.6	7.8	7.1
Special baby care/neonatal unit							
Available cots	—	—	—	—	—	10.0	10.0
Discharges (including deaths)	—	—	—	—	—	142	221
Out-patient services							
Total clinics (antenatal and postnatal)	203	198	196	204	202	202	172
Total attendances (thousands)	7.4	7.5	7.2	9.3	9.7	9.4	9.4
Average attendances per patient	9.0	9.7	9.1	9.9	10.3	11.2	10.0
Average number patients per clinic	36.4	37.9	36.8	45.4	47.8	46.4	54.8

*At the end of 1982, there were 76 beds available at UCH and 38 at the Middlesex Hospital.
Source: Bloomsbury Health Authority

expand ward accommodation and bed capacity at UCH, much of it was needed for the upgrading programme.

A project team, known as the Working Party on Obstetrics, was set up and met weekly to review the work and to plan the pattern and range of services to be provided by the new unit. A nursing subgroup was established to prepare detailed proposals, and the Division of Obstetrics and Gynaecology continued to review the progress of the project and provide direction for the pattern of services within the expanded maternity hospital.

Objectives and planning assumptions

The objectives of the rationalization of the two departments into a single unit were defined as:

(1) To provide a Bloomsbury department of obstetrics of sufficient size to:
    (a) meet the service requirements of the catchment population as determined by the North-East Thames RHA;
    (b) meet the service requirements of the regional neonatal unit;
    (c) provide clinical teaching facilities for medical and nurse training.
(2) To provide an efficient department as measured by agreed standards for running costs, throughput and occupancy.
(3) To provide a department of a standard consistent with the practice and teaching of modern obstetrics.

The District Management Team also believed that the planned rationalization

should preserve the consumer choice which mothers now have in the different policies of the two present units, and include the opportunity for home delivery for suitable women. There should be improvements in antenatal care which should include the extension of antenatal facilities in the community.

Although it was not an objective of the rationalization, one important consideration was that the project should release sufficient space in the Middlesex Hospital, at an early date, for the permanent relocation of the RNOH.

An underlying assumption for the rationalization was the expected trend in birth rates. Following a fairly consistent increase from 1977 to 1980, both regional and national rates dropped off in 1981. Bloomsbury, however, did not follow the national trend (Exhibit 2). Looking ahead, the proportion of women of child-bearing age within Bloomsbury was increasing, but the absolute number of such women was expected to fall over the next decade, due to a general decline in the district's population. The project team concluded that 'since there is no evidence to prove that the birth rate is increasing, it seems reasonable to assume that the number of live births will not increase'.

Exhibit 2: *Bloomsbury District: relative birth rates*

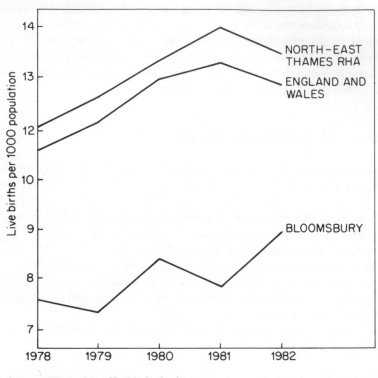

Source: Bloomsbury Health Authority

The average length of stay of a patient in the UCH department was similar to that of other maternity units in the region despite the extra demands and more complex obstetrics problems arising from the presence of the neonatal unit. The beds at the Middlesex had been less utilized. National and local trends had consistently been for a reduction in the average length of stay, and for planning purposes it was assumed that an average length of stay of 6 days would be acceptable, with an occupancy rate of 80 per cent. This compares with the 1981 rates of 6.4 and 76.6 per cent at UCH and 7.8 days and 75.3 per cent at the Middlesex (see Exhibit 1).

While a 6 day average stay was regarded as realistic, it would nevertheless have some impact on consumer choice. For example, those patients from the Middlesex who currently chose when to go home might no longer be able to do so. If the length of stay were reduced much below the planned levels, this could also mean discharging some patients before they felt ready to leave. It would also require additional expenditure to ensure a high quality domiciliary midwifery service with good links between hospital, community, health visitors and general practitioners, to ensure that discharged mothers could cope.

The catchment area

Throughout the discussions, there was uncertainty over the volume of the Middlesex workload that would transfer to UCH. The two units were geographically so close and equally accessible, that location was unlikely to be a factor here. The booking policies, however, had been quite different. The Middlesex Hospital had the capacity to care for any patient that requested services, either for first or subsequent babies, and had a reputation for caring for the relatives and friends of staff, past staff, doctors and doctors' wives, as well as local patients, in a relaxed and much more leisurely atmosphere. UCH did not have the same reputation for leisurely home comforts, and thus some patients who would otherwise have gone to the Middlesex would probably choose to go elsewhere.

UCH had a much more stringent booking policy. Of the 210–250 patients booked each calendar month, the first 150 were accepted from any locality, although not more than 20 were second or subsequent babies from outside the District. The latter were expected to have difficult deliveries since they were not accepted if the first baby was a normal delivery. The remaining bookings were retained for mothers (including late bookings) from within the District and for emergency bookings of patients with obstetric problems.

In the context of bookings policy 'District' had been taken to mean patients residing within the boundaries of the former Camden and Islington Area Health Authority, but since reorganization, had been extended to cover the North-east District of Westminster. Patients from within this catchment area were never turned down. Such patients accounted for 56 per cent of UCH bookings (52 per cent Camden and Islington, and 4 per cent from the Boroughs of Kensington, Chelsea and Westminster) and 49 per cent of the Middlesex workload (21 per cent Camden and Islington plus 28 per cent Kensington, Chelsea and Westminster). The remaining patients came from elsewhere in the North-east Thames Region (UCH 23 per cent, Middlesex 17 per cent), North-west Thames Region (UCH 17 per cent, Middlesex 25 per cent) and other regions (UCH 4 per cent, Middlesex 9 per cent).

This catchment area for booking purposes reflected a generous interpretation, and exceeded the boundaries of Bloomsbury's obstetric planning population, as laid down by the RHA. This comprised Bloomsbury (39 per cent of Camden plus 32 per cent of Westminster), plus South Islington. In fact, only 30 per cent of the UCH and Middlesex patients resided in this formal catchment area. As the regional centre, UCH was also obliged to cater for neonatal cases from anywhere within the North-east Thames Region. Regional officers indicated that Bloomsbury should not be planning capacity beyond these formal requirements. Informally, however, they tended to accept that some allowance should be made for hidden specialties (such as thalassaemic cases), and the longer length of stay for neonatal cases.

The District Management Team felt that selection of hospital was a major ingredient of consumer choice, and recognized that some Bloomsbury residents would themselves wish to be served by another District. They argued that

> the assumption has to be made that Bloomsbury will be expected to maintain its current workload. It is not for the Health Authority unilaterally to withdraw or reduce such a service. . . . A service reduction would anyway be feasible only if those other Districts from which we currently accept bookings for normal deliveries could provide alternative facilities. This is a matter to be determined by the RHA concerned, but there is no evidence known to Bloomsbury that these Districts have spare capacity.

It was therefore suggested that the UCH booking system be continued with the numbers adjusted to take account of the increased workload and bed availability.

Teaching requirements

The University Grants Committee recommended that 100 obstetric beds were required for each 100 medical students. In Bloomsbury this would indicate a requirement for 220 beds. Historically, this number of beds had not been available, and some eight different hospitals had been used by the UCH and Middlesex Medical Schools for clinical experience. For example, in 1982, 48 students were taught on beds within the Islington District (adjacent to Bloomsbury), which left 172 students with a teaching need at the combined obstetric unit. At that time, 105 UCH students were taught on 76 beds at UCH which resulted in large groups of students being present each month on the wards.

Current workloads were more than adequate for the training of nurses and midwives. Indeed, total nurse training requirements could be accommodated on the basis of the current UCH workload alone.

Client groups and bed requirements

Four major client groups could be identified by the planners and the resulting numbers were used to quantify bed requirements.

(1) *Local residents*. A total of 1856 babies were born to local mothers in the two units in 1980. In this context, local is defined as in the current UCH bookings systems. On the assumption that the Authority would continue to provide this level of service and by applying the upper limit of the Peel formula* of 27.5 beds per 1000 live births, the bed requirement for this population was *51 beds*.

*The Peel formula was devised in the 1970s and is used by the Department of Health and Social Security to determine bed numbers required in hospitals. Since the late seventies, reduced length of stay and tendencies towards more domestic style management have meant that the throughput target could in fact be higher than that envisaged by Peel, and this trend was thought likely to continue.

(2) *Medical referrals to the neonatal unit.* The number of neonatal and special baby care cots in the two units was currently being increased from 28 to 48. Little detailed information was available on the occupancy of these cots but it was estimated that eight were used by local residents and the remainder were available for use by babies born to mothers elsewhere in the region. Pressure on cots was growing, reflecting the increasingly complex cases referred to UCH, and the improved medical expertise in keeping alive babies of 24 weeks plus gestation. This had led to an increase in average cot stay length from 13.8 days in 1980 to 18.9 days in 1981, and a correspondingly longer stay by mothers in the supporting obstetric beds. On an assumption of 13.3 days stay for mothers (the 1981 figure) and an 80 per cent occupancy rate in both the neonatal and obstetric beds, *21 beds* were required to support this service.

(3) *Mothers referred to the unit because of difficult obstetric histories or other obstetric problems.* These include diabetes, hypertension, infertility, thalassaemia, cardiac patients, drug addicts and radiotherapy patients. The estimated numbers of such cases exceeded 400 patients. If an *in vitro* fertilization programme started, then these mothers would also probably want to have their babies in the unit, and the best estimate of these numbers was 67 patients per annum.

(4) *Mothers resident in locations other than those specified.* These were estimated as some 1576 patients per annum.

Unfortunately, these four categories were to some extent overlapping. The data was simply not available to determine how many of the patients included under either categories 1 or 4 were also included in the special cases (category 3) or admitted because of the neonatal unit (category 2). Bed requirements were also therefore quantified on the basis of the overall past workload of both the Middlesex and UCH. This involved using the formula

$$\frac{\text{discharges} \times \text{length of stay}}{365} \times \frac{100}{\text{per cent occupancy}} = \text{bed requirement}$$

On the basis of discharges = 4626 (the 1981 level for Middlesex and UCH), average length of stay = 6 days, and occupancy rate = 80 per cent, application of this formula gave a requirement of 95 beds. Using this overall figure of 95 beds, and deducting 72 beds for client groups 1 and 2, left 23 beds for groups 3 and 4 — specialist cases, referrals, neonatal cases, *in vitro* fertilization and patients from outside the catchment area.

There was some debate within the Health Authority about the assumptions of need underlying the 95-bed assessment, and so two other options were identified which limited the catchment area. The first option was 75 beds which did not require any additional beds at UCH, but which would allow for substantial upgrading of the accommodation for both patients and staff, and for improved antenatal care. Although no extra beds were needed, the upgrading would nevertheless require considerable additional space. Improving ward facilities by providing extra bathrooms, dayrooms, laundry and beverage-making facilities, and single rooms, had a considerable knock-on effect, by reducing the number of beds in each nursing unit, and consequently making additional wards necessary.

The second option was for an intermediate number of 88 beds. This would require only a limited increase in beds at UCH and would again allow substantial upgrading. The 75-bed option implied limiting the service to local residents, plus beds in support of the regional neonatal unit. The 88-bed option meant that services could still be provided (at current demand levels) to North-east Thames RHA, and much of North-west Thames RHA (say excluding patients from Ealing, Hammersmith and Hounslow), but to no patients from any other region.

Initial estimates of revenue savings

At the end of 1982, the Health Authority agreed that planning could go ahead on the basis of 95 beds in the new unit. But now the District Administrator had revised upwards his estimate of the capital cost of the new unit to around £2 million. Some members of the Authority began to express concern about the costs of the proposed work. In particular, they sought clarification of the incremental savings from the 75- and 88-bed options when compared with the 95-bed option, and the effect these options might have on the provision of improved facilities and equipment for both medical staff and patients.

In January 1983, the District Treasurer produced a paper which examined the revenue implications of the proposed rationalization in 'broad brush terms'. The paper was limited to variable and semivariable costs and focused primarily on the 95-bed option. The data generated and the assumptions used are set out in Exhibits 3 and 4. Exhibit 3 shows the current department costs at both the Middlesex and UCH, and also the forecast costs for the new (95-bed) combined department, based on cost figures supplied by the various staff groups (nurses, medical staff, estate management, etc).

Many of the staff groups assumed that, because they would be handling the same number of patients (with 95 beds), their costs would be unaltered. In two cases, domestic services and estate management, small cost increases were predicted, because these charges were based on square footage, and the new, upgraded combined unit was expected to occupy a greater floor area. The nurses, however, estimated that they could achieve savings of some £128 000 by moving to the new combined unit.

The District Treasurer felt that the figures in Exhibit 3 generally under-estimated the potential revenue savings. A set of target costs were therefore estimated for the new combined department, based on the existing UCH department costs per head. These figures (shown in Exhibit 4) indicated that there could be potential revenue savings of £327 000. This was considerably more than the savings of £133 000 already identified by the staff groups (Exhibit 3).

Exhibit 3:   *Initial cost comparisons between stay-put and rationalization options*

Existing department costs	UCH	Middlesex	Combined department
	£000	*£000*	*£000*
Direct patient-related costs			
Medical staff	303.7	153.6	457.3
Nursing staff	836.3	393.0	1101.5
Theatre staff	15.7	11.2	26.9
Administration and clerical	27.3	6.4	33.7
Drugs and dressings	49.3	20.0	69.3
CSSD and MSSE*	109.4	30.7	140.1
Pathology and imaging	28.8	11.7	40.5
Provisions	29.2	14.3	38.8
Linen services	14.3	5.8	20.1
Hotel services			
Domestic cleaning	118.0	40.0	163.7
Portering	44.3	13.1	57.4
Catering staff	52.4	27.2	69.8
Estate management	187.8	55.2	246.5
Total	1816.5	782.2	2465.6
Total bed complement	76	38	95

Notes
1. All pay and prices are at November 1982 levels.
2. No detailed analysis of the division between obstetric and gynaecological work carried out by medical staff has been made.
3. Nursing staff costs exclude the neonatal unit staff.
4. It is assumed that as the workload in the combined unit will remain the same, medical staff costs will not vary. However, there could be slight variations in the cost of junior staff when rotas in the combined departments are agreed.
5. The nursing staff requirements include one additional community midwife to cope with the anticipated increased workload in Bloomsbury.
6. It is assumed that clinical non-staff costs will remain unchanged in line with the workload.
7. Provision costs will reduce in accordance with numbers fed.
8. Space-related estate management costs have been adjusted for the combined unit, taking into account the areas and volumes of the two existing units and the proposed new unit.
*Central Sterile Supplies Department (the supply of dressing packs, etc) and Medical and Surgical Supplies and Equipment (instruments, supplies, etc).

Source: Bloomsbury Health Authority

Exhibit 4: *Initial target cost estimates for the new 95-bed combined unit**

Cost category	Existing UCH department cost/bed £000	Target total cost of 95-bed unit £000	Total cost UCH + Middlesex £000	Difference £000
Direct patient-related costs				
Medical staff	4.00	380.00	457.30	77.30
Nursing staff	11.00	1045.00	1229.30	184.30
Theatre staff	0.21	19.95	26.90	6.95
Administration and clerical	0.36	34.20	33.70	(0.50)
Non-staff areas	3.04	288.80	313.50	24.70
Hotel services	5.30	503.50	538.00	34.50
Total	23.91	2271.45	2598.70	327.25
Estimated cost/case	£554	£491	£562	£71

*Assuming no increase in the volume and quality of service, rationalization of the two existing departments should release revenue resources for reinvestment by the Authority. As a guideline marginal costs of additional beds on the UCH site have been assumed not to increase the average costs of existing beds. Without taking developments into account, a rough target cost for the 95-bed unit has been estimated.

Source: Bloomsbury Health Authority

On the basis of this work, the District Treasurer estimated that if the 75-bed option were adopted, then virtually all of the costs of the Middlesex department (except estate management) could be saved, including the costs of medical staff who would eventually be redeployed. The estimated saving from closure of the Middlesex was thus put at £710 000, out of total Middlesex costs of £782 000. No detailed figures were produced for the 88-bed option 'in the absence of detailed consideration of the proposal by the Working Party'.

When it was presented in February 1983, the District Treasurer's paper met with a mixed reception from the Services Committee of the District Health Authority, which was charged with making recommendations on the project. In particular some of the assumptions were questioned, and there was discussion of the fact that the only savings appeared to be coming from the nurses. There was also some debate about the medical staff costs, which included gynaecological work as well as obstetrics, since the current budgetary system made it difficult to separate the two.

The Chairman of the committee stated that he would like to see an analysis that quantified the savings achievable from efficiencies within existing services.

This could be done, he said, 'by comparing the best version of maintaining two separate units with the best version of providing a centralized unit'. These costs could then be used as a baseline against which to compare the marginal costs of various options for the development and improvement of services. He also emphasized the importance of breaking down the total costs of the different options to distinguish between unavoidable capital/revenue costs, and discretionary costs arising from quality improvements. In addition, he pointed out that the costs of the 95-bed upgrading option should include the estimated costs of relocating the departments currently housed in the Darbyshire Nurses Home.

At this point members of the Services Committee again questioned the extent to which the Authority would have to trade off improvements in facilities against the increased capital cost of a larger number of beds. One member with a background in nursing recalled:

> We were involved in difficult discussions about the workload, length of stay and occupancy, but all the time we had an uneasy feeling that we were doing routine work on people who came from outside of our district, maybe a long way away. Also we knew that we were planning a unit that would not have any more money spent on it for 20 to 30 years and yet, if we went for high bed numbers with little upgrading, we were likely to end up with people sleeping in wards that were still somewhat like dormitories. Meanwhile we had two private hospitals starting up locally which planned to take 1500 births per annum. We could easily lose many of our higher social class mothers to those hospitals, which could have a negative effect on the service in our departments.

Revised estimates, including capital costs

As a response to this type of questioning, in March 1983 the District Administrator's office produced an extremely detailed paper which dealt with six options: 95, 88 and 75 beds, all both with and without upgrading. By now it was clear that the 88- and 95-bed options 'without upgrading' were misnomers since some upgrading was required simply to ensure the increase in throughput.

The report included basic information on the capital, revenue and service implications of each option; the anticipated costs for decanting (moving into and out of temporary accommodation) and relocating departments disturbed by the rationalization; cost estimates of providing purpose-built accommodation for the new unit; manpower implications; and sensitivity analysis. Following this more detailed investigation, a number of cost estimates were revised, even for the stay-put option. The most important change was on medical staffing (compare Exhibit 3 with Exhibit 6 below). This difference arose partly from a more detailed breakdown to include a new subcategory 'other staff', which comprised pathology, Central Sterile Supplies Department (CSSD) and theatre staff. More importantly, however, medical costs were revised downwards to

Exhibit 5: *Comparative capital costs of stay-put, 75 and 95 beds with upgrading options*

Cost category	Budget costs (£'000)		
	Stay-put option	75-bed option	95-bed option
(a) Maintenance costs			
UCH backlog[1] (external redecoration, theatre ventilation, fire escapes)	83	—[5]	—
UCH work required within 10 years (rewiring, lifts, double glazing)	240	240	240
Darbyshire Home: backlog maintenance (rewiring, heating, decoration, flooring)	48	73	156
Middlesex Obstetrics (heating, water, etc)	35	—	—
Total	406	313	396
(b) Relocation costs[2]			
Medical School, Dr Shaw's Lab, Child Psychiatry	—	270[6]	270
Residential Units	—	100[6]	300
(c) Rationalization costs			
Obstetrics Hospital: basement alterations[3]	—	100[6]	100
Obstetrics Hospital: ground and fifth floors	—	165[6]	165
Second bed lift and goods lift[3]	—	—	295
Darbyshire Home: basement/third floor[3]	—	324[6]	324
Additional beds (20): fourth/fifth floors	—	—	330
Improved delivery suite[3]	—	—	180
(d) Quality improvement costs[4]			
Improved theatre	—	90	90
Improved delivery suite	—	180	0[7]
Improved accommodation on wards	—	974	974
Improved staff amenities (anaesthetic offices)	—	33	33
Provision of dedicated ultrasound	—	288	288
Improved anaesthetic equipment	—	30	30
Second bed lift and goods lift	—	295	0[7]
Replace windows	—	75	115
Total	—	2924	3494

Notes
1. Many of the capital costs relating to backlog maintenance aspects became incorporated into the overall costs for the 75- and 95-bed options
2. Relocation areas not yet identified; costs are based upon a standard upgrading cost related to an equivalent floor area to that at present occupied.
3. While these items constitute necessary rationalization costs, they also give rise to quality improvements.

reflect only that portion of medical staff time devoted to obstetrics, and to exclude the time spent on gynaecology.

The team also highlighted the urgency, pointing out that the plans for the 95-bed 'with upgrading' option assumed a start on site in January 1984 (that is, in only about 9 months hence). This timetable was necessary if the RNOH was eventually to be relocated in the Middlesex — even though temporary accommodation could probably be found. The first item on the report's list of recommendations was: 'Reach decision on option to be pursued'.

The Services Committee found the paper unbalanced in that, once again, the Project Team had only fully worked up the 95-bed upgraded option, and information and costings for the other options were extrapolated from this work. However, they nevertheless found the data useful. On the basis of this report and another produced by the District Works Officer (which outlined the improvements that could be achieved at various levels of capital expenditure from £1 million to £2.5 million), the Committee decided to drop the 88-bed option. It also noted:

That although a payback period of 94 years for the 95-bed upgraded option was considerable, any scheme to build a totally new obstetric hospital was liable to cost in excess of £8 million and would be unlikely to attract regional funding given the current policy of property disposal and refurbishment of existing buildings.

However, there was some concern that the low revenue savings relative to the high capital cost of the 95-bed upgraded option could also meet some resistance from the region. The high cost might draw too much of Bloomsbury's credit with the region, and could prejudice other capital projects. Alternatively, the region might refuse funding, or simply finance rationalization costs, leaving the district to pay for quality improvements. The risk here was that the project would not then be considered high enough priority, or would be too expensive to finance from the district's discretionary capital funds. On the other hand, if the 75-bed option were implemented, the region might possibly claim back part of the revenue savings on the grounds that these arose from a workload reduction that had lowered the district's RAWP target (see Appendix).

During April, Service Committee members visited the two departments to see some of the real problems on site. Following this visit, members agreed that the

Notes to Exhibit 5 (continued)

4. The items identified as 'quality improvements' do not imply a luxurious level of service provision. They fall short, for example, of the facilities which would be offered in a modern, purpose-built unit. It was nevertheless felt that these quality improvements would produce a modern, attractive and functional unit.
5. Note that in the 75-bed without upgrading option, expenditure on backlog maintenance of £83 000 would be required.
6. These costs apply only to the 75 beds with upgrading option; the relocations and rationalizations are required to free up the space necessary for the quality improvements.
7. Already included under necessary rationalization costs.

Source: Bloomsbury Health Authority

Exhibit 6: *Comparative revenue costs of 75- and 95-bed options*

Cost category	Budget costs (£'000) November 1982 pay/price levels		
	Stay-put option*	75-bed option	95-bed option
(a) Staff costs			
Medical staffing	193	131	186
Nurse staffing	1229	859	1037
Administration and clerical	48	38	57
Other staff	132	103	132
(b) Non-staff costs			
Drugs and dressings	69	55	69
CSSD and MSSE	106	85	106
Pathology and imaging	41	32	41
Provisions	43	31	39
Linen services	20	14	18
(c) Hotel services			
Domestic cleaning	167	125	155
Portering	57	44	47
Catering staff	79	52	52
Estate management	205	162	183
(d) Costs of quality improvements			
Improved accommodation on wards	—	63	64
Additional costs from layout changes	—	45	38
(e) Costs of discretionary developments			
Improved theatres	—	—	12
Ultrasound	—	29	29
Anaesthetics	—	60	60
Domestic night cover	—	13	27
Gross Costs	2389	1941	2352

*Revenue implications of rehousing RNOH have been ignored
Source: Bloomsbury Health Authority

existing accommodation and facilities were clearly inadequate, and that the option of continuing with no upgrading was most undesirable. When it met at the end of April, therefore, the Services Committee suggested that work should concentrate on the following options: the baseline case of staying put, but upgrading the current Middlesex and UCH obstetrics departments to bring accommodation up to an acceptable minimum standard: 75 beds with

Exhibit 7: *Summary of sensitivity of financial information for 95-bed option*

Cost category	(1) Percentage of total costs*	(2) Percentage of variation (±)	(1) × (2) Percentage sensitivity
Medical staffing	9	15	1.4
Nurse staffing	49	5	2.5
Administration and clerical	3	5	.2
Other staff	6	25	1.5
Drugs and dressings	3	10	.3
CSSD and MSSE	5	10	.5
Pathology and imaging	2	10	.2
Linen services	2	10	.2
Provisions	1	10	.1
Domestic cleaning	7	5	.4
Portering	2	10	.2
Catering staff	2	10	.2
Estate management	9	10	.9
Total	100		8.6

Conclusion: Based on these estimates, the information is approximately ± 8/9 per cent

*Total costs here exclude quality improvements or discretionary developments

Further sensitivity analysis: occupancy and length of stay
(a) *Occupancy* If occupancy failed to meet the target of 80 per cent and reached the present level of 75 per cent, or fell below to 70 per cent, this would indicate reductions in the number of cases of 6.25 per cent and 12.5 per cent respectively, assuming the same length of stay. Assuming this would have no implications for staffing levels, this would produce revenue savings of approximately £17 000 and £34 000, but would increase the cost per in-patient case by 5 per cent and 11.5 per cent respectively.
(b) *Length of stay* If length of stay failed to meet the target of 6 days per in-patient case, and was instead 6.5 days, output would be reduced by 7.5 per cent. Assuming this would have no staffing implications, there would be savings of £20 000. The cost per case would increase by 6.5 per cent assuming occupancy remains at 80 per cent.

Source: Bloomsbury Health Authority

upgrading; and 95 beds with upgrading. They felt that the total cost of each option should be broken down into the capital and revenue costs for backlog maintenance; relocation and rationalization; and quality improvements (together with a statement of the service benefits/implications of each major quality improvement). The Project Team met these requirements by providing the papers set out in Exhibits 5–7. The Committee justified this extra work in the following terms:

the costing of the backlog maintenance element in each of the options provides a basic guide to the minimum expenditure necessary. This can then be compared with the cost of the full upgrading which will also incorporate some service developments/

quality improvements. By costing each quality improvement individually it should be possible to compare the relative costs of, for example, improving the antenatal clinic and providing improved accommodation on the wards, which should enable the Authority to make decisions on priorities in the event of a cost reduction exercise.

In addition to preparing the information requested by the Committee, the Project Team also provided clarification on the capital costs of the baseline case. The costs of staying put, but upgrading both departments to minimum contemporary standards would be £2.9 million at UCH (see the 75 beds with upgrading case in Exhibit 5) and £0.5 million at the Middlesex.

The obstetricians' response

When the obstetricians realized that the Services Committee was still considering the 75-bed option, they were quick to respond with their objections. These centred on three main issues: the methods of calculating costs; the service provision; and the teaching issues.

On the subject of revenue costs they were concerned that inadequate checking had been carried out and cited the example of medical staffing where they considered the savings of only £7000 on the 95-bed option to be far too low. They argued that the 'bids' had not been crosschecked to ensure that they were reasonable and felt that this had resulted in serious inflation of the revenue costings. The doctors were also annoyed that the savings figures assumed an artificial division of their time between obstetrics and gynaecology, and that the medical staff costs quoted assumed some provision for gynaecology where they had no control over the budget.

They also argued that the Authority did not appreciate the severe effects upon patient choice and availability of service if the number of deliveries presently being performed in Bloomsbury was reduced. In a letter to the Chairman of the Services Committee, Denys Fairweather, the Professor of Obstetrics and Gynaecology at UCH, who was also Dean of the Faculty of Clinical Sciences, pointed out that

> If the Middlesex Unit is closed, 1000–1200 deliveries are involved. If the slimmed down Obstetric Hospital has also to compensate by restricting the booking of more normal cases, the assumption that length of stay can be reduced to 6 days is quite fallacious. As the proportion of abnormal to normal cases rises the number of operative deliveries/length of stay will increase. . . . Again, the reduction to 95 from the overall total of beds currently available between the Middlesex and UCH is the maximum contribution towards rationalization which could reasonably be expected if levels of service and responsibilities are to be maintained.

Professor Fairweather also questioned the basis of the planning used for the new obstetric unit:

For example, the time lag in the introduction of the UCH neonatal unit has meant that there is a much greater demand for the unit, and the type of care required has moved towards intensive rather than special care. In the original plan, the ratio of babies needing intensive care to those needing special care was 1:2; when the unit first opened the ratio was 1:1.12; but now it is reaching 2:1. Obviously this has implications for staffing levels but these have not been taken into account.

But the Dean's main source of concern seemed to be the teaching of medical students, an issue which he addressed most forcibly:

It seems to have been assumed that, for medical student teaching, if the decision is to end up with only 75 beds, the resulting educational shortfall can be met simply by sending more students to other hospitals. Please understand the difference between the education which can be given at a 'teaching' or 'university' hospital *vis à vis* the District General Hospital.

The HA also appear to be unaware of the fact that in Islington, obstetrics has recently been rationalized involving a reduction of total available beds. This, together with the fact that Islington gives priority to its pupil midwife school, means that, at most, only about 50–60 students per annum can be given training there. It will be quite impossible to give adequate training at UCH to the remaining 170 students (that is 60 more than we presently train) on a reduced number of beds.

In a later comment Professor Fairweather pointed out that the Authority could also stand to lose money if too many students were moved out to other districts such as Islington: 'If this is done the Authority will lose its teaching money — the SIFT Allowance — which amounts to £28 000 per student'.

The decision

The Obstetrics Project Team met in July to reconsider the various options in the light of the users' (the obstetricians) views. The original papers had assumed the same target throughputs on all options, so that the 75-bed option resulted in a 21 per cent service reduction. The Team accepted, however, that because of the regional neonatal unit, the 75-bed option would imply a higher abnormal: normal births ratio, so that the actual reduction in throughput would be greater than 21 per cent. Since normal deliveries were the basis for teaching, this also impacted on teaching requirements. The Project Team recognized that 'the 95-bed option is the only one which comes near to approaching teaching requirements'.

The Project Team concluded that:

taking into account the teaching requirements, support for the regional neonatal unit, the right of women to choose the hospital in which their baby would be born, and the implications for choice and service provision of pursuing the lower bed options, the only solution which could be considered further was the one providing 95 beds.

The Services Committee met in August 1983 and, after considerable discussion, most members felt that they should put forward a recommendation on the lines of that indicated by the users — that is, a minimum of 95 beds in the new unit. The high capital cost and low revenue savings of this option meant that upgrading would have to be restricted to priority items only, namely the additional provision of dedicated ultrasound, second bed lift and minimum essential improvements to the delivery suite.

The Committee also felt that a maximum capital limit of £2 million should be set for the project, and that it should be submitted to the North-east Thames RHA as a priority bid for capital. The RHA would probably regard this as a reasonable bid, although the revenue savings of only £238 000 did not represent a good return on capital. It was felt that the Authority's attention should be drawn to the potential precedent of future service provisions being determined by teaching requirements. In addition it was stressed that the low saving on the project meant there would have to be commensurate savings elsewhere in the district.

The chairman of the Committee, however, disagreed. He registered his disappointment that the users and the Services Committee were arguing for an option which put quantity before quality. He was in favour of a lower bed option with higher revenue savings and therefore the ability to support a higher level of upgrading. He stated that unless he was able to persuade the Committee to change its mind, he would have to dissent from their recommendation.

Appendix : The Organization of the National Health Service and the Bloomsbury Health Authority

In 1974, the NHS underwent a major reorganization, following a report by McKinsey, which set up a three-tier system of regional, area and district health authorities to administer hospital services and coordinate the services provided by family practitioners (general practitioners, dentists, opticians and pharmacists) and local authorities. The structure proved to be unwieldy, and in April 1982, one of the tiers — the area health authorities — was abolished.

The Secretary of State for Social Services was responsible to Parliament for the NHS, with civil servants at the Department of Health and Social Security (DHSS) providing advice and information. Beneath the DHSS were 14 regional health authorities (RHAs) each caring for between two and five million people. Each region contained one or more undergraduate medical schools, and the associated teaching hospitals tended to be the focus for specialized facilities such as renal dialysis or cardiac surgery. (The neonatal unit at UCH was an example of such a 'special facility'.) The RHAs planned the allocation of money they received from the DHSS — about £250 million — and administered all major capital projects within their region.

Each RHA was subdivided into 10–18 districts, each with its own health authority (HA). These health authorities were directly responsible for the provision of health services in their area, typically providing care for about

230 000 people. As with RHAs, the HA consisted of about 15 unpaid members with roughly one-third from the local authority, one-third from the medical professions, and one-third from the local community. The HA met monthly and was responsible for making policy decisions on the allocation of resources to the different services within the district and for the efficient running of all those services. Consumers' views were represented to the HA through the local community health council.

The detailed running of the district and background work for the HA (including formulation of policy options) was carried out by the district management team (DMT). The DMT had a general administrator (the district administrator), a nursing officer, a community physician, a finance officer, and a representative general practitioner and consultant.

One of the aims of the 1982 reorganization and the abolition of area health authorities was to delegate responsibility and to bring decision-making closer to the consumer. The intention was that this should not only increase efficiency but also promote sensible policy decisions based on what was happening on the ground.

Bloomsbury Health Authority

Following the 1982 reorganization, Bloomsbury HA was formed, as part of the North-east Thames RHA, from five former health organizations spanning two regions:

South Camden — a teaching district based on UCH;
North-east Westminster — a teaching district based on the Middlesex Hospital;
St Peter's Hospital Group — a postgraduate group specializing in urology;
Royal National Ear, Nose and Throat Hospital — postgraduate teaching group;
Royal National Orthopaedic Hospital — postgraduate teaching group.

The three postgraduate groups were previously run by boards and governors directly responsible to the Secretary of State.

Geographically, Bloomsbury HA comprises a core area of Central London, including the West End, and areas immediately to the north and east. In the north, it includes St John's Wood, Primrose Hill, Camden Town and parts of Kentish Town. In the west, it includes parts of Maida Vale and the whole of Marylebone, with the western boundary marked by Edgware Road, Marble Arch and Park Lane. The southern part of the area embraces Mayfair, Soho and the Strand, and extends down to the River Thames. In the east, the Bloomsbury HA includes Holborn, parts of Clerkenwell, King's Cross, St Pancras and parts of Tufnell Park. Finally, the central area includes the West End shopping district, Regent's Park, Euston, Somers Town and Bloomsbury itself.

The Authority has a very small local population (132 000) but within its estate it has 17 separate hospitals — currently 2 per cent of the NHS building stock.

The Authority employs in excess of 9000 staff and has an annual budget of some £110 million. This situation presented the Authority with an opportunity to achieve economies of scale through the rationalization of acute services (those dealt with by hospitals). It was also under pressure from the region, since Bloomsbury had constantly been in excess of its RAWP* targets since its formation at a time when the region aimed to distribute its resources more evenly. (Areas in Essex were seen to be consistently under-funded whilst Inner London areas were always overbudget.)

This pressure had resulted in Bloomsbury HA anticipating a reduction in revenue resources of £8–15 million over 10 years. These revenue savings were expected to be achieved whilst preserving levels of service, by maintaining the same case load. The rationale here was that Bloomsbury had a lot of empty beds in its hospitals and that reducing the number of beds and length of stay, whilst increasing throughput, would generate revenue savings.

Capital funding for the HA came from the region and the DHSS. The Health Authority was expected to submit bids for capital spending to the region. Those over £5 million were submitted on a 5 year cycle and had to meet with the approval of the DHSS. Bids under £5 million were dealt with by the region as part of a 3-year planning cycle.

In addition, a district health authority could transfer up to 1 per cent of its revenue to the capital account, and in Bloomsbury this amounted to about £1 million per annum. Proceeds from the sale of land or buildings reverted to regional funds, with the district having a call on the first £200 000 and able to bid for the balance. (In practice districts were normally allowed to retain the whole sum.)

Capital needs in Bloomsbury over the next 10–15 years were likely, because of the nature of the estate, to far outstrip Bloomsbury's own resources. The HA would therefore be heavily dependent on regional funding for its rationalization programme. Equally, it would need to 'produce' as much capital as possible from its own activities, for example, by achieving high revenue savings from the various rationalization schemes.

*The Resource Allocation Working Party (RAWP) recommended a system for equalizing resources between HAs based on the resident population weighted by morbidity and patient flows with allocations for regional specialities and some credit for teaching.

PART B

COST OF CAPITAL AND PERFORMANCE MEASUREMENT

6. Norcros

In May 1977, Norcros was engaged in a significant capital expenditure programme to expand and renovate the facilities in many of its factories in preparation for a general improvement in economic conditions. While expenditure on fixed assets in 1976 had been only £2.6 million, the corresponding figure for 1977 was expected to exceed £7 million. When associated expenditures were included, such as start-up costs and working capital, total expenditure on new projects would probably reach £12 million. In the course of preparing the capital budget and appraising the various project appraisal requests from the Norcros divisions, the company was once again faced with the question of what rate of return they should be earning from their different businesses.

The company and its history

Norcros started life as a public quoted company in June 1956. Originally, it was set up by John Sheffield as a tax shelter for the remaining assets of the Sheffield family. These consisted largely of ironstone deposits in Lincolnshire, and a small label and specialist printing company. The family's wealth had already been seriously depleted by death duties and by 'surtax direction'. These tax problems could, at that time, be significantly reduced by forming a public holding company.

John Sheffield recognized that many other successful family businesses were in a similar position. Norcros also, therefore, set out to provide a convenient 'umbrella' organization for companies of this kind. In particular, Norcros hoped to attract companies which did not wish to lose their independence by joining a large industrial holding group, but which were nevertheless too small to go public on their own.

Sheffield's judgement proved correct, and 23 small family companies joined

This case was written by Paul Marsh as a basis for class discussion rather than to illustrate either effective or ineffective handling of an administrative situation. We are grateful to Julian Franks for help in preparing an earlier version of this case.

Copyright © 1987 Elroy Dimson and Paul Marsh, London Business School.

the Norcros fold during its first 5 years. These companies were characterized by a satisfactory past profit record, and surplus cash. The latter was important since it was used to finance the next acquisition in the chain. These acquisitions broadened the group's interests into a wide variety of different products and sectors including printing, electrical engineering, dry cleaning machinery, haulage and winding gear, iron, steel and metal merchanting, textile trading, kitchen furniture, air conditioning equipment, motor car manufacture, ship-building and many other fields.

In the early stages of Norcros' growth, the original family managements maintained almost total autonomy over their individual companies, and Norcros simply acted as a kind of loose 'club'. Initially, this policy proved successful, and both profits and the share price rose rapidly. By mid-1961, however, it became clear that the pace of the acquisitions policy had somewhat over-extended the company. Borrowings had started to build up, but the complete lack of central control made it difficult to estimate the magnitude of the problem.

These cash problems led to a refinancing operation in early 1962. This coincided with the acquisition of Dow Mac Products, a concrete manufacturer, which was to be the last acquisition until the end of 1965. Meanwhile, Norcros went through a rationalization phase, divesting five unprofitable subsidiaries, and closing a sixth. Budgetary controls were slowly introduced, and although this met with opposition and resentment from the previously autonomous subsidiaries, it gradually helped the group to improve its liquidity and financial stability. The 1964 Annual Report noted 'a marked improvement in financial control and group management'.

In 1966, Norcros carried out a major review of its entire business, which was to guide its strategy right up until the late seventies. A special report to shareholders explained that the new strategy involved focusing on the 14 companies which had the strongest growth potential, and reorganizing these into four main operating divisions. The new divisions were construction, consumer products, engineering, and printing. Each was to have its own divisional chief executive who would report direct to group top management.

No further diversification was to take place for the time being, in order to allow 'all resources of management, men and money to be concentrated on these four sectors'. The aim was to weld these four divisions together 'into a corporate body with a common identity, having a common purpose, and operating with a unified plan'. This would be achieved through central financial control, built on forward budgets, and short, intermediate, and long-term plans.

The special report also explained that 'capital spending, which means the allocation of the resources of the entire group, and thus the shaping of its future, is now rigidly controlled by top management'. It was recognized that these various extensions of head office control represented an 'internal revolution' which would 'disturb many settled ways in the group'. The objective, nevertheless, was to 'build a group identity, to make out of a previously overdiversified holding company an operating unity with a clear and hard sense of purpose, whose members will identify themselves with the success and name of Norcros'.

Norcros in 1977

The strategy and structure which Norcros had identified a decade earlier was still very much in evidence in 1977. The company was still organized into the same four UK operating divisions, although an overseas division had now been added. Several companies which did not fit with Norcros' structure and/or growth requirements had been divested, and a further 13 companies had been acquired. On acquisition, these companies were allocated to one (or more) of the Norcros divisions, and thus integrated into the corporate structure.

By far the largest acquisition was the purchase of Crittall Hope in March 1974 for a purchase price of £11 million. This was a substantial move for Norcros, since prior to the acquisition, Norcros itself had an equity capitalization of only £16 million. Following the integration of Crittall Hope, the composition of Norcros' four UK operating divisions was as follows:

Consumer division

The consumer division consisted of two main companies, Hygena and Crittall Warmlife. The former produced the Hygena range of kitchen storage furniture and the White Space bedroom furniture range. Hygena held over 20 per cent of the UK kitchen furniture market, and produced both quality and budget, ready assembled and self-assembly modular kitchen units. 'White Space' bedroom furniture was a range of self-assembly wardrobes, cupboards and chests with fitted shelves and drawers which could be close-fitted to a room of any shape or size. It was the brand leader in the built-in bedroom storage furniture market.

Crittall Warmlife had three product ranges, namely domestic double glazing, foam insulation for cavity walls, and a range of horticultural products, including various types of greenhouses and other products designed for the growth and protection of plants. Crittall Warmlife held a strong share in each of these markets.

Construction division

The companies in the construction division manufactured airconditioning equipment, precast concrete, and windows. Temperature Limited manufactured airconditioning units for households, offices, hotels and supermarkets, and also specialized equipment for the armed forces and British Rail. Air Flo Heating Supplies manufactured sheet metal ducting for both domestic and commercial applications — for example, warm air central heating.

Dow-Mac Concrete manufactured precast concrete, specializing in pre-stressed units. It was the major supplier of prestressed concrete sleepers to British Rail; the largest UK manufacturer of concrete bridge beams for motorways and roads; and it also manufactured the various structures used increasingly in the building industry for office blocks, multistorey car parks and schools. Dow-Mac's latest product was a patented, prefabricated railway level crossing for British Rail.

Crittall Windows was the largest manufacturer of steel and aluminium windows in Europe. Crittall Construction specialized in the manufacture of aluminium, steel and stainless steel curtain walling. The company was also involved in the growing market of ventilation, in which it was already the second largest supplier of associated equipment. Cego (Engineering) (formerly part of Crittall Hope) manufactured metal and plastic fittings for the UK window manufacturing industry. It also manufactured aluminium extrusions and undertook some galvanizing. Finally, the construction division also included Security Services (a computer agency) and a 50 per cent share in Darlington and Simpson Rolling Mills, which produced hot and cold rolled light steel sections, principally for use in steel windows.

Printing and packaging division

The printing and packaging division of Norcros included Norprint Limited which was the largest designer, manufacturer, and marketer of specialized labelling, identification and marking systems in Europe. Its labelling systems were used for brand and product identification, inventory and date coding, price marking, and numerous other applications. Norprint had more than a 20 per cent share of the self-adhesive labelling market. Major application areas were packaging and canning lines in the food and other industries, and product marking in supermarkets and retail outlets.

Darley Business Forms produced bespoke stationery for the expanding computer continuous stationery and business form market. P.P. Payne had a dominant position in the supply of printing fabric label requirements for the textile industry, and also in the manufacture of strapping and tying systems, based on the extrusion of non-metallic products, particularly polypropylene. Finally, the Autotype Company specialized in coating photographic films and papers used for silk screen, photogravure, and lithoprocessing and printing, and was the world's leading supplier of these technical products.

Engineering division

The companies in the engineering division were grouped under two headings: cranes and heavy engineering, and light engineering. Adamson Butterley designed and manufactured specialized cranes for steelworks, as well as general purpose cranes for docks and container stations. It was also an important

Exhibit 1: *Norcros sales and profits by operating division*

| | (£ million) | | | |
| | 1976 | | 1975 | |
Division	Sales	Pretax Profit	Sales	Pretax profit
UK operating divisions				
Construction	42.4	1.75	38.0	1.30
Consumer	30.0	1.33	26.0	.43
Engineering	32.3	1.44	29.3	1.33
Printing and packaging	22.3	2.66	20.8	3.25
	127.0	7.18	114.1	6.31
Overseas division	15.4	2.53	9.5	1.25
Associate companies	13.5	1.29	9.2	1.18
Head office	0	1.05	0	1.12
Total	155.9	12.05	132.8	9.86

supplier to the steel and coal industries of heavy mechanical handling equipment, hoppers and automatic loading equipment. Other products included railway bridges for British Rail; stainless steel products, notably for the dry cleaning and laundry industry; general steelwork for a wide variety of industries; and a range of presses for the machine tool market.

In terms of light engineering, Lion Foundry was the major supplier of cast iron products required by the Post Office, including telephone kiosks, pillar boxes, and manhole covers. It also manufactured cast-iron parts for forklift trucks, fire escape stairways and walkways, and Mehanite, a special, high-grade cast iron for the automotive and textile industries where strength and abrasive resistance qualities were required.

TRF Pland manufactured stainless steel sinks for kitchens, hospitals, schools and catering establishments. Radiant Superjet designed and manufactured a variety of products for the gas and oil industry, including gas and oil burners, and gas radiant heaters for space heating and industrial purposes. Windley Brothers specialized in the market requiring high precision measuring instruments. Finally, Lowton Metals purchased, processed and resold scrap steel and non-ferrous metals.

The sales and pretax profit figures for each of the Norcros divisions are shown in Exhibit 1.

Corporate financial strategy and techniques

In the early 1970s, Norcros developed a clear financial strategy. This strategy had proved robust, and remained constant even during the 1974–76 period of very high inflation. In 1977, it continued to form the basis of short-term budgets and long-range plans. The company summarized their financial strategy as follows:

(1) To preserve the intrinsic value of the shareholders' net worth in terms of current money values as a resource capable of generating future earnings.
(2) To earn a rate of return on capital employed of at least 25 per cent.
(3) To generate earnings in terms of current money values at a compound growth rate in excess of inflation.
(4) To increase the proportion of earnings derived from overseas economies by way of exports and overseas investments.
(5) To maintain a reasonable balance between foreign assets and liabilities thus reducing the exposure of the shareholders' net worth to currency fluctuations.
(6) To provide a reliable and increasing flow of dividends to equity shareholders, to compensate risk capital investment.
(7) To maintain with suppliers, lenders and partners the highest standards of financial reputation.

Exhibit 2: *Norcros sources and uses of funds*

Sources and uses (£ million)	1971	1972	1973	1975	1976
Sources of funds					
Profit before tax	3.6	4.8	6.4	11.6	12.1
Depreciation	.9	1.0	1.0	2.3	2.1
Sale of subsidiary/associate	.0	.7	1.8	.2	0
Issue of share capital	.8	.1	0	5.7	4.7
Loans raised	1.0	1.4	2.2	12.8	7.3
Total sources	6.3	7.9	11.5	32.6	26.1
Uses of funds					
Net expenditure on fixed assets	1.3	1.8	4.7	3.4	2.6
Increase in working capital	.1	−.5	4.2	5.7	8.5
Acquisition of companies	.8	.7	0	12.8	.1
Taxation paid	1.4	1.0	1.6	3.2	2.6
Dividends to shareholders	1.0	1.1	.9	1.3	1.8
Short-term deposits (encashments)	−.1	2.6	.3	−.2	7.7
Loans repaid	1.1	.6	.1	6.5	2.8
Movement in bank facilities	.7	.4	−.2	−.2	.0
Total uses	6.3	7.9	11.5	32.6	26.1

Note
Figures for 1971–73 are for the year ended 30 November; figures for 1975 are for the 16 months ended 31 March 1975; and figures for 1976 are for the 12 months ended 31 March 1976. All numbers are rounded to the nearest £0.1 million, so totals do not sum precisely.

The financial performance of the group over the period 1971–76 is summarized in Exhibits 2, 3 and 4. Exhibit 2 provides information on sources and uses of funds. Exhibit 3 shows summary profit and loss and balance sheet information, together with a set of performance ratios for the group. Exhibit 4 provides detailed information on Norcros' capital structure.

The financial techniques of Norcros were based on the concept of valuing assets, liabilities and performance in current money values as a means of managerial control. The financial system was designed to influence future

Exhibit 3: *Norcros financial performance and ratios*

Financial summary (£ million)	1971	1972	1973	1975	1976
Group sales	37.7	44.1	56.4	123.5	142.4
Pretax profit	3.9	5.1	6.8	11.7	13.5
Earnings for ordinary shareholders	1.9	2.7	3.5	4.5	5.6
Share capital plus reserves	7.0	8.8	13.0	20.7	28.6
Capital employed[2]	15.0	16.9	24.6	53.6	68.8
Fixed assets (net book value)	8.8	10.1	15.3	27.8	29.1
Fixed assets (at cost or value)	13.0	14.6	25.1	50.0	50.2
Net current assets[3]	4.4	4.1	4.8	18.8	29.4
Pretax profit/sales (per cent)	10.5	11.6	12.1	9.5	9.5
Return on capital employed (per cent)	27	31	29	25	23
Sales/stock	7.9	8.6	7.8	5.3	5.7
Sales/debtors	4.0	4.3	3.8	4.2	4.2
Sales/fixed assets (at book)	4.3	4.4	3.7	4.5	4.9
Current assets/current liabilities	1.4	1.3	1.3	1.5	1.8
Return on shareholders funds (per cent)	28	31	29	25	23
Earnings per share (pence)[4]	5.7	7.6	9.9	9.8	11.0
Assets per share (pence)[4]	22	27	39	46	54
Gross dividend per share (pence)[4]	2.8	2.9	3.1	4.2	5.5
Share price (pence at end of period)[4]	78	105	42	48	77
Dividend yield (per cent)	3.6	2.8	7.5	8.8	7.2
P/E Ratio	13.8	13.8	4.2	4.9	7.0

Notes
1. 1971–73, year ended 30 November; 1975, 16 months ended 31 March; 1976, year ended 31 March.
2. Capital employed = net current assets plus fixed assets plus investments plus current loans plus bank overdrafts.
3. Net current assets = stock plus debtors plus short-term deposits plus cash *less* creditors *less* current loans *less* overdraft *less* corporation tax payable *less* proposed final dividend.
4. Earnings per share, assets per share, dividends per share, and share prices have been adjusted for the one for one scrip issue in April 1973, and for the 'bonus' element of the rights issue in September 1975. Earnings per share and assets per share figures are based on the average number of shares outstanding during the accounting period.

Exhibit 4: *Norcros capital structure*

Balance sheet summary (£'000)	1971	1972	1973	1975	1976
Capital employed					
Issued ordinary shares[2]	4 036	4 046	8 093	10 708	13 628
Reserves	2 989	4 787	4 947	10 031	14 969
Taxation equalization	510	697	1 382	7 370	9 131
Deferred credits	0	0	524	770	642
	7 535	9 530	14 946	28 879	38 370
Issued preference shares[3]	2 198	2 198	2 198	2 198	2 198
Minority interests	82	110	139	694	1 033
Long term loan capital[4]	3 824	3 843	5 891	19 323	21 582
Current loans	374	593	662	1 529	4 702
Bank overdraft	1 022	583	789	977	939
Total	15 035	16 857	24 625	53 600	68 824
Net assets					
Net fixed assets	8 792	10 071	15 259	27 752	29 081
Investments	476	1 484	3 163	4 548	4 698
Short-term deposits and cash	693	1 855	468	922	8 732
Net current assets[5]	5 074	3 447	5 735	20 378	26 313
Total	15 035	16 857	24 625	53 600	68 824

Notes
1. 1971–73, year ended 30 November; 1975, 16 months ended 31 March; 1976, year ended 31 March.
2. The number of 25p ordinary shares outstanding was 15 492 000 (30/11/71); 15 539 000 (30/11/72); 32 657 000 (30/11/73); 42 383 000 (31/3/75); 54 512 806 (31/3/76); 55 569 000 (18/5/77). As at 18/5/77, the market price of the shares was 65p.
3. 2 198 000, 5 per cent cumulative preference shares of £1 each (market price £51 per £100 nominal on 18/5/77).
4. As at 31/3/76, Norcros' long-term loan capital consisted of: £2.485 million 7.25 per cent Unsecured Loan Stock 1977/82 (market price £71 on 18/5/77); £9.991 million 14 per cent Unsecured Loan Stock 1974 (market price £97.5 on 18/5/77); £5 million 15.75 per cent Debenture Stock 1990/95 (market price £107.5 on 18/5/77); £4.106 million of other long-term loans (unquoted).
5. Net current assets = stock plus debtors *less* creditors *less* corporation tax payable *less* proposed final dividend.

events through forecasting probable performance and measuring its effect on shareholders' net worth, earnings and cash flow.

In the annual cycle, each operating company prepared a 4 year plan describing the potential market, the commercial objectives in terms of sales, profits and cash flow, and the additional resources required in terms of factory space, plant and machinery and working capital. After examination and debate, these plans then formed the basis of a group plan and enabled Norcros to assess the future financial requirements of the group as a whole, and its future performance in relation to shareholders' net worth, earnings, cash flow and dividends.

From the first year of the plan, a budget was derived for each company, each department, each factory and each product. This then became a managerial task and finance was provisioned to enable the task to be fulfilled. Throughout the year, each company then provided detailed performance forecasts over the 3 months immediately ahead, and reported the actual performance in the latest completed month. This information was compared in all parameters with the equivalent budget.

The main control on a day-to-day basis was exercised through cash flows. No overdrafts were permitted in operating companies and Norcros performed the role of banker. Cash generated by trading was transferred to Norcros, who in return supplied the cash required for trade expansion and expenditure on fixed assets. Capital expenditure was approved in principle at the time the budgets were prepared. Each project then had to be subsequently applied for with full project justification. Once approved, Norcros control then took the form of a phased supply of the necessary cash.

To provide an incentive to the senior managers of the operating companies, Norcros paid a bonus based on the agreed targets for profit before tax. This bonus was a percentage of salary, with executives receiving 20 per cent for the achievement of target, and further increasing percentages up to 75 per cent for performance better than target.

Charging for the use of assets

To ensure an awareness throughout the group of the hidden costs of employing assets, Norcros charged a standard percentage to each company each month on the assets employed in the activity. The balance sheet categories included stocks, debtors, creditors and fixed assets. This monthly charge, currently 7.5 per cent per annum, was deducted as a normal cost before measuring profit.

Norcros head office maintained that this system yielded a number of advantages. First, it made managers throughout the group aware of the opportunity cost of money tied up in assets, and also it made them equally aware of the cost of time. This was achieved by levying an interest charge on specific events, such as the credit period of debtors and creditors, the length of ownership of fixed assets, and the length of time goods remained in stock. The effect was valued, and charged to the profit statement. Furthermore, the interest charge was dynamic, by being based on monthly opening balances. If stock went up in a month, there was an immediate increase in the charge. If debtors went down in a month, there was an immediate benefit to the profit statement.

Second, the system made departmental profits easy to measure. Since the interest was calculated on assets managed, the charge to a given factory based on its fixed assets, work-in-progress, stocks and so on could be further subdivided as required. For example, parts passing from one department to another were priced including the interest content on the assets involved. Subassemblies passing between factories also contained the interest element attracted by the assets employed to that stage. Similarly, finished goods went into stock at standard prices which included the appropriate interest on the assets involved in their manufacture. In the marketing departments, the interest charge on debtors could be divided readily between outlets of trade, individual customers, exports and so on, so that the particular manager involved was aware of the situation. Finally, overhead departments also bore interest charges so that the interest costs of their assets managed was specifically taken into account. It was felt that this was particularly important in the case of departments such as works engineering and computers.

Third, charging for the use of assets meant that loss-making activities were identified in stark relief. From past experience, Norcros had found that such activities usually contained excessive assets, such as underutilized plant, slow-moving stocks or slow debtors. The Norcros system fairly penalized such situations by charging them with specific costs. It also discouraged inappropriate marginal cost pricing. Calculations for selling-price guidance included interest according to the terms of trade. For example, in the case of exports, interest was provided on the length of time in finished goods stock, goods in transit, export debtors and cash in transit.

Finally, the Norcros system, whereby plant and machinery attracted interest without a deduction for depreciation, meant that factory managers were stimulated to dispose of underutilized or inefficient items. This was intended to encourage modern plants of optimum size. The encouragement was underlined by the fact that the senior management bonus scheme was 'fairly devised,

Exhibit 5: *Interest rates on government securities*

Security	Maturity	Gross redemption yield (per cent) in May 1977
Treasury bills	3 months	8.0
High coupon gilts	5 years	10.0
(coupons of 12	10 years	11.0
per cent or more)	20 years	12.7
Middle coupon gilts	5 years	9.6
(coupons of more than	10 years	9.8
6 but less than 12 per cent)	20 years	12.0
Low coupon gilts	5 years	6.7
(coupons of less	10 years	8.5
than 6 per cent)	20 years	10.2

automatically containing the vital element — cost of time'. This was achieved by linking bonuses to profits before tax, but after deducting the charge for the use of assets.

Within the Norcros divisions, the system of charging for the use of assets was not always universally acclaimed. One criticism was that the system assumed that each company had no equity capital. The companies thus had to pay interest on all their assets, which were anyway, for this purpose, valued at cost rather than book. This meant that if one assumed, say, a 50 per cent debt to equity ratio, some companies were paying interest charges of well over 20 per cent on the assumed debt portion of their capital structure. This was far higher than the current market interest rates faced by their competitors (Exhibit 5). Since the interest costs had to be passed on through higher prices, it was argued that this could make Norcros companies uncompetitive.

Another criticism was that the system was inequitable in that it focused on pretax rather than posttax profits, and thus failed to reflect the significant tax advantages enjoyed by divisions which were investing heavily. Others within Norcros felt that the system was sensible, but that any proposals to finesse it by introducing multiple or differential rates should be resisted. They argued that there were strong advantages to keeping the system simple.

Required rates of return

A major problem facing Norcros was the determination of required rates of return for new capital projects. While Norcros did not feel in any way that they faced capital rationing, they naturally wanted to ensure that only profitable new projects were undertaken. Given their shareholder orientation as a group, Norcros wished to estimate what level of return their shareholders required, and link this in with their capital budgeting criteria.

However, Norcros also used significant amounts of borrowed money (see Exhibit 4). While their gearing was not excessive by current industry standards (for example, in May 1977, the debt to debt-plus-equity ratios for the following industries were: cement 38 per cent, construction 36 per cent, heavy engineering 28 per cent, light engineering 28 per cent, paper and packaging 26 per cent and furniture 28 per cent), Norcros nevertheless felt that their debt ratio should be reflected in the hurdle rates they applied to new investments.

There was also a debate about whether Norcros should use a single discount rate for all new projects, or whether they should vary this rate by division and company, or to reflect the risks of individual projects. Certainly there seemed to be evidence that the risk of shares varied considerably, both between and within industries (Exhibit 6).

Finally, there was concern that any hurdle rates used in capital budgeting should be consistent with Norcros' existing method of charging for the use of assets. For example, if different discount rates were used for different projects,

Exhibit 6: *Risk index (beta) estimates*

Norcros	1.02	**Engineering (general)**		**Furniture and bedding**		**Paper and packaging**
		Bestobell	.92	Austin, F	.86	Alliance Alders	.81
Building materials		Birmid Qualcast	1.06	Christie-Tyler	.76	Associated Paper Mills	1.04
Armitage Shanks	1.03	Brown, John	1.10	Gomme	1.06	Beatson Clark	.99
BPB Industries	1.08	Butterfield Harvey	1.28	Hensher	.98	Bemrose	1.10
Carron	1.14	Chubb	1.11	Jentique	.70	Bunzl Paper	.75
Crittall Hope	1.26	Cohen 600 Group	.93	Lebus	.93	Clyde Paper	.96
Crossley Building Product	.95	Dobson Park	.89	Parker Knoll	.86	Dickinson Robinson	.99
Evered	.81	Dowty	.99	Peerage	.92	Inveresk	.90
Glass and Metal	.97	Duport	1.03	Relyon	.94	Metal Box	.97
Hepworth Ceramic	1.00	Fairey	1.02	Silentnight	.88	Metal Closures	.88
Johnson Richards	.99	GKN	1.03	Stag Furniture	.99	Redfearn	.94
Leaderflush Doors	.89	Glynwed	1.05	Times Furnishing	.83	Reed International	1.16
Magnet and Southerns	1.37	Hawker Siddeley	1.00	Uniflex	.59	Rockware	1.15
Morley	1.20	Laird Group	1.05	Wrighton	1.04		
Pilkington Bros	.99	Morgan Crucible	1.17			Sector average	1.01
UBM	1.06	Ransome Hoffman	.84	Sector average	.91		
		Renold	.94			**Special steels**	
Sector average	1.14	Senior Engineering	1.00	**Heating and ventilating**		Ductile Steels	.93
		Serck	1.04	Haden Carrier	1.13	Dunford and Elliot	1.09
Cement		Smiths Industries	.93	Myson Group	1.20	Johnson and Firth Brown	.89
Aberthaw	.92	Tube Investments	1.02	Wolseley Hughes	1.08		
Associated Portland	1.35	Vickers	1.05	Biddle Holdings	1.00	Sector average	.84
Mixconcrete	1.31						
Ready Mixed	1.36	Sector average	.97	Sector average	1.08		
Rugby Cement	1.31						
Tunnel	1.08						
Sector average	1.30						

Contracting and construction

Company	Beta
Aberdeen Construction	1.08
Bryant Group	1.03
Costain	1.17
Crest Nicholson	1.39
Fairclough (Leonard)	1.15
French Kier	.95
HAT Group	1.06
Laing, John	1.19
Norwest Holst	1.03
Press, William	1.21
Richards and Wallington	1.01
Taylor Woodrow	1.44
Turriff Construction	1.25
Wimpey, George	1.24
Sector average	1.18

Engineering (heavy)

Company	Beta
Babcock and Wilcox	1.33
British Rollmakers	.77
Capper-Neill	.90
Clarke C-J-T	1.13
Davy	.97
Hall (Matthew)	1.12
Harland and Wolff	1.48
Head Wrightson	.96
International Combustion	1.23
Simon Engineering	1.00
Steetley	.83
Swan Hunter	1.27
Whessoe	1.38
Sector average	1.20

Founders and stampers

Company	Beta
Deritend Stamping	.72
Lake and Elliot	1.15
Leys Foundries	.95
Lloyd, F.H.	.72
Midland Industries	.94
Mitchell, Somers	.92
Triplex Foundries	.74
Sector average	.82

Instruments and machine tools

Company	Beta
Averys	.85
Brown Boveri	.64
Desoulter Bros.	.72
Elliott B	.92
Eva Industries	.81
Herbert, A	1.12
Spear and Jackson	.92
United Gas Industries	.84
United Scientific	1.08
Wolf Electric Tools	.69
Sector average	.84

Mechanical handling

Company	Beta
Blackwood Hodge	1.24
Brammer	.66
Fenner, J.H.	.98
Fluidrive	.94
Morris, Herbert	.78
Sector average	.97

Transport, freight and fuel

Company	Beta
Cawoods	1.11
Charrington Gardner	.92
Ewer, George	.78
Howard Tenens	.71
Lep	.84
Mitchell Cotts Transport	.92
Transport Development	1.02
United Carriers	.97
Sector average	.99

Note

These estimates are taken from the London Business School's *Risk Measurement Service*. They are based on 5 years' data ending May 1977 (except for Crittall Hope which is measured using 5 years' data prior to May 1974 when it was acquired by Norcros). Only the more important companies in each sector are included. Sector averages are the market value-weighted mean betas for all of the companies in the sector in question.

did this imply that the existing method of charging for the use of assets should be modified to accommodate different interest charges in each division, and if so, how could this be achieved? Furthermore, if capital projects subsequently failed to achieve the hurdle rates set for them, or if companies failed to cover their interest charges, would this necessarily be indicative of poor management performance?

Senior management within Norcros recognized the danger of applying purely financial criteria and taking a short-term view in judging new projects. Often investment decisions were driven by competitive considerations, and projects had to be undertaken, simply to stay in business, irrespective of their rate of return. At the same time, however, there was a general recognition that financial criteria were important. Senior management therefore wanted to ensure that the criteria used within Norcros had been fully thought through.

7. Chandler Group

Over the course of the 1970s the board of Chandler Group became increasingly concerned that the company should earn an adequate return on capital. It was clear to the directors that if they were to maintain the business as a going concern, historical cost figures would be an inadequate basis for measuring performance. In 1981, they therefore complied with Standard Statement of Accounting Practice 16 (SSAP16), which introduced a system that adjusted conventional accounting statements for the impact of inflation. These adjustments were intended to indicate whether the company was profitable after allowing for the value of its assets to the business (see Exhibit 2 below).

At the beginning of 1986, Christine Dennison, the newly appointed Finance Director, sent a memorandum to the senior managers of each of the company's five divisions. In it, Christine suggested extending the use of inflation-adjusted accounting to divisional performance measurement and to forecasting and forward planning. The company's policy towards internal financing is summarized by this extract from her memo:

> Every business that hopes to remain a going concern in its own right must aim at a return on capital which will be high enough for the business to be self-financing. The unit of financial measurement is cash, that is, the currency of the territory where the business operates. In the case of the Chandler Group parent company, which has overall responsibility for operations in many countries, the currency in respect of which all the sums finally have to be added up is sterling. This is the currency in which the Board is accountable to its shareholders.
>
> Currencies all round the world suffer from varying rates of inflation or (infrequently) deflation. This has to be accepted. Cash has to be counted at its current value at the time in question, with allowance made in any judgements or assessments for the current or expected rate of inflation.
>
> A step change in the size of a business may be financed by a 'rights issue'. However, normal changes from year to year should be financed by retained profit.

Christine Dennison's memorandum went on to explain how accounts which are corrected for inflation provide better information on the profits which are

This case was written by Elroy Dimson, Ewan Labrom and Jennifer Smerdon, drawing on an earlier case by Ian Cooper and Julian Franks. It is intended to serve as the basis for class discussion rather than to illustrate either effective or ineffective handling of an administrative situation. The identity of the company has been disguised.

available for financing the business. She then proceeded to identify five main uses of inflation-adjusted accounts and forecasts:

> First, inflation-adjusted accounts provide a measure of earnings that corresponds more closely (than historic earnings) with the economic reality of the business. Second, such accounts can highlight periods when the company is not earning enough to maintain itself as a going concern. Third, inflation-adjusted forecasts can indicate what rate of growth is sustainable and the policy measures consistent with it. Fourth, adjustment enables us to compare the profitability of different divisions. Finally, these performance figures can be used to allocate capital funds between different parts of the business.

The memo concluded by proposing the introduction of this new system in 1986. Christine attached a sample set of reports using 1985 data, and invited comments.

The company

Chandler is a large engineering concern, whose sales in 1985 totalled over £1 billion. It is organized as a parent holding company with five main groups of wholly owned subsidiaries. The divisional subsidiaries are engaged in the production of steel, aluminium, heavy engineering, light engineering and household products, respectively. The first two divisions are somewhat larger than the others; the last two are smaller. A detailed breakdown of turnover, profits and assets is given in Exhibit 1(a).

Only 45 per cent of total group sales are in the UK domestic market. The balance consists of exports from the United Kingdom (18 per cent) and overseas production (37 per cent). Inflation, both in the United Kingdom and in the various overseas countries in which Chandler operates, as well as fluctuations in exchange rates, have caused the company to be concerned that its operations should be evaluated correctly.

The company has experienced low real rates of growth over the last 5 years, and the breakdown of sales has remained stable. The pattern of profitability has, however, altered significantly. For example, return on sales for the steel division has declined by 25 per cent in the last 3 years, while return on sales for the household products division has increased by nearly 30 per cent. While year-to-year movements in sales margins have been notoriously difficult to predict, it is felt that margin improvements are one of the keys to better performance by the divisions.

Method of adjusting for inflation

In its annual and half-yearly group accounts, Chandler adjusts for the impact of inflation by using the current cost accounting standard, SSAP16. Exhibit 2

Exhibit 1: *Chandler divisional activity for the year ended 31 December 1985 (£ million)*

(a) Turnover, profits and assets in accordance with historic costs

Division	Turnover	Profit before interest	Net assets
Steel products	315	10	125
Aluminium products	257	11	162
Heavy engineering	208	10	99
Light engineering	102	2	59
Household products	155	9	56
Total	1037	42	501

(b) Divisional profits in accordance with SSAP16

Profit breakdown	Steel products	Aluminium products	Heavy engineering	Light engineering	Household products
Historical operating profit	10	11	10	2	9
Depreciation adjustment	(2)	(5)	(2)	(1)	(1)
Cost of sales adjustment	(3)	(1)	(2)	0	(1)
Monetary working capital adjustment	(1)	3	(3)	4	(1)
Current cost operating profit	4	8	3	5	6
Interest	(8)	(10)	0	0	(2)
Gearing adjustment	2	2	0	0	1
Inflation adjusted profit	(2)	0	3	5	5

gives details of the steps involved in making inflation adjustments. The notion underlying the process was described in a 1983 memorandum from Barry Hall, Christine Dennison's predecessor:

> . . . A company which is a going concern should maintain the value of its real assets (fixed assets and inventory) that are financed by shareholders. Assets which are financed by debtholders incur interest charges. These charges are, at least in part, a payment for inflation, and therefore do not need further adjustment for any increase in replacement cost. . . . Profit adjusted for the impact of inflation has to be sufficient to cover all payments to outside parties, including taxes and dividends.

Exhibit 2: *Current cost adjustments under SSAP16*

Balance sheet

Assets are to be recorded at their 'value to the business'. This is the lower of net current replacement cost and recoverable amount. Recoverable amount is the greater of net realizable value (on disposal) and the amount recoverable from further use.

Profit and loss account

Three main adjustments to trading profit, calculated on an historical cost basis before interest, are required to arrive at current cost operating profit. In addition, a gearing adjustment is required if the company is not financed wholly by equity.

(1) *Depreciation adjustment.* This is the difference between the value to the business of the part of fixed assets consumed during the accounting period and the amount of depreciation charged on an historical cost basis.

(2) *Cost of sales adjustment (COSA).* This is the difference between the value to the business of inventory consumed and the cost of inventory charged on an historical basis. If individual current costs of items sold cannot be easily identified, the cost of sales adjustment will normally be calculated by applying to the opening and closing historical cost inventory figures a relevant price index for the type of inventory held.

(3) *Monetary working capital adjustment (MWCA).* This represents the extent to which a firm suffers the impact of price changes on its debtors. The loss on monetary assets is partially offset by the protection given by trade credit when suppliers' funds carry the burden of price changes. Hence, MWCA represents the amount of additional (or reduced) finance needed for monetary working capital as a result of changes in the input prices of goods and services used and financed by the business. It is calculated in a similar way to the COSA. The specific index of price changes affecting stocks is normally employed to calculate MWCA.

(4) *Gearing adjustment.* This is necessary to reduce the current cost operating adjustments to the extent that operating capability is being financed by debt. Interest charges represent the cost of debt financing. Since interest charges reflect inflation, the gearing adjustment avoids double counting of these costs. The adjustment is determined as follows. First, calculate the 'average net borrowing' and 'average net operating assets'. Second, estimate the gearing proportion, which is equal to the 'average net borrowing' divided by 'average net operating assets'. Finally, apply the gearing proportion to the sum of the three current cost operating adjustments (depreciation, COSA and MWCA). This gearing adjustment is a credit to shareholders' profit.

As an example of the size of the adjustments that are required to account for inflation, Exhibit 3 shows Chandler's 1985 inflation-adjusted profit and loss account. The major differences from the historic accounts are:

(1) Additional depreciation   − £11 million
(2) Cost of sales adjustment   − £7 million

(3) Monetary working capital adjustment   + £2 million
(4) Gearing adjustment   + £5 million

The first two allow for inflation in the value of plant and equipment and in inventory. The monetary working capital adjustment shows the company's net exposure to inflation from the excess of trade creditors over trade debtors. The gearing adjustment represents the amount of the extra cost which is financed by debt, and therefore is not a charge on shareholders' funds.

Exhibit 1(b) shows the divisional breakdown of these four inflation adjustments, and how the profits of each subsidiary are affected. When profits are stated in accordance with SSAP16, the steel products division tumbles from top to bottom ranked out of the five subsidiaries, while the division which is the lowest earner in historical terms (that is, light engineering) generates the largest inflation-adjusted profit.

Responses to the memorandum

Within 2 weeks of sending the memorandum about inflation-adjusted reporting, Christine had received a number of replies and requests for further information.

Exhibit 3: *Current cost profit and loss account, in accordance with SSAP16 for 1985*

P and L summary		£ million
Turnover		1037
Operating profit shown by historical accounts		42
Current cost adjustments		
Depreciation	(11)	
Cost of sales	(7)	
Monetary working capital	2	
		(16)
Current cost operating profit		26
Interest		(20)
Current cost profit before taxation		6
Taxation		(4)
Current cost earnings		2
Gearing adjustment		5
Dividends		(8)
Decrease in retained earnings		(1)

Several of the respondents had noted that, after inflation adjustment, the 1985 profit was insufficient to cover the proposed dividend. Gareth Deacon, the Managing Director of the Aluminium Division, asked whether this was truly a drain on the cash resources of the company. 'Has the money that we raised from our rights issue in May 1985 gone to cover the dividend payment?' he asked. 'At the time we raised the money, we were saying it was needed for investment in new businesses and in modernization of existing plant. Is none of it now available for use in the business?'

Most of the comments regarding inflation-adjusted figures concentrated, however, on the measurement of divisional performance. The impact of the various adjustments on the reported profits of the different divisions was dramatic. For example, the Aluminium Division accounted for 45 per cent of the total additional depreciation owing to the advanced age of most of its plant. In contrast, most of the cost of sales adjustment came from the steel and heavy engineering divisions, which were experiencing rapid increases in input prices during the period.

Gareth Deacon was clearly angry that the depreciation adjustment, which was calculated on a 20 year, straight-line basis, overestimated the true cost of his plant. The plant had been extremely profitable during the early part of its life, and he considered it completely unjust to burden current operations with these inflated depreciation charges. Furthermore, Deacon pointed out, 'the spurious impression of aluminium being an unprofitable division would inevitably lead to its being starved of the funds it needs for modernisation and improvements in efficiency'. He concluded his response by threatening dire action if the adjustment remained unaltered.

Richard Giles of the Steel Division was concerned that the holding gains on inventories were being offset by the cost of sales adjustment. His predecessor had left Chandler Group under something of a cloud, after holding excessive stocks of steel during a period of prolonged price weakness, followed by destocking at the bottom of the price cycle. By contrast, Giles had had the foresight to build inventories in anticipation of recent price rises, but evidently this was not to be reflected in the inflation-adjusted profit for the division. He argued that this could scarcely provide an incentive for profitable management of the company's stocks of raw materials and work in progress.

Similarly, Jonathan Brett, the Managing Director of the Heavy Engineering Division, queried the validity of the gearing adjustment. Much of the borrowing of Chandler was taken on by the parent company rather than by the subsidiary companies which formed the divisions. In making the gearing adjustment for individual divisions, this central borrowing was not taken into account. Jonathan was convinced that this would bias the evaluation of divisional performance. In addition, his divisional accountant added another criticism:

The gearing adjustment seems to reward borrowing by divisions whose asset and input prices rise faster than the interest rate (which presumably reflects the overall rate of inflation), and punish those whose holding gains occur at a rate lower than the interest rate. The latter carry interest charges significantly greater than the amount of the gearing adjustment. Indeed, this is true for Chandler as a whole, which had interest charges in 1985 £15 million greater than the gearing adjustments.

On the same topic, Mark Chandler, Chief Executive of the firm, denied the validity of excluding holding gains on inventories financed by equity, however large the gains. He wanted to know whether this procedure could be correct even if the holding gains were to exceed the costs of holding the inventory. He asked whether it would make any difference if the company were to set up a new subsidiary which was a specialist trader in metals.

Gareth Deacon's reply to Christine's document included further resentment about the gearing adjustments:

It appears to me that part of the holding gains on inventories and fixed assets which are financed by debt are included in the figure for profit after interest and taxes. If this is true, what is the rationale behind this adjustment? Why are divisions which have historically been financed by fixed interest debt treated differently from their counterparts which use overdraft facilities at a variable rate of interest? And surely the gearing adjustment will encourage an increase in the use of fixed interest debt finance?

The final major concern about the use of inflation-adjusted figures for performance measurement was voiced by Mark Chandler. He wanted to know whether the company should use current cost operating profits to allocate capital on a divisional basis, and the problems that might arise if this were done. In particular, he wanted to know how the current cost profits ought to be normalized to take account of the capital employed within the division, and whether the divisional performance measures should be estimated before or after the deduction of tax.

Forward planning

In response to a general demand from the senior divisional managers, Christine Dennison sent out further information about the use of inflation-adjusted figures for forecasting and forward planning. The model to be used, and the methodology behind it, were described in detail. The model would be used to generate alternative proforma balance sheets, profit and loss accounts and funds flow statements, samples of which were distributed by Christine (see Exhibits 4, 5 and 6).

The model was written in the form of a spreadsheet, using Lotus 1–2–3^{TM} as the programming language, and could be run on a desktop personal computer. The requirements for employing the model are set out in Exhibit 7. Using the computer, numerous scenarios could be tested based on assumed values for five underlying parameters — real growth rate of fixed assets, inflation rate, margin on sales, tax rate and level of gearing. Christine concluded by saying 'The

Exhibit 4: *Model for projecting inflation-adjusted balance sheets based on SSAP16*
Parameters for model: Same as for Exhibits 5 and 6

Balance sheet summary (£ million)	Opening	Closing
Fixed assets		
Replacement cost[1]	1000	1086
Depreciation[2]	(500)	(530)
	500	556
Working capital		
Stock[3]	400	445
Debtors *less* Creditors[4]	100	111
	500	556
Net assets	1000	1112
Equity[5]	600	639
Loans[6]	400	443
Fixed asset revaluation[7]	—	30
	1000	1112

Notes

1. *Gross fixed assets*

Opening balance	1000	Historic cost balance 400
Inflation*	60	6 per cent × opening balance
Asset disposals	(53)	5 per cent × 1060 [see Exhibit 7a]
Asset purchases	53	
Growth in fixed assets	26	Ensures 5 per cent real growth in
Closing balance	1086	net book value

2. *Depreciation*

Opening balance	500	
Inflation	30	6 per cent × opening balance
Asset disposals	(53)	
Historic cost depreciation	30	7½ per cent × historic cost balance
Additional depreciation	23	Replacement cost *less* Historic
Closing balance	530	cost [see Exhibit 7b]
Net book value = 1086 − 530 =	556	500 + inflation + growth

3. *Closing stock* = Opening value + 6 per cent inflation + 5 per cent growth*

4. *Debtors* less *Creditors* = Opening value + 6 per cent inflation + 5 per cent growth*

5. *Equity*

			Gearing adjustment	
			100%	*40%*
Opening balance	600			
Cost of sales adjustment	24			
Monetary working capital adjustment	6	COSA	24	10
Gearing adjustment	(21)	Depreciation	23	9
Retained earnings	30	MWCA	6	2
	639		53	21

6. *Loan movement*

Opening balance	400	
Gearing adjustment	21	
Additional loans	22	40 per cent × increase in sum of net
	443	debtors + fixed assets + stock

7. *Fixed asset revaluation* = 6 per cent × opening balance (1000) *less* Backlog depreciation (30)

*NB: Normally inflation would be based on *average* rather than opening values.

system is designed ultimately to focus management attention on required trading profit, and whether the business can realistically generate this profit in the years to come.'

Responses from the managers circulated with the additional information package indicated that several were uneasy about using inflation-adjusted figure in this way. They noted that, in particular, the target growth rate has a dramatic impact on required trading margin. Trading margin was also felt to be, in many cases, outside the control of divisional management. John Bridges, the Managing Director of the rapidly growing Consumer Products Division, was quite adamant that it was incorrect to place the burden of financing growth on internally generated funds.

By the end of February 1986, Christine had compiled a thick file of comments on the use of inflation-adjusted figures for evaluation and forecasting purposes. She had to make a decision about whether or not to implement the system, and she also had to reply to the questions raised by the senior divisional managers and by the chief executive of the Chandler Group. Since she was new to the company she was anxious to create a good impression.

Exhibit 5: *Model for projecting inflation-adjusted profit and loss accounts based on SSAP16*
Parameters for model: 5 per cent growth 6 per cent inflation 10 per cent margin
35 per cent tax 40 per cent gearing

P and L summary	£ million
Turnover	1280
Replacement cost of sales[1]	(1152)
Interest[2]	128
	(36)
Tax[3]	92
	(32)
Dividend[4]	60
	(30)
Retained earnings	30

Notes
1. Costs of sales = 90 per cent × turnover
2. Interest charge = 3 per cent over the ongoing rate of inflation multiplied by the opening loan balance [see Exhibit 7f]
3. Tax = 35 per cent × profit after interest but before taxation
4. Net dividend = 5 per cent × opening equity capital [see Exhibit 7f]

Exhibit 6: *Model for projecting inflation-adjusted funds flow based on SSAP16*
Parameters for model: 5 per cent growth   6 per cent inflation   10 per cent margin
35 per cent tax   40 per cent gearing

Funds flow summary	£ million	£ million
Requirements		
For fixed assets		
Historical depreciation	30	
Additional depreciation	23	
Growth in fixed assets	26	
		79
For stock		
Inflation	24	
Growth	21	
		45
For monetary working capital		
Inflation	6	
Growth	5	
		11
Total		135
Sources		
Provided internally		
Depreciation from historical accounts		30
Additional depreciation	23	
Cost of sales adjustment	24	
Monetary working capital adjustment	6	
Gearing (40 per cent)	(21)	
		32
60 per cent growth of fixed assets and stock		29
		91
Provided by lenders		
Gearing adjustment	21	
40 per cent growth of fixed assets and stock	18	
40 per cent additional monetary working capital	5	
		44
Total		135

Exhibit 7: *Employing Chandler's model to project inflation-adjusted accounts*

(a) Identify the capital expenditure required to maintain the planned growth in fixed assets. In the case of plant and machinery, Chandler assesses this is at 5 per cent of cost as adjusted to current pounds.

(b) Deduct from this the depreciation already provided in the 'historic' accounts; the balance is the additional depreciation for the year required because of inflation.

(c) Assess the additional funds due to inflation which are required to maintain normal efficient stock levels. If growth is expected, assess the further additional stock required. Both these elements have to be identified.

(d) A similar assessment has to be made in relation to monetary working capital.

(e) The sum of the additional requirements identified under items (a) to (d) above is then apportioned between equity and loan capital (included under this heading is both short-term and long-term borrowing). The proportion of borrowing to equity is referred to as the gearing percentage. Although gearing percentages are to some extent flexible, no business should assume that it will be allowed to increase its gearing percentage indefinitely. The real requirement is that, over a period of years, the gearing percentage should be held at a similar level which is acceptable to lenders and appropriate for the business. In Chandler's case, this might range between 20 per cent and 40 per cent on the inflation adjusted capital. The chosen gearing percentage determines how much of the additional requirements identified above may prudently be financed by borrowing and how much has to be financed by equity.

(f) Retained profit is arrived at after providing out of 'profit before financing expenses' the following three items: first, interest on borrowings (in Chandler's case, it is considered appropriate to allow for interest at a rate of 3 per cent over the ongoing rate of inflation); second, tax on profits (in Chandler's case, it is considered that the effective tax rate might range from 25 per cent to 40 per cent of inflation-adjusted profits; at any particular time, Chandler would specify the rate to be used in calculations); third, a dividend of 5 per cent on the inflation-adjusted equity capital (if historical capital were used as the base the rate would have to be higher — perhaps 7½ per cent). In practice, the normal dividend requirement might be varied from time to time by Chandler, depending on the particular situation.

(g) The profit before financing expenses may be achieved by any of a wide range of permutations and combinations of sales volume and trading margins, the parameters of which are determined by the nature of the market and the competitive efficiency (in a very general sense of the word 'efficiency' — including, for example, the rate of turnover of capital) of the business.

8. British Airports Authority

In early 1984, the British Airports Authority (BAA) ran an eye-catching series of advertisements in major newspapers and on London Underground posters. The message of the campaign was clear: BAA's premier airport, Heathrow, was not only the busiest international airport in the world, it was also financially successful. One advertisement proclaimed that the 1983–84 financial year had produced a record trading profit of £51.6 million; that revenue from trading concessions had grown substantially by 17 per cent; and that during the year, the BAA had invested £132 million in new facilities, the highest figure ever.

Another advertisement, specifically geared to the record of Heathrow stated: 'Heathrow is outspending every other major airport both in terms of extensions and improvements. . . . As if that weren't enough, this entire expansion programme has been paid for out of our own money. Heathrow is neither subsidized by the Government, nor propped up by the poor beleagured tax payer.'

However, the improving fortunes of Heathrow were not universally acclaimed. Some airport users considered that part of the profits had been made at their expense. In a letter to the *Financial Times* in July 1984, the Chairman of the Steering Committee of the British Airport Users Action Group wrote 'BAA would like to divert attention from Heathrow's excessive rate of return, which is nearly three times greater than the average for UK industrial and commercial companies. The return is exacted from the airlines and their customers regardless of Heathrow being a low-risk monopoly business.'

This was not the first salvo to be fired in the battle between the airlines using Heathrow and BAA. Three years earlier, airlines operating at Heathrow decided that, following recent increases, airport user charges were excessive, and so they started proceedings in the High Court in an attempt to gain repayment of all or part of their fees. The airlines claimed that the structure of airport charges between Heathrow, Gatwick and other BAA airports was unreasonable; that

This case was written by Pamela Pocock and Paul Marsh as a basis for class discussion rather than to illustrate either effective or ineffective handling of an administrative situation. Extracts from Cmnd 7131 are reproduced with the permission of the Controller of Her Majesty's Stationery Office.

BAA was aiming to achieve its overall commercial and financial objectives through unfair exploitation of those depending on it for services at Heathrow; and that this policy led to an indefensibly high rate of return on capital employed at Heathrow. BAA for its part, stated in its Annual Report for 1980–81 that the action would be 'vigorously defended'.

Background to BAA

The BAA was created as a government-owned public enterprise, through the Airport Authority Act 1965, and commenced trading in April 1966. It operated under the terms of a Consolidation Act, the Airports Authority Act of 1975.

Exhibit 1(a): *BAA financial performance: balance sheet*

	Current cost figures (£ million) for the year ending 31 March				
Balance sheet	1978	1979	1980	1981	1982
Fixed assets					
Fixed assets[1,2]	507	516	616	826	860
Deferred expenditure/trade investments	4	5	6	8	12
Total fixed assets	511	521	622	834	873
Current assets					
Debtors	14	22	30	34	36
Loans to public authorities	10	9	19	0	0
Certificates of tax deposits	6	10	0	0	0
Cash	0	8	1	26	20
Total current assets	30	49	50	59	56
Current liabilities					
Creditors and provisions	22	30	37	47	53
Corporation tax	9	14	13	22	18
Short-term loans	0	0	0	4	5
Total current liabilities	31	45	50	73	76
Total net assets	509	526	622	820	852
Long-term liabilities					
Commencing capital debt	53	53	53	53	49
Subsequent loans less repayments	11	10	9	4	8
Reserves	401	463	560	763	794
Deferred taxation	45	0	0	0	0
Capital employed	509	526	622	820	852

Notes
For notes 1 and 2, see Exhibit 1(d). Totals may not sum due to rounding.

BAA owns and manages seven major airports in the United Kingdom — Heathrow, Gatwick and Stansted serving London, and Glasgow, Edinburgh, Prestwick and Aberdeen in Scotland. Together, these airports handle 75 per cent of all passengers and 87 per cent of air cargo traffic in the United Kingdom.

Exhibit 1(b): *BAA financial performance: profit and loss account*

	Current cost figures (£ million) for the year ending 31 March				
Profit and loss account	1978	1979	1980	1981	1982
Income					
Traffic	61.8	88.5	102.7	152.3	160.4
Commercial	63.3	73.7	88.6	101.7	117.1
Total	125.1	162.2	191.4	254.0	277.5
Expenditure					
Traffic	76.4	113.0	128.5	156.4	169.7
Commercial	35.2	36.8	53.4	59.8	68.1
Total	111.7	149.8	181.9	216.1	237.8
Trading profit					
Traffic	(14.6)	(24.5)	(25.8)	(4.1)	(9.3)
Commercial	28.1	36.9	35.3	41.9	49.0
Total trading profit	13.4	12.4	9.5	37.9	39.7
Profit (loss) on disposal fixed assets[3]	(3.3)	(1.2)	(2.8)	(.4)	(.5)
Monetary working capital adjustment[4]	0	0	(1.0)	(1.2)	(.7)
Interest received	1.2	3.3	5.4	6.8	6.0
Current cost profit before interest and tax	11.3	14.5	11.0	43.1	44.5
Taxation	18.9	13.8	12.5	21.0	16.0
Interest paid on borrowings	4.0	4.0	3.9	3.8	3.8
Current cost profit (loss)	(11.6)	(3.2)	(5.3)	18.3	24.7
Extraordinary item (head office move)	0	0	0	0	(2.3)
Current cost profit after extraordinary items	(11.6)	(3.2)	(5.3)	18.3	22.4
Statement of retained profits/reserves					
Total reserves at start of year		400.5	463.0	560.2	762.9
Current cost profit		(3.2)	(5.3)	18.3	22.4
Revaluation adjustment		65.7	101.5	183.2	8.2
Monetary working capital adjustment		0	1.0	1.2	.7
Total reserves at year end	400.5	463.0	560.2	762.9	794.1

Notes
For notes 3 and 4, see Exhibit 1(d). Totals may not sum due to rounding.

Exhibit 1(c): *BAA financial performance: profitability of Heathrow versus BAA total*

	Current cost figures in £ million for year ending 31 March									
	1978		1979		1980		1981		1982	
Income/Expenditure items	All	LHR	All	LHR	All	LHR	All	LHR	All	LHR
Traffic income										
Landing fees[5]	48.9	36.6	72.4	51.8	84.5	60.0	123.2	85.5	125.7	84.6
Parking fees	7.3	4.9	11.4	8.0	13.0	9.5	22.0	17.1	26.3	20.4
Apron/other services	5.7	2.3	4.8	1.7	5.2	1.4	7.2	2.1	8.4	2.7
Total	61.8	43.8	88.5	61.5	102.7	71.0	152.3	104.7	160.4	107.6
Commercial income										
Concessions	40.8	30.1	48.5	35.2	57.0	40.5	65.3	43.8	74.4	48.5
Rents and services	22.3	17.3	25.0	18.7	31.3	23.0	36.1	26.6	42.4	30.5
Miscellaneous	.3	.2	.2	.1	.3	.2	.3	.2	.3	.2
Total	63.3	47.6	73.7	54.0	88.6	63.7	101.7	70.5	117.1	79.1
Total income	125.1	91.4	162.2	115.5	191.4	134.7	254.0	175.2	277.5	186.8
Expenditure items										
Staff costs	32.4	18.9	49.8	28.4	67.2	38.8	75.8	43.8	81.0	46.5
Rents and rates	7.4	4.8	9.7	5.5	10.0	6.3	11.8	7.2	16.5	9.5
Utility/general services	14.8	10.7	16.8	11.8	21.3	15.5	25.5	18.2	28.9	20.5
Equipment and supplies	4.0	2.5	5.1	3.0	5.8	3.4	5.6	2.9	7.5	1.9
Maintenance and repairs	8.3	5.2	10.6	6.4	11.2	6.7	14.8	7.8	17.1	9.3
Other expenses[5]	7.5	5.1	16.1	12.4	16.0	12.1	32.2	22.4	30.8	22.2
Depreciation etc.[6]	37.3	20.0	41.8	22.3	50.4	27.0	50.6	26.5	56.0	29.8
Total expenditure	111.7	67.3	149.8	89.9	181.9	109.7	216.1	128.8	237.8	139.7
Trading profit (loss)[7]	13.4	24.1	12.4	25.6	9.5	24.9	37.9	46.4	39.7	47.0
Attributable to:										
Traffic	(14.6)	2.0	(24.5)	(2.1)	(25.8)	(1.5)	(4.1)	17.8	(9.3)	14.6
Commercial	28.1	22.0	36.9	27.6	35.3	26.4	41.9	28.7	49.0	32.4

Notes

All denotes total for all BAA airports; LHR denotes London Heathrow. For notes 5, 6 and 7, see Exhibit 1(d). Totals may not sum due to rounding.

Exhibit 1(d): *Extract from notes to BAA accounts for the years 1977–78 to 1981–82*

1. *Fixed assets* other than those under construction are stated at their gross replacement cost on the following bases, and accumulated depreciation at year end is similarly uplifted.

All assets were professionally valued at 1 April 1976, and then again at 1 April 1981. In the intervening period, land values were estimated by the Authority's Chief Estates Surveyor, while motor vehicles and office machinery were updated by reference to indices issued by the Central Statistical Office. Other values were updated using the Department of Environment 'Index of the Cost of New Construction'. However, this index was discontinued in 1978, and the Authority established separate indices for each major asset category at 1 April 1978 on the basis of a revaluation at that date of a sample of assets covering all airports by Wakeman Trower and Partners, Quantity Surveyors and Construction Cost Consultants (see also relifing in 1980, footnote 6 below).

2. *Capital expenditure* at cost for BAA was £36.8 million (1977–78), £33.3 million (1978–79), £54.2 million (1979–80), £78.4 million (1980–81) and £83.1 million (1981–82). Of this, expenditure at Heathrow was £20 million, £14 million, £25 million, £32.6 million and £34 million respectively, for each of the 5 years, while expenditure at other BAA airports was £16.8 million, £18.5 million, £26.3 million, £36.9 million and £45 million respectively.

3. *Loss on disposal of fixed assets.*   The breakdown of these figures (in £'000) is: For 1979–80, Heathrow 90, other airports 2748; for 1980–81, Heathrow 188, head office 160, other airports 32; for 1981–82, Heathrow 110, head office (17), other airports 372. No CCA breakdowns are available for earlier years.

4. *Monetary working capital* consists of debtors less creditors, excluding capital expenditure and deferred expenditure provisions. The adjustment has been calculated using the averaging method on the quarterly values of monetary working capital. The index used is a weighted average of changes in the BAA's internal staff costs, the Index of All New Construction for building work, and the RPI for other external costs.

5. *Landing fees and security charges.*   From 1 April 1978, the Department of Trade introduced a levy upon the BAA of 80p per arriving passenger to cover security costs. This levy is recovered in the landing fee charges and paid to the Department of Trade who then reimburse the BAA for expenses incurred in the security activity. The total income from landing fees shown in the accounts from 1978–79 onwards (Exhibit 1(c)) reflects the security levy collected; the net expenditure incurred is included under other expenses (Exhibit 1(c)), while additional security staff costs are included under staff costs (Exhibit 1(c)). The total security levy amounted to £15.6 million (1978–79), £18.9 million (1979–80), £32.4 million (1980–81) and £34.2 million (1981–82), while the corresponding figures for Heathrow were £10.9 million, £13.4 million, £22.5 million and £23.1 million respectively.

6. *Depreciation* is calculated on a straight-line basis using estimated useful lives of assets as determined by studies undertaken by the Authority in 1977 and 1980. The useful lives of assets fall within the following ranges: Terminal buildings (15–40 years); other freehold buildings (40–58 years); runways, taxiways and aprons (23–59 years); aerodrome lighting (15–32 years); car parks (10–45 years); roads, bridges, tunnels and drains (30–55 years); fixed plant and equipment (7–54 years); motor vehicles and mobile equipment (4–22 years).

Following the relifing exercise in 1980, accumulated depreciation was restated to represent the proportion of elapsed life to total life.

The gross replacement cost and accumulated depreciation figures shown in the accounts include significant sums (£145 million at 31 March 1982, £121 million at 31 March 1981) in respect of fully depreciated assets still in use. These assets, which produce an insignificant amount of income, are considered non-essential and it is not the Authority's present intention that they should be replaced. Depreciation has therefore not been charged on these assets in the accounts.

7. *Trading profit (loss) by airport;* Gatwick's trading profit (in £'000) was 258 (1979–80) and 1552 (1981–82), with losses in all other years; Aberdeen showed a profit of 433 (1980–81) and 746 (1981–82) but losses in all other years. All other airports (except Heathrow) showed losses in each year (that is, Stansted, Glasgow, Edinburgh and Prestwick).

The Authority states that its primary task is to 'plan, develop and operate these airports to meet the present and future needs of the international and domestic air transport systems in order that travellers and cargo may pass through them as safely, swiftly and conveniently as possible'. It also coordinates the activities of the many organizations which operate at the airports, including airlines, customs, immigration, police, fuel companies, cargo agents and concessionaires. BAA's aim for the future is to ensure that the UK civil air transport industry maintains its position in the forefront of world aviation, so that UK trade and tourism can flourish.

BAA provides a range of services including planning, developing and maintaining airport buildings, runways and roads; and providing fire services, apron control, terminal management, security, passenger services and information systems, restaurants, shops and car parks. BAA itself concentrates on providing airport services, such as security, fire, rescue and snow clearance, while other services which are not unique to airports, such as catering, retailing, car hire and parking are franchised out to private competition. Thus BAA's own turnover is only a small fraction of the total turnover attributable to businesses located at, or operating from, its airports. For example, in 1981–82, total turnover at Heathrow was some £3 billion, of which £1.9 billion was accounted for by the airlines, £700 million by franchises, £200 million by hotels and freight services located around the airport periphery, and just under £200 million, or only some 7 per cent of the total, by BAA itself.

Under the Airports Authority Act, the BAA acquired a responsibility to deploy its resources efficiently and economically. In response to this requirement, BAA claimed that 'it has financed its operations wholly from internal resources for 13 of the 17 years of its existence and up to March 1983 had paid £65 million in corporation tax. Since its formation, the BAA has been a consistenty profitable enterprise'. (See Exhibits 1(a) to 1(d).)

BAA's profits in fact come from two principal sources, traffic charges and commercial operations (see Exhibits 1(b) and (c)). Traffic charges are designed to reflect the cost of providing and operating facilities for aircraft and passengers, and are levied for landing, parking and apron services, following the broad charging approach adopted by all major European airports. They are based largely on passenger numbers and aircraft weight, but also vary with the time of day, period of the year, whether the flight is domestic or international, and whether the aircraft is 'quiet'. This differs from the method normally

Exhibit 2: *Notional comparison of user charges for major international airports*

Airport	Exchange rate	Notional income[1]		Total charges[2]
		LHR	South-east	
		£ million	£ million	£ million
London		87	99	147
Tokyo	541 yen	102	135	135
Paris	9.72 Ffr.	91	122	122
Frankfurt	4.22 DM	94	124	124
Rome	1944 lira	48	63	63
Madrid	157 peseta	38	50	50
Amsterdam	4.62 guilder	76	100	123
Copenhagen	13.06 krone	58	75	75
Athens	90.97 Dr	31	41	41
Zurich	4.01 Sfr	81	106	106
New York (JFK)[3]	$2.16		90	141
Atlanta			6	68
Los Angeles			18	77
Dallas			23	80
Washington			36	96
Miami			27	91

Notes
1. Notional income is for the airport operator in column 1 using the current local rates but assuming the traffic patterns of either Heathrow (LHR) or the total South-east airports of BAA.
2. Total charges are based on traffic patterns for the South-east. European airports include a government security levy for the United Kingdom and a navigation service charge for the United Kingdom and Amsterdam.
3. All US airports have an estimated $51 ticket tax revenue added to their total charges; these also include terminal rentals where appropriate.
Source: British Airports Authority, Annual Report and Accounts 1979–80.

adopted in North America, where airlines either build their own terminals or lease terminal areas and meet the operating costs directly, and where other capital investment in airports is funded by a government ticket tax. Consequently, landing and parking fees are designed to recover only the residual costs remaining after these other sources of finance have been exhausted, frequently after allowing for concessions and other income accruing to the airport operator. For this reason, it is particularly difficult to make comparisons between European traffic charges and equivalent services in the United States (see Exhibits 2 and 3).

The second source of profits is from concessions, rents and services (see Exhibit 1(c)). In 1981–82, these accounted for nearly 70 per cent of total trading profits. The major revenue earners here are from duty and tax free trading. BAA point out that if this source of income were ever to disappear, this would have a serious impact on profitability, and would ultimately lead to an increase in air fares.

Exhibit 3: *Estimated passenger costs by cost item (per passenger-kilometre) 1982[1]*

Route groups	Total operating costs (US cents)	Aircraft operating costs (per cent) Costs less fuel and oil[2]	Fuel and oil	Other operating costs (per cent) Landing /airport charges	En-route charges[3]	Station expense[4]	Passenger services	Travel agents' fees[5]	Ticket sales, promotion	General admin. and misc.
All routes	7.9	25.0	27.2	3.7	1.5	9.2	11.3	7.9	8.9	5.3
North–Central America	8.4	27.3	26.2	2.4	0	14.3	10.7	6.0	7.1	6.0
Central America	13.2	25.0	24.2	5.3	0	8.3	6.8	9.0	12.1	9.0
North America	9.3	29.0	24.7	2.2	0	16.1	10.8	5.4	6.5	5.4
North–South America	8.2	28.0	28.0	2.4	1.2	8.5	9.8	9.8	8.5	3.7
South America	11.5	28.7	27.8	7.0	.8	7.0	7.8	9.6	10.4	.8
Europe	14.2	23.9	21.1	7.0	3.5	12.7	9.9	7.7	10.6	3.5
Africa	12.7	26.8	33.1	6.3	.8	7.9	6.3	5.5	7.9	5.5
Europe–Middle East	10.2	29.4	24.5	2.9	2.0	8.8	9.8	7.8	9.8	4.9
Europe–Africa	8.3	22.9	30.1	3.6	1.2	7.2	12.0	7.2	9.6	6.0
North Atlantic	6.2	24.2	27.4	1.6	1.6	8.1	12.9	8.1	8.1	8.1
Mid-Atlantic	6.9	26.3	27.5	2.9	1.4	7.2	13.0	7.2	8.7	5.8
South Atlantic	9.4	27.7	31.9	3.2	2.1	7.4	10.6	6.4	9.6	1.1
Asia Pacific	7.5	25.3	25.3	5.3	1.3	8.0	12.0	9.3	9.3	4.0
Europe–Asia Pacific	6.7	23.9	31.3	3.0	1.5	6.0	11.9	7.5	9.0	6.0
North/Mid-Pacific	5.6	23.2	33.9	1.8	0	7.1	10.7	10.7	7.1	5.4
South Pacific	6.4	21.9	28.1	1.6	0	9.4	15.6	7.8	7.8	7.8

Notes
1. Passenger costs have been derived for each route group taking into account the contribution made by the revenue earned for the carriage of freight and mail. The margins of uncertainty in the estimates mean that the figures should be taken as indicative only.
2. Aircraft operating costs include flight operations expenses (cockpit crew salaries and expenses, rentals and insurance of flight equipment), aircraft maintenance and overhaul, and aircraft standing charges such as depreciation and interest charges.
3. En-route charges covers air traffic control on the journey.
4. Station expenses include most costs at the airport, for example loading, checkin and engineering.
5. The commission that is paid to travel agents.

Heathrow and the South-east airports system

The South-east of England is by far the most important region in the United Kingdom for the supply of airport services, the vast majority of which are provided by BAA (see Exhibit 4). The only exception is the municipally owned Luton Airport, which has a small market share, and is not considered suitable for development.

Within the South-east system, Heathrow is by far the largest airport. It is regarded by BAA, the airlines and the flying public alike as Europe's premier airport, because of the large number of destinations served by scheduled services, the greater frequency of services, and the resultant excellent interlining services. Quite simply, Heathrow lies at the crossroads of world aviation.

Exhibit 4: *Heathrow's market share compared with other UK airports*

Year	All UK airports	All BAA airports	All South-east airports[1]	Heathrow	Manchester[2]
Passengers (millions)					
1977	45.9	34.4	32.5	23.4	2.8
1978	52.8	39.4	36.9	26.5	3.4
1979	57.0	42.3	39.4	28.0	3.5
1980	57.8	42.8	39.7	27.5	4.3
Air transport movements ('000s)					
1977	759	447	367	243	47
1978	862	504	408	269	51
1979	924	541	434	276	50
1980	954	564	441	277	58
Cargo (tonnes '000)					
1977	705	602	573	438	34
1978	748	641	612	460	31
1979	797	675	647	496	23
1980	744	630	610	466	24
Income (£ millions)					
1977	163	125	119	91	15
1978	217	162	153	116	21
1979	264	191	180	135	24
1980	345*	254	235*	175	32

Notes
1. Includes non-BAA airports
2. Manchester is the largest non-BAA-owned airport in the United Kingdom
* Estimated by the Chartered Institute of Public Finance and Accounting in their Local Authority Airports Accounts and Statistics

The number of air transport movements at BAA's South-east airports increased from 307 000 in 1970–71, to 379 000 in 1981–82, while over the same period, the number of passengers nearly doubled, from 20 million to 38 million. Projections by both BAA and the government indicated that demand would continue to grow throughout the remainder of the century (see Exhibit 5). Following more than a decade of debate about how this demand should be met, the government made a major policy statement on airports in December 1979. They announced that they would not be building a major new international airport of the kind considered by the Roskill Commission in 1971, nor did they intend to resurrect the Maplin project, even in a revised form. Instead, the policy would be first to encourage the fullest use of regional airports, and second, to meet the increased demand in the South-east, as it developed, by providing additional capacity based on the existing airports, namely Heathrow, Gatwick and Stansted. Over time, this would involve three major new investment projects, namely a fourth (but not a fifth) terminal at Heathrow (due to open in 1985); a second terminal (but not a second runway) at Gatwick; and the expansion of Stansted to 15 million passengers using the existing runway.

Meanwhile, pending construction of the fourth terminal, capacity at Heathrow was virtually exhausted. Even looking beyond 1985, however, BAA was concerned about capacity, which would be constrained by the sizes of the four terminals and by the ceiling, imposed by the government, of 275 000 annual air transport movements from the time that Terminal 4 opened. BAA were opposed to this limit, since Heathrow's physical capacity at that point would be some 300 000 air transport movements (depending on the aircraft

Exhibit 5: *Planning forecasts of demand — BAA airports total*

Forecast item	1983 Actual	1990	1995
Passengers (million)			
BAA South-east	39.7	62.9	79.9
Scotland	5.7	7.9	9.3
BAA Total	45.4	70.8	89.2
Air transport movements ('000s)			
BAA South-east	388	457	512
Scotland	176	202	204
BAA Total	564	659	716
Cargo ('000 tonnes)			
BAA South-east	590	955	1265
Scotland	31	61	75
BAA Total	621	1016	1340

Source: Memorandum by the British Airports Authority to the House of Commons Transport Committee

mix). Nevertheless, the limit would have to be observed, since it had been imposed by the government in response to the overwhelming environmental and planning objections raised at the time of the Terminal 4 planning enquiry. The environmental lobby, plus the constraints on land availability, made any further expansion at Heathrow unlikely for the foreseeable future.

These constraints, combined with the possibility of increased capacity elsewhere, had led BAA to consider the South-east airports as an integral system, for which it had developed a 'South-east Airports Distribution Strategy'. This had three main features. First, it aimed to transfer individual services from Heathrow to Gatwick, particularly where such transfers would best complement Gatwick's route network. Second, it involved low fare traffic transferring from Heathrow to Stansted in addition to the scheduled traffic that Stansted would generate in its own right. And third, some charter traffic would be encouraged to transfer from Gatwick to Stansted, where most of it would anyway be better served.

As a matter of government policy, it had already been agreed that no new airlines should be allowed to operate out of Heathrow. In a statement on 9 October 1979, John Nott, the Secretary of State for Trade, announced:

> The relief of congestion at Heathrow and the provision of scheduled services from Gatwick will continue to be an important objective of the government's civil aviation policies and of all negotiations about the air services of existing operators at Heathrow. As an incentive to those airlines which transfer their services from Heathrow, BAA should maintain its present policy which is to widen the present disparity in the landing and other charges at Heathrow and Gatwick.

(Fees at Heathrow were already some 50 per cent higher than at Gatwick.)

Immediately following the October 1979 statement, BAA's Chairman sent a telegram to all airlines using Heathrow, making it clear that all carriers faced the same choice — accept a limit on their services at Heathrow, or move all or some of them to Gatwick. Actually persuading the airlines to move, however, proved a much more difficult task. Plans to transfer Canadian services to Gatwick were eventually dropped, while the debate over the transfer of Iberian Services dragged on for many months.

The White Paper

Since the late 1970s, nationalized industries in the United Kingdom have come under increasing pressure to meet certain financial targets laid down by the government. The philosophy behind this requirement was set out in a White Paper, 'The Nationalised Industries' issued in March 1978 (Cmnd 7131) which states:

> The Government must be concerned in the strategies and operational decisions of public importance, of industries which are basic to the national economy; in seeing

that these industries, which are not subject to the private sector discipline of the threat of bankruptcy, and are in some cases relatively free from market pressures, are efficient; and in ensuring that there is an acceptable return on the public capital invested in them.

The White Paper argued that although some nationalized industry profits may look large, they were by no means large when they were related to the net assets of the industries which were generating them:

The real rates of return are still generally well below those in the private sector. . . . An adequate level of nationalized industry profits is essential to the continued well-being of the industries and their customers and of the economy as a whole. They provide some of the funds for the very large investment programmes necessary to maintain supplies and services to the public. This keeps down the industries' new borrowing requirements, thus helping the burden of taxation and enabling the Government to maintain other important public expenditure priorities.

Continuing with its theme of investment, the White Paper stressed that when planning their investment programmes, the nationalized industries should take account of the cost to the nation of the investment resources they use — the 'opportunity cost of capital'. In assessing what that opportunity cost of capital ought to be, the White Paper suggested that 'capital and other resources invested in the nationalized industries should produce a return to the nation comparable to that which they would have achieved elsewhere in the economy'.

After deliberating on the pretax real returns which had been achieved by the private sector in the past, their likely future levels, and the cost of finance to the private sector, the government decided that 'nationalized industries should treat the opportunity cost of capital to be earned on new investments over their working life as 5 per cent in real terms before tax'. The government stressed that this 5 per cent was 'the return on investment which the government expected the industries to achieve on their new investments as a whole, and not only on projects suitable for individual appraisal'.

The White Paper went on to explain that the government:

will no longer specify a general test discount rate to be used for all appraisals. The primary responsibility for operating methods of appraisal, designed to achieve 5 per cent on new investment as a whole, will be with the industries themselves. But they will consult their sponsor departments on these methods including, for example, the choice of discount rates, and allowance for risk and for appraisal optimism. For management reasons they might choose to appraise revenue earning investments at a rate higher than 5 per cent as a means of covering the costs of associated non-revenue investment which are also part of the cost of supply. But where investment decisions are solely concerned with the choice of the best techniques for producing a given output, or with issues concerning the phasing of capital expenditure, the appropriate discount rate would be the opportunity cost of capital rate.

Pricing policies

The White Paper stated that the 5 per cent required rate of return (RRR) would also be applied to pricing as well as investment decisions. It differentiated here between industries where prices were set by market forces and those which had scope to determine the prices that they charged. For the latter category, the government saw its main role as determining the overall financial target, and hence the general level of prices set by that industry. So that 'where an industry already makes estimates of its long run marginal costs these could be applied directly, using the 5 per cent RRR to calculate the capital element', and these marginal costings would then be used as the basis of pricing policy.

This approach to pricing would then be used to translate the required rate of return into accounting terms. The White Paper explained the procedure thus:

> In the case of industries where the outputs of old and new assets are indistinguishable, total revenue would be derived directly from the price needed to earn the RRR on new investment; where the price which can be charged for the output of old assets is different from that which would be charged for that of new assets, it will be necessary to take account of this in deriving the total revenue figure. Costs, including depreciation, would then be deducted and the resultant net profit would be expressed as a return either on assets (as valued according to the accounting policies of the day) or some other appropriate base.
>
> Whereas the RRR would be applied to new investments which might have very long lead times, the period to which an industry's financial target would apply would be much shorter. If the industry was operating in stable conditions and without major discontinuities, there would be a reasonably stable relationship between the RRR and the financial target, but this may not apply in other cases where investment characteristically takes the form of large and irregular projects, or where very long term and major restructuring was in progress. Nevertheless, even in these circumstances the systematic application of a standardized approach to the costs and revenue streams associated with proposed investment would help in making strategic decisions on it.

The point was also made that changes in accounting policy, such as the treatment of depreciation, would not necessitate any changes in prices or outputs. In addition, the required rate of return was specified as a real, DCF rate, and as such, was independent of accounting conventions such as the treatment of depreciation or the valuation of assets.

Setting the targets

Finally, the White Paper explained that the 5 per cent RRR would also be an important determinant of the financial targets which were to be set up for each industry. These targets were 'central to the guidelines which the industries expect from the Government', and each industry would 'be held accountable for its performance measured by that target'. The financial targets would be set in accounting terms, and typically expressed as a target return on net assets.

As the White Paper explained,

> The level of each financial target will be decided industry by industry. It will take account of a wide range of factors. These will include the expected return from effective, cost conscious management of existing and new assets; market prospects; the scope for improved productivity and efficiency; the opportunity cost of capital; the implications for the Public Sector Borrowing Requirement (PSBR); counter-inflation policy; and social or sectoral objectives. When the target has been settled for the industry, the Secretary of State will announce it to Parliament. He will indicate the main assumptions on which it is based.

BAA's financial target was announced in Parliament on 26 February, 1980 by John Nott, the Secretary of State for Trade. It was given as an 'average rate of return of 6 per cent per annum on net assets revalued at current-cost over three financial years 1980–81 to 1982–83. The target is related to current-cost operating profit after taking account of depreciation but before interest charges and tax. . . . [It] is designed to be consistent with BAA's progressing towards a rate of return on their airport operations of 5 per cent in real terms on their new investment.' Targets for other nationalized industries are given in Exhibit 6.

Exhibit 6: *Financial targets for some UK nationalized industries*

Industry	Target
British Airways	11 per cent average rate of return on mean net assets, 1975–76 to 1978–79
British Transport Docks Board	20 per cent at least on mean net assets by 1980
Telecommunications	6 per cent a year on mean net assets revalued to replacement cost, from 1976–77 to 1978–79
Posts	2 per cent return on turnover for each of the financial years 1978–79 and 1979–80
Giro	12½ per cent annual average return on public dividend capital plus retained profits over the period 1975–76 to 1977–78

Notes
1. With the exception of Posts and Giro, the above target returns are set after depreciation, but before interest on medium- and long-term borrowing. They are set before interest to show how the industry has managed its resources, irrespective of the way it is financed.
2. Telecom's target is in real terms after historic and supplementary depreciation and with the net assets base revalued from historic to replacement costs.
3. The Post's return is after historic and supplementary depreciation and after charging interest.
4. The Giro return is after interest on the National Loans Fund (NLF) debt remaining following the 1977 capital reconstruction.

Source: White Paper *The Nationalized Industries* Cmnd 7131, HMSO March 1978.

When John Nott announced the financial targets and performance indicators for BAA he expressly added the rider:

> The implication of the financial target for the Authority's pricing policies will depend upon a number of factors. . . . For its part, the government will expect the Authority to take account of the government's policy towards the London area airports system, including transfer of traffic from Heathrow, in its user charging structure.

Commenting on the target in BAA's Annual Report for 1979–80 Norman Payne, Chairman of the Authority, wrote:

> This will be difficult to achieve and will require some increase in future landing fee income in real terms. It has been BAA practice to raise prices on 1 April each year to compensate for inflation. However, as at 1 April 1978 and 1979, the BAA underestimated the effects of inflation, and consequently required a further landing fee increase of 10 per cent to catch up. This was implemented on 1 November 1979. From 1 April 1980, with a heavy capital programme ahead (£700 million over the next 5 years), we had aimed to increase our prices slightly above the current inflation rate. However, in order to achieve the financial target, it has been necessary to increase traffic charges by an average 35 per cent.

In common with other nationalized industries, the goals set for BAA were not purely financial. John Nott also announced that the BAA would be expected to achieve its target by improvements in the productivity of both its capital and

Exhibit 7: *Some operating statistics for BAA*

Statistic	1977–78	1978–79	1979–80	1980–81	1981–82
Terminal passengers (millions)					
All BAA airports	34.81	39.82	43.15	42.57	42.97
Heathrow	23.59	26.57	28.54	27.20	26.47
Costs at constant prices (£ million)[1]					
All BAA airports	128.2	169.8	179.8	180.1	180.4
Heathrow	81.4	106.2	107.7	114.1	109.9
Employees					
BAA employees[2]	5023	6490	6804	6634	6375
Head office staff	766	808	851	825	745
Heathrow[2]	2730	3602	3853	3767	3599
Security	887	2037	2222	2137	1981

Notes
1. Costs exclude depreciation and net payments to the security fund. They have been estimated on the basis of the following inflation rates: March 1979, 9.6 per cent; March 1980, 20.8 per cent; March 1981, 16.6 per cent; March 1982, 11.6 per cent.
2. BAA and Heathrow employees includes security staff but excludes head office staff. In calculating government performance indicators, 'employees' includes head office staff but specifically excludes security staff.

Source: BAA Annual Report and Accounts, 1977–78 to 1981–82.

employees. In particular, over the period of the financial target, the Authority was set two specific productivity targets. First, it was 'to seek to ensure that, after allowing for changes which might occur in the activities of the BAA (for example in passenger search and apron handling services), the number of passengers handled per employee grows at an average rate of 3 per cent per annum'. Second, BAA was asked 'to seek to reduce expenditure per passenger before depreciation (excluding any excess of payment of levy to the aviation security fund over reimbursement of security expenditure from that fund) on average by 2.5 per cent per annum'.

These productivity targets were to prove particularly difficult to meet (Exhibit 7). BAA attributed this, however, to the static traffic pattern over the period 1980–82, and the 'deepest economic recession since the 1930s', which had not been anticipated when these efficiency improvements had originally been agreed. Certainly, the optimistic traffic forecasts of the early 1970s had failed to materialize, and this had been a period of intense competition and reduced trading profits within the airline industry.

The airlines' argument

For the airlines using Heathrow, the November 1979 and April 1980 price increases were the last straw. Eighteen airlines, known as the Air Canada Group after their alphabetical leader, therefore brought charges before the High Court of Justice under English law, against both BAA and the Secretary of State for Transport, in an attempt to regain payment of part of their fees. The Group claimed that BAA's power to impose user charges under the 1975 Airports Authority Act (and under Common Law) was limited to a power to impose fair, just and reasonable charges which were not discriminatory.

The Air Canada Group alleged that the recent price increases were unfair. BAA was able to impose them only because it enjoyed, and was abusing, its monopoly power. Because of this, they also brought charges under Article 86 of the Treaty of Rome, which is an antitrust statute. The airlines also claimed that BAA had failed to consult them adequately about the price increases, as it was required to by the 1975 Act. A similar set of charges were brought separately by a nineteenth airline, Pan Am, who further alleged that BAA's recent price increases unfairly discriminated in favour of British Airways, and reflected 'an unpublished policy of being nice to British Airways'.

The charges against the Secretary of State (as opposed to BAA) were that the recent price increases 'were caused by the unlawful directions of the Secretary of State'. The airlines claimed that the Secretary of State had, in mid-1979, instructed BAA not to borrow, but instead to finance all capital and other expenditures from internal sources over the next 3 years. The airlines alleged that this was carried out for the purely domestic political purpose of reducing and containing the PSBR, and had nothing to do with aviation policy or the performance of BAA's duties under the 1975 Act.

Restricting BAA to internal funding meant that the company would need to increase its profits if it was to continue with its heavy capital expenditure programme. The airlines alleged that the Secretary of State would have known this when he subsequently set BAA's financial target. Therefore, in setting a high target, he would have recognized and intended that BAA could achieve this only by a substantial (and unfair) increase in user charges from November 1979. This price increase was needed if BAA was to generate sufficient profits to fund its capital spending internally, thereby preventing any further call on public funds, or increase in the PSBR. By his actions, the Secretary of State had therefore required BAA to abuse its dominant position under Article 86 of the EEC Treaty.

The airlines alleged that BAA, for its part, had agreed to the 6 per cent target even though previously it had argued that a lower 3–4 per cent return on net assets (RONA) target would be consistent with the 5 per cent RRR specified in the White Paper. The airlines claimed that BAA had accepted this higher target purely because the price rises it implied would enable them to fund their capital expenditure programme internally. They argued that BAA had acted unlawfully in following the instructions of the Secretary of State, since these had contributed to the imposition of unfair price rises, and BAA had failed to exercise its independent judgement.

The airlines complained that BAA's user charges not only exceeded the full and proper cost of providing services (together with a reasonable rate of return), but that they also unfairly discriminated against Heathrow, in favour of Gatwick and Stansted. As Heathrow users, they objected to subsidizing other, less profitable airports. They also argued that it was quite unreasonable of the BAA to seek to finance peak capital expenditure, virtually without recourse to borrowing. This meant that airport users faced an 'excessive and unreasonable burden of paying immediately and in advance the full capital cost of major new facilities likely to have a working life of many years'. They argued that BAA should have either cut capital expenditure, or financed it externally, probably by borrowing.

The Air Canada Group also pointed out that, as a nationalized industry with monopoly power, BAA was subject to the White Paper guidelines. Thus even if one accepted the appropriateness of the 6 per cent RONA financial target (which the airlines felt was too high), it still had to be assumed that the financial target had been calculated on the assumption that prices were based on long-run marginal costs (LRMC), which include the prescribed 5 per cent rate of return on capital resources.

The airlines felt that it was virtually impossible to estimate LRMC directly and reliably, since any such estimates were highly dependent on forecasts and assumptions about the uncertain future, which would anyway be highly subjective if provided by BAA. Nevertheless, since the target itself had been set so as to be consistent with LRMC, the concrete evidence that achieved returns at Heathrow had consistently exceeded the 6 per cent RONA target was prima facie evidence that the general level of prices charged ahd been above LRMC, and that BAA was thereby earning excessive profits at Heathrow. The airlines could find no other reasons which would explain the high levels of achieved return, such as greater efficiency, or a series of fortunate incidents ('good luck').

BAA's response

BAA responded by denying that it had abused any dominant position in the provision of airport services. Indeed, BAA argued that Heathrow did not even have a dominant position, since it faced extensive competition in passenger, cargo and interlining traffic from other airports in the South-east, from elsewhere in the United Kingdom, and from the continent. They claimed that Article 86 of the EEC Treaty did not, therefore, apply.

Because of this, BAA maintained that the November 1979 and April 1980 user charge increases were in no sense unlawful. While BAA had consulted with the Secretary of State to agree a financial target, BAA had received no instructions to increase user charges. On the contrary, the price rises had been initiated by BAA, and although they had been approved by the Secretary of State, they did not result from any interference on his part. BAA denied that traffic charges had been increased 'in order to' achieve the financial target. The increases would have been necessary anyway, whether or not a target of 6 per cent had been agreed with the Secretary of State.

For his part, the Secretary of State denied that at any material times, his dominant purpose had been the reduction and containment of the PSBR. Even if it had, however, he argued that this would have been quite properly within his powers under the 1975 Act. The Secretary of State did not deny that he had adopted policies designed to encourage the transfer of airlines and services from Heathrow to Gatwick. This was intended to relieve congestion at Heathrow, and to reflect the relative costs incurred in meeting demand in the London airport system. BAA had agreed with and implemented these policies by, amongst other things, charging significantly more for services at Heathrow than at Gatwick.

BAA also reiterated its long-held philosophy that it was impossible to look at Heathrow in isolation, and that instead one had to look at the South-east airports as part of a single system. Where costs incurred at any one airport within the system result from traffic demand throughout the system as a whole, the total traffic in the system should contribute to meeting those costs. In the South-east, Heathrow and Gatwick were generating revenue surpluses, while Stansted, which was at an earlier stage of development, was not. Stansted's losses represented the price being paid to ensure that it was able to offer capacity for growth in traffic when Heathrow and Gatwick were full. BAA argued that it was therefore perfectly reasonable to use revenues from airports in surplus to finance operating losses or capital expenditure at one or more of its other airports, which were at different stages of development. Indeed, this was one of the advantages of having the airports in a single ownership group. They pointed out that this was standard practice in multiplant private sector firms, where individual plants were not generally operated in financially watertight compartments.

Given the severe limits on expansion at Heathrow, BAA had therefore been developing Gatwick and planned to develop Stansted. The Authority's intention was 'to bring the facilities at Gatwick up to a standard at which it can rank with other major international airports in Europe, and which will permit an increase in the frequency of services and interlining that is possible'. BAA clearly believed that such an investment was totally defensible, however financed, and that 'this had provided a more widely acceptable alternative to Heathrow, so making it easier to relieve congestion to the benefit of Heathrow users'.

BAA also pointed out that in setting traffic charges, it took into account only those costs which were incurred by the use of the facilities which it provided for the airlines. Profits from commercial activities, particularly duty-free, had to be regarded as a separate business, subject to competitive forces. Furthermore, they pointed out that since the profits at Heathrow stemmed mainly from these commercial activities, any cross-subsidization which occurred between airports was in fact financed from that source, and not from other charges. BAA pointed out that it was nevertheless important for them to maximize income from commercial activities if they were to achieve financial self-sufficiency.

The need to self-finance

BAA also took the airlines to task for complaining that Heathrow revenues had been used to subsidize investment, 'although they do not say how such capital expenditure should have been financed'. The BAA board had in fact met in July 1979 and decided that levels of congestion at BAA airports were unacceptable, and there could be no question of a cutback in the capital expenditure programme. In order to generate sufficient cash over the next 3 years without recourse to borrowing, user charges therefore had to be increased.

The limitations BAA faced on borrowing were part of a general pressure on nationalized industries to minimize their new borrowing requirements. However, BAA anyway had an organizational culture which was geared to self-financing of major projects. Indeed, the Authority had formulated a policy that aimed for 100 per cent self-financing, except in periods of severe recession or exceptionally high spending, when they might fund up to 40 per cent of capital expenditure from borrowing. This was partly motivated by high real interest rates, but was mainly intended to help BAA keep control of its own investment programme. As one of BAA's senior managers put it: 'There is always a feeling that when things are in the balance — and you are borrowing — then you will have the Treasury and the politicians calling the shots'. This policy was well-known. In a paper, 'BAA, policies and programmes; an information document for consultations with air transport customers', the Authority stated that: 'In agreeing a (financial) target with the government, the Authority has taken cognizance of the need to generate surplus funds for the replacement of assets and investment to meet the growth of traffic, and the desirability of achieving financial self-sufficiency'.

This need to be self-financing was therefore also taken into account when setting user charges. But the Authority maintained that there was nothing unusual in its approach to the funding of the greater part of its capital expenditures from internal sources: 'The practice is widespread in the UK economy. More specifically, self-financing is common among nationalized industries.' Exhibit 8 shows the extent to which capital requirements of nationalized industries were financed from internal sources between 1976 and 1981. In addition, the Authority contended that some of the factors which

Exhibit 8: *Financing of capital requirements by the nationalized industries*

Organization	Internal sources of funds as a percentage of capital requirements (at outturn prices)				
	1976–77	1977–78	1978–79	1979–80	1980–81
National Coal Board	18	15	—	—	—
Electricity (England & Wales)	90	97	113	80	89
N. of Scotland Hydroelectric	18	23	31	31	46
South of Scotland Electricity	130	130	115	56	74
British Gas Corporation	157	264	226	194	174
British National Oil Corp	6	5	6	112	184
British Steel Corporation	7	—	—	—	—
Post Office[1]	81	114	106	84	109
British Airways Board	91	55	68	28	—
British Airports Authority	88	91	110	100	82
British Transport Docks Board	223	192	218	138	91
British Waterways Board	—[2]	—	—	—	—
National Freight Corporation	0	9	9	30	71
National Bus Company	—	—	—	—	—
Scottish Transport Group	0	11	17	20	14
British Aerospace	na[2]	252	54	51	105[3]
British Shipbuilders	na	—	—	—	—
Total	49	60	55	42	48

Notes
1. Including British Telecom throughout this period
2. Negative figures are denoted by —, and non-available figures are indicated by na
3. Up to December 1980
Source: *The Government's Expenditure Plans*, White Papers, Cmnd 7439, 7841, 8175 and 8494.

influence private sector decisions on self-financing are not relevant to nationalized industries: 'A private company will normally have a self-financing ratio of significantly less than 100 per cent, primarily because this is believed to be in the shareholders' interest. These considerations do not arise in a public enterprise where the degree of self-finance does not make any difference to the risks borne by the government'.

Pricing and LRMC

As BAA explained in its Annual Report for 1981–82,

> in order to achieve financial efficiency, the BAA has created its own charging policy and developed this on the principle of LRMC. This entails identifying the cost imposed over the long term by a unit of demand, such as a particular series of flights. While it may not be possible to do this precisely for every service, certain policies do flow from the principle. [First,] peak traffic costs more and will be reflected in the charging structure. [Second,] . . . where costs incurred at any airport within the system result from traffic demand throughout the system as a whole, the total traffic in the system should contribute to meeting those costs. [Third,] a differential between airports will appear, in the same way as between peak and off-peak, if one airport had considerable spare capacity. [Fourth,] where capacity is fully used, and cannot be expanded, the long-run marginal cost to the economy of a service occupying a unit of capacity is the value of the service that has been denied that capacity — in other words the rationing price.

In discussing the application of LRMC to Heathrow, BAA argued that:

> Adopting the principles of LRMC pricing, the marginal costs of Heathrow are essentially the capital and operating costs incurred to provide airport services for future additional traffic, expressed in terms of costs per unit of demand. Since the need for additional facilities arises from operators wishing to provide services at an airport which is already at capacity, the resultant costs should clearly be borne by these airlines. The major investment project planned to meet the future growth of traffic at Heathrow is Terminal 4 and its related apron and other facilities. The estimated costs of the project can be used to give a reasonable measure of LRMC.
>
> However, this project relates only to the expansion of terminal and parking facilities. The BAA is not planning to expand its runway capacity to any significant extent, and the LRMC of the runway facilities at Heathrow cannot therefore be calculated on the basis of the costs of any planned expansion of these facilities. In these particular circumstances the economically efficient pricing policy is generally to use prices to bring the demand for runway capacity into balance with supply. This can be done by including the marginal costs of runway congestion.

BAA argued that its landing fees appeared high only when comparisons were based on Heathrow summer peak charges. The principle of marginal cost pricing had resulted in higher charges at such times, when compared with other European airports. Comparisons were often difficult here, however, given that many European airports were more directly controlled, and had less independence than BAA. This meant that business objectives were often overridden in favour of wider political considerations. Even taking this into account, however, BAA claimed that its charges per passenger taken over the year were similar to those at other European, US and UK regional airports. They also pointed out that airport user charges were anyway a relatively small part of overall airline costs and were therefore unlikely to generate substantial problems for the airlines.

Risk and ROCE

BAA not only responded to the Air Canada Group allegations, but it also made a number of points about the application and interpretation of the financial targets. The Authority differed with the airlines over the degree of risk involved in investment projects at an airport. It was the view of BAA that the 5 per cent RRR applied to low risk projects and that more risky projects required a premium. The appropriate size of this premium had been determined partly on the basis of sensitivity analysis of the Heathrow Terminal 4 and Gatwick Terminal 2 projects. For example, while the best estimate of the rate of return for the Heathrow Terminal 4 project was 8.5 per cent, there was an 89 per cent chance that the rate of return would equal or exceed 5 per cent, when allowance was made for the possibility of unfavourable cost or revenue experience. BAA claimed on the basis of this that 'a mean rate of return of 8 per cent would be associated with a high probability of exceeding 5 per cent'. It further added 'even if a combination of circumstances do conspire to produce a low rate, there would be measures that we could take to control the gap'.

In its Annual Report for 1979–80, BAA therefore stated that 'the real internal rate of return sought by the Authority on individual capital projects will not be less than 10 per cent for those related to traffic and 8 per cent for projects related to the less risky property and accommodation investments'. BAA argued that it had to impose these higher cutoff rates, since this was the only way it could be sure of meeting its target of a 5 per cent RRR on all new investments, taken as a whole. The premiums were partly needed to allow for the 'dilution' effect of various non-revenue-producing projects, and partly, to compensate for risk. The rates chosen were designed to reflect the risks inherent in capital investment in inflexible assets, which were fixed by location, and which were associated with long-lived, long lead time projects, designed to meet uncertain demand, generated by others as and when it arrives.

BAA supported this view by reference to Maplin:

These points are clearly demonstrated by the events of the 1970s. In the early part of the decade, expectations of a substantial increase in air traffic movements lay behind the development of plans for a new London airport at Maplin. These expectations were later revised downwards due to factors such as the recession following the 1973–74 oil crisis and the rapidly growing usage of wide-bodied aircraft, and Maplin was cancelled. Had the Maplin project gone ahead, it would have led to substantial overcapacity in the airport system serving London and the South-east, with serious financial implications for the BAA. This illustration demonstrates the vulnerability of the BAA's demand projections and investment decisions both to unforeseen circumstances (the oil crisis) and to technological change (the introduction of wide-bodied aircraft).

The Authority was also concerned about the application of the RONA target. In particular, it objected to the fact that its return had been compared with those of UK industrial and commercial companies (excluding North Sea activities) which had been taken from government statistics, rather than from company accounts. BAA contended that RONAs taken from these sources would differ for at least two important reasons. First, asset values in official statistics are based on average asset lives, while company accounts will reflect the lower of the depreciated current replacement cost or the recoverable amount. Second, in a recession, a relatively large number of assets will have a recoverable amount below their depreciated current replacement cost — and in some cases, assets which are still included in the official statistics will have been written off in the company's accounts. To substantiate these claims, BAA produced its own values for the average RONA, produced using company accounts data (Exhibit 9).

Exhibit 9: *Comparison of average RONAs for British commercial and industrial companies*

	Average RONA prepared by		
Year	Government[1] *per cent*	Bank of England[2] *per cent*	Phillips and Drew[3] *per cent*
1975	4.9		6.0
1976	4.9		7.0
1977	7.1		8.5
1978	7.7		8.5
1979	5.3	8.2	8.0
1980	4.0	7.4	7.0
1981	3.2	7.5	8.0
Average 1975–80	5.7		8.0

Notes and sources
1. Net pretax rates of return at current replacement cost for UK industrial and commercial companies excluding North Sea, published in *British Business*, 17 September 1982.
2. Profit before interest charges and taxation as a percentage of end-year capital employed excluding goodwill, for a sample of nearly 250 non-oil companies, published in the *Bank of England Quarterly Bulletin*, September 1982.
3. Pretax before interest CCA RONA for 120–150 major non-oil industrial and commercial companies, rounded to the nearest ½ per cent, prepared from company accounts by Phillips and Drew.

Looking at the specific question of its own RONA, the Authority spent some time arguing about the problem of valuation of assets and, in particular, the difficulty of valuing land at an airport. The value of land given in the accounts was the notional replacement cost of existing sites (in accordance with SSAP16) and was at that time £12 800 per acre (£31 600 per hectare). But, BAA argued, there could be other ways of valuing the land. For example, they could assume conditions of effective competition, in which case the land value would be higher. Alternatively, they could base the valuation on the future earning potential of the land in its present usage. Then again, they could approximate the value of the land for the terminal buildings to that of industrial land. Or they could use the per annum land values assessed for Terminal 4, that is £12 000 per acre (£29 650 per hectare), and capitalize that. Finally, they could base the valuation on the equivalent price of the commercial space within existing terminals.

BAA also had doubts about the extent to which the published data on the RONAs for industry in general reflected the target, or *ex ante*, RONA used for a range of projects within these industries. In the view of BAA: 'As a result of the uncertain environment in which industry and commerce operates, the *ex post*, or achieved, RONA might not be a good indicator of an *ex ante* RONA which was considered to be reasonable and which was expected to be achieved'. They also stressed that the period 1975–80 was not perhaps a fair datum period for the comparison.

Finally, BAA questioned the link between the required rate of return as laid down by the White Paper, and the calculation of RONA. The Authority made three points. First, the RRR is a forward-looking concept relating to the rate to be achieved on new investment, whereas RONA measures the accounting return on existing assets. Second, the timescale for RRR and RONA are different: RRR measures return over the lifetime of an investment, RONA measures the accounting return for a single year. Third, RONA is not a unique concept but depends on the accounting conventions and assumptions used, for example, to calculate depreciation and asset lives.

So, BAA argued, the RRR could be converted into a RONA only on the basis of a variety of assumptions, and, even if these assumptions were agreed and accepted, the resultant target RONA for the Authority as a whole should not be considered as a maximum earned at any one location, nor should it be applied rigidly to one year out of the three covered by the target.

Enter the expert witnesses

Throughout 1981, the evidence produced by the Air Canada Group and BAA mounted up, with each side trying to outdo the other with the niceties of its arguments. To complicate matters further, both sides appointed expert witnesses. These individuals were expected to study the economic arguments, and then to produce evidence to support one party or the other.

PART C

COMPANY VALUATION

9. Bula Mines (A)

Bula Limited, a privately owned company, was set up to exploit a deposit of zinc and lead ore in the Republic of Ireland. In 1974, the Irish Government arranged to purchase 24 per cent of the equity and were given 25 per cent of the equity free of charge by the owners. An arbitration panel was set up to value the company. The arbitrators had to decide on the price at which the government would acquire its stake in the mine, and were to hand down their decision on 12 November 1976.

The story

In 1970, a rich deposit of lead/zinc ore was discovered beneath the farmland of one Pat Wright, an elderly Irish farmer. Lacking the resources or expertise to develop this himself, he sold the land (about 120 acres or 300 hectares) to Bula Ltd, a company owned by Tom Roche, managing director of Cement Roadstone, his son-in-law, Michael Wymes, and a colleague, Richard Wood. The terms were £500 000 cash, £300 000 when mining commenced and a 20 per cent stake in Bula Ltd. By July 1974, Bula had negotiated a participation agreement in outline with the Irish government. The government agreed to buy 24 per cent of the equity in Bula, and to accept a further 25 per cent as a gift. The price at that time was not agreed, and was to be the subject of arbitration. Estimates by Bula then valued the company at about £10 million, while the government had been advised that the mine was worth much less than this.

Further information released then revealed the following holdings in Bula Ltd:

Roche Family	30 per cent
Wymes Family	30 per cent
Patrick Wright	20 per cent
Richard Wood	20 per cent

This case was written by Elroy Dimson as a basis for class discussion rather than to illustrate either effective or ineffective handling of an administrative situation.

Copyright © 1987 Elroy Dimson and Paul Marsh, London Business School.

The terms of payment were to be:

Half payable within 3 months of agreement
One-quarter payable after 1 further year
One-quarter payable after 2 further years.

The freehold of the land belonged to Bula, as did all mining rights and minerals underneath the land. This is unusual and stems from a quirk of the law under which Pat Wright originally purchased the land. This fact means that the value of the mine was higher than normally would be the case, since otherwise, under a Minerals Acquisition Order, the Irish government could lay claim to the minerals and then license the mining company as a producer of the ore. However, the circumstances of the land freehold prevented this.

In October 1974, Bula announced the retention of RTZ Consultants to carry out a feasibility study of the part of the zinc and lead ore body owned by Bula. The ore body itself is in an area called Navan. The other part of the ore body is owned by a company called Tara, which does not own its section of ore freehold. However, Tara was further advanced at that time in its evaluation of the ore body. The split ownership of the Navan ore caused the government much embarrassment. The original idea was to purchase compulsorily both the Bula

Exhibit 1: *Comparison of the Tara and Bula mines*

Information	Tara	Bula
Estimated ore body	63 million tonnes	19.6 million tonnes
Probable extraction rate per year	2.2 million tonnes	1.0 million tonnes
Estimated initial production date	Early 1977	Late 1977
Predicted employment: Construction	1100	600
Production	800	300
State holding of equity	25 per cent	49 per cent
Cost of state holding: First 25 per cent	Nil	Nil
Remainder	Nil	Fixed by arbitration
State representation on board	Two directors[1]	Two directors
State receipts: Company tax on profits[2]	50 per cent	50 per cent
Royalty on profits	4½ per cent	Nil[3]
Other receipts	Annual rent	Nil[3]
Estimated overall proportion of mine profits accruing to state	67 per cent	74 per cent[4]

Notes
1. Or 25 per cent of the board membership of Tara.
2. Capital allowances of 120 per cent of investment expenditure may be written off against taxable profits.
3. No royalty is payable by Bula because the Bula ore body is privately owned.
4. Or 62 per cent excluding the stake to be purchased by the government.
Sources: Irish Times, 13 December 1975 and RTZ Consultants report.

and Tara sector, and lease them to Tara to operate. However the compulsory purchase order on the Bula section failed as related above, leaving the government no option but to allow separate development.

Technical appraisal continued, and facts began to trickle out. In July 1975, RTZ Consultants delivered their report to Bula. By December 1975, a detailed comparison of the Tara and Bula mines was published (Exhibit 1).

At about this time, it was revealed that it would be necessary to divert the River Blackwater, in order to fully mine the deposits. Costs would be shared by Tara and Bula, and were estimated to be about £2 million. However, this proposal started to draw a lot of protests from environmentalists and fishermen, who took the view that the salmon would be disturbed. The companies replied that diversion was necessary to get at almost 12 million tonnes of ore.

In order to provide a satisfactory basis, both for Bula's planning effort and for valuing the government's share in the mine, Bula commissioned a detailed feasibility study of its whole mining operation. The study was undertaken by Bechtel, a prestigious international firm of mining consultants.

Technical data

Comprehensive technical data was provided by Bechtel in their report dated April 1976. The report was essentially a feasibility study of the whole Bula mine undertaking. The ore reserve figure in the Bechtel study was that calculated by RTZ Consultants, using evidence gleaned from 202 drill holes bored on the Bula site: 'The geological interpretations and the in situ undiluted reserves developed by RTZ Consultants and presented in their July 1975 report were checked and accepted by Bechtel. These have been used to estimate mineral reserves and for the preliminary mine planning.'

This technical information was accepted as the best available by almost everybody involved in valuing the mine. In particular, there was general

Exhibit 2: *Bula Mine's estimated ore reserves*

Category of reserves	Quantity (tonnes) *millions*	Lead reserves *per cent*	Zinc reserves *per cent*	Combined lead/zinc *per cent*
Measured (open pit)	9	1.1	7.2	8.3
Measured (underground)	5	1.9	9.0	10.9
Total measured reserves	14	1.4	7.8	9.2
Additional indicated reserves	6	0.8	4.4	5.2
Total measured and indicated	20	1.2	6.8	8.0

Sources: Irish Times, 8 February 1977, and Irish Independent, 12 September 1975.

agreement about the quantity and quality of the ore body (Exhibit 2). Neither were capital costs a subject for controversy: Bechtel's projection that the mine would require an initial investment of approximately £22.6 million during calendar years 1977 and 1978 seemed reasonable. Diversion of the river and further underground work would be required before underground mining could commence. This would cost a further £5 million at 1977 prices.

Some people felt differently about the operating costs, which were projected by Bechtel to be at the rate of £5 a tonne for open pit working, and £8 a tonne once underground operations were phased in during 1986. The objections were raised primarily by financial analysts, who pointed out that Bechtel's cost figures were substantially below the expenses disclosed in the annual accounts of other Irish mining companies (see Exhibit 3).

Another point of contention was the likely course of metal prices over the life of the project. A study by R. J. Lee, published in 1976, had shown that the annual average price of zinc in the United Kingdom and United States during the period 1900–1974 had changed very little in real terms, though there appeared to be a 25-year cycle in zinc prices. It was therefore asserted by a financial journalist that 'the current price of zinc, $795 per tonne, totally understates the value of the metal. It is the price at the bottom of the zinc demand cycle. If the metal demand/price cycle repeats itself as it has done for the past 25 years then zinc will rise rapidly in price over the next 3–5 years' (J. O'Neill, *Irish Business*, March 1977). Under this scenario, zinc, and perhaps lead, prices would rise faster than operating costs.

The converse point of view was held by another writer: 'Uncertainty surrounds the likely future movements of metal prices. If these were to increase relative to costs then obviously future cash flows would increase. However, this is thought unlikely to happen. . . . Operating costs in Bula are likely to increase relative to the value of metal and so net income is likely to fall' (J. O'Reilly, *Irish Times*, 8 February 1977.) Despite the disagreement over the likely course of prices and costs, virtually all published valuations of the Bula project assumed that sales revenues would move in line with the general level of inflation. For

Exhibit 3: *Operating expenses as a proportion of total income for Bula and comparable companies*

Company	1973 per cent	1974 per cent	1975 per cent	Projected per cent
Northgate	45	55	80	
International Mogul	46	56	65	
Bula (Bechtel projections)				
Open cast				28
Underground				45

Source: Irish Times, 8 February 1977

example, it was forecast by O'Neill that, at 1977 prices, sales revenues would remain at the level of £19 million per year from 1979 to 1995 inclusive, while O'Reilly estimated revenues of £18 million per year through till 1996.

Valuing Bula Mines

The task of valuing the mine was undertaken by the London Institute of Arbitration. Advisers were retained by the Irish Government and by Bula Limited. The RTZ Consultants and Bechtel reports were made available to both parties. The advisers were asked to submit a written valuation of the mine to the arbitration panel during the course of summer 1976.

10. London European Airways

The London European Airways Company (LEA) was founded in January 1984 by Nigel Harford and Michael Harwood who perceived that an opportunity existed for a new airline to offer scheduled services between Luton International Airport and major European cities — in the first instance Amsterdam and, subject to licences and operating rights, Paris and Frankfurt. The service was to be aimed primarily at the business traveller, with considerable emphasis placed on flight timings and quality of cabin service.

The founding directors had both gained valuable experience in establishing and operating a similar service whilst they were employed by Euroflite, the company which operated the Luton–Brussels route using small commuter aircraft (see Exhibit 1 for career details of the directors). They concluded from their experience that any airline seeking the market share necessary to become financially viable would need to operate an aircraft that would be acceptable to passengers as an alternative to the Trident, Airbus, Boeing 757 and DC9 used by Heathrow-based airlines on their European routes. The aircraft would also need to have sufficient capacity to break even at low percentage load factors. The Viscount aircraft met both these requirements.

Having established the suitability of the Viscount, the founding directors commissioned market research and commenced the detailed planning work necessary to obtain a Civil Aviation Authority (CAA) licence to operate a scheduled service between Luton and Amsterdam. This licence was granted in August and applications were lodged for similar licences for Luton/Paris, and Luton/Frankfurt. These destinations are three of the most popular in Europe; indeed, Paris and Amsterdam are the busiest and third busiest of all international scheduled routes out of London.

This case was written by Elroy Dimson and Paul Marsh as a basis for class discussion rather than to illustrate either effective or ineffective handling of an administrative situation. We are grateful to Paul Arwas and Nicholas Walker for help on an earlier draft.

Copyright © 1987 Elroy Dimson and Paul Marsh, London Business School.

Exhibit 1: *Career details of London European Airways directors as of 1984*

Nigel Harford (aged 40), Managing Director, is a marketing-orientated general manager with 15 years (1969–84) experience in the aviation industry including commuter airline management, air charter operation, aviation consultancy and aircraft sales. He is a former Council member of the General Aviation Manufacturers and Traders Association and a former Board Member of the Air Transport Operators Association.

Nigel Harford was closely involved in the setting up of Euroflite (which introduced the only existing year-round scheduled air service from Luton), was a director from its inception, and was Managing Director from 1982 until its sale in 1983. Previously he was UK Sales Director of the American Aircraft Company, Houston, Texas, and Operations/Sales Director of Cabair with responsibility for UK sales of Grumman American Aircraft and for air-charter operations with a fleet of 14 aircraft.

Michael Harwood (aged 44), Finance and Administration Director, is a financially orientated general manager with 11 years (1973–84) experience in the aviation, business travel and freight forwarding industries, and 7 years (1964–71) financial management experience with large international groups. He is a Fellow of the Institute of Cost and Management Accountants and a Sloan Fellow of the London Business School.

Following service as a pilot in the Fleet Air Arm, he joined Standard Telephones and Cables in 1964 and was, at various times, responsible for financial control, data processing and accounting functions within six separate groups and divisions.

Subsequently he was financial controller of the Wines and Spirits Division of Whitbread, Chairman and Chief Executive of Alltransport International Group Travel Division and a founder director of the Richmond Business Management group of companies with subsidiaries engaged in business travel and air freight forwarding. He was Managing Director of Euroflite from 1980 to 1982.

John Cumberland (aged 40), non-executive director, is Chairman of Curtis, Edington, Say and Partners, the marketing agency handling the LEA account. From its formation in 1981 until 1983 he was the managing director of Hoverspeed. He gained invaluable experience there in successfully reorganizing and marketing the cross-channel service.

Richard Shuker (aged 38), non-executive director, is Managing Director of Richard I. Shuker, a company which provides services in relation to the Business Expansion Scheme. He represents in particular the interests of investors through Bexfund and is a director of that fund's managing company. He has degrees in economics and law. From 1979 until 1983 he was Company Secretary of Friends' Provident Group.

The airport

Luton International Airport is designated by the government as one of the four London Gateway Airports (see the map in Exhibit 2). The airport lies 33 miles (53 km) north-west of Central London, and 1.5 miles (2.4 km) from the

Exhibit 2: *Catchment areas of the four London airports*

The Luton Catchment Area consists of:
(1) The area north and north-west of Luton, extending along the M1 and A1 corridors to Northampton and Kettering (1 hour's drive) with a population of 1.3 million. North of this are the catchment areas of Birmingham and East Midlands airports; to the east is the Stansted area; and to the west is Heathrow.
(2) The north-west outer London area served by the M1 and A1 to the North Circular Road at Brent Cross, containing a population of 1.7 million.
(3) The southern catchment area, including many north London suburbs such as Hampstead, Finchley and Wembley, which, although closer to Heathrow, have shorter travel times to Luton. LEA feel this will be reinforced by the completion of the M25 outer orbital motorway.

London–North of England M1 motorway, to which it is connected by a link road. It has good public rail and road transport to Central London and the North, with trains running every 20 minutes from Luton Station (7 minutes from the airport) to London, a 36-minute journey.

The airport, which is owned and operated by Luton Borough Council, has been profitable and this has encouraged the recent investment of some £10 million to improve its facilities. The passenger terminal can now handle up to 3.5 million passengers per year, compared with its previous throughput of 1.8 million. The passenger area contains bar, restaurant, snack bar, shopping, banking, car rental, and other facilities. There is also ample low cost short-term and dedicated long-term parking for the scheduled service passenger within 1–2 minutes walk of the terminal building. Separate checkin desks, immigration and security channels are available for scheduled service passengers, thereby avoiding any delays or inconvenience arising from charter aircraft operations.

The proposed service and aircraft

The service offered by LEA was to be aimed primarily at the business traveller. The Amsterdam service would start in February 1985 and operate twice daily on weekdays only, leaving Luton at 7.30 and 16.00, and Amsterdam at 10.00 and 18.30, local time. Flight frequency would increase to a possible maximum of four round trips daily by the third year. Flight timings were chosen for the convenience of business travellers, who make up over half of London/ Amsterdam traffic, and who travel principally in the mornings and evenings.

Following detailed market research (see below) into the requirements of the business traveller, LEA had selected the 71-seater Viscount turboprop aircraft (Exhibit 3). This aircraft has low capital cost and reasonable operating costs,

Exhibit 3: *Artist's impression of the LEA Viscount*

allowing break-even at relatively low load factors, and yet provides adequate capacity to cope with peak demand. LEA felt this was important, since any turned-away peak demand would tend to switch elsewhere permanently. Market research also showed that the Viscount was highly acceptable to passengers who, while not unduly concerned about aircraft type, generally preferred a 71-seater to small commuter planes.

LEA had contracted with British Air Ferries to buy one Viscount, for delivery in February 1985, and had an option to purchase a second. The maintenance contract included provision of a replacement aircraft in the event of the aircraft being unserviceable. Further aircraft would be required for the Paris and Frankfurt routes assuming that the necessary licences were obtained. In due course, the Viscount(s) would be replaced by larger aircraft, such as BAC 111 or DC9, as and when justified.

Considerable emphasis was to be placed on the quality of cabin service, and the quality and standard of presentation of meals and bar service. Morning flights would include the choice of a cooked English breakfast, or fresh croissants and fruit, served on china with filtered coffee and freshly made tea. Imaginative snacks, wines and complimentary cocktails would be served on afternoon and evening flights. Up to four cabin crew would be carried. The flight time to Amsterdam would be 52 minutes, compared with 44 minutes for a BAC 111 from Heathrow. However the lack of congestion and short taxiways at Luton would make the overall journey time identical.

Market research indicated that approximately half the incoming Dutch traffic would be bound for Central London. LEA therefore intended offering a free coach service from Luton airport to the station, plus a free railpass for Luton–London travel. Alternatively, they would provide a luxury dedicated coach service, linking Luton arrivals to a variety of London destinations. In either case, passengers leaving Amsterdam at 10.00 local time could be in Central London by 11.30.

Competition and pricing

At the time of LEA's creation, there were no scheduled services between Luton and Amsterdam, Paris or Frankfurt. Euroflite operated a scheduled service to Brussels, and Air UK ran a scheduled Stansted–Amsterdam service (see Exhibit 4 for details of scheduled international services from Luton and Stansted).

The vast bulk of scheduled London–Amsterdam traffic went through Heathrow and Gatwick. British Airways and KLM operated a pooled route from Heathrow, offering a daily total of 1900 seats on 11 flights in each direction on Tridents and 757s (BA) and DC8s, DC9s, and Airbuses (KLM). From Gatwick, British Caledonian ran a four times daily service on 104-seat BAC 111s. Approximately 56 per cent of the one million annual passengers were business-oriented, and 61 per cent were foreign-originating. Flights were most

Exhibit 4: *Scheduled services from Luton and Stansted as at 1984*

Luton Services

(1) *Euroflite to Brussels* is a twice-daily service using a 16-seater Jetstream. Traffic has built up slowly to a current load factor (March 1984) of 42 per cent, which is approaching break even. Euroflite state that 80 per cent of passengers pay full fare, and that freight traffic averages £20 per flight. Euroflite is owned by the McAlpine Group.

(2) *British Midland Airways to the Channel Islands* (summer only)

(3) *Euroflite to Rotterdam.* The licence was granted in August 1984, but operations have not commenced. Euroflite applied for Luton–Amsterdam but were turned down in favour of LEA. They are appealing against this decision.

Stansted Services

(1) *Jersey European to Brussels.* This licence was originally granted to Air Anglia who never operated the route. Jersey European operated a Twin Otter service for 2 years before withdrawing in 1983. Euroflite claim that the introduction of the Stansted–Brussels service had no impact on their Luton traffic.

(2) *Air UK to Amsterdam* is a four times daily service using a Shorts SDS 330 30-seater, unpressurized aircraft (originally, Air UK operated twice daily with a larger aircraft). Volumes have grown steadily from 2000 (1981), to 15 000 (1982), 21 000 (1983), and a forecast 28 000 passengers in 1984. The route is operating just above break-even. A third of the traffic is Dutch-originating. Half the passengers pay full fare, and of the remainder, 19 per cent are interline, and 31 per cent Pex. Cargo revenues are quite small.

Note
Total London–Brussels traffic volumes are roughly half total London–Amsterdam volumes.

frequent and traffic heaviest in the mornings and evenings, reflecting the importance of business traffic. The overall route load factor was over 75 per cent, and it was often difficult to make late bookings for morning or evening flights. Traffic has gradually expanded in recent years (see Exhibit 5), and LEA expected this to continue.

LEA expected most of their traffic to come from passengers currently using Heathrow. They anticipated that UK passengers who found Gatwick most convenient would continue to do so, although some London-bound, foreign-based travellers might be persuaded to use Luton rather than Gatwick as a London gateway. Similarly, analysis of LEA's catchment area (see below) indicated little overlap with Stansted, so that potentially they could capture only about 8 per cent of Air UK's traffic. This lack of overlap and competition with Stansted was expected to remain the case, regardless of any further development of Stansted Airport. The LEA directors knew of no Dutch carriers interested in starting scheduled services to Luton or Stansted.

Exhibit 5: *Air passenger traffic: historic growth and forecasts*

(a) **Total passenger traffic, all South-east airports**

| Year | Actual traffic | Total passengers in millions DTI forecasts | | | BAA forecast |
		Low	Mid	High	
1977	32.5				
1978	36.9				
1979	39.4				
1980	39.7				
1981	40.1				
1982	40.3				
1983	42.5				
1984	47.0				
1985		44.7	47.8	50.9	
1990		52.6	61.5	70.3	66
1995		59.7	74.5	89.3	84

(b) **London–Amsterdam total traffic volumes**

Route	Total passengers (thousands) 1981	1982	1983
Heathrow–Amsterdam	846	873	892
Gatwick–Amsterdam	160	168	163
Stansted–Amsterdam	2	15	21
Total: London–Amsterdam	1008	1056	1076

Note: Forecasts provided by Department of Trade and Industry (DTI) and British Airports Authority (BAA)

LEA's London–Amsterdam fares would be identical to those charged from Heathrow. The LEA directors expected the vast majority of passengers to pay the full economy (or Y-class) fare. This had been their experience on the London–Brussels route, which had a similar business/leisure passenger mix, and where 95 per cent of passengers paid full fare.

For the sake of prudence, however, LEA assumed that only 92.5 per cent of passengers would pay full fare. Of the remainder, they assumed 2 per cent interline (half fare), one per cent children (half fare), 3 per cent Eurobudget (85 per cent fare) and 1.5 per cent Pex (two-thirds fare). The latter two fare classes were restricted to off-peak flights, booked and paid for at the same time, with no subsequent changes or refunds. Pex returns also involved a Saturday night stay. The availability of such fares reflected recent government moves which had led to significantly lower (but restricted availability) fares on several European routes, including London–Amsterdam. LEA felt that by carefully controlled marketing of its surplus seat availability, it would be able to earn small additional revenues from reduced-fare ticket sales, without diluting the revenue from, or level of service provided to, its essential core of full-fare business traffic.

LEA's catchment area

LEA commissioned Comma Computer Marketing Services to carry out market research on potential Luton–Amsterdam traffic volumes. This research proceeded by first defining Luton's catchment area; then assessing the volume of existing London–Amsterdam traffic falling within this catchment area; and finally, estimating how much of this LEA might capture.

To define the catchment areas for the four London airports, the map of the South-east was divided into 'grids', and the driving times from each grid to each airport were estimated, assuming use of the fastest route. Travel times by public transport were also assessed. Each airport's catchment area was then defined as the area enclosing locations from which it is quicker to reach that airport, by either public or private transport, than any alternative airport.

Exhibit 2 shows the four resultant catchment areas. Luton's area contains a population of 3.9 million, versus 5.2 million for Gatwick, 4.2 million for Heathrow, and 3.1 million for Stansted. The majority of potential passengers for LEA comprise those who currently travel through Heathrow but live in, or are travelling to, destinations in the Luton catchment area. Of Luton's catchment population, 1.2 million (living to the north) would normally drive past Luton to get to Heathrow, arriving at Heathrow up to 1 hour later. Of Luton's catchment population, 20 per cent live within 30 minutes of the airport, 25 per cent within 30 to 45 minutes, and the remainder live within an hour's travel.

Market potential

The market researchers next estimated how many London–Amsterdam passengers started or ended their journeys in the Luton catchment area. They based this on a major traffic survey of air travellers to and from the United Kingdom (CAP 430) conducted in 1978 by National Opinion Polls (NOP) for the CAA. Exhibit 6 shows the 1978 Heathrow–Amsterdam traffic flows (there were no Luton or Stansted flights then) broken down by UK origin or destination. The rightmost columns show the percentage of each origin/destination's population which falls in each airport's catchment area (for example, Camden passengers are 100 per cent in the Luton area, whereas Southwark passengers are 60 per cent in the Heathrow and 40 per cent in the Stansted areas). These percentages were then applied to the actual traffic figures to deduce potential traffic through each airport, assuming equally acceptable services were available.

Exhibit 6: *London–Amsterdam passengers by origin-destination*

| Origin or destination | Per cent of total passengers in category | | | | Percentage traffic share | | |
| | business | | leisure | | | | |
	UK	Foreign	UK	Foreign	Luton	Stansted	Heathrow
Inner London							
City of London/Westminster	12	51	3	51	30	10	60
Lambeth/Wandsworth	4	.7	6	2			100
Kensington/Chelsea/ Hammersmith	5	5	5	8			100
Camden	1	2	2	2	100		
Southwark/Lewisham	1	.9	1	1		40	60
Tower Hamlets	.3	.6	.4	.3		100	
Hackney	.4	.1	0	0	60	40	
Greenwich	.9	.4	0	0	20	80	
Islington	.4	1	0	0	80	20	
Other Inner London	2	7	.2	5	10	10	80
GLC Essex	1	1	3	1		100	
Outer London							
GLC Herts/Middlesex	9	9	13	5	60		40
GLC Surrey	6	1	6	2			100
GLC Kent	1	.4	3	0	20	60	20
Surrey/Sussex/Berks/Hants	15	4	15	4			100
Kent	1	.5	.8	.4	20	60	20
Metropolitan							
Essex	3	.3	.5	.2		100	
Herts/Beds	3	4	5	2	100		
Bucks/Oxon	5	1	.8	.3	20		80
Beds/Bucks	2	.4	0	.1	100		
West Sussex/Hants/Berks	.9	.5	.6	.8			100
Non-metropolitan							
Essex	.2	0	.8	.9		100	
East Sussex	.3	.3	0	1		20	80
Kent	.3	.1	2	.4	20	60	20
Oxon	2	.7	4	.7	20		80
Southampton/Isle of Wight	2	.6	.9	1			100
Other							
All other regions	21	7	26	11	12	15	73
All origins and destinations	100	100	100	100	25	11	64
Total passengers (thousands)	208	289	106	254	215	97	545

The airport traffic potentials are summarized in the first four columns of Exhibit 7. They indicate that Luton–Amsterdam and Stansted–Amsterdam have potential annual traffic volumes of 215 000 and 97 000 respectively, based on 1978 traffic levels. This compares with total traffic on the Heathrow–Amsterdam route of 892 000 in 1983.

The market researchers' final step was to estimate how much of this potential traffic LEA could capture. To do this, they conducted a telephone survey of 1791 randomly selected households in the Luton catchment area. Respondents were asked about their past travel patterns and future forecasts. Experienced travellers were asked their preferences between the proposed twice daily Luton Viscount service, and travelling to an alternative airport with more frequent services. From the 1171 responses obtained, they concluded that LEA could expect eventually to attract 65 per cent of the potential Luton catchment area traffic. Assuming similar attitudes among foreign travellers and equally convenient flight timings, LEA could also eventually expect 65 per cent of foreign-originating potential traffic.

LEA knew this could not be achieved immediately, partly because their first-year flight timings were not ideal for Amsterdam-originating passengers, but also because it would take time to build awareness. Their actual traffic forecasts of 22 000, 37 000 and 50 000 for years 1–3 reflected this. LEA pointed out that these figures represented only 2.5, 4.1 and 5.6 per cent of the total Heathrow–Amsterdam traffic in 1983, and that the year 3 total was only 36 per cent of the figure suggested by market research. These figures also took no account of anticipated growth in the overall market (see Exhibit 5), nor of any increase in

Exhibit 7: *Potential traffic and LEA's traffic forecasts*

| Category of travel | Annual traffic flows (thousands of passengers) to and from Amsterdam | | | | | | | |
| | Potential traffic for each airport[2] | | | | Lea total | Lea traffic forecasts | | |
	Total[1]	Heathrow	Stansted	Luton	Attainable[3]	*Year 1*	*Year 2*	*Year 3*
UK business	208	141	26	41	26	8	13	19
UK leisure	106	68	15	24	15	2	3	4
Subtotal UK	314	209	41	64	42	10	16	22
Foreign business	289	171	30	87	57	9	14	20
Foreign leisure	254	164	26	64	41	3	6	8
Subtotal foreign	543	336	56	151	98	12	20	28
Total traffic	857	545	97	215	140	22[4]	37	50

Notes
1. All London airports, excluding Gatwick.
2. Figures based on CAP 430 survey and catchment area analysis (see Exhibit 6).
3. The total traffic attainable by LEA is 65 per cent of the theoretical Luton potential (previous column), based on the replies to the market research company's telephone survey.
4. These figures are rounded to the nearest thousand. The unrounded forecasts are 21 846 (year 1), 36 681 (year 2) and 50 478 (year 3).

journeys stimulated by the new service (the telephone survey had suggested that 30 per cent of the existing Luton air travellers would fly to Europe more frequently if scheduled services were available from Luton).

Finally, to ensure that their market research would be as reliable and indisputable as possible, LEA commissioned Martin Collins, Visiting Professor in Market Research at City University Business School, to monitor the research and report on its validity. Professor Collins concluded: 'my overall impression is of a competent and technically acceptable study, intelligently structured to meet the constraints of time and cost. . . . The targets set by LEA appear to represent prudent judgements'.

Sales and marketing

Promotion of the Company was to be assisted by travel specialists Curtis, Edington, Say and Partners, headed by John Cumberland, former Managing Director of Hoverspeed, and a non-executive director of LEA (see Exhibit 1). A total budget of £175 000 was allocated for sales and marketing during the pre-launch period and first 12 months of operation.

The planned advertising campaign reflected the results of qualitative market research by Messrs Hurdle and Trew into the requirements of Luton catchment area business travellers. The emphasis was to be on local radio and local business press advertising, bus backs, tube cards, exhibiting in local business related trade shows, together with extensive direct mail campaigns and personal visits from LEA's own sales staff to business travel managers, company directors, chambers of commerce, and business travel agents. A significant element of the marketing budget was reserved for advertising and promotion in Holland. The Schipol (Amsterdam) Airport authorities welcomed the service, and would instruct and entertain groups of agents and travel managers who would be invited to sample the service by flying to Amsterdam in otherwise unoccupied seats.

British Airways had agreed to accept LEA tickets on BA flights, and a similar arrangement, and possibly a full interline agreement was anticipated with KLM. Travellers who missed flights in Luton or Amsterdam would thus not need to purchase another ticket before rerouting via Heathrow. LEA would be fully installed on the Travicom reservations system, which handles 80 per cent of UK business travel, within 3 months of start-up. LEA seats would also be bookable on KLM's 'skytrack' system, available through 3000 'CORDA' terminals in Dutch travel agencies, in KLM, and to other user airlines around the world.

Licences

On 2 August 1984, following a contested application and a public hearing, the Civil Aviation Authority (CAA) granted LEA a licence to operate a scheduled service at an unrestricted frequency carrying passengers, cargo and mail on the Luton–Amsterdam sector effective upon the completion of satisfactory financial arrangements. Euroflite, the competing applicant, was refused a licence, and had subsequently given notice of appeal to the Secretary of State. However, in the light of the CAA's stated reasons for awarding LEA's licence, and on all past precedent, the LEA Directors were confident that this appeal would fail. In the Directors' judgement, it was extremely unlikely that the CAA would grant any further licences on this sector for at least 3 years, and even then only if the route would support a second airline. The consent of the relevant Dutch authority would, in the opinion of the Directors, simply be a formality given the existing bilateral agreement between the two governments.

The company also applied for licences to operate from Luton to Paris and from Luton to Frankfurt. It was anticipated that these applications would be contested and would be considered by the CAA at separate public hearings during early 1985.

Staff and premises

The management team of the company was to consist of Nigel Harford (Managing Director), Michael Harwood (Finance and Administration Director) and a Chief Pilot/Operations Manager.

Approximately 20 other staff would be recruited to join the company early in 1985. In particular, flight crews would initially comprise three further pilots and seven hostesses. The sales force would comprise two salespersons in the United Kingdom and a general sales agency organization in Holland. The remaining staff would be employed in aircraft engineering, operations control, reservations, accounting and general administration. Operation of the Airline's reservations computer, passenger and freight handling, catering, checkin and security checking would be delegated to third-party specialists.

Apart from the checkin desks available to the company in the airport concourse, the company had been offered and intended to accept a lease on 1800 square feet (about 170 square metres) of office accommodation on the ground floor of Luton International Airport Administration Building, with its own entrance and car parking facilities.

Financial projections

The following projections are based on a single-route operation (Luton–Amsterdam) and reflect the figures submitted to the CAA with the Company's successful licence application, with adjustments to take account of price and other changes between that date and the time when the estimates were prepared.

Forecast item	Year 1	Year 2	Year 3
Revenue (£'000)	£1 816	£2 984	£4 072
Profit before tax (£'000)	£26	£463	£827
Projected number of passengers ('000)	22	37	50
Round trips per weekday	2	3	4
Percentage load factor	30	33	34

The principal assumptions on which the Directors calculated these figures are set out below:

(a) The service will commence in February 1985. However, since seasonality is not of great importance on the London–Amsterdam route, the projected figures are considered equally applicable to alternative start dates.

(b) Fares will be equivalent to those currently charged by British Airways on the Heathrow–Amsterdam route. There will be no material change in average air fares or other competitive factors on this route.

(c) Revenue consists of gross income from the sales of tickets and freight, together with net income from duty free sales which will average £1 per passenger. A full range of duty free goods will be available on flights at prices below those at Luton and Schiphol.

(d) Freight income will be approximately £110 000 in the first year of operation, rising to £130 000 in the third.

(e) 80 per cent of tickets sold will be subject to commission at the rate of 9 per cent.

(f) Direct flight operating costs will average £1659 per round trip in the first year rising to £1700 in the third.
Passenger-related costs will average approximately £6.31 per passenger

(g) (£3.69 for passenger taxes, 73p for the security levy, 18p for the reservation, 56p for baggage handling, 85p for the meal and 30p for the drink).

(h) The company will purchase a Viscount aircraft plus spares for £400 000 financed by hire purchase over 4 years at an interest rate of 15 per cent per annum.

(i) Overheads (including depreciation of aircraft) will be approximately £594 000 in the first year, rising to £803 000 in the third. Since these projections assume a single route operation, all overheads are chargeable to that one route.

(j) Other expenses, mainly amortization of start-up costs, will amount to £75 000 per annum over the first 3 years. Of this, approximately £125 000 has already been incurred. The remaining £100 000 will be spent on advertising, promotion, crew training, etc during the immediate pre-launch period.

(k) Working capital requirements (debtors less creditors) are expected to average 7 per cent of total revenue.

(l) The projections assume that adequate finance will be available, and take no account of any interest earned on any surplus cash balances. The current yield on short-term gilts is around 11 per cent.

(m) The forecasts have been prepared at current price levels. It is implicitly assumed that ticket sale prices will increase at the same rate as cost inflation. The anticipated annual inflation rate over the next 3 years is approximately 5 per cent.

(n) Exchange rates will be 4.25 Dutch florins and 1.24 US dollars to the pound.

(o) There will be no material change in economic conditions or in legislation or government policy in the United Kingdom or Holland which will adversely affect the Company's business.

A detailed breakdown of expenses and revenues is provided in Exhibit 8, and information on tax rates and allowances is given in Exhibit 9. LEA commissioned chartered accountants Stoy Hayward to review their figures, and to compare them with third-party estimates where available. Stoy Hayward concluded that 'as far as the accounting policies and calculations are concerned, the projections have been properly compiled on the basis of the assumptions . . . In our opinion, the basis on which the directors have prepared their projections appear reasonable'.

Financing

When the CAA licence was granted in August 1984, a total of £100 000 had already been invested in LEA. Nigel Harford and Michael Harwood had started the company by subscribing £5000 in cash for shares. In March 1984, Bexfund, a venture capital organization had provided £45 000 as seed corn capital for market research and the licence application. In return, they received 32 per cent of the shares (the total issued capital at this stage was 10 million half-pence shares). The founding Directors also provided the company with a £50 000 interest free loan, and in addition, there was a small bank overdraft.

The London Venture Capital Market (LVCM), a sister company of Bexfund (both were wholly owned by the Ravendale Group) had also underwritten an issue of shares to the public, to raise a minimum of £550 000 after expenses. The issue expenses including printing, advertising, capital duty, accountancy and legal charges, fees to the receiving agents and registrars, and a 6 per cent commission to LVCM were all payable by LEA. LVCM was a licensed dealer in securities and would 'endeavour to arrange' that a market in the shares would be made and maintained on an over-the-counter basis.

Exhibit 8: *Detailed financial projections*

Breakdown of airline expenses and revenues		£'000		
		Year 1	*Year 2*	*Year 3*
Flight	Flight/cabin crew	102.6	144.1	196.5
operating	Aircraft fuel and oil	344.0	516.0	688.0
costs	Maintenance	57.9	86.6	115.8
	Landing, departure, navigation	169.2	273.3	390.3
	Handling and parking	188.8	283.3	377.7
	Subtotal	862.5	1303.3	1768.3
Passenger-	Commission on ticket sales	121.2	203.6	280.1
related	Baggage handling/reservation	16.1	27.1	37.4
variable	Passenger meals and drinks	25.1	42.2	58.0
costs	Passenger taxes and security levy	96.6	162.2	223.1
	Subtotal	259.0	435.1	598.6
Fixed	Insurance	24.5	24.5	24.5
costs	Flight crew training (not amortized)	4.5	7.0	9.5
and	Depreciation of aircraft and spares	99.6	157.5	215.4
overheads	Depreciation of ground equipment	5.5	5.5	5.5
	Sales staff	31.2	31.2	31.2
	Reservation staff and system	31.2	38.4	38.4
	Advertising and promotion	100.0	100.0	100.0
	Directors' salaries	86.9	93.8	93.8
	Other ground staff salaries	76.0	83.7	83.7
	Computer rental	25.0	25.0	25.0
	Rent and rates	10.0	10.0	10.0
	Other administration and general	51.4	71.2	94.3
	Coach and rail fares	24.0	36.0	48.0
	Hire purchase interest	24.0	24.0	24.0
	Subtotal	593.8	707.8	803.3
Other	Amortized development and			
expenses	preoperational costs	71.5	71.5	71.4
	Amortized flight crew training	3.3	3.3	3.4
	Total expenses	1790	2521	3245
Revenue	Passengers and baggage	1684	2827	3891
items	Freight	110	120	130
	Profit from bar and duty free	21.8	36.7	50.5
	Total revenue	1816	2984	4072
Profit	*Net profit* (before tax)	26	463	827
	Passengers carried	21 846	36 681	50 478

Exhibit 9: *Corporation tax rates and capital allowances*

Investment made during period	Corporation tax rate	First year allowance*
	per cent	*per cent*
1 April 1983 – 13 March 1984	50	100
14 March 1984 – 31 March 1984	50	75
1 April 1984 – 31 March 1985	45	75
1 April 1985 – 31 March 1986	40	50
1 April 1986 onwards	35	25

*Allowance received in first year of expenditure, with a 25 per cent writing-down allowance (on a reducing balance basis) in subsequent years. For example, for an investment made after 31 March 1986, the initial allowance is 25 per cent. Thus for an asset with an initial cost of £100 this means that the amount allowable against corporation tax is £25 in the first year, 25 per cent of (£100–£25) = £18.75 in the second year, and so on. Payment of tax for London European Airways will occur approximately 1 year after the liability is incurred.

LEA estimated that net proceeds of £550 000 would provide sufficient capital for the Luton–Amsterdam route. However, an additional £150 000–£200 000 would provide sufficient funds for two additional routes, assuming the first commenced in late 1985, and the second in late 1986. The draft prospectus had been prepared, and in October, discussions between LEA and LVCM were centred around the questions of how many new shares they should issue, and at what price.

11. Hesketh Motorcycles

Early in the summer of 1980, Alexander Hesketh met venture capitalist Duncan Fitzwilliams. He explained why he needed a financial partner in his motorcycle business:

> We have spent about £500 000 bringing our superbike to the preproduction stage. To see it through to volume production will cost us at least as much again. The project has a good chance of paying off, but there is no way we can risk putting so much money into one venture.

Over the previous year, a number of smaller companies had bypassed the onerous requirements for obtaining a full Stock Exchange listing, and had made successful placings of unlisted shares (Exhibit 1). These were traded on a matched-bargain basis under the Stock Exchange's Rule 163:2, but the Exchange had recently issued a proposal to set up an Unlisted Securities Market (USM), which would facilitate dealing in such shares. Duncan Fitzwilliams responded:

> I think we could do better than just looking for a partner for you. Why don't you consider an offer for sale of shares? Your company would be the first to be offered on the new Unlisted Securities Market.
>
> The way to do it would be for our company, Venture Link, to sign up a group of underwriters. We would then market the shares direct to the public and to institutional investors. You should be left with shares which are worth a good deal more than the half million pounds you originally put into the business.
>
> Let me prepare an outline prospectus and invite some fund managers to lunch. You would have to give a presentation on the company, and offer to show them round your workshops.
>
> If they are interested in underwriting the issue, we can follow it up. If not, other than the time we put in on your behalf, there's nothing lost.

Lord Hesketh agreed, and after further discussion, he decided to go ahead with Fitzwilliams' proposal. As the draft prospectus developed, the feeling grew that

This case was written by Elroy Dimson as a basis for class discussion rather than to illustrate either effective or ineffective handling of an administrative situation.

Exhibit 1: *Public sales of unlisted shares in UK companies*

Date	Company name	Method of issue	Issue proceeds
1979			*£ million*
January	Edinburgh Securities Co. Ltd	Placing	1.3
March	Applied Computer Techniques	Placing	0.2
April	John Baker (Insulation) Ltd	Placing	0.3
November	McLaughlin and Harvey Ltd	Placing	0.6
November	Quest Automation Ltd	Placing	1.3
December	Bil-Kil Chemicals Ltd	Placing	0.5
December	Lontrim Group Ltd	Placing	0.3
1980			
January	Thermo-Skyships Ltd*	Prospectus	3.2
March	Webber Electro Components Ltd	Placing	0.3
April	Energy Finance and General Trust	Placing	0.4
April	R.H. Morley Group Ltd	Placing	0.3
May	Air Call Ltd	Placing	1.1
June	Kennedy Brookes Ltd	Placing	0.1
July	Harrison Cowley (Holdings) Ltd	Placing	1.1
July	SPO Minerals Co. Ltd	Placing	1.2
July	United Electronic Holdings Ltd	Placing	1.5
August	Baker Electronics Ltd	Placing	0.5
August	Carlton Real Estates	Placing	0.1
August	Rolfe and Nolan Computer Services	Placing	0.4

*Subsequently renamed Airship Industries

the company should be looking for about £1.3 million, after expenses. This would cover further cost escalation and any other unforeseen contingencies. It was expected that some £500 000 of this sum would be utilized during the preproduction period on the acquisition of jigs, tools, test equipment and other items of a capital nature. The directors of Hesketh's company felt satisfied that, on these figures, the company would have sufficient working capital to enable it to achieve its production plan.

The company

In 1972, Alexander Hesketh became involved on his own account in the business of Grand Prix motorcar racing under the name of Hesketh Racing. In July 1974 he promoted the formation of Hesketh Motorcycles Limited (HML), which subsequently acquired the business of Hesketh Racing from a company effectively controlled by Lord Hesketh and the Trustees of the estate of his late father. HML had at its disposal a group of talented designers and engineers who produced the Hesketh Formula 1 car which, driven by James Hunt, finished fourth in the 1975 Grand Prix World Manufacturers Championship.

The financial burden of maintaining a motor racing team without certainty of sponsorship is very heavy and it became clear to Hesketh that motor racing on its own was unlikely to prove profitable. HML therefore eventually withdrew from direct involvement in Formula 1 racing. However, through its motor racing experience, the production team had acquired considerable engineering skills which were used to build up a substantial and profitable specialized automotive engineering business involving the contract overhaul of Formula 1 and Formula 2 engines, the manufacture of specialist parts, including suspension components, complete chassis, oil tanks, water pumps and engine pumps, the production of high-precision steel and aluminium machinings and the contract testing, using dynamometers, of diesel and petrol engines for leading manufacturers. During 1977, Lord Hesketh began looking for other ways of exploiting his company's engineering skills, with the aim of developing a proprietary volume product. Among the many possibilities considered were various forms of transportation, of which the motorcycle, due to the rising cost of fuel, the increasing congestion of road traffic and the growth of leisure time, seemed to present the most attractive marketing opportunities.

The current share of the world motorcycle market held by British manufacturers had been reduced to negligible proportions, due mainly to the dominance of the large-volume Japanese manufacturers, with their technologically advanced and competitively priced products. Nevertheless Hesketh's assessment was that an opportunity existed, and would continue to exist, in both domestic and export markets for a British-made motorcycle in the high-capacity (over 750 cc), high-performance, 'superbike' sector. After an intensive and critical analysis of competitive designs and engineering, Hesketh decided towards the end of 1977 to embark on the design of a new high-performance superbike combining individuality and exclusivity with the best traditions of British engineering. The aim was to capture a profitable share of the rapidly growing high-performance sector of the market.

The market for 'superbikes'

Over the period 1975–79, the share of the total UK motorcycle market held by superbikes grew from 2 to 5 per cent (see Exhibit 2a). This represents an average compound rate of growth in the number of superbikes sold in the United Kingdom of some 30 per cent per annum, compared with just under 3.5 per cent per annum for non-superbikes. The superbike growth rate in the first 6 months of 1980 (as compared with the corresponding period for 1979) was half the 1975–79 growth rate, but this was mainly due to a sharp decline in sales of motorcycles with a capacity of between 751 cc and 900 cc. In the range of 901 cc

Exhibit 2: *The market for 'Superbikes', 1975–80*

(a) **Sales of 'superbikes' as a proportion of all motorcycle sales**

| Year | Europe (excluding Italy) | | United Kingdom only | |
	Number of motorcycles	*Number of superbikes*	*Number of motorcycles*	*Number of superbikes*
1975	497 444	12 500	174 751	3800
1976	594 295	18 812	188 627	4800
1977	621 863	25 000	176 031	5002
1978	511 750	35 000	174 095	6995
1979	534 000	53 375	206 812	10270
1979 1st half	—	—	94 742	6041
1980 1st half	—	—	112 645	6912

(b) **National shares of the UK 'superbike' market in 1979**

Manufacturing country	*Principal manufacturers*	*Number of superbikes sold*
Japan	Honda, Suzuki, Yamaha, Kawasaki	6600
Germany	BMW	2270
Italy	MotoGuzzi, Ducati, Laverda, Benelli	1200
United States	Harley-Davidson	200
United Kingdom	Triumph	—

*'Superbikes' are defined in this table as being of 800 cc capacity or greater. Motorcycles sales figures exclude moped sales.
Source: Motor Cycle Association of Great Britain Ltd.

to 1050 cc, UK sales in the first 6 months of 1980 were up by over 50 per cent on the same period of 1979, although this rate of growth may have been exceptional and is not believed to have occurred in other European countries.

Comparable statistics are not readily available in relation to the market for motorcycles on the continent of Europe. However, it is believed that while, as in the United Kingdom, during the early part of the 1970s continental demand for motorcycles of all types grew very rapidly, there was virtually no growth in the demand for motorcyles below the superbike category during the second half of the decade; in marked contrast, sales of superbikes continued to grow at an impressive rate. Superbikes are believed to have constituted about 2½ per cent of all continental motorcycle sales during 1975 but by 1979 estimated superbike sales had risen to over 50 000 machines per annum, representing about 10 per cent of all continental sales. The Japanese manufacturers' share of the continental superbike market appears still be growing and is probably slightly higher than their share of the equivalent UK market (see Exhibit 2b).

The product range

Hesketh's plans were based on the assumption that the number of superbikes sold in the United Kingdom during 1981 to 1983 would be about 12 000 per year, and the number sold in the rest of Europe would be over 50 000 per year. Hesketh sought to capture 5–7 per cent of the available UK superbike market and 1–2 per cent of the continental superbike market during this period. He also hoped to make a limited number of sales into other countries such as Japan, Australia, South Africa and Canada, where a substantial demand for superbikes exists. The United States, although potentially a very large market, is difficult for a foreign manufacturer to penetrate, due to the variety of regulations and legislation in force in the individual states. The company therefore decided to restrict the initial marketing of its products in the United States to California. If the marketing plan were to be successful, Hesketh expected to be exporting well over half its annual production by 1983.

In 1980, only one model, the V1000 Sports Tourer, had been brought to the preproduction stage. This is described and illustrated in the Appendix (p. 128). However, Hesketh intended to add other models to the range, all built around the same basic engine and gearbox unit. By 1983, the range was planned to consist of three models:

Sports Tourer. This is a slim, compact motorcycle haivng a low centre of gravity, and consequently good handling characteristics. The bike offered a top speed of 140 miles (225 km) per hour, and was well received by UK dealers (see below). Introduction was planned for late 1981.

Full Tourer. This machine has the standard engine, full weather-protection fairing and rear-detachable luggage. This configuration is very popular both on the Continent and in the United States. Hesketh intended to introduce it in the latter part of 1982.

Cafe Racer. This machine has a more finely tuned version of the existing engine, a single seat, dropped handlebars and individual styling. The sales statistics of other manufacturers indicated a substantial worldwide demand for this type of machine, which HML planned to introduce in 1983.

These three models, which formed the main Hesketh range, were to be supplemented by the introduction in the second or third year of production, of limited runs of specialized types of motorcycles such as low riders, production racer replicas and special-order personalized motorcycles. In addition, Hesketh intended to enter the market for items such as police motorcycles, engine units for specialist frame-makers and accessories of various types, including clothing and headgear. These accessories could be marketed, although not necessarily manufactured or assembled, by HML. A significant proportion of turnover would also arise in due course from the sale of spare parts.

Market research

In order to evaluate market response, Hesketh asked a market research company to organize a dealer meeting on behalf of HML. Twenty dealers were invited to view the motorcycle in April 1980 to provide critical appraisal, to indicate interest in acquiring a franchise, and to estimate volume sales against given price structures. The people invited represented up-market dealers mainly selling a mix of European, American (Harley-Davidson) and Japanese superbikes. Of the 20 invited, 17 attended.

The dealers were also informed that no more than about 20–25 dealers would initially be appointed in the United Kingdom, and discounting from the list price would be discouraged. All of those in attendance indicated that they wished to sell the Hesketh. In a formal questionnaire, they indicated that at a price of £3750, annual potential sales would total 607 units, while at £4995, sales would amount to 271 units.

Most of the dealers stated that 'it's a £4000 machine'. The predictions at the lower price range were far more confident, and the impression was that the volume of sales at the £4995 price range was only an educated guess. The dealers' comments were generally very favourable ('it's much better than expected', 'excellent styling', 'first British bike not made in a blacksmith's shop'), and their interest centred more on maintaining quality, length of warranty period and spares back-up than on eventual price.

As a considerable commitment would be required of the dealers, it was considered essential by all those present that each dealer would be given a reasonable sized territory. All dealers expressed a desire to avoid the current tendency, which prevails at the lower price end of the market, to discount from the recommended price. They also discussed variations of the standard machine, that is, the cafe racer and full touring models. Dealers commented that a three-model range would significantly increase sales volume.

Dealers felt that the Hesketh motorcycle fell clearly in the expensive up-market category. The competition in this segment is represented by BMW, Harley-Davidson, Honda CBX, Kawasaki 1300, Laverda and the very low volume special order manufacturers, such as Munch (West Germany) and Van Veen (Holland).

With the exception of these last two, the superbikes fall into two main types, Japanese and European/American. The Japanese models (Honda, Suzuki, Yamaha, Kawasaki) are three, four or six-cylinder mass-produced models, aimed mainly at the American market. They are competitively priced, and at the time of the dealer meeting they sold in Britain in the range of £1700–£3300. The success of the Japanese has been based on the broad appeal and competitiveness of their machines. This was seen by dealers as a weakness, for it had led to bland design, and had left gaps in the market for more positively designed machines which appeal to 'big bike' enthusiasts.

To some extent, these niches are being exploited by the European and

American motorcyle manufacturers (see Exhibit 2b above). These machines are mainly two-cylinder (though Laverdas have three cylinders and Benellis have four), and because of low production volumes they sell at higher prices than their Japanese counterparts. The features which these motorcycles offer are simple design and maintenance, good fuel consumption, light weight and excellent handling. Their traditional concept and styling tends to appeal to European buyers. The dealers were, however, critical of the detail finish on some of these models, and also pointed to the high retail prices of these bikes.

The marketing plan

In the light of the company's market research, it was decided that the Hesketh range of motorcycles would be sold through carefully selected dealers. It was planned that each dealer would be required to give contractual undertakings in relation to the maintenance of stocks of spares and the promotion of HML's product range in their dealership area. Hesketh expected to appoint up to 25 dealers to cover the British Isles, with overseas dealers to follow in due course.

The company decided that the recommended retail price of the V1000, when first available, would be in the region of £4000 including VAT. If it were to have been available in late 1980, the price would have been about £3750 including VAT. For comparison, the prices of 1000 cc production superbikes ranged from approximately £2050 to approximately £4800, the price range reflecting the widely differing specifications and performances of these machines (Exhibit 3).

Exhibit 3: *Selective price comparisons with competing superbikes*

Model	March 1980	January 1981 (estimated)
	£	£
Honda CBX 1000	2899	3150
Laverda 100 Jota	3199	3500
Kawasaki Z1300	3199	3500
BMW R100RS	3399	3700
Hesketh V1000	**3750**	**3950**
Harley Davidson FX5-80	3939	4300
Harley Davidson FLH-80	4279	4700
Harley Davidson FLH-80 (low rider)	4369	4800
Harley Davidson FTL-80	4759	5200
Munch (West Germany)*	8500	9200
Van Veen (Holland)*	12 500	13 500

*Low volume, special order manufacturers

The V1000 was priced towards the upper end of the superbike range, but the directors of HML believed that the superbike market was not predominantly price-sensitive and that, having regard to its design and performance, there would be a ready market for the V1000. In addition, they were confident that its running costs would be lower than those of its competitors because of its fuel economy and of their intended policy of offering competitively priced spares. The latter policy was also expected to result in UK insurance premiums being lower than those for comparable imported motorcycles.

The production plan

The first production models of the V1000 were planned to be available for delivery in the early summer of 1981. No sales revenues were therefore expected in HML's financial year ending 31 March 1981. The sales effort in the following year was to be concentrated mainly on the UK market, while the first sizeable export deliveries were planned to take place during the year ending 31 March 1983.

The production plan therefore envisaged assembly of sufficient motorcycles to provide as many demonstration models as might be required during the year ending 31 March 1981, with total delivery of all models in the Hesketh range of 1000, 1700 and 2000 units respectively in each of the subsequent 3 years. Once an annual production level of 2000 units had been achieved, Hesketh planned to consider a further expansion of production, having regard to any additional capital expenditure involved.

Production of the V1000 and of subsequent models was to be undertaken by means of an assembly operation and, initially, HML did not intend to be significantly involved in the manufacture of components. Substantial funds were needed to purchase jigs and tools to be made available to selected manufacturers for use in the volume production of the relevant components. A system of selective quality assurance testing was to be applied to all deliveries of components before they were accepted. HML would then assemble, test, market and deliver the completed motorcyles. These would, in their turn, be subjected to rigorous final inspection and quality control procedures.

Premises and staff

HML was negotiating to take an underlease for a period for 21 years on industrial premises at Daventry, Northamptonshire, comprising a factory with an area of 25 200 square feet (2340 square metres), including 3500 square feet (325 square metres) of office accommodation and a parking area sufficient for 60 cars, at a commencing annual rental of £44 000 subject to review every 5 years. Daventry is some 10 miles (16 km) from Easton Neston, Towcester, where the development of the V1000 had been carried out.

Exhibit 4: *Senior management of Hesketh Motorcycles Ltd as at August 1980**

Non-executive Chairman Sir Barrie Heath, aged 64. Previously, Group Chairman of Guest, Keen and Nettlefolds Ltd, he is a director of Barclays Bank Limited, Pilkington Brothers Limited, Smiths Industries Limited and Tunnel Holdings Limited, and a member of the European Advisory Council of Tenneco Inc. He has wide experience of production engineering, particularly in the motor industry.

Deputy Chairman Lord Hesketh, aged 29. Development of the V1000 was made possible by the financial support provided by Tristar, of which he is Chairman and which is effectively controlled by him and the Trustees of his late father's estate. Lord Hesketh devotes a large part of his time to the affairs of HML, particularly in regard to the marketing and promotion of its products.

Managing Director Anthony Horsley, aged 36. Responsible for the overall supervision of the V1000 programme. He was previously Managing Director of Tristar and other companies in the Tristar group of companies but resigned his executive positions within the Tristar Group in order to devote his full time to HML. Contracted to serve as Managing Director for a period of 3 years commencing on 1 September 1980.

Technical Director Geoffrey Johnson, AMIET, aged 45, is Technical Director of the Tristar Group. Responsible for the design and engineering of the V1000 and for the technical programme required to bring it to the production stage and to introduce additional models to the range. He was formerly Chief Engineer of engine design in the Austin Morris Division of British Leyland, and before that, Chief Designer to British Racing Motors Limited (BRM).

Financial Director Leslie Hartwell, FCCA, MBIM, aged 44, is Financial Director of the Tristar Group and of other concerns connected with the Hesketh family's interests. He has occupied senior executive positions with Slough Estates Limited and Richard Johnson and Nephew Group Limited. Responsible for controlling the financial affairs of HML and for introducing the production control, stock control and accounting systems needed to administer its operations.

Non-Executive Director David Simpson, aged 46. A Director of Heritable Group Holdings Limited and Managing Director of Godwin Warren Holdings Limited, Chairman of Godwin Warren Engineering Limited and Chairman of Mokes and Co. Limited. Prior to these appointments, he was labour relations manager at Vauxhall Motors Limited, Plant Director of a manufacturing division of Chrysler (UK) Limited and Director of Manufacturing of Leyland Cars Limited.

*It was expected that a further appointment to the Board, to fill the post of Production Director would be announced shortly, and that additional directors and executives, including a full-time Finance Director and a marketing manager, would be recruited as needed. A further non-executive director, to be nominated by Venture Link Limited, might also be appointed.

The company intended to sublet, on an annual basis, a self-contained unit of 4200 square feet (390 square metres), including 850 square feet (80 square metres) of office accommodation, at a proposed rental of £7800 annually, until such time as the additional space might be required. Subject to completion of the negotiations and legal arrangements occupation of the factory and part of the office space was expected to begin in November 1980; the remainder of the office space was to be ready for occupation in the spring of 1981. These premises provided sufficient space for HML's immediate requirements.

In the initial preproduction stage, the nucleus of the staff required by Hesketh was planned to consist of some ten experienced employees who had all been engaged in the development of the V1000. Additional staff would be recruited locally, as required, and trained by HML. It was expected that the total workforce, including part-time workers, would be some 30 people by 31 March 1981, rising to about 75 once a production rate of 2000 machines per annum was achieved. Having regard to current employment conditions in the engineering industry in the Midlands, the company expected no difficulty in recruiting staff of the required calibre.

The backgrounds of the senior management of HML are summarized in Exhibit 4.

Future prospects

By mid-1980, full production drawings and specifications for all the components required for the V1000 had been prepared and submitted to possible suppliers for the purpose of obtaining written estimates. Internal company estimates were also made of the size and cost of the direct and indirect labour force required and of the overhead and other expenditures involved. The suppliers' and HML's own estimates were then used to calculate the overall unit cost of the motorcycle at different levels of production. All estimates were adjusted, where appropriate, for the possible effects of inflation between the dates of the original estimates and the anticipated start of production. The unit cost would, of course, be affected by the introduction of different models into the range at a later date.

Volume deliveries of the V1000 were not planned to commence before May 1981. HML therefore anticipated making a trading loss in its financial year ending 31 March 1981, partially offset by interest earned on invested funds. Thereafter, profitability would depend on a number of factors, including the selling price of the V1000 and associated spares, the number of motorcycles produced and sold, the volume of sales of spare parts and the cost of materials and labour.

However, on the assumption that production was confined to the V1000 Sports Tourer, Exhibit 5 sets out the expected profitability of the operation making no allowance for profits derived from the sale of spare parts or

Exhibit 5: *Projected profitability of the V1000 Sports Tourer*

Profit breakdown*	1000 Units per annum £'000	1500 Units per annum £'000	2000 Units per annum £'000
Recommended retail	3950	5925	7900
VAT and dealers' margin	1114	1671	2228
Net selling price	2836	4254	5672
Materials			
Engine and gear box	1100		
Frame and running gear	800		
Assembly materials	40		
Total materials	1940		
Direct labour	116		
Total prime cost	2056		
Gross margin	780		
Overheads			
Indirect labour	110		
General overheads	130		
Research and development	100		
Marketing expenses	100		
Warranty	30		
Total overheads	470		
Operating profit before exceptional item	310	700	1050
Amortization of £495 000 deferred R and D expenditure	60	90	120
Operating profit after exceptional item	250	610	930

*At March 1981 prices. Certain items disguised to preserve confidentiality.

accessories or for interest earned on the temporary investment of surplus funds. The table, which is based on the historical cost convention, provides for the writing off of the deferred research and development expenditure incurred on the motorcycle up to 30 June 1980, amounting to some £½ million.

The balance sheet for Hesketh Motorcycles Ltd is shown in Exhibit 6. Other than its capitalized research and development, it is clear that as of 1980, HML owned no other assets. It would not be able to pay dividends until sufficient distributable profits were available, after allowing for any needs to finance further expansion.

Exhibit 6: *Balance sheet for Hesketh Motorcycles Ltd as at 30 June 1980*

Summary balance sheet	£
Current assets (motorcycle parts)	4 385
Fixed assets (book cost: £13 004)	10 365
Investment in non-motorcycle subsidiary (subsequently sold)	2
Deferred research and development expenditure*	494 681
Total assets	509 433
Share capital	90
Revenue deficiency	(21 419)
Loan from ultimate holding company	530 762
Total liabilities	509 433

*Costs of research and development were incurred between the following dates:

1 month ended 31 December 1977	7 500
15 months ended 31 March 1979	176 581
Year ended 31 March 1980	261 217
3 months ended 30 June 1980	49 383
	494 681

The total research and development expenditure is allowable as a deduction against future trading profits liable to corporation tax. Any further research and development expenditure incurred after 30 June 1980 will be written off as incurred.

The following amounts have been capitalized within the above total of £494 681:

Depreciation	2 639
Directors' renumeration	12 535
Bank and loan interest	14 633

The terms of the flotation

The time came for Lord Hesketh to make his presentation to the institutions which had expressed interest in underwriting the sale of shares in HML. Representatives had been gathered together from a small number of investment organizations, as well as from HML and Venture Link, the issue sponsor. Hesketh's presentation was received enthusiastically. The investment managers then turned to listen to Duncan Fitzwilliams:

This offer would be unique in at least two ways. It is the first manufacturing company without a prior trading record where the Stock Exchange is likely to permit over-the-counter dealings. And it would be the first prospectus to appear with the names of the underwriters on the cover.

In a moment, I am going to ask you whether you would be prepared, in principle, to be associated with the offer. But first, let me explain the terms which we visualize for the issue. . . .

Appendix: Technical information on the Hesketh V1000

It took some 2½ years from the original conception to produce a motorcycle which, following rigorous testing of several prototypes, was ready for volume production. The overall specification, design, styling and engineering of the Hesketh V1000 were the responsibility of the HML team, and a subcontractor was employed to assist the company in the design and engineering of the completely new British engine and gearbox. Prototypes of the V1000 have been extensively road and bench tested and were test driven by some of Britain's leading experts on high-performance motorcycles, who were also consulted on its design and styling during its development.

The Hesketh V1000 is a 90 degree in-line Vee Twin motorcycle of 1000 cc capacity. This configuration allows a low centre of gravity, making for better handling characteristics and permitting a slim compact motorcycle which presents a smaller frontal area, reducing wind resistance and assisting performance and fuel economy. The 90 degree in-line Vee-Twin engines give optimum smoothness, virtually free from the vibration frequently experienced with other types of superbike engine, whilst four valves per cylinder produce exceptional power without detriment to fuel economy.

The V1000 has a top speed of over 130 miles (208 km) per hour and an average fuel consumption in excess of 50 miles per gallon (18 km per litre) is attainable under normal riding conditions. The performance, handling and styling of the V1000 compare favourably with those of competing superbikes.

The design of the V1000 combines a number of features not currently available on other superbikes, including a coaxial chain layout, which maintains a constant chain tension (greatly improving the life of the chain), and a parallelogram brake linkage system on the rear wheel, which allows the rider to apply the brake with greater safety when cornering.

The Hesketh V1000 Sports Tourer

PART D

ACQUISITION AND DIVESTMENT

12. Thorn-EMI (A)

On 16 October 1979, Thorn Electrical Industries surprised the City with a bid for EMI. The terms of the offer were 7 Thorn shares for every 20 shares in EMI. Based on Thorn's pre-bid share price of 410p, the bid valued EMI at £160 million.

EMI: history and business

EMI was an international music, leisure, and electronics conglomerate. It operated directly in 30 countries, and employed around 47 000 people. Its worldwide activities included the manufacture and sale of records and tapes; music publishing; medical, industrial and defence electronics; domestic electronic products; cinemas, hotels and restaurants; film production and distribution; television productions; live theatres; bingo; squash; ballroom dancing and other branches of entertainment, including a 50 per cent stake in the UK's largest commercial TV station. The divisional and geographical breakdown of EMI's activities is shown in Exhibit 1.

Until the 1950s, EMI was a traditional record company, with side interests in defence technology. But despite its reputation as the world's oldest and largest record company, it was running at a loss. In 1954, a new managing director, Joseph Lockwood, was brought in. He reorganized the music division, streamlined distribution, and bought Capitol Records. Lockwood's actions transformed losses into steady profits; but the signing of the Beatles turned these steady profits into a torrent of gold. Sales in 1963–64 rocketed by 80 per cent, and the company was faced with the enjoyable challenge of how to invest this massive cash flow.

EMI's solution was the traditional one, namely diversification. It set itself the objective of becoming an all-round leisure company. Its acquisitions in the mid

This case was written by Paul Marsh and Elroy Dimson as a basis for class discussion rather than to illustrate either effective or ineffective handling of an administrative situation. We are grateful to Patrick Barwise and Robin Wensley for extensive help in preparing and revising this case, and to Robin Wensley for writing the appendix.

Exhibit 1: *EMI — divisional and geographical breakdown of turnover and profit*

Year ended 30 June	1975 Turn-over	1975 Profit	1976 Turn-over	1976 Profit	1977 Turn-over	1977 Profit	1978 Turn-over	1978 Profit	1979 Turn-over	1979 Profit
	£ million	£ million	£ million	£ million	£ million	£ million	£ million	£ million	£ million	£ million
Divisional breakdown of turnover and profit										
Music	258.3	19.7	344.8	27.3	430.3	32.7	439.0	16.8	430.3	1.8
Leisure	66.6	6.0	81.4	5.6	94.9	7.2	131.9	11.8	146.3	18.8
Television	29.1	3.0	38.2	5.6	50.6	8.1	60.8	9.1	71.8	7.8
Non-medical electronics	128.7	5.4	164.9	13.9	182.1	12.1	174.3	13.6	177.4	12.9
Medical electronics	20.4	9.2	42.1	12.5	93.2	14.7	66.5	(13.2)	43.7	(12.8)
Property	—	(0.1)	—	—	—	—	—	—	—	—
Group total (excluding sales between divisions)	503.1	43.2	671.4	64.9	851.1	74.8	872.5	38.1	869.5	28.5
Deduct: Net interest payable		8.2		5.6		10.1		12.1		17.7
Group profit before taxation		35.0		59.3		64.7		26.0		10.8
Geographical breakdown of turnover and profits										
United Kingdom	198.1	16.5	241.9	21.8	291.0	25.2	348.9	30.6	393.9	31.2
Europe	134.5	9.6	170.4	14.5	223.4	16.6	231.6	6.8	207.5	(8.1)
North America	78.2	7.1	128.8	13.1	198.4	16.3	170.3	(4.6)	174.2	2.4
Other countries	92.3	10.0	130.3	15.5	138.3	16.7	121.7	5.3	93.9	3.0
Group total (excluding sales between divisions)	503.1	43.2	671.4	64.9	851.1	74.8	872.5	38.1	869.5	28.5

to late 1960s included the Delfont Organization (live theatre); Associated British Pictures (cinemas, Elstree Studios and film distribution); 50 per cent of Thames Television; the Blackpool Tower Company; and Keith Prowse Music. The spending spree continued into the 1970s. In 1975, it bought the Star Bingo chain, and set about transforming it into EMI 'Leisure Centres'. In 1976, it added more hotels, and bought Screen Gems (music publishing). In 1977, it streamlined its dance halls into EMI Dancing Ltd and began restructuring its restaurant division. Also in the mid-1970s, EMI began to transform itself into a major international film company. First, it invested in big budget films like *Convoy* and *Close Encounters of the Third Kind*, and then financed blockbusters like *Death on the Nile* and *The Deer Hunter*.

During this period, EMI did not neglect its non-leisure activities. In the 1960s, it set about expanding the company's electronics and technological interests, then mostly based in defence contracts, into the lucrative area of commercial electronics. EMI bought Associated Fire Alarms (AFA) in 1968, and Minerva — AFA's major competitor — the next year, putting them together to form AFA-Minerva. Similarly, in the late 1960s, EMI created EMI-

Mec, a manufacturer of automated machine tools, out of earlier purchases. It then bought SE Labs, a company making specialized instrumentation and data products.

However, EMI's tentative entry into the field of high technology was changed out of all recognition by the invention in 1972 of the revolutionary brain scanner by an EMI scientist Godfrey Hounsfield. It was this (which brought its inventor a Nobel Prize for Medicine in 1979 and great prestige to the company) that was finally to blunt the edge of EMI's apparently unassailable profitability. The brain scanner, which evolved out of research done for EMI's defence work, was quickly followed by the body scanner. Both were immediately hailed by the medical profession as revolutionary diagnostic aids. EMI believed that the scanner promised even greater riches than the Beatles. But from 1977 onwards, the scanner provided EMI not with the expected bonanza profits, but with a continual drain on its resources as the research and development (R and D) bill grew steadily larger.

Moreover, competition grew more intense as EMI's success with the scanners led other multinational medical equipment firms (including Siemens and General Electric) to enter the market. This competition — and the devices' complex technology — brought a rash of costly patent litigation, and ever increasing R and D costs. In 1977–78, EMI spent over £12 million on developing new models. Furthermore, in contrast to other medical equipment firms, EMI had no other products in the medical business. Thus it had to build up its own sales force and service structure, and whereas its competitors' overheads were spread over a number of products, EMI had only the scanners. With lower margins to work with, EMI was ill-prepared to face any decline in demand. This was exactly what happened in 1978 when President Carter, in an attempt to cut American health costs, imposed restrictions on capital expenditure by hospitals which required them to show a 'certificate of need' for equipment costing over $100 000. In one fell swoop, the scanner's major market (60 per cent) disappeared. EMI was forced to further increase R and D to produce a modular version which could be bought in separate parts and then joined together.

The 1970s also saw the start of the erosion of EMI's position in the record industry, which had been built on the success of the Beatles, and not on a range of artists. The UK market share fell from 32 per cent to 22 per cent between 1968 and 1978, and US market share fell to less than 10 per cent. EMI had simply failed to develop a roster of new artists to replace the Beatles — as late as 1973 the release of two Beatles anthologies accounted for 17 per cent of EMI's total profits. While EMI diversified away from music, the major American record companies, notably CBS and WEA, invested heavily, signing up new artists for huge sums and setting up branch operations throughout the world. In contrast to an industry average of 12–13 per cent of turnover being invested in A and R (artists and repertoire), EMI invested around 7–8 per cent. In particular, EMI failed to develop its repertoire in the all-important American market.

Exhibit 2: *EMI — the 10 year record*

	1970 £ million	1971 £ million	1972 £ million	1973 £ million	1974 £ million	1975 £ million	1976 £ million	1977 £ million	1978[2] £ million	1979 £ million
Balance sheet										
Employment of capital										
Goodwill	61.3	64.2	64.2	80.8	81.9	80.3	82.6	108.5	84.9	94.1
Fixed assets	68.8	80.8	84.7	104.2	112.9	130.4	149.5	179.0	234.1	234.8
Investments	14.5	16.2	15.2	14.4	11.5	12.2	13.7	17.6	17.6	13.1
Current assets	111.8	123.1	122.7	155.8	192.6	208.7	282.2	366.6	368.9	365.1
Total assets	256.4	284.3	286.8	355.1	398.9	431.6	528.1	671.7	705.4	707.2
Less: Current liabilities and taxation	104.3	105.6	105.7	132.5	165.6	185.8	243.4	304.8	321.3	298.4
Net assets	152.0	178.7	181.1	222.7	233.3	245.9	284.7	366.9	384.1	408.7
Capital employed										
Capital and reserves[1]	108.2	109.8	115.0	131.2	144.6	154.3	176.9	218.0	243.9	246.7
Minority interests	12.7	11.8	12.5	15.0	9.6	11.0	13.2	13.4	11.2	10.1
Net assets	120.8	121.6	127.4	146.2	154.2	165.3	190.1	231.4	255.1	256.8
Loan capital	31.4	56.8	53.7	76.0	77.2	75.1	80.0	109.3	119.6	142.6
Deferred tax[2]	(0.3)	0.3	(0.0)	0.5	2.0	5.5	14.6	26.3	9.4	9.4
Capital employed	152.0	178.7	181.1	222.7	233.3	245.9	284.7	366.9	384.1	408.7
Fixed assets additions and revaluations										
Net additions	3.9	7.0	6.1	9.3	8.4	14.3	22.7	32.1	33.7	(0.4)
Acquisitions (net of disposals)	4.7	8.2	0.4	16.8	3.2	9.0	0.6	10.1	(1.8)	1.9
Revaluations	(0.2)	0.6	0.2	1.9	2.7	4.6	7.9	4.0	5.7	4.7
Increase in gross value	8.4	15.8	6.6	28.0	14.4	28.0	31.2	46.2	37.7	6.2
Earnings, dividends and employment										
Basic earnings for year										
Pence per share[3]	12.1	6.1	9.8	14.2	17.0	15.8	25.8	28.8	7.6	1.8
Ordinary dividends for year										
Pence per share[4]	8.7	6.2	7.5	7.9	8.3	9.6	10.5	14.0	14.0	4.9
Personnel at year-end (in thousands)										
Total number of employees	42.4	40.8	40.3	46.3	46.6	48.4	49.9	51.3	49.7	47.6

Notes

1. EMI had 111,165,302 shares outstanding as at 30 June 1979.
2. Adjustments have been made to the 1978 statistics to reflect the change in accounting policy relating to deferred taxation.
3. Appropriate adjustements have been made to basic earnings per ordinary stock unit from 1970 to 1974 inclusive to allow for the effects of the rights issue announced on 11 March 1975.
4. Up to and including 1972 ordinary dividends are stated gross; thereafter the figures comprise an aggregate of the cash dividend and the imputed tax credit.

In 1978, EMI was still developing its leisure activities, still pouring money into the scanner and still making significant (albeit reduced) profits from its music division. Although its debts were rising, EMI nonetheless looked too solid to be under threat (Exhibit 2). But behind the scenes it was facing serious problems. All it needed was for the record market to hiccup and EMI would be in severe difficulties.

This was just what happened in 1979 when inflation finally caught up with the world record industry and sales fell by some 20 per cent across the board. The immediate effect on EMI was to reduce its weak cash flow to zero. Suddenly its credit was no longer limitless and within a few months Lord Delfont replaced Sir John Read as Chief Executive, whilst Sir John remained as Chairman. The Board set about rationalizing the company. The first step was to raise cash by selling off peripheral interests, including the head lease on the new EMI Centre for £33 million. However dramatic these sales looked, they solved only the immediate liquidity problem (Exhibit 3). To end the long-term negative cash flow, EMI had to sell something substantial.

It was this crisis that provided the backdrop to EMI's announcement in July 1979 that it was selling 50 per cent of its music division to Paramount Pictures for some £65 million. But after 2 months of negotiation the deal fell through, not

Exhibit 3: *EMI sources and uses of funds*

Sources and uses (£'millions)	1978	1979
Funds from operations	32	24
Less: uses		
Dividend payments	7	11
Tax payments	22	27
Fixed assets	47	42
Purchase of goodwill	1	14
Repayment of long-term debt*	8	14
	85	108
Net deficit	53	84
Funded by		
Decrease in working capital	2	21
Disposals	9	30
New loans	21	43
New equity issues	8	0
Increase (decrease)in overdraft	13	−10
	53	84

*45 per cent of EMI's debt was repayable within 5 years from 1979. Scheduled repayments included £10 million (1980); £31 million (1981); £12 million (1982); £7 million (1983); £4 million (1984).

so much because EMI and Paramount could not agree a firm price, but because EMI refused Paramount's demand for management control.

Thus EMI's crisis continued. While Lord Delfont asserted publicly, 'I am not Chief Executive in order to preside over a bargain basement sale of EMI's assets', privately, behind the scenes, he and the Board were wondering how to rationalize the cumbersome conglomerate. They turned their attention to the defence electronics business and approached a number of companies, including Thorn, who they hoped would be interested. Then on 16 October, Thorn's bid for the whole of EMI stole the initiative from them.

Thorn: history and business

Thorn was a major electrical company, heavily involved in lighting, domestic appliances, TV manufacture and rental, and engineering. It operated in 19 countries and employed around 80 000 people.

Thorn was set up in 1928 by Jules Thorn who had come to Britain in his early 20s as a representative for an Austrian lamp concern. It went public in 1936. After the imposition of import duties, Jules Thorn moved from importing lamps and radio valves into manufacture. He bought his first factory at Enfield in 1933, and began to challenge the established lamp cartel. A few years later, he acquired the Ferguson Radio Corporation, and became involved in the manufacture of radio sets and radiograms as well as lighting.

After the war, Thorn entered a long phase of steady growth. Two key decisions were the negotiation in 1948 of a licence from Sylvania of the US (a subsidiary of General Telephone and Electronics) to make fluorescent lighting, and the purchase in 1968 of Radio Rentals.

The first of these decisions made Thorn a force to be reckoned with in the lighting industry, and gave the company a technical advantage which it put to good use in its highly efficient factory at Enfield. The Sylvania deal, which led to a long association with General Telephone and Electronics, illustrated Jules Thorn's preference for acquiring technology rather than developing it in-house.

The Radio Rentals purchase, at a cost of £185 million, roughly doubled Thorn's size. Although the price was criticized at the time as too high, the deal gave Thorn an immensely strong position in the TV rental market, providing both a sure outlet for its own TV sets and a steady source of profits growth.

By the time Sir Jules retired in 1976, the company consisted of four product groups (Exhibit 4). Thorn Consumer Electronics handled the manufacture and distribution of TV and audio products (mainly under the Ferguson brand name), and the television rental business (under the name of Radio Rentals, DER and Multibroadcast). The Domestic Appliances Group manufactured and marketed cookers, refrigerators, freezers, mixers, washing machines, fires, water heaters and central heating equipment under a number of brand names including Tricity, Moffat, Kenwood, Bendix and Parkinson Cowan. It also ran

400 retail outlets (Rumbelows). The Lighting Products Division was the largest UK manufacturer of electric lamps and fluorescent tubes and lighting fittings and controls. Finally, Thorn had a diversified Engineering Products Group which made industrial control and general engineering products. As part of the engineering group, Thorn had a telecommunications division based on a 51 per cent holding in a joint company with L. M. Ericsson of Sweden.

The postwar era for Thorn under the leadership of Sir Jules had thus been one of growth and success. Sir Jules had built up his company through a series of canny acquisitions of ailing companies, and by buying in technology. Thorn had proved a first-rate production engineering company with great skills in improving other people's products. Its strategy had been based on building up large market shares. By 1976, it had over one-third of the UK markets for lighting, colour and black-and-white TV sets, cookers and refrigerators. It had always shown a strong preference for consumer products, and was less at home with capital goods. At the same time, it had concentrated on the UK market. Although exports were not insignificant, Thorn had never sought to carve out a dominant share of the world market. Finally, the company was highly

Exhibit 4: *Thorn — divisional breakdowns of turnover and profit*

Year ended 31 March	1975 Turn over	1975 Profit	1976 Turn over	1976 Profit	1977 Turn over	1977 Profit	1978 Turn over	1978 Profit	1979 Turn over	1979 Profit
	£ million	£ million	£ million	£ million	£ million	£ million	£ million	£ million	£ million	£ million
UK companies including exports										
Consumer electronics	256.9	51.0	268.6	47.7	316.7	57.4	338.5	62.4	381.0	65.6
Domestic appliances	154.9	13.6	192.6	12.6	260.7	16.2	288.3	18.0	331.5	19.6
Lighting	102.0	4.6	113.0	4.5	126.9	8.1	145.4	10.9	157.3	10.4
Engineering	108.8	10.2	123.4	10.0	167.8	12.1	188.5	14.1	204.2	12.8
Terminated activities	28.1	(6.3)	21.4	(5.5)	—	—	—	—	—	—
	650.7	73.1	719.0	69.3	872.1	93.8	960.7	105.4	1074.0	108.4
Overseas companies										
Consumer electronics	33.5	(1.1)	49.1	2.5	54.9	3.3	58.2	3.0	64.7	7.0
Domestic appliances	17.8	1.5	29.2	2.5	37.6	3.5	40.3	2.6	41.8	1.5
Lighting	65.7	3.4	82.7	3.7	100.2	5.1	105.8	3.2	103.1	3.6
Engineering	17.5	2.4	20.6	1.5	25.0	2.6	26.9	2.2	40.7	1.6
Terminated activities	4.3	(2.1)	2.0	(0.5)	—	—	—	—	—	—
	138.8	4.1	183.6	9.7	217.7	14.5	231.2	11.0	250.3	13.7
Group total (including sales between divisions)	789.5	77.2	902.6	79.0	1089.8	108.3	1191.9	116.4	1324.3	122.1
Deduct: Financing charges		11.1		5.2		6.4		6.1		4.0
Group profit before taxation		66.1		73.8		101.9		110.3		118.1

paternalistic. Sir Jules found it hard to delegate, and did not hand over the reins until he was 76.

His choice of successor, Sir Richard Cave, was somewhat unexpected. Sir Richard arrived with two kinds of solid achievement: a distinguished war record, and 30 years of steady progress through Smiths Industries to its chairmanship in 1973. During his first year or so in Sir Jules' chair, Sir Richard established a number of priorities. One was to 'move towards a more logical relationship between a small but strong corporate headquarters and decentralised subsidiaries'. Second, he brought in sophisticated planning systems 'to get the company used to thinking further ahead'. As Sir Richard explained it, 'We used to be a wonderful paternalistic company in Jules' day. Now we are a wonderful professional company.'

Sir Richard resolved to expand the businesses which showed a high return, but to disinvest in other areas. In engineering, for example, where a number of not very logical acquisitions had been made, some sorting-out was clearly needed. He looked for opportunities to expand Thorn's stake in TV rental, both in the United Kingdom and on the Continent. The bid for the French TV rental company Locatel, still held up by a monopolies enquiry at the time of the EMI bid, was one such example. Sir Richard felt that Thorn generally needed a wider international spread, especially in the United States and western Europe.

Sir Richard also argued that the company needed to move into areas of higher technology. Thorn was basically an electrical company; Sir Richard wanted to extend its commitment to electronics and to do more innovative R and D of its own. Except in the lighting area, Thorn spent little money on R and D whilst perhaps being one of the best improvers in the United Kingdom on other companies' developments. Sir Richard felt that this strategy had substantial dangers in the 1980s. In order to explore ways of moving into areas of high technology, he made a careful study of the US market. One particular area of interest was industrial controls. After making one or two small US acquisitions in 1978, Thorn moved into the bigger league with the purchase of Systron-Donner, a California-based instrument and measurement business.

While these US acquisitions helped the company gain the high technology base it lacked, Sir Richard felt that it was a mistake to limit operations in this field to the United States. Many of the larger US companies in which Thorn would have been interested were priced on very high multiples, and would have involved paying up to 50 per cent in goodwill. At the same time, such acquisitions carried substantial risks, and Thorn clearly recognized that management of these types of companies, at the distances involved, with the skills of Thorn's present senior management team, introduced further difficulties and uncertainties. Sir Richard was therefore very keen to acquire a medium to large size, high technology company in the United Kingdom. He felt this would have to be based in defence, since only defence provided a sufficiently large outlet within the United Kingdom.

Meanwhile, during the late 1970s, Thorn's growth image became somewhat

Exhibit 5: *Thorn — the 10 year record*

Year ended 31 March	1979	1978	1977	1976	1975[2c]	1974[2b]	1973	1972	1971	1970[2a]
	£ million	£ million	£ million	£ million	£ million	£ million	£ million	£ million	£ million	£ million
Balance sheet										
Capital employed										
Share capital[3]	35.9	34.7	33.9	33.9	33.9	33.4	33.4	33.4	33.0	32.7
Reserves[1]	384.2	317.6	216.9	184.5	161.7	147.5	127.1	105.1	82.7	66.4
Minority interests[1]	10.2	8.8	7.7	7.8	7.5	8.2	7.2	6.4	6.0	6.4
Loans	19.1	25.1	25.2	27.3	33.7	33.1	35.0	37.3	40.5	37.6
Deferred taxation[1]	79.1	68.8	125.7	104.1	82.1	55.3	22.5	19.3	11.7	6.5
Capital employed	528.5	455.0	409.4	357.6	318.9	277.5	225.2	201.5	173.9	149.6
Employment of capital										
Fixed assets	139.6	131.7	114.2	99.4	97.8	81.7	70.0	65.9	58.7	53.8
TVs and rental equipment	200.1	183.2	170.5	149.5	131.0	126.2	109.2	101.6	75.4	57.4
Subsidiaries not consolidated	11.1	11.8	12.8	18.1	24.4	33.0	13.0	11.9	14.9	9.3
Net current assets	177.7	128.3	111.9	90.6	65.7	36.6	33.0	22.1	24.9	29.1
Net assets	528.5	455.0	409.4	357.6	318.9	277.5	225.2	201.5	173.9	149.6
Profit and loss										
Results										
External turnover	1208.1	1091.9	992.9	806.9	706.9	618.8	506.8	412.7	342.6	294.1
Trading profit	221.0	207.5	191.2	153.7	144.2	150.6	132.1	95.2	72.5	59.0
Depreciation	98.9	91.1	82.9	74.7	67.0	69.7	58.2	41.9	31.1	24.2
Financing charges	4.0	6.1	6.4	5.2	11.1	6.7	4.1	4.5	4.2	3.6
Profit before taxation	118.1	110.3	101.9	73.8	66.1	74.2	69.8	48.8	37.2	31.2
Taxation[1]	39.4	37.7	50.9	36.7	35.3	37.5	35.7	18.8	14.3	12.7
Profit before extraordinary items[1]	78.2	71.5	51.0	37.1	30.8	36.7	34.1	30.0	22.9	18.5
Dividends and earnings										
Dividend										
preimputation tax system							3.6	9.2	7.8	6.9
postimputation tax system[2]	18.5	15.7	8.9	8.0	6.0	6.9	4.2			
Gross cash flow	186.4	162.0	153.9	126.4	112.9	117.7	111.2	78.7	58.5	45.3
Earnings per share										
preimputation tax system							30.0p	21.7p	16.7p	13.6p
postimputation tax system	55.1p	52.1p	36.1p	27.5p	23.0p	26.2p				

Notes

1. The figures for 1979 and 1978 are wholly comparable with one another since the relevant figures for 1978 have been restated to reflect the change in accounting policy for deferred taxation adopted in 1979. The five items affected by deferred taxation in earlier years have not been restated.
2. Dividend:
(a) 1970: interim dividend reduced by Chairman's waiver.
(b) 1974 and subsequent: not comparable with earlier years due to introduction of United Kingdom imputation tax system.
(c) 1975: interim reduced by issue of shares in lieu of dividend.
3. Thorn had 142 387 930 shares outstanding as at 30 June 1979.

dented. The outlook for 1979–80 was for pretax profits no better than 1978–79's £118 million, which themselves were only 16 per cent up on 1976–77 (Exhibit 5). Furthermore, most of the excellent cash flow from the TV rental side was earmarked to help pay for the expanding markets for video recorders and the 1980s' generation of colour TV sets. These were expected to be home video entertainment centres incorporating teletext and programme recording facilities, and demanding much heavier investment than the 1971–73 generation of

UHF sets now ending their useful lives. Although video promised to be a major growth prospect, there were considerable uncertainties and extensive competition in this area. And for the moment, in 1979–80, the TV rental market was reaching saturation, and the high profits from the switch to colour were now declining. Thorn's scope for domestic expansion in its other traditional lines of business looked decidedly limited. Domestic appliances were not particularly attractive long term. Manufacturing had become heavily concentrated and competitive; margins were poor; and local preferences made exporting difficult. Finally, lighting demand was governed by the level of industrial investment and housebuilding, which in turn moved in line with overall economic growth.

It was against this background that Thorn made its surprise bid for EMI. The bid was by far Sir Richard's boldest throw since he succeeded Sir Jules in 1976.

Events leading up to the bid

Although the bid came as a surprise to the City, it was in fact the culmination of several months and indeed years of strategic thinking and planning within Thorn. As far back as late 1975, before Sir Richard Cave took over at Thorn, there had been very serious discussions between Sir Jules and EMI's Chairman, Sir John Read. The two companies had got together to exchange figures, and the government had been consulted. At that stage EMI was still a 'glamour stock' and the basic proposal had been for a one-for-one share swop. At the time, some of Thorn's institutional shareholders had expressed opposition to the merger. Ultimately, however, the deal floundered, largely because the succession issue at Thorn dominated the discussions, and yet remained unresolved. Negotiations were completely terminated with the arrival of Sir Richard.

By 1978, Sir Richard had already firmly established himself within Thorn, and there was a general feeling at board level that the time was right, and that the company was large and strong enough to do something 'big'. In line with the general strategy of seeking out a high technology UK acquisition, Thorn reviewed a number of candidates. Plessey was seriously considered, but Sir Richard fairly quickly concluded that Plessey was on a recovery path and would make the grade on its own. Thorn then turned their attention to Decca. At first sight, it seemed an ideal acquisition candidate. It was a manageable size and, although it had obvious problems, Thorn felt that with management attention, a great deal could be achieved. It was a high technology, UK-based company, and it also had substantial interests in entertainments, music and records.

Sir Richard felt that the acquisition of the latter would offer substantial advantages to Thorn. He had recently been carrying out a detailed review of the future of the television set in the home during the 1980s. Currently, television sets were receiving three broadcast programmes and were just starting to be used in connection with video cassette recorders (VCRs) and simple information programmes. Over the next 10 years, Thorn concluded that the television set would have to cater for four broadcast stations, sophisticated information programmes (including Prestel and its developments), substantial numbers of VCRs, even greater numbers of video disc players, satellite TV programmes, and (possibly stemming from that), a reintroduction of cable TV.

These considerations were crucial to Thorn for a number of reasons. First, with Thorn's major interest in rental, it was essential to get the timing of these changes right, and to assign the correct priorities. Thorn's leadership in the rental area had, after all, been built up on their readiness to introduce new products early. Yet to achieve profitability, rented equipment has to be in the customer's hands for many years, so that misjudgements on new technology could be very expensive. Second, Thorn saw major new rental and manufacturing opportunities as it looked forward to the coming 'video age'. In particular, they took the view that the videodisc would provide the greater opportunities here. Thorn placed considerable credence on market forecasts for the United States which indicated the use of some 9 million VCRs and some 10 million videodisc players by 1985. At the end of the 1980s, the numbers might enlarge to some 20 million VCRs and some 30 million videodisc players which together would serve some 50 per cent of the television sets in use. Clearly, therefore, the world market would be a substantial one for Thorn to enter into manufacture of this type of hardware. Finally, Thorn saw important opportunities in video software. There was a growing realization, particularly in the United States, that cassette and disc software was most likely to be manufactured and distributed by the existing music companies. Because of this, music and film companies were talking together, investigating the future, and making suitable arrangements. Thorn felt that companies with interests in both software and hardware were particularly well placed for the future.

In thinking about Decca, therefore, Sir Richard was increasingly coming to the view that it was more likely that Thorn would get its requirement on the hardware and rental side right if it had a full stake in the 'software' business. A major interest in the software side would not only give Thorn a real opportunity of understanding and reacting to the changes to come, but would also place them in a similar position to their competitors such as RCA and Philips. It would also give them an advantage over the Japanese who, in Thorn's view, were clearly suffering from a total inability to control and have real understanding of any of the software side.

However, in spite of the initial attractions of Decca, on closer examination, Thorn concluded that the company's problems were far worse than they had anticipated. Thorn drew away from Decca, and began instead to reconsider both EMI and Plessey. Meanwhile, however, in September 1979, EMI's deal with Paramount fell through. EMI, who by now had realized that something had to go, turned its attention to trying to sell its defence electronics division.

EMI Defence Electronics manufactured a number of systems and products for the UK Ministry of Defence, including the Cymbeline mortar locating system; the Searchwater airborne radar system for use in the Royal Air Force

Nimrod maritime long-range patrol aircraft; the proximity fuze for the Sky Flash air-to-air guided missile; the Ranger barrier defence mine-layer for the British Army; and the SARIE and other electronic support measures systems for the Royal Navy. In particular, EMI Electronics had established a leading position in electro-optics, which was one of the fastest growing areas of defence technology, used extensively on systems for detection, surveillance, tracking and other applications. The Defence Electronics Division also manufactured microwave tubes and components and specialist machine tools; and supplied advanced systems for commercial application in offshore energy programmes, and advanced automatic ticket inspection and barrier control equipment for British Rail.

EMI's merchant bankers, Lazards, drew up a prospectus for the sale of its defence interests, and a number of potential buyers were approached including Plessey, Racal, Hawker Siddeley, GEC and Thorn. EMI were seeking a price in the region of £90–£100 million, and Sir Richard had little doubt that they would obtain this.

The final days

EMI's action forced Thorn to take a fairly rapid view of the situation. Sir Richard was extremely interested in both the electronics and music businesses of EMI. He felt there were two basic alternatives. Thorn could be highest bidder for electronics now and make the necessary arrangements on the music side later. This made some sense since Sir Richard felt that Thorn had another 2 years or so before a move was essential on the software side. Alternatively, Thorn could bid now for the whole of EMI. A board meeting was arranged, and the Thorn directors very quickly decided that they really had to look at the whole of EMI.

EMI was therefore approached for informal exploratory talks. In fact, Sir Richard and the EMI directors had been friends for years, and the two companies once almost lived together while EMI made HMV records and Thorn manufactured HMV gramophones to play them on. Sir Richard knew Sir John Read from his days at Ford, and Harold Mourgue, Thorn's Finance Director, was a friend of Sir John. EMI was prepared to talk fairly openly, and although Thorn was provided with no additional detailed figires (beyond those in the defence electronics prospectus), EMI gave fairly clear and friendly indications about the rest of the business. Indeed, EMI seemed pleased to be talking to friends, after their recent experience with Paramount who had attempted to drive an extremely hard bargain.

Thorn next examined the financial implications of acquiring EMI. They first looked at the new money required for Thorn's existing businesses, particularly the rental area, where there would be considerable cash requirements over the next few years for expansion and replacement of equipment. Next they

Exhibit 6: *Stock market performance of Thorn and EMI, 1970–79**

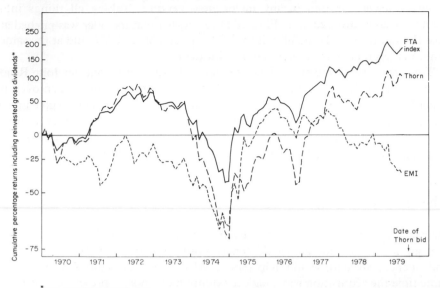

Note logarithmic vertical scale

estimated the cash requirements and likely borrowings of EMI in the future. Finally, they looked at the total position of Thorn-EMI and concluded that on the basis of gearing of 50 per cent (borrowings to capital employed, excluding goodwill, deferred tax and asset revaluations), the joint company would be strong enough to carry out its forward strategy. Furthermore, they projected that in some 3–4 years, the cash flow from their rental area would become very positive so that they would be well over the hump of borrowings.

Thorn held another board meeting to discuss the price they should offer for EMI. Although Thorn had discussed this with Hambros, their merchant bankers, the terms of the offer were very much decided by Thorn. On the date of the board meeting, the EMI share price stood at 95p. The Thorn directors felt that the absolute minimum price that would be acceptable to EMI was 125p. In discussing how much more than this to offer, the directors looked at all the possible counter-bidders for EMI and concluded that there was nobody else in the field who could fit EMI as well as Thorn. They decided, therefore, that the maximum price should probably be in the region of 145p. They had a fairly strong feeling that they would not get slapped down at near the top of this range. Eventually, they decided to make an offer of 7 Thorn shares for every 20 in EMI. Thorn's share price had recently been strong and currently stood at 410p (Exhibit 6), and assuming that Thorn's price held steady, this valued the EMI shares at 143½p. Thorn, however, expected their share price to fall on the announcement of the bid. They recalled the market's view of the 1975 talks; EMI had been receiving a very bad press recently; and the institutions would

143

naturally be somewhat nervous, particularly since Sir Richard was still viewed as being somewhat untried in any major new venture. Taking all things into account, Harold Mourgue, the Finance Director, felt that the offer was pitched at 'just the right price'. Hopefully, it would be acceptable to EMI, and at the same time, just high enough to deter counterbidders.

When the terms were put to EMI, however, Lord Delfont and Sir John Read found them difficult to agree to. Lord Delfont had only recently taken over as Chief Executive and it was only natural that he should be reluctant to give up so soon. Furthermore, EMI did not manage to get its board together rapidly enough to discuss the offer, and by 16 October, Thorn felt it had to show its hand and announce the bid, because of the dangers of a leak.

The commercial logic

Sir Richard and his team set about drafting the press release. In this document, they argued that the merger would benefit both companies. Thorn's commercial and financial strength would help solve EMI's current difficulties, while at the same time the acquisition was a logical extention of Thorn's present interests. It was also claimed that it fitted well with Thorn's publicly stated strategy of building on existing strengths in the consumer and home entertainment markets; moving into higher technology engineering, especially defence; seeking new products to add to the present businesses of consumer electronics, domestic appliances, lighting and engineering; and expanding internationally.

The press release argued that a key element in the commercial logic was the notion of marrying up Thorn's hardware strengths in home entertainment with EMI's software strengths. Thorn made and rented televisions; it also rented the Matsushita VHS videotape system and it hoped to market Matsushita's videodisc system when it came on the market in perhaps 2 years' time. EMI, on the other hand, through its international music and film businesses, coupled with its commercial television interests, had an excellent opportunity, provided it had the financial strength, to play a major part in the manufacture and distribution of the software that would be used in these machines. It was argued that this was a source of considerable potential synergy. EMI had the software, while Thorn could market it. Thorn's rental shops, although located in prime high street shopping sites, nevertheless stood empty for most of the day. Once a set had been rented, the customer need never go in the shop again. Thorn saw an opportunity here to increase the throughput of their rental shops and make them highly productive. Thorn painted a picture of the rental shop in the future containing racks of videotapes, videodiscs, possibly digital audiodiscs, too — a complete home entertainment.

The other key element of Thorn's strategy stressed in the press release was the development of greater expertise in high technology, through the acquisition of EMI's defence electronics division and central research and development department. Thorn argued that this was an essential step in moving Thorn up the technology ladder, since breakthroughs in electronics are typically pioneered in defence and then recycled in civil and consumer electronics.

Thorn also argued that there was industrial logic in acquiring EMI's other divisions. Thames TV, an associated company, would be very helpful to Thorn in the new video era of the 1980s, and would assist the company in providing an understanding of the match between the various aspects of programme material. EMI's 'out of home' entertainment and leisure interests such as dancing, bingo, cinemas, restaurants and hotels fulfilled Thorn's desire for new business areas, while at the same time providing 'a natural extension of Thorn's already major contact with the consumer'. Thorn explained that they were 'getting into the area of dealing with people and all their entertainment needs'. Finally, Thorn argued that the worldwide organizations of both companies would enable the enlarged group to strengthen its international activities.

In drafting the press release, Sir Richard was careful to describe Thorn's offer for EMI as a merger proposal. In many ways, this was an accurate description given the friendly relations and discussions with EMI. Privately, however, Sir Richard and his board did not intend any other outcome than the Thorn management taking full charge of the EMI management. The structure that they had in mind was that Sir John Read should become Deputy Chairman and that Lord Delfont should report directly to Sir Richard with responsibility for the music, entertainment and leisure businesses. The remainder of the EMI businesses, primarily electronics, would immediately become integrated within Thorn's present structure, responsible to the Managing Director, helped by a strong corporate centre, but with decentralized product groups with clear and strong line management arrangements. Sir Richard was convinced that this structure was the best possible for firstly controlling a high technology business, and secondly for spreading the use and understanding of this technology throughout the present Thorn businesses.

The other omission from the press release was any discussion of disposals and asset sales. Clearly, any talk of disposals would not have endeared Thorn to EMI's management and workforce. Thorn did, however, drop a hint in this direction about medical electronics by stating that they felt this division merited special consideration and investigation. Privately, Sir Richard felt that EMI had got this business wrong from the very start, and that the only alternatives now were to take on a very substantial partner or to sell the business entirely. He also believed that to follow Thorn's future strategy in music and high technology wholeheartedly, it would be necessary and right to be prepared to divest certain interests in Thorn's Engineering Division, and also certain areas of EMI, particularly in the leisure and entertainment area. This was a strategy which Thorn could follow without having to make quick and forced sales, so that they could obtain the best price. Naturally, in setting the overall price for EMI, Thorn had speculated about the price tags for the individual EMI divisions. The Paramount offer had valued half the Music Division at £65 million, and the

Exhibit 7: *Characteristics of quoted companies in the leisure, music, television, electrical and electronics industries[1]*

Industry and Company	Earnings before interest and tax (£ million)	Profit after tax (£ million)	Capital[2] employed (£ million)	Book value of equity (£ million)	Market capitalization of equity (£ million)
Leisure					
Associated Communications	24.0	11.8	116.7	82.1	75
Associated Leisure	5.7	3.8	17.6	13.2	26
Black and Edginton	3.2	.9	30.9	18.1	14
EMI	28.5	2.0	314.6	162.0	106
Ladbroke	53.6	29.3	161.0	91.5	105
Television companies					
Anglia TV	2.7	1.5	8.5	8.0	10
HTV	4.5	2.4	15.1	11.8	13
LWT	4.4	2.2	31.5	22.8	24
Trident TV	7.3	3.2	28.4	27.7	27
Hotels and catering					
De Vere Hotels	2.0	1.1	37.0	36.7	25
Grand Metropolitan	182.9	104.3	993.2	564.6	781
Reo Stakis	4.0	2.5	16.7	10.9	21
Savoy Hotel	1.5	.4	25.4	18.2	34
Trust House Forte	87.7	41.9	474.0	294.1	312
Electricals					
Ferranti	15.5	9.6	82.2	52.5	92
GEC	463.6	257.3	1450.0	1039.3	2108
Plessey	72.4	41.3	318.1	239.9	276
STC	42.2	25.9	176.8	123.8	246
Light electronics					
Decca	4.6	−0.7	109.8	87.0	59
Eurotherm	3.3	2.1	6.7	4.9	40
Farnell Electronics	5.1	2.4	13.9	13.2	41
Racal	70.3	41.6	169.0	117.7	600
Thorn	122.1	78.2	568.1	498.7	608
Office equipment					
Rank Organisation	153.8	76.0	592.9	326.9	443

Notes
1. Latest information available at end September 1979. Book value excludes goodwill.
2. Including bank loans, but excluding goodwill.

asking price for the Defence Electronics business had been £90–£100 million. Conceivably, the Leisure Division assets might be worth perhaps £60–£70 million, the 50 per cent stake in Thames TV some £30 million, and AFA-Minerva, a further £15 million (Exhibit 7). On an assets valuation basis, therefore, Thorn felt that their offer left them with plenty of scope for profitable disposals, should these prove appropriate, in those parts of the EMI business that were not central to their strategy.

The press release completed, Sir Richard Cave and the Thorn Board waited with keen interest to see how the Stock Market would react, and what EMI's decision would be.

Appendix: A note on the TV and VCR markets

Television market in the United Kingdom

From 1970 to 1975, and especially from 1975 to 1979, a number of changes have been evident in the television market. The market data provided in Exhibits 8–10 enable us to make the following observations.

Sets-in-use. The substantial drop in the number of monochrome sets-in-use experienced in the early 1970s with the introduction of colour has been halted, while the number of colour sets has continued to grow, albeit more slowly. The number of sets in use now exceeds substantially the number of households, indicating considerable second-set purchase.

Rental. In general the rental sector does better in the case of new developments and/or larger sets. The trends in the market have, however, been against rental in both these areas. Hence, the rental share of sets-in-use has dropped from 58 per cent in 1970 to 47 per cent (estimated) in 1979. The decline has been, however, much slower for 1975–79.

UK retail market. In the retail market, monochrome sales have actually grown faster than colour sales on a percentage basis, although in value terms, colour still represents about 75 per cent of the total.

The switch to smaller monochrome sets has been very evident, with an increased import penetration based on their strength in small screen monochrome televisions. The import proportion of colour televisions has also increased from 19 per cent (1975) to 22 per cent in 1978, whilst the proportion of small screen colour televisions has increased much faster: from 12 per cent (1976) to 24 per cent (estimated) in 1979.

Rental operators. Thorn, through Visionhire and other subsidiaries, has a dominant 30 per cent share of the total rental market. The three other important operators are Electronic Rentals (13 per cent), which has strong links with the Philips group; Granada at 11 per cent and Rediffusion (also with strong Philips links) at 9 per cent.

VCRs and Videodisc

VCRs remain a small, but rapidly growing market. Exhibit 8 shows that consumer offtake of VCRs has risen from 15 000 in 1977 to an estimated 125 000 for 1979 and a forecast 180 000 for 1980. As is often the case with new technologies (see above), rental has been a very important component of sales and is currently estimated at around 75 per cent of all sales. This, despite the fact that a recent *Which?* report advised (July 1979): 'We think that buying a video recorder and taking out a maintenance contract works out cheaper than renting.'

There also remains considerable choice and conflict about the various video systems, the four basic being VCR (Philips); Beta (Sony); VHS (JVC); and SVR (Grundig). Current evidence suggests that worldwide JVC is outselling all its competitors by a wide margin; some have put the figure as high as 5:1 (*Financial Times*, March 1979). At the moment, however, this confusion is perhaps not critical for users since the major use (*Which?*, June 1979) is for recording-playback of television programmes. Similarly in the United States, where the market is much more developed, a recent (March 1979) survey indicated that average households played back 3.4 tapes per week of previously broadcast programmes (and recorded 4.1 programmes per week), and watched only 0.5 prerecorded cassettes per week which were either bought, rented or borrowed. Films and television movies were the most important single type of programme to be recorded.

All this suggests that there may be a market for prerecorded material via the videodisc, when and if it is available on the UK market (Philips has been testing their VLP (Magnavision) product in Atlanta since February with, apparently,

Exhibit 8: *Television and VCR market in the United Kingdom 1970, 1975–79 (million sets)*

	Sets in UK			Sets rented			VCRs
Year	Mono	Colour	All	Mono	Colour	All	All
1970	17.8	.7	18.5	10.2	.5	10.7	—
1975	13.5	9.5	23.0	4.6	6.5	11.1	—
1976	12.3	11.0	23.3	4.0	7.3	11.3	—
1977	11.0	12.5	23.5	3.5	8.2	11.7	.015
1978	10.5	13.8	24.3	3.2	8.5	11.7	.070
1979*	10.5	15.3	25.8	3.0	9.0	12.0	.125

*1979 figures are estimated.

148

strong positive response from both consumers and distributors). On the other hand, competition over disc systems looks like being just as intense as with VCRs with RCA planning to introduce a much cheaper, lower technology system (possibly in 1–2 years time), Sony undertaking expensive development, and both Thomson (France) and JVC having their own demonstration systems.

On top of this, in a recent survey of intentions of potential VCR purchasers in the United Kingdom, 25 per cent expressed interest in recording and keeping tapes temporarily, while over 50 per cent expressed a wish to keep recordings more permanently which might also imply a large market for prerecorded material on VCRs and hence difficult competition for the videodisc.

Exhibit 9: *Value of UK retail and rental market (£ million)*

Year	Retail market			Rental market		
	Mono	*Colour*	*All*	*Mono*	*Colour*	*All*
1975	38.2	199.2	237.4	19.2	175.6	194.8
1976	47.0	206.8	253.8	17.4	165.2	182.6
1977	56.3	244.4	300.7	14.2	184.5	198.7
1978	80.5	291.8	372.3	13.8	212.1	225.9
1979 (estimated)	92.0	305.0	397.0	10.0	215.0	226.0

Exhibit 10: *Source of mono sets (thousands)*

Year	Small screen		Large screen	
	UK made	*Imports*	*UK made*	*Imports*
1975	300	405	206	29
1976	260	525	194	26
1977	340	505	173	17
1978	550	550	145	25

13. Hanson Trust

On 6 December 1985, Hanson Trust announced that it was making a bid for the Imperial Group. The announcement was classic Hanson style — made on a Friday evening after a week in which the company had published an impressive set of annual financial results, and in which it had appeared to be interested in a number of other potential takeover victims. At this time, Hanson was also engaged in a legal tussle over a $900 million contested bid it was making for the US conglomerate, SCM.

Earlier in the week had come the news that Imperial and United Biscuits intended to merge. Lord Hanson, the chairman of Hanson Trust, said that with this announcement, 'Imperial put up the "for sale" sign'. Hanson felt that the terms of the merger greatly favoured United Biscuits, and that this demonstrated, yet again, that Imperial was incapable of correctly valuing businesses.

The chairman of Imperial reacted to the Hanson move by saying that, 'The bid is completely inadequate. There is no industrial logic. We will fight Hanson as tenaciously as we can.' United Biscuits were also unimpressed. Their chairman commented, 'This deal means that Imps would be absorbed in a sprawling industrial combine which shows no particular skills in consumer products,' adding, 'The Imps/United Biscuits proposal offers a far better deal for shareholders.'

The bid from Hanson was the largest acquisition offer to date in the United Kingdom. At £1.9 billion it came at the end of a record-breaking week for British mergers and acquisitions in which £1.87 billion had been offered for Distillers Co. by the Argyll Group, £1.3 billion had been offered for United Biscuits by Imperial, and £1.2 billion had been bid by GEC (General Electric Co.) for Plessey.

This case was written by Elroy Dimson, Ewan Labrom, Paul Marsh and Jennifer Smerdon as a basis for class discussion rather than to illustrate either effective or ineffective handling of an administrative situation.

The players

1. Hanson Trust

Hanson Trust is an industrial conglomerate that has grown through a strategy of acquisition and merger (Exhibit 1). Hanson's objectives are well defined:

Exhibit 1: *Hanson Trust's acquisitions and divestments, 1970–85*

Name of acquisition	Cost of acquisition	Receipt on sale
United States	*$ million*	*$ million*
Gable Industries	2 (1973)	4 (1975)
Seacoast Products — animal foodstuffs	32 (1974)	30 (1983)
Carisbrook — textiles	36 (1975)	16 (1977)
Hygrade Food Products	32 (1976)	163 (1979)
Interstate — food	30 (1977)	93 (1985)
Old Salt Sea Foods	2 (1977)	na (1983)
Templon Spinning Mills	7 (1978)	
Natural Casing Division of Hygrade	see above	9 (1979)
McDonough — conglomerate	180 (1980)	49(1981)[1]
Gulf Resources (5 per cent)	10 (1981)	
USI — conglomerate	532 (1984)	25 (1985)[2]
SCM — bid pending	930 (1985)	
United Kingdom	*£ million*	*£ million*
National Star Brick and Tile	1 (1971)	
Castle Brick — building materials	3 (1972)	
Midland Brick — building materials	3 (1973)	
BHD Engineers	12 (1973)	na (1973)
Angus Milling — grain merchants	1 (1975)	
Rollalong — building site amenities	1 (1976)	
Hamlyn Animal Feeds	1 (1977)	
Henry Campbell — textiles	5 (1978)	
Lindustries — engineering and textiles	25 (1979)	na (1980)
Berec Group — batteries	95 (1982)	
UGI	20 (1982)	
United Drapery Stores	250 (1983)	186 (1983)[3]
London Brick	247 (1984)	
Powell Duffryn — bid failed	147 (1985)[4]	
Imperial Group — bid pending	1900 (1985)	

Notes
1. Cement division only
2. PolyTech division only
3. UDS assets only
4. Amount offered — bid failed

We aim to invest in good basic businesses producing essential products for which there is a clear continuing demand. We avoid areas of very high technology. We do not want to be involved in businesses which are highly capital intensive and where decision making has to be centralised. We want to be concerned with businesses where our 'free form' management approach is appropriate.

Acquisitions are, therefore, carefully chosen because they are likely to respond to Hanson's style of management. Exhibit 2 gives the major areas of activity of the companies which Hanson has acquired. In these companies, Hanson's focus on return on capital and its readiness to close down loss-making operations and sell surplus assets has resulted in dramatic cash flows.

Growth in Hanson Trust is, therefore, achieved by acquiring and turning round companies. In the main, each acquisition has been larger then the previous one. According to press commentators, the theory behind this is that each acquisition gives an immediate boost to Hanson Trust's profits, justifies the cost, and keeps the share price up and institutional investors happy. Hanson's strategy has been highly successful, and between 1980 and 1985 the company's revenues grew by 200 per cent and profits by 400 per cent (Exhibit 3).

Behind Hanson Trust are two men whose names are said to be enough to bring terror to the boardrooms of many UK companies, Lord Hanson and Sir Gordon White. Hanson is chairman of Hanson Trust, and White is chairman of its American offshoot, Hanson Industries. An executive of a previous target company recalled that Hanson's reputation was such that 'when we heard he had made a bid, the directors fell apart. All that the non-executive directors wanted to know was at what price we were giving in.'

The association between James Hanson and Gordon White goes back more than 20 years. Both come from prosperous English families and were well known in the gossip columns before their company hit the financial headlines. An associate notes that 'Hanson and White are witty, personable, and have an enormous appetite for fun and play after hours. . . . But they combine that with an incredible intensity when the gun goes off at 8 am.'

The two men have very different management styles. White prefers deal-making, and says that 'the sharp end of business appeals to me'. He is famous for never actually seeing what he is buying, but for doing all his work from financial reports: 'I've never gone to look, never visited a plant or headquarters. I don't believe in royal visits.' Lord Hanson, in contrast, is the elder statesman of Hanson Trust. He chairs the parent company in the United Kingdom, and represents Hanson Trust to the public and to its shareholders (mostly British institutions).

Hanson started his business career in the family trucking company. In 1948 it was nationalized by the postwar Labour government, and he says that this made him less emotional about the companies he takes over. 'I think my father was a passionate transport man. I became dispassionate when I saw nationalization.

Exhibit 2: *Business and geographical activity for Hanson, Imperial and United Biscuits.*

Breakdown as of 1985	Turnover *per cent*		Profit before tax *per cent*	
Hanson Trust				
United Kingdom				
Allders (department stores)	17		10	
British Ever Ready (batteries)	5		11	
Hanson Brick	7	40	19	53
Lindustries (electrical and gas)	6		9	
Hanson Engineering	5		4	
United States				
Carisbrook (textiles)	7		5	
Consumer products	10		8	
Food products	18	60	5	47
Furniture	5		6	
Hanson Building Products	8		10	
USI (diversified engineering)	12		13	
Imperial Group				
Imperial Tobacco	53		47	
Imperial Brewing and Leisure	20		37	
Imperial Foods	14	100	13	100
Howard Johnson	12		3	
Other activities	1		—	
United Biscuits				
United Kingdom				
UB Biscuits	21		36	
UB Foods	14		20	
UB Frozen Foods	6		—	
DSC (bakery and meats)	4		—	
UB Restaurants	2	53	3	65
UB International (exports for UB)	1		1	
Wimpy (fast food)	2		3	
Distribution services	3		2	
North America				
Keebler (biscuits)	39		27	
Specialty brands (spices, herbs)	4	44	6	34
Other	1		1	
Rest of world				
Productos Ortiz (bakers)	1		(1)	
Westimex (potato crisps)	1	3	1	1
Others	1		1	

Exhibit 3: *Financial results for Hanson Trust plc (£ million)*

	1981	1982	1983	1984	1985
Income statement					
Turnover	856	1148	1484	2382	2675
Profit before tax	50	60	91	169	253
Taxation and minorities	(16)	(18)	(28)	(43)	(60)
Extraordinary items	(0)	(1)	1	(3)	16
Dividends	(11)	(13)	(19)	(33)	(59)
Retained earnings	23	28	45	90	150
Balance sheet					
Tangible assets	129	211	289	685	602
Investments	4	4	11	17	187
Fixed assets	133	215	300	702	789
Inventory	155	242	312	503	452
Receivables	106	150	217	419	353
Cash and investments	198	154	433	521	1257
Current assets	459	546	962	1443	2062
Payables	162	180	265	491	432
Dividend	6	8	13	21	41
Short-term loans	48	133	286	240	433
Current liabilities	216	321	564	752	906
Net assets	376	440	698	1393	1945
Long term loans	191	188	186	797*	640
Long-term payables	16	62	82	183	180
Minority interest	3	2	2	2	1
Shareholders funds	166	188	428	411	1124
Capital employed	376	440	698	1393	1945
Funds flow					
Group profit	50	60	91	169	253
Depreciation	16	23	31	44	53
Sale of fixed assets	8	5	15	10	24
	74	88	137	223	330
Capital expenditure	27	30	40	50	59
Working capital	(4)	21	(26)	(25)	20
Dividends paid	10	12	16	24	39
Tax paid	14	22	23	34	37
Extraordinary items	—	—	—	—	26
	47	85	53	83	181
Share issues	—	—	(175)	—	(505)
Debentures/loans	(56)	(45)	(195)	(583)	—
Assets of subsidiaries	77	95	288	622	(90)
Investments	(3)	2	1	(4)	185
	18	52	(81)	35	(410)
Change in net liquid funds	9	(49)	165	105	559

*Secured long-term bank loan of £540 million granted

Now we're fond of many of our businesses, but we're not in love with them.'

Gordon White started by selling advertising space in the farmers' magazines and sports programmes published by his father's company. He says 'It was really hard slogging. I travelled more than 40 000 miles a year, making 200 cold calls a week. There's nothing better in the world than selling space for learning intuition in negotiations.'

By 1964 Hanson and White had joined forces and were running a group of truck dealerships. They sold out to a small public company called the Wiles Group and joined Wiles' board of directors. Before long the founder, George Wiles, sold his shares to Hanson and White, and Hanson Trust was born. The company began to grow by a process of acquisition, always looking for companies with assets that could be sold quickly if necessary. Explaining this strategy, White commented that, 'Being Yorkshiremen, we always say, "Don't tell me what we can make on a deal. What can we lose?" Many times we could have made that quantum leap into the big league, but we would examine the downside risk under a microscope and just walk away.' Hanson has joked in the past that 'Avoid the downside risk' will be inscribed on White's tombstone.

Hanson and White are assisted by a small headquarters staff in both the United Kingdom and the United States. This central staff is responsible for raising money, analysing acquisitions, monitoring divisional budgets and controlling capital expenditure. Control is maintained through budgets, selection of senior managers, and via incentive schemes.

Hanson Trust takeovers tend to follow a predictable pattern. The first step is normally to slash overheads and dismantle central administrative systems. The company is notorious for its ruthless attitude to existing top management — probably one of the reasons that a Hanson bid generates so much hostility. Centralized top management is normally replaced by one that is decentralized and incentive-motivated. Large bonuses are paid for improvements in profits and return on capital employed.

The second move is to sell off surplus assets that are not generating income such as a headquarters building or spare factory capacity. And frequently part of the original cost is recouped by selling divisions in business areas that do not fit the Hanson criteria or are unlikely to respond to the Hanson style of management. The third step is to impose tight control of all capital expenditure by the Hanson headquarters staff. Immediately after the acquisition a moratorium is put on capital expenditure. During this time the future prospects of the acquired company and its industry sector are assessed. Even after this is done, however, all capital expenditures over £500 in the United Kingdom and $1000 in the United States must be approved by the headquarters staff.

What the hotchpotch of companies owned by Hanson Trust has in common is the management objective that each year, overall, they will make the highest possible return on capital, and significantly increase profits. Hanson and

White's secret is to grow by becoming smaller — decrease the amount of capital, sell subsidiaries that do not perform and demand higher efficiency in all its businesses.

The company has been charged with asset stripping and the case of United Drapery Stores (UDS) is often cited. Having purchased UDS for £250 million, Hanson Trust immediately sold off property assets for £186 million. Having thus reduced the cost to £64 million plus interest, one of the few remaining components — Allders, the company that runs duty-free shops at airports — made Hanson £29 million in one year. 'This may well be asset stripping but it was a brilliant piece of business,' stated *Business* magazine in March 1986. Asset stripping is, however, a somewhat vague and emotive term. Hanson has certainly on many occasions sold off surplus assets, or indeed whole businesses to others to whom they are more valuable. Hanson point out, however, that they have never been involved in selling off individual assets which were essential to the long-term future of the business in question.

In 1973, Hanson Trust's profit record attracted the big paper producer, Bowater. Hanson agreed to a takeover, hoping to repeat the experience with Wiles. However, the bid was referred to the Monopolies and Mergers Commission, and Bowater withdrew its offer.

That same year, 1973, Gordon White decided to leave the United Kingdom for the tax haven of Bermuda. Unable to operate in the United Kingdom for tax reasons, he searched for opportunities abroad for Hanson Trust, soon deciding to concentrate on the United States. Within 4 years, Hanson Industries had swallowed up a number of companies in a wide range of industries and, with the acquisition of US Industries for $531 million in 1984, became one of the largest 150 corporations in the United States. In a 1985 television interview with Alan Whicker, White said: 'It broke my heart to leave England, it really did, but I comforted myself with the thought that really I was working for England, because whatever I could build up (in the United States) would belong to the shareholders of Hanson Trust and those shareholders were all British.'

In its early days, Hanson Trust was regarded by investors as a speculative venture, and was tainted by its close association with Slater Walker after the latter's highly publicized collapse in 1974. In the early 1980s, Hanson Trust became popular with investors and was a core holding of every institutional portfolio. Its meteoric stock market performance over this period is displayed in Exhibit 6 (see below, p. 163).

In the summer of 1985, White began purchasing shares in the US conglomerate SCM. It was a typical Hanson target, with a mixture of operations in low technology industries and plenty of scope for cost cutting and immediate asset sales. In August, Hanson made a tender offer at $60 a share (worth $745 million), and a week later SCM announced a management buyout with the assistance of investment bank Merrill Lynch at $70 a share (worth $868 million). At the beginning of September, Hanson increased its bid to $72 per share ($900 million). Merrill Lynch and the SCM management responded with a $74 offer, accompanied by a 'lock-up' option allowing Merrill to acquire SCM's food and pigments business for $80 million and $350 million respectively should any other party purchase more than one-third of the shares of SCM. These two divisions were considered to be the most attractive parts of SCM, and the effect of such an option would have been to make SCM less attractive to a potential bidder. Hanson contended that their price tag was too low.

Hanson withdrew its $72 per share offer on 11 September, but the same day began buying SCM shares on the open market. By the end of the following day, Hanson held 25 per cent of SCM's shares. The fight then moved into the courtroom, with Hanson eventually being allowed to continue purchasing SCM shares. The Merrill option was to be triggered by purchases of one party of one-third of SCM's shares, and Hanson hovered just below this level for a while. In October, Hanson announced a new cash offer of $75 a share, conditional on the Merrill option being dropped. At the time of the Hanson bid for Imperial in December, the offer for SCM was still tied up in the US courts, although judgement on the legality of the 'lock-up' option was expected early in the New Year.

The submissions required by the US courts have provided some interesting insights into the operations of Hanson Trust. Asked how he valued a prospective acquisition, White replied 'gut feeling'. White had no formal permission for the SCM offer, and Lord Hanson was quoted as saying 'Gordon sent me the (SCM) accounts and I liked the photographs.' In the interview with Alan Whicker, White categorized himself as

> very laid back. I couldn't care less about business, other than the fact that I feel it's like boarding a ship, robbing all the men and raping all the women. It's an adventure as long as it's fun. It has to be fun if you're going to tilt against the Establishment or, and particularly (in the United States), you're going into a very tough fight. Every time you have to gird up your loins to get in there and kill 'em because if not, they'll kill you.

2. Imperial Group

The Imperial Group was the UK's largest cigarette maker with approximately 50 per cent of its profits coming from tobacco products, 50 per cent from brewing and leisure, and the balance from its food subsidiaries. The company had many well-known brands, amongst them Embassy and John Player cigarettes, Golden Wonder crisps, HP sauces, Courage and John Smith beer, and Happy Eater restaurants (see Exhibit 2 for major areas of activity).

Imperial's performance during the 1970s was unexciting, and marked by a continuous effort to diversify away from tobacco products and from the United Kingdom. In July 1981 a boardroom coup led to the departure of the then chairman, Malcolm Anson, after only 15 months in office. Profits had fallen dramatically, and there was dissatisfaction with his decentralized management style.

The new chairman was Geoffrey Kent, who once ran the Courage brewing division and had been with the company for more than 20 years. He became chairman promising 'hands-on management from the centre', and immediately began to divest a number of the more poorly performing businesses. One major policy change was the abolition of the principle that divisions could reinvest earnings as they saw fit, and the introduction of a requirement to justify major capital expenditure to central management. Kent divided Imperial into 24 strategic business units within three divisions (tobacco, food, and brewing and leisure), tightened central control over budgets, and increased corporate monitoring of actual performance against budget. In the tobacco division, for example, production capacity was rationalized and turnover increased. This helped Imperial to maintain a 40 per cent share of the UK market. However, the market for tobacco products in the early 1980s had been steadily declining, and generic and own-label brands had been increasing their share.

Most of the businesses that were divested were from the food division. This division had suffered a number of setbacks. For example, J. B. Eastwood, the egg and poultry producer, had been bought by Imperial just before the UK egg market was hit by dumping from Dutch producers. In 1982, the poultry, egg, meat and animal feeds businesses were sold for a net loss of well over £50 million. Many of the companies sold were bought by Hillsdown Holdings for £48.5 million. Hillsdown turned them around and in the 9 months to September 1985 extracted more than £9 million in operating profits from them. Nor were the food businesses Imperial's only unfortunate acquisitions. It took the company over 10 years to obtain respectable returns from Courage, and the eventual profitability of the business (Exhibit 4) had to be set against the £320 million that was originally paid for Courage in 1972.

Imperial also had the dubious distinction of having made one of the most criticized acquisitions ever by a British company. In 1980 Imperial purchased Howard Johnson, the US hotel chain, for $630 million, nearly twice Howard Johnson's previous market capitalization. Imperial was eager to diversify away from tobacco, and the US exchange rate appeared very favourable (the purchase price was equivalent to £280 million). Imperial's finance director, James McKinnon, said at the time 'Howard Johnson is absolutely unique and just so right for Imperial it isn't true.' However, the move was controversial from the beginning, with many of the institutional shareholders questioning both the strategy and the price.

Howard Johnson turned out to have a major weakness in its chain of Orange Roof restaurants. Little investment had been made in these for many years and, as McKinnon later recalled, 'The menu was not right, the position was not right, and the service was appalling.' Imperial poured money into the restaurants but never managed to make them financially successful, and meanwhile Howard Johnson's overall profit performance deteriorated steadily.

Exhibit 4: *Financial results for Imperial Group plc (£ million)*

	1981	1982	1983	1984	1985
Income statement					
Turnover	3771	4098	4367	4593	4919
Profit before tax	106	154	195	221	236
Taxation and minorities	(15)	(36)	(65)	(69)	(67)
Extraordinary items	(35)	(67)	(49)	(23)	(61)
Dividends	(52)	(52)	(56)	(64)	(73)
Retained earnings	4	(1)	25	65	35
Balance sheet					
Tangible assets	903	865	905	1049	1429
Investments	41	83	66	80	73
Fixed assets	944	948	971	1129	1502
Inventory	488	421	402	417	435
Receivables	402	405	492	423	729
Cash and investments	52	61	149	201	115
Current assets	942	887	1043	1041	1279
Payables	748	596	725	711	790
Dividend	52	52	56	64	50
Short-term loans	37	51	13	60	131
Current liabilities	837	699	794	835	971
Net assets	1049	1136	1220	1335	1810
Long-term loans	250	228	225	194	164
Long-term payables	0	81	106	94	122
Minority interest	2	2	2	9	6
Shareholders funds	797	825	887	1038	1518*
Capital employed	1049	1136	1220	1335	1810
Funds flow					
Group profit	106	154	195	221	
Depreciation	77	77	76	86	
	183	231	272	306	
Capital expenditure	108	94	81	167	
Working capital	(116)	62	(66)	8	
Dividends paid	32	52	52	56	
Tax paid	40	33	25	42	
	64	241	92	273	
Debentures/loans	16	5	27	24	
Assets of subsidiaries	(199)	153	30	1	
Investments	—	(146)	—	—	
	(183)	12	57	25	
Change in net liquid funds	302	(22)	123	8	

*Includes surplus on revaluation equal to £617 million

In the year to October 1984, Howard Johnson's operating profits fell by 40 per cent to $15 million. In the first 6 months of 1985 they were $9.9 million, 40 per cent lower than the same period the previous year.

Towards the end of the summer of 1984, Imperial announced that it was thinking of selling Howard Johnson. Investment bank Goldman Sachs was retained to identify potential buyers, and eventually in September 1985 most of the chain was purchased by Marriott, another US hotel group. The sale price was $314 million, and Imperial was to keep a subsidiary valued at the time at $50 million. Imperial thus made a 42 per cent loss on the original dollar investment in Howard Johnson, but because the proceeds were valued at an exchange rate of $1.43 to the pound while the purchase was valued at $2.25, the sterling loss was less painful.

The immediate impact of the deal was to improve Imperial's liquidity by over $300 million. The company began to look around for another major acquisition, and ran a computerized check on more than 1200 companies in search of a suitable party. United Biscuits was identified and the two companies formally announced merger talks at the beginning of December 1985.

3. United Biscuits

United Biscuits Group was the largest biscuit manufacturer outside the United States. The company had over 100 brands under the McVitie and Crawford labels, and also manufactured snack products under the KP name. United Biscuits held the UK Wimpy franchise, and in 1982 entered the confectionery market by acquiring Terrys of York. Nearly half of the company's sales came from the United States, where it sold cookies under the Keebler brand name. It also had small American interests in sauces and dressings and in olives. Exhibit 2 (above) identifies the major areas of activity of the company.

One part of United Biscuits originated in McVitie & Price, a company which prospered and grew under the chairmanship of a Scottish lawyer, Sir Alexander Grant, who invented the digestive biscuit. The current chairman, Sir Hector Laing, is the grandson of Sir Alexander. As a young boy in Edinburgh, Laing had his introduction to the family business cutting oatcakes from 6 am until school started. Laing returned to the business after the Second World War, and in 1948 McVities merged with Macfarlane Lang to become United Biscuits. The first chairman of United Biscuits was Sir Peter MacDonald, senior partner of a leading law firm and chairman of McVitie & Price. A series of mergers with other family interests built United Biscuits up into the dominant UK biscuit company.

The spirit of family feeling still existed in United Biscuits where team work and entrepreneurialism were highly valued. Sir Hector Laing remained a dominant influence in the company, generating strong employee loyalty and providing a rich source of myth and legend, such as his decision to buy Wimpy

Exhibit 5: *Financial results for United Biscuits plc (£ million)*

	1981	1982	1983	1984
Income statement				
Turnover	1026	1205	1425	1743
Profit before tax	61	68	83	87*
Taxation and minorities	(17)	(23)	(25)	(25)
Extraordinary items	(1)	(4)	35	(3)
Dividends	(16)	(18)	(22)	(24)
Retained earnings	27	23	71	35
Balance sheet				
Tangible assets	292	344	394	496
Investments	1	3	4	2
Intangibles	55	—	—	—
Fixed assets	348	347	398	498
Inventory	93	104	120	138
Receivables	110	143	184	219
Cash and investments	49	33	44	28
Current assets	252	280	348	385
Payables	121	160	216	255
Dividend	16	18	22	24
Short-term loans	38	21	40	55
Current liabilities	175	199	278	334
Net Assets	425	428	468	549
Long-term loans	125	153	171	222
Long-term payables	0	10	39	26
Minority interest	1	1	1	1
Shareholders funds	299	264	257	300
Capital employed	425	428	468	549
Funds flow				
Group profit	61	68	83	87
Depreciation	23	29	33	40
Capital issued	1	2	1	2
	85	99	117	129
Capital expenditure	61	70	98	133
Working capital	22	16	(9)	21
Dividends paid	14	16	18	22
Tax paid	12	18	28	20
	109	120	135	196
Debentures/loans	(26)	(24)	(18)	(51)
Assets of subsidiaries	17	19	6	15
Investments	(4)	—	—	—
	(13)	(5)	(12)	(36)
Change in net liquid funds	(11)	(16)	(6)	(31)

*Estimated profit before tax for year ended 28 December 1985 is £100 million

while shaving one morning, or his whisky-drinking sessions with the night shift at the Edinburgh factory.

United Biscuits' major areas of activity are shown in Exhibit 2 and its recent financial performance in Exhibit 5. The company had a record of sound, if unspectacular, growth and a reputation for good management. In its most recent results, it had reported particularly unexciting profit figures. Despite a sales increase of 22 per cent, the Group's profits were only 4 per cent higher than those of the previous year.

Exhibit 6: *Share price movements, January 1980 – November 1985*

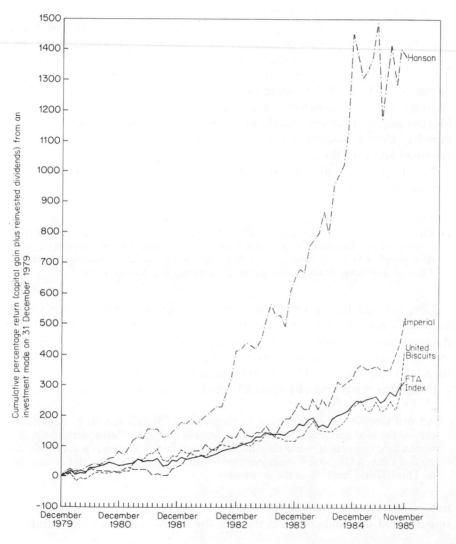

The low profits reported for 1984 were a result of the 'cookie war' in the United States, which began in 1983 and was still continuing in December 1985. United Biscuits' US subsidiary, Keebler, was its first acquisition in the United States, and had an excellent profit record until the middle of 1983; 1983 profits were $55 million with profit margins of around 7.5 per cent. However, in 1982 and 1983 two new companies, PepsiCo and Proctor & Gamble, entered the US cookie market. They introduced the 'dual texture cookie' or 'DTC', which were hard on the outside and soft on the inside; and in early 1984 Keebler followed suit with its own Soft Batch range. Three years later these DTCs had 16 per cent of the US market. All the participants aggressively supported their DTC products by cutting margins drastically, and by 1984 Keebler's profits were down to $42 million, and margins to less than 5 per cent.

In the middle of 1985, United Biscuits was the second largest biscuit manufacturer in the world — only Nabisco was larger. However, in the last 6 months of the year several dramatic changes occurred. Nabisco had strengthened itself in 1981 by merging with Standard Brands, another American food company. In June 1985 it agreed to a $4.9 billion takeover by R. J. Reynolds, the huge US tobacco company. In September 1985 another tobacco giant, Philip Morris, acquired General Foods for $5.6 billion. Within the space of a few months, United Biscuits was faced with two competitors backed by huge resources and cash flows.

Asked why the tobacco giants should be acquiring food companies, Sir Hector Laing said:

The Americans are scared that law suits and other pressure on tobacco will increase. They want to run that side down while building the food side up. Food is regarded as a safe product. The only thing we know is that in the year 2000 people will be eating. Also people's tastes in food are not like their tastes in, say, consumer electronics. They change very slowly, and a dynamic company can foresee them.

Laing believed that the Third World was where future market expansions would occur. 'That's where the population is, and in countries like China living standards are rising, and dramatic growth is possible.' However, it is difficult to create international brands in food products (McDonalds is one of the few successful examples), and heavy investment would be required.

Discussing the proposed Imperial/United Biscuits merger, Laing said:

All that tobacco money is coming in [from Phillip Morris and R. J. Reynolds] to expand the food business. I believe it is targeted at the Third World particularly. If we want a food business of world class and stature, an Imps/UB merger will provide it. If we don't have a UK food company in that league, we will be leaving the development of Third World markets to the Americans

Exhibit 6 displays the longer-term stock market performance of Hanson, Imperial and UB, and compares these to the FT-Actuaries All Share Index.

The bids

Bid 1: The Imperial–United Biscuits merger

On 2 December 1985, Imperial and United Biscuits announced that they were to merge. The terms of the merger were to be an exchange of five new shares in Imperial for every four existing United Biscuits shares.

The combined group would have annual sales of more than £6 billion, and would be one of the largest companies in the United Kingdom. It would own a portfolio of famous brand names, and would have leading positions in each of its three business areas. On 1984 figures, tobacco would make up one-third of the combined group's profits, food 41 per cent, and the balance would be accounted for by brewing and leisure. This compares with Imperial's 1984 profit breakdown of 47 per cent tobacco and 13 per cent food.

The Imperial chairman, Geoffrey Kent, would stay on as chairman of the combined group. It was planned that he would retire in March 1987, and that Sir Hector Laing would then take over. Until that time, Laing would be deputy chairman and chief executive. In December 1985, Kent was aged 63 and Laing 62.

The other senior management positions were to be shared between Imperial and United Biscuits executives. Two United Biscuits managers, James Blyth and Bob Clarke, were to be finance director and chairman/chief executive of the food division, respectively. Gerry Sharman of Imperial (previously chairman of Imperial Foods) was to become director of corporate development and planning, and Michael Pickard was to remain as chairman and chief executive of the old Imperial brewing and leisure division.

A cloud on the horizon was the possibility of a reference to the Monopolies and Mergers Commission (MMC). Although the number of referrals each year is tiny (typically 3–5), and notwithstanding the fact that over 70 per cent of these are granted approval, a reference can ruin the chances of a bid being successful. This is because it can take as long as 6 months for the bid to be investigated, and in fact most referred bids end up lapsing. Since Imperial and United Biscuits would together control 30 per cent of the £426 million UK crisps market and 48 per cent of the £184 million snack market, without taking into account their involvement in generic/own label production, an MMC referral was a worrying possibility. However, one of their defences would undoubtedly be that Nabisco already controlled over 32 per cent of the market, again without including generic/own label products.

The following comments are a sample of those that appeared in the press after the merger proposals were formally announced:

Nominally, Imperial is making an offer for United Biscuits, though the deal is being presented as a merger. The reality looks more like a reverse bid by United for a much larger company, looking to gain managerial control after a short but decent interval, and obtaining access to a much-needed cash generator (the Imps tobacco business) on what look distinctly favourable terms. Even for admirers of United, however, this is not necessarily to be regarded as a coup. (Lex, *Financial Times*, 3 December 1985)

The merger makes sense, although investors' enthusiasm should not be uncontrolled. United Imperial will be strongest in two declining markets — cigarettes and brewing — and one whose growth prospects are much debated — biscuits. Which is not to say that marketing expertise and the control of production and distribution costs cannot generate significant profits growth. (*Investors Chronicle*, 6 December, 1985)

An all-paper takeover of UB would make Imperial rather less liable to be taken over, either as a cash generator or as an asset play. (*Financial Times*, 3 December 1985)

It is no secret that 'Imps' was to the fore on Hanson Trust's UK acquisition list. But whatever the predatory peer's plans may have been, they were rudely interrupted on Tuesday when Judge Shirley Kram refused to uphold Hanson's injunction which prevents Merrill Lynch from extricating SCM's crown jewels. Hanson Trust will seek to overturn this ruling by way of appeal on 16 December. Suffice to say that the Hanson camp is fully occupied stateside. (*Observer*, 1 December, 1985)

Despite the speculation about the reason for the proposed merger, both Laing and Kent were keen to emphasize the industrial logic of the move. 'I do not have a defensive bone in my body', said Laing. In response to suggestions that the proposed merger might be a reverse takeover in disguise, he added 'People are only looking at the food side of the merger. There's a lot more to it than that.'

Imperial issued its formal offer document for United Biscuits on Monday 30 December 1985. At the same time it announced a 14 per cent dividend increase for 1985 and an estimated pretax profits rise of 7 per cent in the year to October 1985. Pretax profits for United Biscuits for the year to 28 December 1985 were estimated in the offer document at about £100 million, an increase of 14.7 per cent from the previous year.

Geoffrey Kent urged shareholders to accept the merger, saying that although one initial effect of the merger would be reduce earnings per share for Imperial shareholders based on the results of the two companies to that date, 'the two boards are confident that, with the opportunities we see both for reducing costs and for developing our markets in the UK and overseas, the rate of growth of the combined companies will be considerably greater than either could achieve on its own'.

In his 30 December letter to shareholders, he pointed to the merged group's 'strong financial position and balance sheet with low borrowings relative to shareholders' funds', as well as to 'the depths of management' of the combined teams. He cited as merger benefits their shared food technologies, lower production and distribution costs, higher share in the frozen food market, expansion of fast-food and restaurant outlets, and strengthened export sales. He also noted that annual cost savings of around £30 million a year had already been identified. Imperial shares closed at 257p and United Biscuits shares at 240p on the day the formal offer document was issued (Exhibit 7).

Bid 2: The initial Hanson–Imperial merger

On 6 December 1985, Hanson Trust announced that it was to make an offer for the Imperial Group. The terms were to be two Hanson Trust shares and £5.32 nominal of 8 per cent convertible unsecured loan stock 2004–9 for every five Imperial shares. Loan stockholders had the right to convert any part of their holdings into fully paid ordinary share capital at the rate of 37.72p nominal of ordinary share capital for every 195p nominal of loan stock converted. The earliest conversion date was to be February 1988 and the latest to be February 2004. The Hanson bid was conditional on the Imperial/United Biscuits merger being dropped. On the day prior to the offer announcement, Hanson shares had closed at 210p. After the offer was announced, the shares closed at 205p. On 6 December, Imperial shares closed at 258p and United Biscuits at 251p (Exhibit 7).

On the day of the bid, Mr Howard Johnson — who had founded the Howard Johnson hotel chain, sold it to Imperial, and seen it sold on to Marriott — is reported to have sent Hanson a telex saying 'You've made my day. Good luck.'

The day prior to the announcement of the offer, Hanson Trust had made public its financial results for the year to September 1985. Pretax profits had increased by nearly 50 per cent to £253 million, and turnover had risen 12 per cent to £2.67 billion.

Talking about the Imperial/United Biscuits plans, Hanson said

> This reverse takeover is clearly a management deal and not in the best interests of Imperial shareholders. Laing and I have equal experience in tobacco and brewing — zero. The difference is that we have 20 years experience of improving companies and he does not — Imperial badly needs a lager for Courage. We will give it one. With us the management will not need to worry about strategy. On tobacco, we will address the problems. I am not setting out to knock the management. I think Geoffrey Kent and I can work very well together.

Hanson calculated that its offer was worth 250p a share to the Imperial shareholders, compared with 200p which it said was implied in the United Biscuits merger.

However, when it came to Imperial's record of diversification by acquisition, the Hanson offer document pulled no punches. It alleged failure of these attempts at diversification, overpayment for acquisitions, and asset sales at too low a price. Four acquisitions were chosen as examples of mismanagement which had cumulatively imposed 'losses' on Imperial shareholders of well over £1 billion — more than Imperial's entire net worth:

> Between 1975 and 1980 your board sold Imperial's valuable holding in BAT Industries for a total of £239 million to finance planned diversification. Today that holding alone would be worth £1100 million. . . . In 1978 Imperial bought J. B. Eastwood (and) in 1982 your board sold the whole business for only £39 million — at a loss of £63 million. . . . In 1978 Imperial sold its holding in Bunzl for £3.6 million

Exhibit 7: *Share and convertible loan stock price data for selected weeks*

Day and Date		Hanson shares (p)	Hanson 8 per cent convertible[1] (£)	Imperial shares (p)	United Biscuits shares (p)	FTA All Share Index
Monday 2 December	1985	210	162	241	274	688
Tuesday 3 December	1985	209	158	234	257	685
Wednesday 4 December	1985	207	158	232	257	680
Thursday 5 December	1985	210	157	232	255	676
Friday 6 December	1985	205	155	258	251	679
Monday 30 December	1985	198xd	148	258	240	682
Tuesday 31 December	1985	198	149	255	240	683
Thursday 2 January	1986	198	149	256	238	687
Friday 3 January	1986	199	150	258	238	691
Monday 6 January	1986	195	149	248	229	690
Tuesday 7 January	1986	200	151	249	230	685
Wednesday 8 January	1986	199	149	246	233	680
Thursday 9 January	1986	191	145	242	231	669
Friday 10 January	1986	197	149	244	232	675
Monday 20 January	1986	193	148	249	235	670
Tuesday 21 January	1986	193	144	257	233	667
Wednesday 22 January	1986	194	144	256	235	674
Thursday 23 January	1986	193	146	254	231	670
Friday 24 January	1986	191	147	254	232	670
Monday 10 February	1986	155[2]	156	272	232	709
Tuesday 11 February	1986	153	155	270	233	707
Wednesday 12 February	1986	154	155	278	229	714
Thursday 13 February	1986	153	156	285	235	716
Friday 14 February	1986	151	156	291	242	719
Monday 17 February	1986	148	156	320	232	718
Tuesday 18 February	1986	150	152	308	220	726
Wednesday 19 February	1986	151	153	308	220	726
Thursday 20 February	1986	148	151	309	218	727
Friday 21 February	1986	161	156	314	225	738
Monday 7 April	1986	182	178	356	263	822
Tuesday 8 April	1986	179	177	349	260	818
Wednesday 9 April	1986	178	176	345	260	811
Thursday 10 April	1986	178	176	345	260	811
Friday 11 April	1986	185	175	363	267	813

Notes
1. The Hanson 10 per cent convertible loan stock 1990–2007 and the United Biscuits convertible preferred shares are new stock, and would not therefore be created and hence quoted unless and until the respective bids succeeded.
2. Note that Hanson had a 1 for 3 scrip issue on 27 January (xc date), and all prices subsequent to that date should be interpreted accordingly.

(and) today that holding would be worth £36 million, a loss to shareholders of more than £32 million. . . . In 1979, in the face of widespread criticism, Imperial bought the US restaurant chain Howard Johnson for $630 million — over twice its net worth. Subsequently (it) sold Howard Johnson for $314 million, resulting in an overall loss to Imperial shareholders in only 5 years of over £300 million.

Kent replied to the initial bid saying that, 'There is no fit between us and Hanson. If you exclude Howard Johnson, our operating profits have risen by 30 per cent a year in the four years since I became chairman. That is a very good performance and I don't see where Hanson would achieve any added value by taking us over.'

Hanson Trust also said that the Imperial bid would not affect its pending US offer for SCM. One of, the directors pointed out that the company had the resources to commit itself to two bids at the same time since the Imperial bid was to be paper-financed while the SCM bid was to be in cash.

Despite the acrimony surrounding the bid, Hanson and Kent appeared to have a strong mutual admiration. Kent said that he informally asked Hanson to join Imperial's board two years previously 'because I thought he was a good businessman'. Hanson was too busy at the time, but was prepared to talk about forming closer links between Hanson Trust and Imperial. Kent immediately rejected the idea and Hanson looked elsewhere. The two men were both members of the board of Lloyds Bank, and in fact sat side by side at meetings. In the past, when takeover speculation about Hanson Trust and Imperial had surfaced, this had caused some amusement to their fellow board members.

The fight against Hanson

Dicussing Imperial's future with Hanson Trust, the Hanson offer document maintained that:

> The successful Hanson Trust technique of 'hands-off' management will be put in place to support the existing managers and staff in realizing the fullest possible potential. Imperial has many famous brands (and) it is essential that line management be free to focus single-mindedly on the nurturing of these . . . that marketing, advertising and promotion be maintained; and research and development encouraged in order to improve these brands' leading positions. All this is precisely what Hanson Trust's philosophy will make possible without the expensive trappings of centralized management, the inevitable confusion of purpose and the constant distraction of the need to diversify. . . . Imperial will be decentralized. Responsibility will be devolved to the operating divisions. Line management will be free to manage. Cash incentives or share options will be introduced or extended. Emphasis will be placed on improving the return on capital employed. . . . There is no present plan to sell any of the Imperial businesses.

Imperial responded to the Hanson offer document with a stinging attack on the past record of Hanson Trust itself. As the *Financial Times* noted on 13 January 1986:

Taking pot shots at the Hanson track-record is not a course of action which merchant bankers have generally recommended to their clients. Hanson's victims have never been able to match the earnings per share growth reported by Hanson itself, with the result that attack has been a dangerous form of defence. Imperial may find that, when it comes to slinging mud, more sticks to its own face than to Hanson's, but it is significant that corporate financiers no longer see Hanson as an invulnerable target.

Imperial's defence document considered the Hanson Trust bid to be totally unacceptable and one that should be rejected out of hand. It stated to its shareholders that:

Hanson's bid grossly undervalues your shares and would also involve you in an immediate capital loss. Your income would be dramatically cut. The income from Hanson would be less than half the income you would receive from Imperial in 1986. A substantial reduction in earnings and assets would be inflicted on Imperial shareholders. Hanson deprives you of voting power; you lose because loan stock holders cannot vote.

Geoffrey Kent accused Lord Hanson of misleading Imperial's shareholders in his attack on Imperial's diversification record: 'It's rather like selling a house at £50 000, seeing the new owner sell it 5 years later for £60 000 and then being accused of having 'lost' £10 000.' Imperial also noted that Lord Hanson himself had said in a television interview on 8 December 1985: 'I think the Imperial Group's existing management is very good, particularly since Geoffrey Kent became the Chairman of the Company. They run their business very well.'

Extension of Hanson's bid

On 6 January came the news that Hanson Industries had been successful in its bid for SCM. Hanson had argued that the directors of SCM had breached their fiduciary duties to the company's shareholders when they granted the 'lock-up' option to Merrill Lynch. SCM had argued in contrast that the use of the 'lock-up' option was reasonable under the 'business judgement rule' which says that the directors are the best judges of how a company should conduct its business. After the victory, Hanson increased its stake in SCM to over 66 per cent.

Back in the United Kingdom, the Hanson offer to Imperial shareholders was to expire at 3.00 pm on 24 January. Hanson Trust had earlier announced that they were to make a capitalization issue to their shareholders of one share for every three held on 10 January. They promised Imperial shareholders that the value of the offer for their shares would not be affected by the issue, and announced new terms of 8 new Hanson shares and £15.96 nominal of new Hanson loan stock for every 15 Imperial Group shares.

Media speculation about the fate of the Imperial bid was varied. There was even a rumour of a 'white knight' riding to the rescue. Meanwhile Lord Hanson was awaiting the outcome of his offer to the Imperial shareholders. Supporting him in the United States was Sir Gordon White, who had said on television the previous year: 'My father always used to tell me that any fool could sell, but it takes a clever man to buy. The real secret, I suppose, is that I can see when something is the right price. If you buy at the right price you're not going to make a mistake.' Monday 27 January saw Hanson extend its takeover bid until 14 February after picking up a 0.53 per cent stake in Imperial from 1608 shareholders, despite an offer that continued to be below Imperial's market value.

Bid 3: Hanson's increased and final offer

On 12 February, Lord Hanson's ambition was given a massive boost as the government, after much deliberation, referred the Imperial–United Biscuits merger to the Monopolies and Mergers Commission. Hanson's bid for Imperial received the all-clear. Immediately, Imperial Group shares rose 8p to 278p (Exhibit 7) — well clear of the Hanson bid terms — in anticipation that Hanson would come back with a revised offer. Surprisingly, United Biscuits shares held relatively firm — shading only 4p to 229p (Exhibit 7) — perhaps on the assumption that a 'for sale' sign still hung over the company. A spokesman for United Biscuits described the government's decision as 'quite extraordinary and monstrous' and, as a result, Imperial and United Biscuits abandoned their merger plans.

However, the takeover battle for Imperial took a remarkable turn on 17 February as Hanson Trust increased its bid from £1.8 billion to £2.32 billion — only to see this topped by a rival £2.56 billion offer from United Biscuits, which was Britain's biggest ever bid. Imperial's share price rose sharply on the offers to 320p, up 29p on the day (Exhibit 7). Hanson accompanied its bid with a forecast that its pretax profits in the year to September would be not less than £340 million, up 34 per cent on the previous year and that its dividends would total not less than 4p net, up 22 per cent. United, for its part, announced a final dividend of 5.15p a share for the year to December 1985 (4.8p in 1984) making a total of 8.0p for the year (7.5p).

Hanson's new offer was 28 per cent higher than the first. For each Imperial share they offered a choice of one ordinary Hanson Trust share plus 153p in cash, or one ordinary share plus 153p nominal of 10 per cent new convertible loan stock, or one ordinary share plus 153p nominal of 12 per cent loan notes 1989. The 10 per cent convertible unsecured loan stock 2007–2012 carried the right of conversion into Hanson ordinary shares at 172p a share over the period 1990–2007. On the basis of Hanson's closing price of 148p on 17 February, the offer was worth 301p for each Imperial share (Exhibit 7). There was, however, a full cash alternative underwritten at 293p a share.

Hanson's offer document, dated 27 February, declared that the bid was designed to give maximum flexibility allowing Imperial shareholders to take any combination of cash, convertible stock, loan notes and Hanson shares. It stated:

The choice is yours. Whatever form of consideration you choose you will make a substantial capital gain. Before the announcement of the merger talks last November each Imperial share was worth 217p. By accepting the increased offer you can receive a total package currently worth up to 346p.

You will receive a substantial increase in income. Imperial forecast a net dividend of 12p per share in 1986. This provides a gross income of only £17.14 on 100 Imperial shares . . . under the all cash election you would receive gross income of £31.56, an increase of 84.1 per cent.

The document went further by reiterating Hanson Trust's track record:

. . . . 22 years of unbroken earnings per share, dividend and profit growth. Imperial's line managers will be given a renewed sense of purpose, free of constricting central bureaucracy and board misjudgements.

There will also be a new financial discipline at the top. This is evidently necessary from the repeated failures of the Imperial board — the BAT disposal, the Howard Johnson fiasco and the sale of J. B. Eastwood which together cost shareholders £1 billion.

The Imperial board has now lost all credibility having recommended the reverse take-over by United.

Bid 4: The United Biscuits offer for Imperial

United accompanied its bid with a market raid on 17 February, picking up 7.7 per cent of Imperial shares by the time the Stock Exchange closed and a further 2 per cent in after-hours dealings. Its offer consisted of five new ordinary shares (ranking *pari passu* with existing stock) plus five new convertible preferred shares plus 275p in cash for every six Imperial ordinary shares. Imperial shareholders would also be entitled to retain the final dividend of 6.6p per share. The new convertibles would have a fixed preference dividend of 7p net and be convertible on 5 August in any year, commencing in 1987, on the basis of 100 ordinary for every 245 preference shares.

There was also a cash alternative for all or any of the new United Biscuits convertibles on the basis of a fixed price of 100p per new convertible. Thus, with United Biscuits' share price falling 10p to 232p on the day of its offer, the bid was worth 332p for each Imperial share (Exhibit 7).

United said that it began making contingency plans for a bid for Imperial as soon as Hanson unveiled its offer in December 1985. Yet it was stirred into action by the referral to the Monopolies Commission. If victorious in its bid, it was prepared to sell Imperial's Golden Wonder business which produced crisps, nuts and snacks, and made pretax profits of £8.1 million on turnover of £117.2 million in the year to October 1984.

Whereas Hanson argued that it should be judged on 'its record in making assets sweat' and that the takeover of Imperial by United, a much smaller company, would be a risky venture, Hector Laing replied that 'United Biscuit's offer contained an industrial logic lacking in the Hanson bid'. In the UK market both Imperial and United Biscuits have restaurant chains (Harvester Steak houses and Happy Eater outlets for Imperial; Pizzaland and Wimpy for United) and frozen food interests (Ross and Youngs for Imperial; McVities for United).

Sir Hector argued that there would be substantial benefits in areas such as distribution and food research. He also envisaged savings in the United States by putting together the two companies' sauce and spice interests. Lastly, he believed that the much greater size would give United the muscle to meet American competition in the growing food markets of the Third World. Nevertheless, one City institution described some of his remarks as 'jingoistic tub-thumping' while another argued that Imperial, with its high dependence on the United Kingdom, was the wrong target.

Under United's plans, Sir Hector Laing would become chairman and chief executive of the combined group immediately, rather than waiting until 1987, when Geoffrey Kent was due to retire. Mr Kent would become an executive director.

The bid received mixed reactions with the *Financial Times* reporting on 18 February:

> The idea that United Biscuits should make an offer for Imperial Group would, in any but the present circumstances, seem plainly ridiculous. Imperial is a very much larger company than United Biscuits and the natural flow of cash is from tobacco to biscuits. To turn that arithmetic on its head — with the result that Imperial shareholders are paid a premium for selling out of a mature business — makes little sense except in a stock market which has come to accept that sense can be measured in underwriting commissions.

Hanson believed that United Biscuits would be completely overstretched (the offer would involve a maximum cash outlay of £346.6 million). It argued that United's management had no experience in managing large acquisitions of diverse businesses. Also, if United were to succeed, the market price of its ordinary shares would drop substantially because of the vast number that would have to be issued and because the bid speculation would disappear.

Based on estimates from brokers Grieveson Grant, United Biscuits alone would see earnings per share of 20.7p in 1985, rising to 25.5p in 1987. If it acquired Imperial, 1986 earnings would be 19.8p and the 1987 tally would be 23.5p. Most brokers agreed that United Biscuits shares would be worth less if the takeover went ahead.

The fight for Imperial shares

On 19 February, Morgan Grenfell spent £360 million on behalf of United Biscuits to increase United's shareholding in Imperial to 14.9 per cent — the maximum it could acquire without providing a full cash alternative to its offer, which was only partly cash underwritten. Three days later, Hanson made a representation to the Stock Exchange seeking clarification of Morgan's relationship with its client in the share buying. Under Stock Exchange regulations, United Biscuits required shareholder approval for investments which might give rise to a commitment greater than 25 per cent of capital and reserves. Morgan Grenfell had been buying shares on its own account. Yet,

United Biscuits' published net worth was £410 million, £50 million more than the value of Morgan's share purchases. The bank argued that the maximum loss which might be suffered on the purchase was £16 million — the difference between the purchase price of 320p a share and Hanson's cash alternative of 293p. Additionally, with an indemnity for United to meet any losses by Morgan on the investment, it considered there to be no breach of regulations. The Stock Exchange agreed but demanded that the practice should not be repeated.

On 22 February, Hanson took its stake in Imperial to 1.3 per cent. On 27 February, the Hanson offer document was mailed to Imperial shareholders. Sir Hector Laing commented that the document contained no new positive arguments. He added, 'Hanson is clearly fearful of not winning and because of this, has left its closing date open to extension'.

On 28 February, the United Biscuits offer was mailed to Imperial shareholders. On 13 March, United Biscuits' holding rose to 17 per cent and that of Hanson to 7.86 per cent. The following day, Golden Wonder was sold for £54 million to Dalgety, the food and agricultural group, but the deal was conditional on United Biscuits succeeding with its bid for Imperial. Mr Maurice Warren, chief executive of Dalgety, considered the price to be 'competitive'. Imperial said that the terms were 'fair and reasonable and in the interests of shareholders'. However, Mr Martin Taylor, Finance Director of Hanson Trust, said Imperial seemed 'anxious to make a forced sale because United Biscuits want them to'. The City had expected Imperial to receive more than £60 million because Golden Wonder's value was thought to be approximately £70 million in a less hurried sale.

A bitter advertising battle followed with both Imperial and United Biscuits fighting against Hanson and both bids being repeatedly extended.

'Hanson's recent growth has been fuelled by acquisition of underperforming companies and also by the use of highly rated shares and convertible securities. The timing and rate of these acquisitions has created growth, but to maintain the momentum, the size of acquisitions must rise inexorably,' claimed Imperial on behalf of United Biscuits. 'The logical conclusion is that the likes of ICI must eventually be swallowed up if the momentum is to be sustained.' It went further by stating that 'Hanson's high gearing after the takeover could lead to the dismemberment of the Imperial Group. Hanson's paper offers are of questionable value, and the cash offer is an attempt to take Imperial over at a P/E ratio less than 11' (Exhibit 8).

Hanson criticized the 'inaccuracies' in Imperial's advertising campaign and issued writs against the company, each of its directors and its advertising agency seeking damages for 'malicious falsehood and defamation'. It also continued to emphasize its performance. 'Earnings per share have grown by 33.9 per cent per annum since 1980 (to February 1986), Imperial's have grown by only 14.7 per cent. Dividends per share have grown by 28.7 per cent per annum since 1980, Imperial's have grown by only 5.8 per cent.'

On 1 April, United Biscuits disclosed that it had received only 0.07 per cent

Exhibit 8: *Comparative risk and return measures for Hanson, Imperial, United Biscuits and industry sectors.*

Risk measures as at end 1985

Company/sector	Market value £ million	Beta	Variability per cent	Specific risk per cent	Dividend yield per cent	P/E ratio
Hanson Trust	2817	0.89	27	23	3.1	13.2
Imperial Group	1928	0.71	26	23	5.4	14.0
United Biscuits	967	1.15	30	23	4.6	13.1
Industrial conglomerates	188[1]	0.99	28	23	4.1	12.7
Food manufacturing	133[1]	0.92	24	19	4.4	12.4
Milling and flour	626[1]	1.03	27	22	3.9	12.3
Tobacco	2299[1]	0.90	29	25	5.2	7.6

Abnormal returns[2]

Company/sector	1984q4 per cent	1985q1 per cent	1985q2 per cent	1985q3 per cent	1985q4 per cent	1986q1 per cent
Hanson Trust	31	−9	−8	3	−5	2
Imperial Group	−5	2	−1	5	21	22
United Biscuits	17	−10	4	−5	27	−18
Industrial conglomerates	12	0	0	0	1	−6
Food manufacturing	2	1	1	−5	9	−3
Milling and flour	14	0	1	−4	14	0
Tobacco	14	−10	1	−16	14	11

Notes
1. Industry sector capitalizations are equally weighted averages; all other industry descriptors are market value weighted averages of the figures for individual companies. The number of companies being averaged are: industrial conglomerates 38, food manufacturers 59, milling and flour companies 4, and tobacco companies 3. Risk measures are estimated from the most recent 60 months' data.
2. The abnormal return for a company is the difference between the return (capital gain plus dividends) on its shares and the return over the same period on a diversified portfolio. The diversified portfolio, which consists of a holding in the FTA All Share Index plus Treasury Bills, is designed to have the same risk (beta) as the company. As at 11 April 1986, 3 month Treasury Bills were trading at 10⅛ to 10 ⁵⁄₁₆ per cent. At that date, government bonds which were trading close to par offered gross redemption yields varying from 8.6 per cent (for bonds maturing in 5–10 years' time) to 8.7 per cent (for bonds maturing in 15–20 years' time).

Source: London Business School *Risk Measurement Service*, various issues.

further acceptances for its offer, bringing its total to 21.96 per cent. The offer was to be extended to 11 April as a final closing date.

On 2 April, Hanson Trust announced that it spoke for 30.2 per cent (14.1 per cent purchased in the market) of the shares in Imperial compared with the 21.96 per cent (14.9 per cent purchased in the market) holding revealed by United Biscuits. Hanson again extended its offer to coincide with United's closing date of Friday 11 April. Under the terms of the City Code on Takeovers and Mergers, Hanson could, in fact, extend their offer to 29 April (this date being 60 days after the posting of the United Biscuits' offer document for Imperial). Indeed, Hanson felt that United Biscuits had made a tactical error in choosing an earlier final closing date than they need have done. They felt that United were trying to force an early decision, and that this signalled a lack of confidence on United's part that their share price, and hence the value of their offer, could be sustained at its current level. By 4 April, Hanson's offer exceeded that of United by 6.5p per share.

During the week prior to the closing date, the following comments appeared in the press:

> I will probably accept the Hanson paper because I cannot afford to miss out on short-term performance of shares. (Quote from a fund manager, *Sunday Times*, 6 April, 1986)

> The institutions appear to be listening long and hard to Laing's plea for the creation of 'a market leader in food manufacturing, brewing and leisure'. (*Observer*, 6 April, 1986)

> United Biscuits, in bidding for Imperial, is also engaged in large-scale diversification . . . Experience over the last two decades suggests that claims about industrial 'synergy' between, say, beer, biscuits and restaurants, need to be treated with caution. (*Financial Times*, 10 April, 1986)

> United Biscuits can claim justifiably that it (rather than Hanson) has more to offer Imperial. It has an impressive record in developing and marketing new brands. (*Investors Chronicle*, 11 April, 1986)

From the start, it had been clear that two issues would dominate the battle: the relative values of the two offers, which in turn depended on the strength of the bidders' share prices; and the question of which company would manage Imperial's assets better. When the final offers were launched on 17 February, United Biscuits initially held the edge on price. The shares of both companies were then swept forward in the subsequent bull market; but following Hanson's acquisition of SCM, its share price was stronger than United's giving Hanson the edge (see Exhibits 7 and 8). By the last week of the battle, however, the prices moved closer; and on 10 April, the offers were virtually identical. It was clear, therefore, that the issue was likely to be settled on management grounds.

The arguments put forward by the rival companies could not have been more different. Hanson said essentially that it should be judged on its record in making assets sweat. United replied that its offer contained an industrial logic lacking in the Hanson bid. There had been two target audiences for these messages: small investors and City institutions. Although small investors traditionally vote their shares the way the management tell them, many had sold their shares in the market. By 10 April, their stake in Imperial had probably been reduced from 25–30 per cent down to 10–15 per cent.

As the battle progressed, it therefore became clear that the outcome would be decided by the institutions. As is normal in takeover contests, both sides took roadshows to the fund managers and put their cases in person. Sir Hector Laing stressed the long-term synergy between United Biscuits and Imperial, while Lord Hanson focused on short and medium-term performance. Analysts and fund managers discussed the presentations in minute detail, and voting intentions were in many cases decided at board level. As each investment institution cast its vote on Friday 11 April, they knew that their decision could have profound consequences for no less than three of Britain's largest companies.

14. Anglian Canners

Anglian Canners Limited manufactures and sells a range of canned food products. At the end of 1976, Anglian's sales were £14.3 million and profit before tax and interest was £815 000. Anglian Canners is one of the two UK subsidiaries of Amalgamated Food Products Inc., a large US multinational corporation with sales in excess of US $2 billion. Amalgamated's other UK subsidiary is a large bakery products company with sales in excess of £60 million, which operates entirely independently of Anglian Canners.

During 1976, a new management team arrived at Amalgamated following the announcement of losses for the second year in succession. After a thorough strategic appraisal, Amalgamated was reorganized into three major divisions — bakery products, meat products, and diversified products. Anglian Canners was placed in Diversified Products Group since the company is Amalgamated's only canning operation anywhere in the World. At the time of reorganization, a new President of the Diversified Products Group was appointed from outside the food industry. He was Mr Charles Hodges, aged 45, previously Vice-President of a major US conglomerate, who had a reputation for being a tough, no-nonsense manager. Mr Hodges and his team immediately began to appraise the performance and future potential of each of the subsidiary companies under their control. In December 1976 they turned their attention to Anglian Canners.

Product lines

The principal product lines sold by Anglian are canned vegetables and fruits, dog food, mushrooms, Irish stew, preserves, lard and certain provisions such as imported meats; 76 per cent of turnover is sold under the company's brand names, and the remainder is private label sales. The latter are heavily concentrated in canned vegetables where they account for nearly half of total output. Exhibit 1 summarizes the major product lines and their 1976 sales.

The original version of this case was written by Stuart St P. Slatter. This abridged version was prepared for use in corporate finance teaching by Paul Marsh. It is intended to serve as a basis for class discussion rather than to illustrate either effective or ineffective handling of an administrative situation.

Copyright © 1977, 1987 Stuart St P. Slatter, London Business School.

Exhibit 1: *Anglian's products, markets and market share in 1976*

Product line	Anglian's sales (£'000)	Per cent of total sales	Gross margin as per cent of sales	Anglian's market share	Market share of brand leader
Canned vegetables					
Processed peas	2488	18	10.0	4	32
Garden peas	1060	7	15.0	4	15
Beans in tomato sauce	2019	14	16.1	2	49
Mixed vegetables	726	5	20.0	12	12
Other	824	6	35.0	2	—
Total	7117	50	16.5	4	—
Canned fruit	270	2	20.3	2	na
Preserves	1209	8	19.2	1	42
Dog food	2137	15	19.7	2	60
Mushrooms	679	5	14.6	16	72
Irish stew	500	3	13.0	17	33
Lard	1541	11	11.3	na	na
Other	853	6	11.5	1	—
Total	14 306	100	16.1 (average)	4	—

The market for Anglian's products

Anglian competes in a number of different segments of the processed food market in the United Kingdom.

Canned fruit and vegetables: The total canned fruit and vegetable market has grown at the rate of 1.4 per cent per year over the past decade. Certain segments such as carrots and canned new potatoes continue to show sound growth, while other segments show slow growth (beans in tomato sauce, mixed vegetables) or even a decline (processed peas and canned fruit). Overall, over the next 3 years, a fairly static market is likely.

Mushrooms: The UK canned mushroom market doubled in size between 1970 and 1974 but is now static or declining as a result of the UK economy turning down. However, the market is still considered to have good long-term growth potential.

Dog food: The canned dog food market has remained almost static over the last 3 years after growing at a rate in excess of 10 per cent a year from the mid-1960s. Total dog food sales are still rising slowly, but dried and semidried products are expanding their market share at the expense of 'wet' meat products.

The preserve market: The preserve market, which includes jams, conserves, marmalade, fruit curd and honey, is relatively static.

Lard: This is also a static market.

Competition

There are 23 canning companies competing in the UK market. This number has declined in recent years as the least efficient firms have found themselves unable to compete effectively. Anglian's competitors tend to be large (often multi-national) companies with dominant brands in one or more market segments. Exhibit 1 indicates Anglian's estimated market share and that of the brand leader in each market segment in 1975.

The major elements of competition are price and customer service (including product availability). Branded products usually obtain slightly higher margins than private label products, but price is of overriding importance in both cases. Consumer advertising is a major competitive factor only in the market for dog food and beans-in-tomato sauce. The preserve market is less of a commodity market and provides manufacturers with greater opportunities for product differentiation. Gross margins (sales less cost of goods sold) for Anglian's major product groups are given in Exhibit 1.

Marketing policies

Anglian sells its products to 1900 accounts throughout the United Kingdom. Twenty-five of these represent 51 per cent of total sales. Anglian is strongest in the North where it distributes to both independent stores and multiples. These distribution strengths represent a deliberate policy to select customers who are small enough for Anglian to be able to meet their requirements, and who are also less likely to demand large quantity discounts. Anglian focus on the North to minimize distribution costs.

The importance of marketing and selling is underlined by the fact that there are two Board members responsible for this area. The Director of Marketing has three product managers reporting to him, responsible for pricing, advertising and promotion, and new product development. The Director of Sales is responsible for the field sales force and sales administration. There are 21 sales representatives and five regional sales managers.

Anglian's retail prices are generally in line with its competitors. However, it is able to obtain slightly higher prices for its mixed vegetables and its branded lard, while in the dog food market, its products are positioned as good-quality low-priced brands. Anglian's marketing policy emphasizes special product promotions with retailers and wholesalers, rather than consumer advertising.

Manufacturing and operations

The company has two plants located about 25 miles (40 km) apart at King's Lynn and Fakenham. King's Lynn is a 16 acre (6 ha) site, of which only 5 acres (2 ha) are in use. It comprises three production locations, totalling 44 000 ft^2 (4050 m^2), built in 1932, 1938, and 1948 respectively, together with offices and a canteen. The Fakenham plant is on a 1.6 acre (0.6 ha) site, and has a 43 000 ft^2 (396 m^2) production area, a 42 000 ft^2 (3860 m^2) storage area, together with office space. Both sites are unmortgaged freehold properties. The fair market values are estimated to be £150 000 at King's Lynn and £80 000 at Fakenham. This is £96 000 in excess of book value.

Three of the five canning lines at the King's Lynn plant are high speed, and as fast as any in the industry. The equipment at the Fakenham plant, however, is less modern, and management feel that it would benefit from new plant and equipment to increase line speed and improve productivity. The plant and equipment at the two sites has a gross book value of £772 000, and a net book value (after depreciation) of £332 000. Although the fixed asset register lists nearly 1200 items of equipment at the two sites, most are small in value, and only 13 items have net book values of more than £5000. Of these, the two largest are the effluent pretreatment plant at King's Lynn, purchased for £76 000 in 1974–75 (current net book value of £62 000), and the retort units at Fakenham, purchased for £26 000 in 1973–75 (current net book value of £15 000). Assets purchased in the last 3 years account for two-thirds of the net book value and one-third of the gross book value. Assets purchased before 1970 account for 20 per cent of the net book value and half of the gross book value. Although this indicates that some of the machinery is old, management pays considerable attention to plant maintenance.

Both plants are operating close to one-shift capacity (3.5 million cases per year for King's Lynn and 1.2 million for Fakenham). The company currently prefers to operate an overtime system rather than a partial second shift because this gives it more flexibility and greater control over labour costs. A second shift would be possible but at King's Lynn this is constrained by plant effluent regulations. Under the current one-shift system, the greatest constraint is retort (cooking) capacity. To overcome shortages of production capacity at peak loading periods, Anglian subcontracts production to other canners. Generally speaking, however, increased demand for Anglian's products in recent years has been matched by an increase in plant productivity.

Anglian maintains good relationships with all its suppliers and tends to keep the same ones from year to year. The company makes annual contracts ahead of the season with local farmers for 80–90 per cent of its fruit and vegetable requirements. If there is a shortage, additional quantities are bought on the open market. The company buys almost 100 per cent of its metal cans from Metal Box Limited, the dominant UK supplier of cans. Terms are negotiated every 2 years and competitive quotations are obtained.

Anglian devote considerable effort to running an efficient physical distribution system. They serve 2900 drop shipment points for their 1900 accounts, and, on average, deliver 543 orders each week, with an average order size of 2.6 tons; 90 per cent of their finished goods are delivered from a 56 000 ft^2 (5200 m^2) distribution warehouse (consisting of two old aircraft hangars) located 3 miles (5 km) from King's Lynn. Anglian currently pay £5000 per annum for this site, and the lease expires in December 1981. Of Anglian's products, 56 per cent are delivered by their own fleet, while the remainder go by common carrier. Anglian's fleet consists of 30 vehicles, made up of 11 articulated lorries (10–17 tons), 17 rigid lorries (6.5–10.5 tons) and two small vans. The total net book value of these vehicles is £110 000.

Employees and management

In total, Anglian employs 576 people. Of these six are board members, a further eight are members of the management team, 55 are in marketing and sales, three in purchasing, 32 in accounts/head office, and 78 are in distribution. Of the remainder, 182 work at the Fakenham plant, and 212 at the King's Lynn plant; 80 per cent of the employees are members of the General and Municipal Workers Union (GMWU), and although a few other unions are represented, all negotiations are with the GMWU. Industrial relations are very good, and management are in favour of a recent suggestion by the Union to set up a 'closed shop'.

The Board of Anglian Canners consists of six full time executive directors: the Chairman and Managing Director, the Directors of Marketing, Sales, Purchasing and Production, and the Controller/Company Secretary. Their ages range from 43 to 58 (average age 50), and their length of service with the company from 7 to 37 years (an average of 20 years). Three of the directors have spent their entire careers with the company. The directors and members of the management team receive a basic salary, plus the normal package of fringe benefits. In addition, there is a bonus, linked to profit before tax, which can add up to a further 30 per cent of basic salary.

Past financial performance

Anglian has achieved an impressive rate of growth in the period 1971–76 (see Exhibit 2). During this period, sales increased from £5.2 million to £14.3 million, and trading profit increased from £177 000 to £815 000. Note, however, that the 1971–76 period was characterized by high inflation rates (retail price inflation was 9, 8, 11, 19, 25 and 15 per cent in the years 1971 to 1976 respectively). Sales growth was also boosted by £1.4 million in 1973 by the acquisition of Fruity Products Limited in 1972. Profit margins have also

Exhibit 2: *Anglian Canners: consolidated profit and loss statements (£)*

	1971	1972	1973	1974	1975	1976
Sales: factory products	2 945 499	3 816 195	5 684 368	7 710 809	9 759 310	11 232 256
bought-in	2 255 426	2 196 463	2 643 831	3 131 994	3 129 209	3 073 343
	5 200 925	6 012 658	8 328 199	10 842 803	12 888 519	14 305 599
Cost of sales						
Factory: materials	963 472	1 274 820	2 015 485	3 392 950	3 556 071	3 907 041
cans/ends	842 143	1 074 637	1 546 435	1 639 110	2 391 575	3 027 381
packing/fuel/power	190 600	256 073	367 190	408 904	673 654	835 788
labour (direct)	139 206	182 226	316 491	371 782	456 622	625 388
overheads	269 437	312 045	456 048	542 125	878 187	899 795
Total factory products	2 404 858	3 099 801	4 701 649	6 354 871	7 956 109	9 295 393
Bought-in goods	1 993 172	1 957 229	2 211 235	2 702 537	2 778 920	2 707 679
Total cost-of-sales	4 398 030	5 057 030	6 912 884	9 057 408	10 735 029	12 003 072
Distribution costs	275 927	330 167	440 678	498 324	599 372	657 261
Advertising and promotion	51 789	93 461	88 713	119 132	190 852	250 580
Selling and marketing expenses	155 087	170 659	209 604	225 959	250 746	265 609
Administration: salaries	72 528	85 765	112 166	119 071	147 882	164 449
others	70 506	56 163	104 559	106 537	147 746	150 009
Trading profit	177 058	219 413	459 595	716 372	816 892	814 619
Interest expense — UK	101 827	78 063	201 320	390 864	349 425	335 146
Interest expense — New York[1]	Nil	Nil	5200	5200	42 290	52 428
Currency loss (gain)	(17 356)	21 275	558	(2303)	54 908	84 637
Chicago administration cost	Nil	Nil	Nil	Nil	14 851	15 605
Additional pension premium	Nil	Nil	Nil	30 000	40 000	Nil
Profit retained in New York	Nil	Nil	23 841	Nil	Nil	Nil
Other	Nil	Nil	Nil	Nil	Nil	22 000
Pretax profit	92 587	120 075	228 676	292 611	315 418	304 803
Tax	Nil	37 500	75 052	143 750	137 475	124 005
Aftertax profit	92 587	82 575	153 624	148 861	177 943	180 798
Compulsory disposal	—	—	48 166[2]	—	—	—
Net income after taxes	92 587	82 575	201 790	148 861	177 943	180 798
Depreciation charged	50 935	52 668	77 131	90 435	113 245	117 132

Notes:
1. From 1971–74, the dollar loan from Amalgamated Food Inc. was not made on an arm's-length basis. If it had been, the interest payments would have been £23 000 (1971), £19 000 (1972), £36 000 (1973) and £48 000 (1974).
2. Profit resulting from compulsory sale to the Greater London Council of leased administration office and freehold warehouse.

increased over this period from 15.4 per cent in 1971 to 16.7 per cent in 1975. This has been achieved through a growth in factory products as opposed to bought-in products (see Exhibit 2). The slight setback in the profit margin to 16.1 per cent in 1976 was due to the severe drought in summer 1976, which affected Anglian's product mix.

No taxes were paid from 1971 to 1974 because of tax allowances, the introduction of stock appreciation relief provisions in the United Kingdom (see Appendix), and the tax losses acquired when Anglian purchased Fruity

Exhibit 3: *Anglian Canners: consolidated balance sheets (£'000)*

	December 28 1974	December 27 1975	December 31 1976
Current assets			
Cash	10	1	3
Debtors and prepayments	1630	1700	1717
Inventories	3625	3326	3848
Total current assets	5265	5027	5568
Current liabilities			
Amalgamated Foods Inc. $ Short-term financing	212	338	390
Amalgamated Foods Ltd. £ Short-term financing	300	302	303
Bank overdraft	2756	1890	1957
Creditors and accrued expenses	1308	1437	1515
Total current liabilities	4576	3967	4165
Net current assets	689	1060	1403
Fixed assets (net)	621	596	586
Deferred assets*	26	19	12
Total net assets employed	1336	1675	2001
Financed by			
Amalgamated Foods Inc. $ Term loan	130	153	182
Deferred taxation	257	395	511
Equity (capital stock, reserves, P and L account)	949	1127	1308
	1336	1675	2001

*Deferred assets represent the written down value of the tax loss carry forward acquired when the assets of Fruity Products were purchased.

Products. As of year-end 1976, Anglian had a tax loss carry forward of £540 000. Of this amount, £125 000 is the balance of Fruity Products' losses, and £415 000 results from the stock appreciation relief provisions. Exhibit 3 shows Anglian's consolidated balance sheet for the past 3 years.

Anglian is financed largely by loans from Amalgamated Foods, and also by bank overdrafts (see Exhibit 3). The overdraft, which currently stands at £1.957 million (see Exhibit 3), is part of a £3.5 million facility provided by Barclays Bank (£1 million at 1.5 per cent above base rate) and by First National Bank of

Chicago (£2.5 million at 1.75 per cent above base rate). Base rates at this time were 13.5 per cent. This compares with yields on (high coupon) short and long-term gilts of 14 and 15.5 per cent respectively.

Future plans

In preparation for his appraisal of Anglian, Mr Hodges requested that Anglian prepare a 5 year sales and profit forecast (Exhibit 4). Apart from the introduction of one new product, mushy peas, the projections assume no other new product introductions and no major changes in marketing strategy. Mushy peas have already been test-marketed and the company plans to 'go national' during 1977. The product is considered to match Birds Eye frozen mushy peas in taste. Sales of this product are expected to reach £700 000 in 1979, but are expected to reduce sales of processed peas by about £250 000. However, the gross margin on mushy peas is 23 per cent compared with only 10 per cent on processed peas.

The sales projections assume that production capacity will increase by an additional 150 000 cases per year as a result of the replacements and additions

Exhibit 4: *Anglian Canners: forecast profit and loss statements in real terms*

	(£'000 in real terms as at December 1977)				
	1977*	1978	1979	1980	1981
Net sales	17 104	19 154	19 649	20 198	20 492
Cost of goods sold	14 336	15 971	16 299	16 729	16 974
Gross margin	2768	3183	3350	3469	3518
Gross margin (per cent)	16.2	16.6	17.0	17.2	17.2
Overheads					
Warehousing and distribution	695	771	778	789	793
Advertising and promotion	330	372	380	387	390
Operating overheads	593	593	604	604	604
Total overheads	1618	1736	1762	1780	1787
Profit before tax, interest, and depreciation	1150	1447	1588	1689	1731
Total depreciation	89	165	214	251	263
Profit before tax and interest	1061	1282	1374	1438	1468
Profit before tax and interest as percentage of sales	6.2	6.7	7.0	7.1	7.1

*Budget

Exhibit 5: *Anglian Canners: projected net capital additions (1977–81)*

| | £'000 in real terms as at December 1977 | | | | |
	1977	1978	1979	1980	1981
Plant and equipment					
King's Lynn	106	210	213	153	95
Fakenham	219	215	130	90	90
Motor vehicles					
(net of disposals)	16	23	23	23	23
Other	10	—	—	—	—
Total	351	448	366	265	208

Exhibit 6: *Anglian Canners: projected earnings (1977–81)*

| | £'000 in money terms, i.e. at future prices | | | | |
	1977	1978	1979	1980	1981
Profit before depreciation,					
interest and tax	1150	1566	1923	2251	2538
Depreciation	(89)	(169)	(226)	(272)	(294)
Profit before					
interest and tax	1061	1397	1697	1979	2244
Interest	(550)	(648)	(664)	(613)	(493)
Profit before tax	511	749	1033	1366	1751
Tax at 52 per cent	(266)	(389)	(537)	(710)	(911)
Profit after tax	245	360	496	656	840

Major assumptions

1. 1977 figures based on December 1977 budgeted costs and prices. For 1978–81, the annual rates of inflation used are 15.4 per cent for 1978 and 10 per cent thereafter. The corresponding monthly rates are 1.2 per cent in 1978 and 0.8 per cent thereafter. Cash flows are assumed to occur evenly in 12 monthly instalments throughout the year. To convert from the figures in real terms (as at December 1977) given in Exhibit 4 to the figures in money terms given above, the appropriate monthly inflation rates are applied to each of the cash flow instalments. Thus, for example, the 1978 trading profit figure is shown as £1 447 000 in £ December 1977 in Exhibit 4. This is assumed to occur in twelve equal instalments of £120 583 in £ December 1977. To convert from £ December 1977 to money terms, the first of these instalments is inflated by 1.2 per cent, and the last of the 12 monthly instalments for 1978 is inflated by 15.4 per cent. Following this procedure, cash flows shown in real terms (£ December 1977) should be inflated by the following rates to obtain cash flows in money terms for future years:

1978	8.23 per cent
1979	21.12 per cent
1980	33.29 per cent
1981	46.62 per cent

2. Interest on borrowings has been assumed at the current market rate of 15 per cent per annum for 1977 onwards, and calculated for simplicity on year-end debt levels.

Exhibit 7: *Anglian Canners: projected balance sheet (at 31 December 1977–81)*

| | £'000 in money terms, i.e. at future prices | | | | |
	1977	1978	1979	1980	1981
Net assets employed					
Net fixed assets	848	1164	1381	1462	1473
Inventory	4789	5804	6663	7538	8412
Receivables	2052	2488	2856	3231	3605
Other current assets	105	118	140	160	183
Payables	(1796)	(2177)	(2499)	(2827)	(3155)
Net assets employed	5998	7397	8541	9564	10518
Capital employed					
Shareholders' funds	1553	1913	2409	3065	3905
Deferred tax	777	1167	1704	2414	3325
Total borrowings	3668	4317	4428	4085	3288
Capital employed	5998	7397	8541	9564	10518

Assumptions
1. Inflation assumptions as in Exhibit 6.
2. Current legislation concerning stock relief will continue for the foreseeable future and no tax will be payable during the period due to the tax loss carry forward position. Tax is budgeted at 52 per cent.
3. Receivable, inventories and payables have been estimated as a percentage of sales: receivables (12 per cent); finished goods inventories (22 per cent); raw materials (6 per cent) and payables (10.5 per cent).

that management plans to make to plant and equipment. Exhibit 5 summarizes the planned net capital additions from 1977 to 1981.

In anticipation of Mr Hodges' visit, Mr Moore, Anglian's chief executive, asked Jack Lebetkin, the company's controller to project the company's financial requirements up to the end of 1981. Exhibits 6 and 7 show Anglian's projected financial requirements together with the assumptions that Mr Lebetkin used in arriving at the forecast.

Mr Hodges' visit

Mr Hodges arrived in the United Kingdom in late December 1976. He met Anglian's management and was duly presented with their projections and forecasts. Although, for obvious reasons, he had not mentioned this to Mr Moore, one of the options he was actively considering was to sell Anglian Canners to another company. He personally felt unexcited about Anglian's prospects and the company was something of a misfit in Amalgamated's new structure. In addition, Amalgamated's board felt very negative about continued investment in the United Kingdom.

In looking at the figures, Mr Hodges was anxious to assess the minimum price below which the sale of the company would not be worthwhile. He also wanted to know what sort of price Amalgamated could reasonably expect to obtain.

Appendix: UK taxation and deferred tax

In 1976, the UK corporation tax rate was 52 per cent. Tax was payable on trading profits net of capital allowances, but before deducting accounting depreciation. For tax purposes, plant and machinery was completely written off in the first year (that is, a 100 per cent first-year allowance), while industrial buildings carried an allowance of 54 per cent in the first year and 4 per cent per annum (straight-line) thereafter. There was no restriction on the period for which tax losses and allowances could be carried forward. Tax was paid, on average, with a delay of 1 year. The United Kingdom operated an imputation tax system and corporation tax was deemed to include personal tax at the standard rate of 35 per cent.

Accounting profits in the United Kingdom were calculated using the FIFO method of stock valuation, and hence holding gains on stock were subject to corporation tax. To remove the worst effects of this, the government had introduced a system of 'stock relief'. Under this legislation,

Stock relief = (closing stock — opening stock — 15 per cent of trading income net of capital allowances)

and this stock relief figure was deducted from trading income net of allowances to obtain the taxable figure. Stock relief was symmetrical and decreases in stock values were subject to tax clawback. The amount of clawback, however, could not exceed the total amount of stock relief obtained in the past.

Although the government had given assurances that stock relief would not in the future be withdrawn, the UK accounting profession took a conservative attitude to both capital allowances and stock relief for the purposes of reporting profits. The accounting tax charge was calculated as 52 per cent of FIFO profits after accounting depreciation but before capital allowances. Differences between this accounting tax charge and the actual amount of tax paid were then reflected in changes in a specially constructed deferred tax account.

PART E

FINANCING DECISIONS

15. Commercial Union Assurance

In September 1974, Commercial Union Assurance Company (CU) astonished the financial community by announcing a £62 million rights issue, one of the largest ever made in the United Kingdom. One of the most unusual features of this issue was its timing. The Financial Times-Actuaries All Share Index had fallen by 64 per cent since its peak in May 1972, and virtually no new issues of any size had been made on the London market for nearly 2 years (Exhibit 1). In addition, the issue was made just prior to a general election.

CU, founded in 1861, was one of Britain's largest insurance groups, underwriting virtually all classes of insurance on a worldwide basis. Its net premium income in 1973 was £642 million of which 23 per cent was generated in the United Kingdom and Ireland, 15 per cent in western Europe and 40 per cent in the United States. In spite of its age and venerability, CU had a brash and plushy image for an insurance company. It inhabited one of the finest office properties in Britain, a gleaming, finely shaped modern skyscraper, 27 floors high, from which its executives operated from luxurious airy offices with plenty of natural light. In recent years, the company's aggressive acquisitions policy, its determined marketing campaigns and its progressive views on the insurance industry had helped to give it a distinctive character and image, together with a reputation for responding vigorously to its commercial environment. In spite of this, CU was as much a part of the City establishment as the other insurance companies, as the glittering galaxy of eminent bankers and financiers on its board bore witness.

Over many years, CU had followed a policy of agressive growth, acquiring several other UK insurance companies. In 1973, it acquired Delta-Lloyd, the second largest insurance company operating in Holland, and thereby at a stroke doubled its presence on the Continent. Over the past 5 years, the company had achieved one of the fastest rates of progress of all the composites. Premium income grew by 15 per cent a year (Exhibit 2), investment income by 21 per

This case was written by Paul Marsh as a basis for class discussion rather than to illustrate either effective or ineffective handling of an administrative situation.

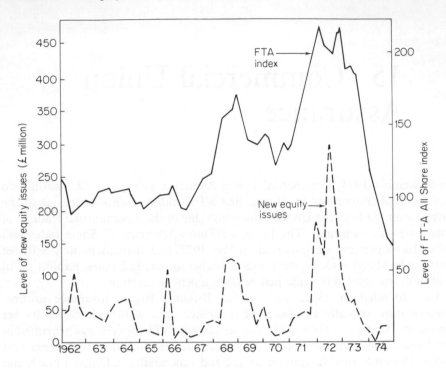

cent, and trading profits by 25 per cent. Pretax profits over this period achieved a 20 per cent per annum growth with particularly good figures being recorded in 1971, but only a relatively modest 10 per cent increase in 1972. Earnings per share had advanced by 12 per cent per annum from 7.4p in 1968 to 12.8p in 1973.

Background to the rights issue

A major event leading up to the issue was CU's abortive bid for St Martins Property Corporation. CU, who had held 10 per cent of St Martins shares for several years, launched a £70 million bid for the remaining equity in August 1974. There were two reasons for this bid. The first was to rebalance CU's property portfolio following the sale of 80 per cent of its interest in its London head office building for £66 million. The second reason for the bid was quite simply to improve CU's solvency ratio.

Insurance companies writing short-term business (that is, by and large, non-life insurance) were required by Department of Trade regulations to maintain a minimum solvency margin. The reason for this was that with most of this business, there was no fixed liability. On accident, industrial injury and health insurance, they did not know how much they might have to pay out. Inflation and humanitarian considerations meant that the payouts often exceeded the most pessimistic assumptions. In addition, there was always the possibility of a major disaster such as an earthquake in San Francisco. The solvency margin was defined as the ratio of shareholders' capital and free reserves to annual premium income. Under the then DTI regulations, this ratio was not allowed to fall below 10 per cent, otherwise the insurance company in question was technically insolvent. However, in practice, companies liked to maintain 30 per cent solvency margins — that is, three times the minimum set by the Department of Trade. As part of the process of harmonizing financial regulations within the EEC, the DTI was anyway planning to raise its minimum ratio to 16 per cent. It also stood to be raised even further than this by a change in the definition of ranking assets.

In the early 1970s, all insurance companies found this ratio slipping. First, while inflation had increased, companies' premium income, profitability and the ability to generate free reserves to maintain solvency margins had not been growing at anything like the same rate. Secondly, the disastrous slump in security prices in 1973–74, particularly in the United Kingdom, greatly reduced

Exhibit 2: *Commercial Union Assurance: profits and solvency margins*

Profits and solvency margins	Year ending 31 December (£ million)					6 months ending 30 June (£ million)	
	1969	*1970*	*1971*	*1972*	*1973*	*1973*	*1974*
Net written premiums (fire, accident, marine)	344.5	389.5	467.8	567.2	642.2	301.9	388.9
Increase over previous year*	7	13	20	21	13	13	29
Retail price inflation*	5	7	10	6	9	10	21
Underwriting	−4.0	−4.2	0.7	0.2	−5.5	−5.3	−2.7
Investment income	25.6	32.9	38.6	45.0	59.5	24.4	35.0
Life profits (including associate companies)	2.2	2.8	2.4	4.9	5.3	2.6	1.9
Trading profit	23.8	31.5	41.7	50.1	59.3	21.7	34.2
Loan interest and minorities	2.3	5.9	8.2	10.8	16.2	6.6	9.6
Profit before tax	21.5	25.6	33.5	39.3	43.1	15.1	24.6
Tax	5.5	7.4	10.8	13.3	16.7	6.1	10.8
Profit after tax	16.0	18.2	22.7	26.0	26.4	9.0	13.8
Earnings per share (pence)	8.7	9.9	11.6	12.7	12.8	4.4	6.8
Solvency margin (per cent)**	46	40	53	46	37	na	29

*Annual percentage rates
**Shareholders' capital plus free reserves (that is, net assets attributable to ordinary shareholders plus preference capital) to net written premiums

the value of their investments and hence their free reserves. This problem was particularly acute for CU which had one of the 'weakest' balance sheets of all the composites (see Exhibit 3 and also the comparative solvency ratios given in Exhibit 6). At the time of the St Martins offer document, the directors estimated that net assets attributable to the ordinary shareholders had fallen to £185 million. On the basis of the latest half-yearly figures for net written premiums, this implied that CU's solvency ratio then stood at 26 per cent, compared with levels of 37 per cent and 46 per cent for the previous 2 years respectively (see Exhibit 2).

Exhibit 3: *Commercial Union Assurance: consolidated net assets (excluding life funds)*

	(£ million)		
Consolidated net assets	Balance sheet *31 December 1972*	Balance sheet *31 December 1973*	Directors' estimate *20 September 1974*
Investments and assets			
Government securities	227	314	
Debentures and preference	179	164	
Ordinary shares	403	324	
Mortgages and loans	66	131	
Property	126	189	
Other (including fixed assets)	14	25	
	1015	1147	
Current assets			
Agents and companies (net)	128	152	
Current and deposit accounts	87	84	
Other current assets	63	89	
	278	325	
Total assets	1293	1472	
Less liabilities and provisions			
Outstanding claims and provisions	490	588	
Unearned premiums (accruals)	237	290	
Tax, dividends and minorities	28	39	
Other funds and provisions	80	95	
Loans and preference capital*	163	209	
Deferred tax	38	16	
	1036	1237	
Net assets attributable to ordinary shareholders	257	234	170

*Preference capital outstanding in 1972, 1973 and 1974 was £1.75 million

CU claimed that this solvency ratio presented no immediate difficulties. Nevertheless, they did point out that eventually, in a year or two, if the ratio constraint became binding, they might have to halt the growth of their premium income, and forgo any opportunities which might crop up for expanding their business. Furthermore, the solvency margin had become a key variable in management's monitoring of its operations, so much so that it was now calculated on a weekly rather than on a monthly basis. The board claimed that the acquisition of St Martins provided a convenient way of increasing the company's share capital and reserves. Unfortunately for them, however, St Martins received a higher bid for £107 million in September 1974 from the Kuwait Investment Office. CU was unwilling to enter into a contested bid in opposition to cash-rich Arabs, and instead moved to increase its capital base with a rights issue.

Reasons for the issue

The rights issue was announced on 24 September 1974 at the same time as CU revealed that it was withdrawing its bid for St Martins. The decision to go ahead with the rights issue had been taken at a board meeting less than a week before, and the arrangements for the issue had been made with remarkable speed. The issue was underwritten by four leading merchant banks, Kleinwort Benson, Baring Brothers, Lazard Brothers and J. Henry Schroder Wagg, and the underwriting operation had been kept a very closely guarded secret. John Linbourn, CU's finance director, explained that 'the company has acted quickly to avoid a dreadful period of uncertainty following the St Martins bid. . . . There is no point in waiting until you have to do something!'

When asked why the company was making a rights issue now when the shares were at their lowest level for 16 years, John Linbourn replied, 'It's a grave mistake to wait and assume the Stock Market is going to improve.' But surely there were better ways of increasing the capital base than by a rights issue?

> We've kept a check on all the major property companies and investment trusts, but none of them fitted our needs. This way, all the benefits from the extra shares go to our shareholders. We decided to issue shares, rather than a loan stock or a package, to keep it simple. We have completed the subunderwriting only today, and a complicated package would have taken longer to get accepted. The shares would have been damaged more if there were rumours of a rights issue before the announcement.

John Linbourn would not, however, say how CU would spend the new money, although he did indicate that in the short term, it would be invested in short and medium-dated Gilts. Nor was the circular letter which gave shareholders details of the issue any more informative. The solvency arguments were reiterated and the letter pointed out that shareholders' funds were now estimated to have fallen (at 20 September 1974) to approximately £170 million

Exhibit 4: *Commercial Union Assurance: sources and uses of funds (excluding life business)*

Sources and uses	1969	1970	(£ million) 1971	1972	1973
Sources					
New cash from trading	18	44	74	71	95
Loan capital	2	—	18	10	—
Other loans	17	55	2	17	45
Total	37	99	94	98	140
Uses					
Property	2	3	40	23	33
Normal investment*	16	79	−8	84	78
Cash deposits	16	18	27	−13	−24
Acquisitions for cash	—	—	31	4	60
Movements in reserves	3	−1	5	—	−7
Total	37	99	94	98	140

*Including short-dated securities

implying a solvency margin of about 23 per cent. No specific uses for the new money were detailed, however, and CU merely stated that 'the proposed issue will enable (the company) to continue to take advantage of opportunities for profitable expansion, and thus place us in a better position to maintain our record of steadily increasing profits and dividends'. It was widely felt in the City, however, that CU would soon now make a bid for a smaller, more digestible property company, but this time in cash.

CU emphasized, however, that while it may have needed to increase its capital, it had no immediate cash worries. Insurance was traditionally a cash flow business (Exhibit 4), and in any event, the company held over £250 million across the world in cash and short-dated securities. Part of the board's thinking in deciding on the issue was undoubtedly the desire to be at the head of the queue of companies which were likely to come to the market for fresh capital, rather than at the tail. Gordon Dunlop, the group's 47-year-old chief executive, a blunt man, who had been very much the driving force behind CU's changed image, pointed out that 'the first guy who does it is away to the races, the rest are left with their mouths open'.

Terms and issue details

The proposed rights issue involved the sale of 103 973 617 new shares on the basis of 1 for 2 at 60p to raise £62.4 million. The ex-rights date and the last acceptance date were scheduled for 22 October and 11 November respectively. The fee payable to the four merchant banks which underwrote the issue was 2½ per cent (£1.56 million) out of which they paid subunderwriting commission of 1⅝ per cent and a fee to Cazenove and Co., the brokers to the issue. The unusually high fee for subunderwriting reflected the fact that an extraordinary general meeting had to be held to authorize additional capital. This delayed the issue, and extended the period during which the subunderwriters were at risk to over 6 weeks. Total issue expenses including capital duty, the fee to the merchant banks and administrative expenses amounted to approximately £2.2 million, leaving net issue proceeds of £60.2 million.

The new shares ranked *pari passu* in all respects with the existing ordinary shares. CU were forecasting a total dividend for the full year (1974) of 10.217p per share. This represented a 12½ per cent increase in dividend per share.

Market reaction/press comments on the issue

On the day of the issue announcement, CU's shares fell by 12p to 72p per share (Exhibit 5). While City opinions differed on the reasons for this price fall, there was a general consensus that the news of the issue had formidable implications for the insurance industry as a whole. In particular, the speed of the announcement suggested to many City experts that the impact of inflation on insurance solvency margins was biting much harder and more quickly than previously thought (see Exhibit 6 below).

Exhibit 5: *Commercial Union Assurance: comparative share price performance*

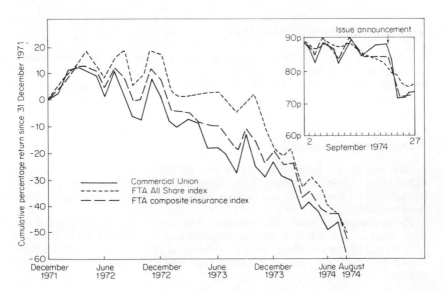

Exhibit 6: *Composite insurance companies: comparative statistics*

	Share returns to 31 August 1974 (per cent)		Estimated risk measures		Solvency margins (per cent)	
	Last year	*Last 5 years*	*Beta*	*Standard* deviation (per cent)*	*Latest balance sheet*	*Estimate at 25 September 1974*
Commercial Union	−40	−20	0.97	28	37	24
Eagle Star	−60	−39	1.43	39	45	29
General Accident	−37	+17	1.12	34	48	30
Guardian Royal Exchange	−40	−7	0.93	30	54	30
Phoenix	−43	−16	1.13	34	47	31
Royal Insurance	−38	+33	0.87	27	57	23**
Sun Alliance	−42	+10	1.02	29	44	29

*Annualized standard deviation of continuously compounded returns
**Royal Insurance's reserves were probably higher than the 23 per cent shown in the table as its properties had never been revalued; at a realistic value, the percentage might be nearer 30 per cent. In addition, both Royal Insurance and Commercial Union had a provision for 'extreme weather' which none of the other companies had. In Commercial Union's case, if this provision is added back, its current solvency ratio increases to about 27 per cent.

The financial press's reaction to the issue focused on the attractiveness of CU shares to investors, the timing of the issue and whether or not the issue would succeed. Press comments included the following:

Evening Standard (24 September 1974)

. . . At this price the new shares yield an incredible 17 per cent. Few shareholders are likely to pass up the opportunity of taking what looks like a real bargain. I gather that the biggest shareholders — National Westminster Bank with 5 per cent and a couple of German banks who together have about the same stake — are very happy with the deal.

Financial Times (25 September 1974) (Lex)

. . .But why has CU been willing to fork out over £1¼ million to the underwriters? In fact the idea of doing something like a one for one at 30p was, apparently, considered but rejected on the grounds that there is no room for leaving anything to chance in these markets. . . .
   The unfairness to shareholders, of course, lies in the fact that if they cannot take up their rights for one reason or another, then the underwriters will get in at what most people would agree is a 'cheap' price — yielding 17 per cent and comparing with 84p before the news. This matters far more than any theoretical sums about earnings dilution.

The Times (25 September 1974)

. . .Certainly, it is a breach of all conventional wisdom about stock market funding in the depths of a bear market. Few companies could expect to escape with an ex-rights yield as low as the CU's 15 per cent, so one would have to presuppose a handsome prospective return on capital to make a rights issue worthwhile. And there are obvious question marks about the receptivity of shareholders to heavy new cash demands. . . . although a spate of rights issues would undoubtedly be depressing for the market as a whole, some companies may already be close to anticipating the point at which the price of a rights issue is largely immaterial.

The Guardian (25 September 1974)

. . .Institutions are believed to hold about 70 per cent of CU's shares, so it is widely expected that most of the issue will be taken up. The price of 60p is low against Monday's closing share price of 84p. This should also make the issue attractive to private shareholders. The yield is 17 per cent.

Daily Mail (25 September 1974) (Patrick Sergeant)

. . .Firstly, why now? Secondly, why a rights issue? Thirdly, why offer shares at 60p where they yield 17 per cent on the forecast dividend? CU have to earn 22% before tax on the money merely to pay the dividend.

Fourthly, do CU regard 17 per cent as the right yield for the shares of one of our leading international companies whose direction, management and standing are as good as any in the country? Fifthly, do they think they must grab the money now because shares have further to fall and it would cost them more later?

. . .Although the new CU shares will yield more than Consol 2½ per cent yesterday, thus wiping out the reverse yield gap, the market will be relieved that CU do not expect leading shares to fall far enough to bring their dividends into line with CU's.

Financial Times (26 September 1974) (Lex)

. . .Commercial Union's underwriting went a sight better than it would have done if the underwriters had really been expected to be troubled in a big way in the immediate future.

Investors Chronicle (27 September 1974)

. . .But the fact remains that insurance companies, with their long-standing connections with merchant banks and other institutions are uniquely well placed to raise large amounts of money. Other companies, whose need for cash might be more urgent, could well find that their pleas fell on comparatively deaf ears.

The Economist (28 September 1974)

. . .Few industrial companies today could make a rights issue a tenth of the size of the £62.4 million that Commercial Union Assurance launched on a stunned bear market on Tuesday. It is not just that the City sticks together, especially before election time, or that insurance companies who are the prime underwriters of new issues have a special incentive to scratch each others' backs. Insurance is probably still a better bet than industry during superinflation.

Financial Times (28 September 1974) (Onlooker)

. . .As long as the share price holds up, and it appears firm at present at around 77½p, it is in the shareholders' interests to raise the necessary capital to take up the rights. Otherwise the underwriters to the issue will be picking up CU shares at a bargain price.

Financial Times (28 September 1974) (Lex)

. . . What will not do, however, is the dotty notion that the yield at which CU had its massive rights issue underwritten — 17 per cent — has some crucial message for the market as a whole. Whether CU was right to go ahead with the issue and get it underwritten, may be a matter for debate. But it had another important responsibility as well — to make as sure as it possibly could in these dreadful markets that the rights were going to be worth something. If it had arranged the underwriting at a higher price, and the shares had subsequently slipped below that level, it would have done its existing shareholders a major disservice.

Sunday Times (29 September 1974)

. . .One of the knottiest problems was to fix the terms. By agreeing to pay an effective 17 per cent for fresh money and a service fee equivalent to 2½ per cent, CU set a precedent. For if a company of that calibre is ready to pay so much, what about smaller, financially weaker groups?
. . .By Monday, Cazenove's sent out underwriting offers to about 400 institutions asking them to underwrite the issue. Over 300 accepted to underwrite a total of £46 million with the banks agreeing to take up the rest should shareholders shy away. Very few institutions refused. But then the terms were such that they would 'prove irresistible' says Cazenove's senior partner Luke Meinertzhagen. And CU is paying its advisers and underwriters fees of around £1½ million.

Sunday Telegraph (29 September 1974)

The sharp readjustment of insurance shares after Commercial Union's £62 million rights issue owed more to the relative attractiveness of the 17 per cent yield CU is offering than to any fresh bearish views about the sector.

Sunday Express (29 September 1974)

Keep some money by to pick up some of the new shares in Commercial Union. When dealings start next month, there will be the possibility of buying unwanted new shares cheap and without having to pay stamp duty.

16. British Telecom

British Telecom (BT) is the principal supplier of telecommunications services in the United Kingdom. It operates one of the largest telephone networks in the world, with some 20 million exchange lines. The company's main business is providing local, national and international telephone services. It is also the major supplier of telephone apparatus, and it provides a range of other services including telex, radiophone, radiopaging, data communications and information services. In 1983–84, BT's turnover was nearly £7 billion, and its operating profit was £1.5 billion (see Exhibit 1 for a 5 year profit history). The company employs some 240 000 people.

In early 1984, BT was still nationalized. Plans for privatization, however, were well advanced, and the government intended to sell 51 per cent of BT to the public in the late autumn. The flotation would be the largest share offering the world had ever seen, by a factor of five. It promised to be the most complex and daunting corporate finance endeavour even undertaken. BT would possibly become Britain's largest quoted company, bigger even than British Petroleum.

In April, the senior management of BT and the government were engaged in tough negotiations on two key issues which had to be resolved before the flotation. The first related to the future regulation of tariffs, and the second to the company's capital structure. Both issues, in turn, hinged on a third, not yet fully resolved question, namely the degree of competition which BT would face, and its likely effectiveness. The government wanted agreement on regulation and capital structure by Easter, so that it could announce the outline flotation arrangements to Parliament.

Historical background

The world's first commercial telecommunications operations began in 1839 with the establishment of a telegraph line between Paddington and West Drayton in London. The development of the telephone by Alexander Graham Bell,

This case was written by Paul Marsh as a basis for class discussion rather than to illustrate either effective or ineffective handling of an administrative situation. We are very grateful to Deryk Vander Weyer, Deputy Chairman of British Telecom, Tom Sharp of the Department of Trade and Industry, and Mark Burch of Kleinwort Benson for their time, help and invaluable comments. We are also grateful to Antonio Mello for research assistance on an earlier draft.

Exhibit 1: *Five year profit record and sources and uses of funds*

Profits and funding	Year ended 31 March (£ million)					
	1980	1981	1982	1983	1984[1]	
Turnover	3601	4570	5763	6414	6876	
Operating costs						
Staff costs	1609	2110	2394	2571	2715	
Depreciation	410	475	647	765	907	Profit
Other operating costs	928	1154	1538	1826	2036	
	2947	3739	4579	5162	5658	and
Less: Own work capitalized	(200)	(283)	(308)	(328)	(316)	
Total operating costs	2747	3456	4271	4834	5342	loss
Profit before interest	854	1114	1492	1580	1534	account
Net interest payable	537	544	556	549	544	
Profit before tax	317	570	936	1031	990	
Tax	—	—	—	—	—	
Extraordinary items	107	—	—	—	—	
Retained profit	424	570	936	1031	990	
Add: Depreciation	410	475	647	765	907	
Funds generated	834	1045	1583	1796	1897	
Foreign loans raised (repaid)	58	(64)	20	(29)	7	Sources
Lease finance	25	18	51	32	34	
Total sources of funds	917	999	1654	1799	1938	and
Increase in tangible assets	959	1239	1458	1517	1513	
Increase in investments	7	11	18	33	20	uses
Repayment of government loans	179	11	(108)	112	154	
Increase (decrease) in stocks	15	24	(3)	65	71	of
Increase (decrease) in debtors	495	(98)	240	269	210	
Increase (decrease) in creditors	(389)	(229)	126	(417)	(171)	
Increase (decease) in net liquid funds	(349)	41	(77)	220	141	funds
Total uses of funds	917	999	1654	1799	1938	

Note
1. Results for the year ended 31 March 1984 were not published until July 1984. As at April 1984, however, good estimates of these full-year figures were available internally within BT.

patented in 1876, led to the establishment of private telephone lines. These were linked together for the first time by a public telephone exchange opened in London in 1879. In the early days, telephone services were provided by the General Post Office (GPO) in competition with private sector companies. In 1896, the GPO took over the private sector trunk service, and in 1912, it became the monopoly supplier of telephone services throughout the United Kingdom (except in the City of Hull).

This government-owned monopoly, with telecommunications operating within the GPO, continued for some 70 years. Over this period, there were sigificant developments in telecommunications. But in the 1970s the pace of change quickened still further. Major technological developments were bringing fundamental changes in transmission systems, exchange equipment, and customer apparatus.

Telecommunications networks were being converted from analogue to digital systems for transmission of speech, text, computer data and television. Transmission via optical fibres promised significant advantages over coaxial cable. Internationally, satellites were increasingly being used for voice, data, facsimile and broadcasting transmission. Cellular radio technology promised vastly improved mobile telephone services. Mechanical and electromechanical switching equipment in telephone exchanges was being replaced by digital equipment, incorporating computers, and permitting a much wider range of facilities. The telephone itself was evolving into a complex electronic device, and major developments were taking place in computer and word processor networks and transmission, private automatic branch exchanges (PABXs), telex, teletext and electronic mail.

These changes were bringing telecommunications, broadcasting, computing, and information technology together in a way that was revolutionizing the industries involved. BT itself was carrying out development work on integrated systems. These would handle both the existing and new forms of traffic which were emerging through the growth of information technology, such as electronic funds transfer, credit card verification, high-speed transmission of data and facsimile, and video conferencing.

Steps towards liberalization

Against this background, a new Conservative government came to power in 1979. It had a desire to 'roll back the frontiers of the State', to stimulate competition, and to 'create a prospering, mainly free enterprise economy'. In September 1979, Sir Keith Joseph, Secretary of State for Industry, announced a government review of the GPO's telecommunications monopoly. As a result of its findings, Sir Keith announced, in July 1980, that the government intended to liberalize the telecommunications market.

The British Telecommunications Bill was therefore introduced. The eventual passage of this Act in July 1981 transferred the telecommunications business of the Post Office to a new public corporation, British Telecommunications. The Secretary of State was given powers to license competing telecommunications services, and to require BT to 'open up' its network by permitting the attachment of a wider range of privately supplied subscriber apparatus. Only the provision of a user's first telephone remained its prerogative. The equipment market, ranging from telephones to PABXs, was thus opened up with just one proviso, namely that suppliers' equipment had to meet certain standards, and be approved. Finally, the Act enabled BT's lines to be used by others to provide value-added services, such as data processing and storage, and answering facilities, where BT previously had a monopoly. The reorganization took effect on 1 October 1981, when BT became an independent corporation.

In October 1981, it was announced that Mercury was to be the chosen vehicle for network competition. Mercury obtained a 25 year renewable licence to operate a national and international digital network to compete against BT's trunk traffic. Mercury had been set up by Cable and Wireless, British Petroleum and Barclays Merchant Bank, to provide a customized service in long-distance communications for business and corporate clients by establishing its own UK optical fibre network. This was to be in a 'figure of eight' from London–Bristol–Birmingham–Leeds–Liverpool–Birmingham–London. It would cover most of the major business centres in England, and some 60 per cent of the UK's business population. It was estimated that it would cover just under 20 per cent of BT's overall traffic. Mercury could also interconnect with the BT network and enter the profitable international communications sector to Europe and the United States. It was not yet clear whether other operators would also be licensed.

During 1982, the changes introduced by the Act began to take effect. Increasingly, BT's network was used by other firms to provide value-added services, and the private sector started selling telephones directly to the public. Mercury's plans were also well advanced. While many commentators doubted how effective Mercury's competition would be, BT took the threat very seriously, and was redoubling its efforts to prepare itself for the new competitive environment (see below).

The privatization announcement

Within a year of the 1981 Act, there was a further major development in government policy. In July 1982, Patrick Jenkin, the new Secretary of State, announced that the government would introduce legislation to turn BT into a public limited company, and to permit the sale of a substantial part of its equity. The government would also be creating a regulatory body, and introducing a major change in licensing arrangements.

These developments had not been heralded in the 1981 Act, nor in the government's 1979 election manifesto. Previously, privatization plans had related mainly to the reversal of controversial nationalizations such as that of British Aerospace. Since taking office, the government had sold off 50.6 per cent of British Aerospace to the public for £150 million, 50 per cent of Cable and Wireless for £182 million and the whole of Amersham International, a radiochemicals company, for £64 million. It had also raised £276 million from its stake in BP by selling 5 per cent of it, and sold the entire government holdings in ICL, Ferranti, British Sugar, Fairey and the National Freight Corporation for a total of £163 million. But so far, nothing of BT's size or political significance had been attempted or announced.

A number of factors contributed to this major mid-term policy development. First, it was felt that the flotation would extend, and maintain the momentum of, telecommunications liberalization. The government also believed that exposure to the scrutiny of private investors would further stimulate BT to improve its efficiency, and that efficiency would be better gained from market forces than from central State direction. As Cabinet Minister Norman Tebbit put it, 'the nationalized industries have been letting us down for years'. The government wanted the new privatized BT to become the 'flagship' of Britain's electronics information industries, using its huge procurement power and market muscle to lead smaller companies into the battle for world markets.

The second factor favouring privatization was the government's financial picture. A major problem faced by this 'monetarist' government was to contain public spending as part of the fight against inflation. In particular, the cost of the nationalized industries threatened the public sector borrowing requirement (PSBR) limits. Nearly all the nationalized industries were demanding more money to finance their modernization programmes. The March 1982 public spending estimates forecast that the nationalized industries would need £5.3 billion of public support until the end of the government's life, compared with an earlier estimate of only £800 million. The alternative to increased borrowing was for the companies to raise prices, but this would have led to higher inflation.

BT's financial needs were contributing to this problem. Spurred on by the prospect of competition from Mercury, BT wanted to speed up its modernization programme. In mid-1981, they estimated their spending needs as £2 billion per year over the next 5 years. Despite BT's high self-financing ratio of 80–85 per cent, this implied significant borrowing. In June 1981, BT's external financing limit (EFL) was raised from £180 million to £380 million, although BT had argued strongly for £500 million. It complained that government borrowing curbs were delaying its investment programme. To fund the deficit, BT raised prices by 10 per cent in August 1981. This followed two increases of 12.5 and 20 per cent in the previous year.

To help solve its funding needs, BT in 1981 received outline agreement to issue profit-linked 'Buzby Bonds' to raise perhaps £150–£200 million direct from the City. On further consideration, however, the government recognized serious problems with this idea. It would be very difficult to give investors sufficient reassurance that their profit-linked returns would not be subject to government interference on pricing policy, while simultaneously giving the government the degree of control it felt it needed over a public sector enterprise which would still be subject to the PSBR. It was estimated that, because of this, the bonds would need to promise a return 3–4 per cent above the yield on gilt-edged. Given the costs involved and the relatively small amounts envisaged (relative to BT's capital spending programme), this idea was eventually shelved.

The government saw privatization as a possible alternative solution. Moves towards privatization and competition should increase efficiency, which in turn, would reduce the drain on state finance. Privatization would free BT 'from the web of government interference and control'. Once 51 per cent was sold, BT would be outside the PSBR and the government's EFLs. It could seek finance from the market, instead of from the Exchequer, or by putting up prices. The government would also raise a significant amount from the flotation, thereby reducing its overall borrowing needs.

As a profitable concern in a growth industry, BT was an appealing candidate for privatization. The government estimated that the sale could raise up to £4 billion to help underpin its financial strategy. A further attraction to some individuals was the opportunity to achieve a quantum leap in wider share ownership. Sir Geoffrey Howe's first budget specified this as an objective, but so far little progress had been made. While estimates varied, probably only around 1–1.5 million UK citizens held shares (excluding employee shares) directly, and this figure had been declining for years. Supporters of wider share ownership saw the BT offer as a chance to market shares to employees, telephone subscribers and small investors, and thereby turn the tide in the direction of a share-owning democracy. At the time of the privatization announcement, little was said about this objective, although later it assumed major importance. Ideology received a major boost from pragmatism here through a strong perception that the flotation would anyway be too large to be marketed to institutions alone. It was also felt that significant holdings by private investors could make BT more difficult to renationalize.

The Telecommunications Bill

The Telecommunications Bill, which was to provide the enabling legislation for privatization, was introduced in November 1982. Immediately prior to this, there was a series of important behind-the-scenes discussions between BT and the government on the form which BT would take. One option was to split it up, as was happening to American Telephone and Telegraph in the United States, and sell parts of it separately. Though favoured by some individuals, others argued that this simply substituted local monopolies for a national monopoly, while at the same time diminishing BT's ability to compete on a world scale. A break-up would also have infuriated both BT's unions, who were already angry about privatization, and BT's management, who lobbied intensively against this option. A break-up was anyway deemed impractical, mainly because of BT's lack of adequate, decentralized financial and information systems, and the substantial senior management changes which would have been needed. Resolving these problems would have meant delaying privatization for several years. The decision was therefore taken to privatize BT intact.

The Telecommunications Bill eventually received House of Commons approval on 29 March 1983. Kenneth Baker, Information Technology Minister, told MPs, 'There is no justification for retaining BT's monopoly. This Bill is the greatest measure of denationalization and liberalization ever presented to Parliament. . . . State control is control by a bureaucratic elite, it is not control by the people. . . . State capitalism is the worst form and the most debased form of capitalism there is.' Stan Orme, Labour's Shadow Industry Minister responded, 'We will continue to oppose this Bill, and all those who seek to make a profit from public assets. . . . We will restore the public telecommunications monopoly to BT. We believe it should be owned by the nation as a whole.'

However, just as the Bill began its committee stage in the House of Lords in May 1983, a general election was called. The Conservatives were returned with an increased majority, and the Bill was reintroduced in essentially the same form. After over 300 amendments, the Bill eventually became law on 12 April 1984. Under its terms, BT was to become a plc on 1 July 1984, paving the way for an October flotation. The Act also created an Office of Telecommunications (OFTEL) headed by a Director General which was to act as the telecommunications regulatory authority. BT's exclusive privilege to run telecommunications systems was removed by the Act, and was to be replaced by a licence.

BT's operating licence, which would spell out the pricing formula by which the company was to be regulated (see below), would be published in late May, and brought before Parliament for approval. This licence would require it to maintain a universal telecommunications service throughout the United Kingdom, including rural areas, and to continue to provide public call boxes, services for the disabled, and '999' calls. BT would have to allow other carriers, notably Mercury, to connect to its circuits in exchange for a fee. BT was also required to set up separate accounting and reporting arrangements for equipment-making and marketing, and phase out cross-subsidies to these businesses from public network revenues.

Management, systems and structural changes

Ever since 1977, when a Review Committee on the Post Office (the Carter Report) recommended significant changes in organization and management, the Post Office, including its telecommunications business, had been undergoing a major internal shake-up. The objective was to change the Post Office's corporate culture from a civil service mentality to that of a profit-oriented, market-led organization. From early on, it was recognized that to achieve this, it would be necessary to install a credible management team, with wide private-sector experience.

The first significant appointments came in 1980 when the new government appointed Ronald Dearing and Sir George Jefferson as Deputy Chairmen of the Post Office, and as prospective Chairmen of the two new corporations, the Post Office and BT. Sir George took over formally as Chairman of BT when it became a separate corporation in October 1981. Prior to joining the Post Office, he had been a Board Member of British Aerospace. Sir George was joined in 1981 by Deryk Vander Weyer, who became a part-time Board member, and subsequently Deputy Chairman in October 1983. Deryk Vander Weyer had been Chairman of Barclays Bank UK, and brought much-needed experience of banking and the City. Both men had a strong marketing orientation. Further board appointments were made to add additional outside business experience. The tier of senior management was also strengthened by external recruitment, to help change the corporate culture.

In addition to the management changes, a key priority was to install an effective financial information system. This was needed to provide a tighter grip on costs and also, to make sure the flotation prospectus carried conviction. In the past there had been no profit centres, and no devolution of financial responsibility, since income and expenditure had been handled quite separately. BT management thus had only a rather imprecise notion of where its cash came from and flowed to, and this had contributed to major forecasting errors, particularly in funding requirements (see below).

Changes were also made in financial reporting practices. Nationalized industries had been ahead of private sector companies in their adoption of inflation accounting. In line with this, BT's accounts had been prepared under the historic cost convention, modified by the charging of supplementary depreciation to reflect the estimated replacement value of its fixed assets. In readiness for privatization, it was decided to put BT's accounts on a basis comparable with other private sector companies. This would make it easier for the market to assess BT's worth.

From 1 April 1983, BT therefore ceased charging supplementary depreciation, shortened the estimated useful lives of a number of fixed assets, and charged to revenue expenditure certain other assets (such as telephones) which had previously been capitalized. Exhibit 1 shows the reconstructed 5 year profit record following these changes. Exhibit 2 shows the various retrospective adjustments. In 1982–83, for example, the changes increased reported profit before tax from the £365 million originally reported to a new figure of £1031 million. The increase of £666 million comprised £626 million from the cessation of supplementary depreciation, and £40 million from the other adjustments. The auditor's report on BT's accounts for the year ending 31 March 1984 was, for the first time, wholly unqualified.

In terms of operations management, BT had launched an efficiency drive that considerably reduced the waiting list for telephones, and the time taken to repair faults. The planned introduction of new digital equipment and System X exchanges was also accelerated. Meanwhile, BT was developing its marketing

Exhibit 2: *Financial results by services*[1]

Turnover and profit	1980	1981	1982	1983	1984[2]
			£ Million		
Turnover					
Inland Rentals — business	154	211	292	334	350
Inland Rentals — residential	495	651	795	887	908
Inland Rentals — apparatus	298	427	600	791	894
Subscribers' calls	1649	2079	2471	2547	2725
Call office receipts	69	85	91	97	102
Private circuits	105	135	192	265	
Telex	54	83	107	129	672
Miscellaneous[3]	134	142	223	223	
Total inland	2958	3812	4771	5273	5651
International	643	758	992	1141	1225
Total	3601	4570	5763	6414	6876
Reported profits					
Inland rentals — business	(55)	(81)	(2)	1	
Inland rentals — residential	(190)	(279)	(233)	(323)	1155
Inland rentals — apparatus	(116)	(70)	(60)	55	
Subscriber's calls	449	495	651	536	
Call office receipts	(56)	(68)	(73)	(77)	(50)
Private circuits	(31)	(17)	(4)	26	
Telex	(14)	3	(16)	(26)	108
Miscellaneous	(24)	(42)	(26)	(24)	
Total inland	(37)	(58)	237	168	1213
International	166	182	221	197	321
Total	129	124	458	365	1534
Add: Supplementary depreciation	426	518	541	626	na
Add: Interest payments	537	544	556	549	na
Add: Retrospective adjustment	(238)	(72)	(63)	40	na
Historic cost pretax profits	854	1114	1492	1580	1534

Notes
1. All figures are taken from the accounts referring to the year in question — 1980 figures are taken from the 1980–81 accounts etc. Each year, there have been retrospective adjustments to the prior year figures, and BT warn that 'the figures are not totally reliable, and the methods used are under review'. Totals may not sum due to rounding.

2. Figures for 1980–83 are shown after interest and supplementary depreciation. Figures for 1984 are preinterest historic cost profit figures. The 1984 figures were not published until July 1984. As at April 1984, however, good estimates of these full year figures were available internally within BT.

3. The miscellaneous figure and the subsequent totals are adjusted to include the (small) retrospective changes to the annual turnover figures.

operations. By April 1982, Sir George Jefferson was claiming

> There is a new spirit of enterprise growing in the organization, and a determination to seek out business. The introduction of new services and products provides tangible evidence of this. Significant progress has been made in improving services, and the task of modernizing the huge network has continued to be pushed forward vigorously.

Major structural changes were also occurring. The once top-heavy organization was decentralized into semiautonomous profit centres, and proper management controls were put in place. By early 1984, BT had reorganized itself into five operating divisions:

(1) *Local Communications Services* (LCS) which provided the local telephone service and which was also the gateway to the trunk and international telephone networks. This was by far the largest of the five divisions, employing some 200 000 people. At 31 March 1984, there were some 20 million lines in service, an increase of more than half a million over the previous year. On average, more than 60 million calls were made each day. LCS was also responsible for the sale and rental of apparatus, including telephones and business exchanges, and the public call box service.

(2) *National Networks* ran the trunk telephone service. It also offered a range of specialized services for business users including the inland telex network and high speed links between computers. For radio and TV broadcasters, it provided networks for the switching and transmission of sound and vision programme material.

(3) *BT International* (BTI) provided international telephone services, maritime and offshore communications, and specialized international business services, including telex and private circuits. It owned 44 ratio stations, three satellite earth stations, and had interests in 54 submarine cables. The breakdown of financial results by services in Exhibit 2 shows that BTI had been consistently profitable.

(4) *BT Enterprises* (BTE) supplied, mainly through LCS, telecommunication apparatus for both businesses and consumers, most bought from outside manufacturers. It also operated national radiopaging and radiophone systems, Yellow Pages and the Prestel information service. It was investing in cellular radio.

(5) *Development and Procurement* carried out R and D, principally at its laboratories at Martlesham in Suffolk. This was widely regarded as one of the world's leading telecommunication research centres. In 1983–84, BT spent nearly £180 million on R and D. This division was also responsible for the procurement of all equipment used by BT.

BT's capital expenditure programme

Procurement was clearly going to remain a key activity. Sir George claimed that BT's public network was one of the most antiquated in western Europe. While this may have been over-harsh, UK investment in telecommunications per inhabitant had certainly been lower in recent years than in Germany, France, and Scandinavia. The company's modernization plans allowed for capital expenditure of about £2 billion in each of the next 4–5 years. Orders for System X digital exchanges had been accelerated, and the aim was a fully digitalized system by the mid-1990s. BT also planned to replace the entire trunk transmission network with optical fibre by 1992.

This capital expenditure programme was justified partly on the grounds of cost savings, and partly on quality and improved customer services. In reality, it was much more than this, and many of BT's managers viewed it as the crucial bridge between BT's 'past' as a utility, and its 'future' as a high technology company in a far more competitive environment. Senior management treated the threat of Mercury and other competitors very seriously. BT's success would depend critically on its ability to respond rapidly to customer needs, with high standards of quality. This in turn required the rapid introduction of modern equipment and technology.

Indeed, the image BT wished to project was of a company poised on the threshold of a technological revolution, alive to commercial opportunities, and impatient to compete in a wide range of emerging growth markets, from office automation to satellite systems. As Sir George Jefferson explained, 'there will come a time when electronic information services, transmitted on computer-controlled networks, will replace conventional telephone traffic as the main source of the organization's revenues'. Many of the new activities would be in competitive, international businesses, reflecting the increasingly global nature of the telecommunications industry. 'We're in an international business, and must not be parochial,' commented Colin Crook, Managing Director of BT Enterprises. 'We have to be as at home in Silicon Valley and on the Stanford University campus as we are up in Cambridge or down the M4 motorway.' Certainly, BT's ambitions already extended overseas, where it was scouting for possible acquisitions and joint ventures.

The modernization programme and the many future investment opportunities, including acquisitions, raised an obvious question, namely where the money would come from. This problem had not been helped by the recent, March 1984 Budget changes in corporation tax. Until this point, BT's tax allowances had shielded it from corporation tax, but it would soon be coming into a tax paying position. City analysts estimated that the phased withdrawal of 100 per cent first year allowances would add some £700 million to BT's tax liability in the second half of the decade.

An additional problem was estimating the likely magnitude of the future funding requirement. BT's track record here had been unimpressive. The February 1983 White Paper on Public Expenditure revealed BT as the worst offender amongst the nationalized industries in terms of its funding requirement forecasting error. In 1982–83, BT undershot its forecast by £663 million. Thus in spite of earlier complaints that it needed to borrow more and raise prices to fund investment, BT was able to finance its £1.5 billion increase in tangible assets (£455 million less than forecast) internally, with a negative EFL of £323 million. BT attributed this to delays in delivery of equipment, cheaper suppliers' prices, improvements in its internal efficiency, and the general impact of the recession. The *Financial Times*, however, stated that 'The Government believes the Corporation has been guilty of faulty financial forecasting'. There was also talk of 'flabby financial control'. Nor was this the first misforecast by BT, and the bias was invariably in the same direction. Within the DTI, there was a sense of *déjà vu*. Clearly, realistic forecasts of capital expenditure were necessary not only for internal financial planning, but also in order to inform the debate on both regulation and capital structure.

Regulation and competition

The demands of the investment programme was one factor behind the sharp disagreements between BT and the government in late April 1984 on the questions of regulation and capital structure. The privatized BT was to operate within a framework of regulation designed to protect the consumer from any abuse of BT's monopoly, and, at the same time, to encourage competition. To the extent that regulation would constrain BT's profitability, or that a heavy debt burden would syphon off funds for interest payments, this was seen within BT as a threat to its cash position, and hence its investment programme.

At least in the short and medium term, BT would retain much of its monopoly, in spite of the government's stated policy of increasing competition. The government had licensed only one other national network operator, Mercury, and in October 1983 pledged to issue no more licences, either domestically or internationally, until November 1990. Furthermore, the sale of capacity on private circuits connected at both ends to public switched networks would not be licensed before July 1989. However, competition was expected to develop from cellular radio and cable TV operators, and also in the supply of customers' apparatus.

Although BT would have only one UK network competitor, BT believed this would produce a noticeable impact. They argued that the threat of competition should not be judged simply by the number of competitors, nor by their crude market share. Mercury would, after all, be 'cream skimming'. It would have a very modern, fully digital network, a low cost structure, and could attack some of BT's most profitable markets. It could develop niches in fast growing areas, and pick off selected clients, such as the banks, oil companies and Ministry of Defence. BT felt that Mercury's opportunities, and hence their competitive threat, were much greater than was immediately apparent.

Apart from the impact of competition, the main instrument of regulation would be BT's licence. The licence not only set out BT's public service requirements (see above), but also prescribed limits on BT's pricing policy.

There was to be a ceiling of 'RPI-X' on any overall change in prices for a designated 'basket' of services, where RPI represented the percentage increase in the Retail Price Index. 'X', and the precise definition of which services would be in the basket, had yet to be decided. Once agreed, the RPI-X formula would remain in place for 5 years. OFTEL was reponsible for enforcing licence ,conditions, initiating changes, and monitoring competition. It would have legal powers to investigate offences, and direct that they be corrected.

The RPI-X approach, proposed by Professor Littlechild, differed markedly from the US method of regulating utilities. In the United States, price increases have to be justified to a regulatory commission, which imposes a ceiling on return on capital employed (ROCE). It was felt this had two drawbacks. First, management had little incentive to improve efficiency or margins, since any increase in ROCE would be returned to customers through lower prices. Second, the allowed return was set in such a way that US utilities were not self-financing, and needed regular recourse to the capital markets. The advantage of 'RPI-X' control was that it operated directly on consumer prices (which was the political imperative), while allowing BT to retain the benefit of improved efficiency.

By late April, the negotiations between BT and the government had boiled down to a debate about the magnitude of 'X' and the contents of the basket. The government had compromised to RPI-3, while BT was still arguing for RPI-1. BT claimed that a limit of RPI-3 could squeeze its cash resources soon after privatization, making it difficult to service its debt, pay taxes and dividends, and finance £2 billion a year in capital investment. BT cited City concerns that tighter tariff controls would diminish its investment appeal, and could threaten the flotation. For example, the *Financial Times* of 31 March 1984 commented, 'The official pricing formula will be far and away the most important determinant of BT's market value. Each extra percentage point by which prices are pegged below the RPI will result in a £30 million fall in profits in year 1, with a compound effect thereafter.' Sir George Jefferson pointed out 'the crucial question is whether the shares come to the market regarded as a growth company in a high technology industry, or as something more akin to a dull utility'. Sir George had no doubts that BT could be a growth stock provided the government did not burden it with too much debt, and provided the regulatory framework was not so restrictive as to hinder BT's expansion.

The government, while clearly concerned about BT's attractiveness as an investment, nevertheless stood firm. They argued that tariff restraints would provide an incentive to BT to cut costs and improve efficiency. They were, however, prepared to be accommodating on the definition of the 'basket' (there had been much debate, for example, about whether trunk calls should be in or out). To give BT additional flexibility, they proposed that the basket should include line rental, and almost all inland telephone calls. Prices for BT's other services (45 per cent of turnover) were not to be regulated. Provision was also to be made for any permitted increase foregone in 1 year to be carried forward for up to 2 years. BT for its part decided to give an undertaking not to increase residential rentals by more than RPI + 2 to satisfy the political concerns of a substantial group of Conservative backbenchers.

The pension fund liability

Meanwhile, a parallel set of negotiations was taking place on capital structure. The BT team was led by Deryk Vander Weyer, and advised by Warburgs, their merchant bankers, and Cazenoves, their brokers. The government team was led by the DTI, with the Treasury closely involved, and advised by merchant bankers, Kleinwort Benson, and brokers Hoare Govett.

In all preflotation discussions, the DTI and Treasury worked closely together. Each, however, had slightly different priorities. The Treasury's main interest was in the size of assured receipts from both the sale and debt service, together quite separately with a wish for effective competition to encourage efficiency in the telecommunications sector of the economy. The DTI's main concern was the health of the newly privatized company and its main competitor, Mercury, and the effectiveness of the practical arrangements both for selling off BT, and putting in hand the new regulatory system.

All parties recognized that BT's balance sheet and capital structure had to be resolved before there could be any discussion about pricing or marketing. (The first three columns of Exhibit 3 show BT's historical balance sheets.) The first priority was to sort out what should happen to the £1.25 billion pension fund liability. BT felt this should be assumed by the government. The government, however, took a different view.

The pension fund liability had a long and controversial history. Until 1969, the Post Office, including telecommunications, was part of the civil service. The pension obligation fell on the government, and there was no separate pension fund. In 1969, the Post Office became a public corporation, inheriting the pension obligations. Pension liabilities for service after 1 October 1969 were to be paid by contributions to a newly established fund. But the question then arose of funding the past service liabilities for the 400 000-odd people employed at the time of the change.

The initial arrangement in 1969 comprised a fund of £1.5 billion (face value) 2½ per cent Consols, an undated government stock. The government was to redeem this by making annual payments of £45 million to the fund to 'repurchase' the stock at the ruling market price. These payments were originally expected to last for 25 years, but the fall in Consol prices meant that all the notional stock was redeemed in less than 15 years.

The poor performance of Consols showed up rapidly in pension fund valuations. The Actuary's Report in 1974 disclosed a deficiency of £1092 million, relating to service prior to 1969. This would have to be made up by additional payments from the Post Office to the Fund. The Post Office Board claimed that the government should fund this deficit, since it arose from the

Exhibit 3: *Historical and proposed balance sheets*

Balance sheet	Actual figures year ended 31 March (£ million)			Proposed adjustment 31 March (£ million)	Proposed balance sheet (£ million)
	1982	1983	1984[1]	1984	31 March 1984
Fixed assets					
Tangible assets	7367	8119	8725	—	8725
Investments	62	95	115	—	115
Total fixed assets	7429	8214	8840	—	8840
Current assets					
Stocks	72	137	208	—	208
Debtors	1466	1735	1945	—	1945
Short-term investments	—	124	252	—	252
Cash	49	38	55	—	55
Total current assets	1587	2034	2460	—	2460
Creditors: falling due within a year					
Short-term borrowings	221	114	118	—	118
Foreign loans	162	113	145	—	145
Lease finance	18	24	40	—	40
Trade creditors	750	1003	1170	—	1170
Other creditors, including tax	249	277	306	—	306
Accrued expenses	69	74	40	—	40
Deferred income	140	271	280	—	280
Total creditors	1609	1876	2099	—	2099
Total net assets	7407	8372	9201	—	9201
Long-term liabilities					
National Loans Fund (NLF)	3057	2944	2790	(2790)	—
Unsecured loan stock	—	—	—	2750	2750
Foreign loans	317	338	313	—	313
Lease finance	104	130	148	—	148
Pension fund covenant	1250	1250	1250	(1250)	—
Capital and reserves					
Preference shares	—	—	—	750	750
Reserves	2679	3710	4700	(960)	3740
Share capital	—	—	—	1500	1500
Total capital employed	7407	8372	9201	—	9201

Note
1. Results for the year ended 31 March 1984 were not published until July 1984. As at April 1984, however, good estimates of these full year figures were available internally within BT.

civil service days, and from the government linking its payments to Consol prices. The only alternative was higher prices for postal and telecommunications services. The government, however, disagreed. The Post Office had accepted the original arrangements with no proviso for a review. Many businesses were faced with pension fund deficiencies, and there was no case for preferential treatment. Furthermore, if past contributions had been high enough to avoid the deficiency, these would anyway have been met by charges to the customer, and not the taxpayer.

This was the start of a long debate. Meanwhile, the deficiency was still growing. Although the Carter Report in 1977 attempted to resolve this issue, its recommendations proved unacceptable. By 1978, the Post Office had decided that the government would not give in, and that some other mechanism was needed to alleviate the burden on its customers. At that time, the postal business was struggling to break even, while telecommunications was highly profitable. In practice, any deficiency payments were thus likely to fall largely on telecommunications customers.

The Post Office decided there were good reasons for formalizing the deficiency as a liability on telecommunications. The government had set return on asset targets for the two businesses in different ways. Telecommunications' target was on profit *before* interest while the Post Office target was on profit *after* interest. If pension fund payments could be represented as interest, rather than deficiency payments, there was a case for telecommunications assuming the deficiency. Expenditure which affected performance against target would be replaced by expenditure which did not. The target could then be met without raising prices. Profit *after* interest would be lower, with less internally generated funds available to finance capital expenditure. But since telecommunications was then self-financing, this presented no immediate problems.

In 1978, the Post Office therefore drew up a scheme whereby the pension fund deficiency was formalized as a covenant running from 1978 to 1992, borne entirely by the telecommunications business. In practice, this meant that telecommunications was burdened with a debt to the pension fund of £1.25 billion, on which it had to pay interest at an effective rate of 14.5 per cent (2 per cent above current gilt yields), and where the principal had to be repaid over the period 1986–92. The government accepted this arrangement in return for an agreement to freeze rather than increase postal and telecommunications charges. Cynics commented that this would help dampen inflation during the sensitive run-up to the general election.

BT was split from the Post Office in 1981, and separate pension schemes were set up in 1983. Despite further argument, the government insisted that BT should retain its covenant liabilities, and make interest (and, in due course, principal) payments not only to its own pension fund, but also to the Post Office scheme. In BT's 1982–83 accounts, the covenant was shown as a 'long-term liability' of £1.25 billion. Covenant payments were nearly £200 million per year, and were included in 'net interest payable'.

In negotiations on its preflotation balance sheet, BT argued that the government should take over this £1.25 billion liability, since it was a hangover from BT's civil service past. They pointed out that potential investors would be worried if BT had to service this controversial liability out of future profits, and that they would not understand the rationale for it. In marketing terms, it would be a disaster. The government agreed, but had no intention of simply taking it over without a quid pro quo. They therefore suggested that it should remain a liability of the residual statutory corporation (which would remain fully in the public sector), instead of being transferred across to the new BT plc. The government would then service the covenant out of the interest payments it received from BT's newly consolidated borrowings from the government.

While leaving the liability with the residual statutory corporation was agreeable to BT, replacing it with an equivalent amount of debt was not. However, 'procedural' agreement to adopt this mechanism did manage to shift the debate away from the historical rights and wrongs of the pension fund question, and BT's deep sense of outrage. Instead, negotiations could now focus on the key issue of how much debt the new corporation should have.

Capital structure

In the past, BT had borrowed money to finance its medium and long-term needs from the National Loans Fund (NLF). On 31 March 1983, BT had £2944 million of NLF loans outstanding, although the 1984 accounts were expected to show a reduction of some £154 million (see Exhibit 3). However, since BT was a nationalized public corporation, the dividing line between its NLF debt and its reserves was a function of history rather than a question of ownership. Only BT's £451 million of foreign loans were held 'externally', and even these carried government guarantees.

The current debt level reflected history since all BT's past new financing had come from debt rather than equity, resulting in an arbitrary balance sheet split between debt and reserves. BT's management argued that the resultant debt ratio was far too high, and was not even a sensible starting point for discussions. They maintained that a new capital structure was needed, designed for BT's long-term health, and that this should not be influenced by short-term considerations designed to maximize government proceeds from the share sale and from subsequent debt servicing.

BT management argued that the 'ideal' capital structure would have a low level of debt. An internal memorandum pointed out that it was a 'major concern' of the board to achieve a significant reduction in BT's debt, 'thus considerably reducing the interest it has to pay. Debts could either be written-off, or converted to equity.' Unless this was done, BT claimed that cash flow projections derived from their financial forecasting model indicated that the company would have to indebt itself still further to fund dividends, tax payments, interest charges (which totalled £549 million in 1983 — see Exhibit 1) and capital expenditure. BT's overriding concern here was with cash availability. They wanted a capital structure which gave them the financial flexibility to meet not only their planned expenditures, but also left them scope for acquisitions, or the development of new activities. They did not want to be constrained by high gearing, and 'kept short' by high debt servicing payments.

BT's projected cash flow position had already been hit by the phased withdrawal of 100 per cent allowances in the 1984 Budget (see above). At the same time, these budget changes made debt seem less attractive to BT, since the tax advantage of debt over equity appeared to have been largely removed. Thus while interest payments would continue to shield BT from corporation tax, BT argued that the effective corporation tax rate on distributed profits was now quite low. Standard rate personal tax at 30 per cent would continue to be payable on dividends as advance corporation tax (ACT). But since the overall corporation tax rate (including ACT) was scheduled to fall to 35 per cent, the incremental amount of corporation, as opposed to personal, tax on distributed profits was now quite small.

BT management argued that the company's gearing would have a direct impact on the dividend payments which it could afford. With a low debt to equity ratio of say 15–20 per cent, BT could comfortably pay annual dividends of around £550 million. Assuming BT's equity was worth around £8 billion, this would meet the yield of 7 per cent which City opinion seemed to favour (the figures currently bandied about for the value of BT's equity fell in the range £6–£8 billion, with figures at the lower end regarded as more likely, unless BT's debts were significantly reduced). However, if current debt levels were maintained, BT claimed that such dividend payments would be out of the question, since £550 million in dividends plus £550 million in interest would consume more than two-thirds of estimated (1984) pretax profits. This would be unacceptable, since Warburgs had advised them that the market would look for dividends to be covered at least twice out of post-tax profits. Under this scenario, BT would either have to greatly slow down its capital expenditure programme, or else fund it by taking on even more debt. The latter might be difficult, since high initial gearing would reduce management's ability to raise further funds, and could leave a taint of too much debt, which would linger for a long time.

BT management did not see it as part of their duty to maximize the sale price of the shares. Indeed, too high an issue price could make it difficult for them 'to perform' subsequently. BT nevertheless recognized the importance the government attached to pricing. In putting their case to government, they therefore pointed out that any lowering of the dividend yield (because of constraints on cash) would automatically reduce BT's investment value. This view was borne out by stockbrokers De Zoete and Bevan who commented,

> The most obvious way to attract investors (other than simply lowering the issue price) is to increase the dividend yield. Although the long-term rate of return from an

investment is equal to the sum of the initial dividend yield plus the dividend growth rate, in the short term, beleaguered managements are well aware that raising the dividend is the surest way to cause an increase in the share price.

The government considered BT's arguments and found them wanting. Certainly, a key concern was to make BT an attractive investment. Kleinworts, their merchant bankers, had confirmed that the shares would be valued on yield, and that 7 per cent would indeed be an appropriate figure. While this was nearly double the average yield on industrial shares (Exhibit 4), it was still well below the average for quoted US telephone companies (Exhibit 5). The government would have preferred a much lower figure, but even on the basis of 7 per cent, they refused to accept BT's claims. In particular, they were deeply distrustful of BT's forecasts. Past experience made them more inclined to believe annual capital expenditure forecasts at the bottom end of the range £1.8 million to £2.3 million, rather than BT's top end estimates. The government also believed profits and cash flow would be stronger than predicted. Even with no debt write-offs, they believed that BT could pay dividends of £550 million, fund its capital expenditure, pay taxes and service its debt quite comfortably.

Initially therefore, the government argued that there should be no write-offs. They certainly did not wish to provide any free gifts to the new shareholders at the expense of the taxpayer. They were particularly sensitive here to criticisms by many politicians (on both sides of the House) who felt that write-offs of debt (or 'forgiving debt') represented a cost to the Exchequer. Like BT, the government was also concerned with its own cash flows, and recognized that, whereas it would continue to receive all of the secure flow of interest on BT's debt, it would get only 49 per cent of BT's less certain dividends. There was also some feeling that BT should not be allowed to build in too much contingency and 'financial flexibility', since a 'lean and tight' organization would have a greater incentive to be efficient. Privately, the government was not keen on BT making predatory acquisitions. Furthermore, while they wanted BT to be internationally competitive, they felt that a lowly geared BT might be disproportionately powerful, particularly given its continuing effective monopoly in many areas. They did not want to put BT at an unfair advantage over current and future competitors.

One other important consideration led the government in the same direction. Ministers knew that the BT flotation would be seen as a major test of their privatization policy, and the political success of the issue was by now the paramount concern. A failure would be an enormous setback to the privatization programme, whereas a success would open up a host of future options. The major problem, however, was the sheer size of the issue.

It had originally been thought that, because of its size, the 51 per cent stake might have to be sold in more than one tranche, and indeed, the Telecommunications Bill contained specific provision for this. The government and BT wished to avoid this, however, since it would have involved an awkward period of transition. Until 51 per cent was privatized, BT would remain within the

Exhibit 4: *Comparison of BT with other UK quoted companies*

Company	Figures in £ million (except where indicated) for last accounts as at 31 March 1984									Figures as at 31 March 1984		
	Share capital and reserves	Preference shares	Long and medium-term loans	Other long-term liabilities[1]	Short-term loans	Capital employed	Cash and marketable securities	Gearing[2] (per cent)	Interest[3] cover	Market capitalization (£ million)	Gross yield (per cent)	P/E ratio
Allied Lyons	1210	9	396	77	65	1756	59	37	5	1141	5.2	12.0
Amersham International*	49	0	4	6	10	69	4	25	13	115	2.8	15.6
Asda-MFI	243	2	1	63	15	322	80	6	582	1179	2.0	26.1
Associated British Ports*	152	0	8	29	0	189	16	4	10	118	3.4	13.3
BAT Industries	3168	0	844	617	418	5047	723	33	8	3292	5.2	6.0
Beecham Group	976	0	262	67	49	1353	299	30	8	2256	4.4	14.1
BOC Group	1035	3	657	210	125	2028	88	63	3	1078	3.2	15.6
BP*	9626	12	4283	5955	1185	21 061	915	35	10	8589	7.3	9.9
British Aerospace*	739	0	259	265	34	1298	310	29	5	468	5.6	5.2
Britoil*	363	0	251	592	14	1219	321	28	17	1255	5.7	8.8
BTR	692	0	562	89	271	1614	126	107	4	2564	2.5	18.8
Cable and Wireless*	478	0	133	191	148	951	184	42	12	1598	2.3	17.2
Ferranti*	143	3	2	18	32	198	40	23	14	594	1.2	23.0
General Electric Company (GEC)	2409	0	118	647	103	3276	1570	7	23	5163	2.4	13.3
Glaxo Holdings	542	0	14	68	94	718	144	18	16	3074	1.5	27.3
Grand Metropolitan	1554	13	857	159	154	2735	51	60	3	2407	3.4	15.0
Hanson Trust	429	0	182	87	283	983	327	90	3	1265	2.4	17.2
ICI	3333	9	1268	931	538	6079	774	43	5	3707	5.6	9.8
Imperial Group	887	0	225	108	13	1233	149	24	7	934	7.9	8.7
Plessey	490	0	34	169	40	734	325	11	20	1737	2.1	21.2
Racal	369	0	118	49	25	561	154	34	7	1155	1.8	16.3
STC	262	0	9	54	33	357	24	13	19	1073	3.2	16.0
Thorn-EMI	574	64	159	169	180	1148	26	54	5	1160	3.6	18.7
Unilever	1708	5	123	522	215	2573	407	15	9	1730	4.7	9.2
BT	5240	750	3211	0	303	9504	307	81	4	na	na	na

Notes

1. Other long-term liabilities include deferred tax, other deferred liabilities, and minority interests.
2. Gearing is here defined as (total debt plus preference)/equity. Equity is defined as share capital plus reserves plus minorities plus deferred liabilities.
3. Interest cover is profit before interest and tax divided by interest payable.
4. BT figures as at 31 March 1984 as finally proposed by the government (see final column, Exhibit 3).
*Indicates recent privatization/government share sale.

Exhibit 5: *Comparison of BT with overseas quoted telecommunications companies*

	Figures in US$ million as at 31 March 1984 (except where stated)							Figures as at 31 March 1984		
Company	Share capital and reserves	Preference shares	Long and medium-term loans	Other long-term liability[1]	Short-term debt	Capital employed	Gearing[1]	Market capitalization ($ million)	Gross yield (per cent)	P/E ratio
AT and T[2]	13 763	1494	9300	3726	850	29 133	67	16 084	7.7	12.4
Ameritech[3]	6769	0	4923	3238	0	14 930	49	6398	9.1	6.9
Bell Atlantic[3]	8299	0	4847	3851	0	16 997	40	6918	9.1	7.3
Bell South[3]	8765	0	6435	4164	0	19 364	50	8973	8.5	7.5
NYNEX[3]	7310	0	5448	3656	0	16 414	50	5886	10.0	6.3
Pacific Telesis[3]	6184	511	5807	3204	0	15 706	67	5628	9.4	7.2
Southwestern Bell[3]	6559	0	4984	2221	0	13 764	57	5576	9.8	6.4
US West[3]	6375	0	4847	3254	0	14 476	50	5660	9.4	6.4
Bell Canada[4]	5307	424	4418	2331	414	12 894	69	6946	9.1	7.4
Hong Kong Telephone[5]	2175	0	0	661	9	2845	0	5452	3.6	12.8
British Telecom[6,7]	5240	750	3211	0	303	9504	81	na	na	na

Notes

1. Defined as in Exhibit 4.
2. On 1 January 1984, American Telephone and Telegraph Company divested itself of its 22 wholly owned telephone operating companies by spinning off seven regional holding companies (see note 3 below). AT and T retained ownership of the former AT and T Long Lines interstate trunk organization, Western Electric Company, its manufacturing arm, Bell Telephone Laboratories Inc., AT and T Information Systems Inc., and AT and T International Inc., as well as those portions of the former operating companies that provide interexchange service and customer premises equipment. AT and T balance sheet figures are as at 31 December 1984. All figures in US dollars.
3. One of the seven regional holding companies divested by AT and T on 1 January 1984. All figures in US dollars.
4. Balance sheet figures as at 31 December 1983. All figures throughout th s row in Canadian dollars.
5. Balance sheet figures as at 31 December 1983. All figures throughout this row in HK dollars. Company 80 per cent owned by Cable and Wireless as at 31 March 1984.
6. Figures throughout this row as at 31 March 1984 in £ million, as finally proposed by the government (see final column, Exhibit 3).
7. Comparisons between BT and the other companies require caution. Prior to 1 January 1984, AT and T was probably the most similar, but the split into eight companies with separation between trunk and local lines has left nothing directly comparable. The US companies and Hong Kong Telephone are subject to rate of return regulation, rather than RPI-X. In practice, this has meant that they are rarely able to finance their growth internally. There are also restrictions on the activities in which the US telecommunications companies can engage, notably data communication. Finally, BT's depreciation rates are noticeably higher than those used in the United States, and in fact, BT's profits for 1983–84 would have been 18 per cent higher if US depreciation rates had been employed.

PSBR and still be seen as subject to interference, and the 'dead hand' of government. Indeed, certain major institutions indicated they would not support the sale if there was any prospect of transitional state control. This was taken seriously, since this was not a flotation where the government could afford a divided camp amongst the institutions. There was also a belief that, with a phased sale, the share price would be depressed by subsequent tranches 'overhanging the market'. However, a single sale, which immediately put 51 per cent into private hands (the 'BP solution') would avoid these problems, and be acceptable to investors, since governments of all political persuasions had a proven track record of not interfering with BP.

Fortunately, Kleinworts and the City gave strong advice that a single-tranche sale would be possible, if carried out on a partly paid (instalment) basis, with extended intervals between instalments. The decision was therefore taken to sell the entire 51 per cent in one go. The flotation was still seen as close to the limit, however, and serious doubts remained about how much of the issue would be absorbed by the UK institutions. Assuming that the issue was worth approximately £4 billion, then this contrasted with the £2.5 billion which UK institutions added to their equity portfolios during 1983. It was therefore estimated that the government would be able to rely on selling only about half the issue to UK institutions even on a party paid basis. The remainder would have to be actively marketed to the UK public and overseas investors. If BT's debt was significantly reduced by conversion to equity, this would make the 51 per cent stake even larger, and more dificult to sell as a single tranche.

BT management were horrified at the notion of no write-offs. They pointed out that the company's historical debt ratio (long-term debt divided by total equity) based on the March 1983 balance sheet was 126 per cent (see Exhibit 3), and that this was absurdly high for a private sector company. They conceded that the flow of retentions would reduce this over time, but pointed out that with no write-offs, the 31 March 1984 debt ratio would still be a massive 96 per cent (see Exhibit 3). They claimed that this was far higher than for other UK quoted companies (see Exhibit 4), and that this level of gearing would greatly increase BT's investment risk, which was already high, given the increasingly competitive and uncertain nature of the telecommunications industry. They felt that this, together with the low interest cover of only 2.8 times (for 1983–84), would alarm potential investors, who would prefer a 'sound' balance sheet, which they would regard as a significant selling feature.

BT management argued that there was another reason why BT should have a lower debt ratio than other companies. Unlike other quoted companies, BT felt they would have no access to the equity market in the near future. A rights issue would be out of the question, at least until the new shares were fully paid. By the same logic, acquisitions would have to be for cash, not shares. Even once the shares were fully paid, a rights issue would be unpopular, particularly if the government was successful in attracting a large number of private investors as shareholders. The government's remaining 49 per cent would anyway be 'overhanging' the market, although the government had undertaken to sell no more shares before 1988. BT's equity would therefore 'have to last a long time'. Because of this, and given the capital requirements of the business, the rising tax burden, and the need for a generous dividend, BT reiterated strongly that the government should 'write-off' a significant amount of its long-term debt.

The government gave serious consideration to the arguments about investor perceptions. They wanted to get the highest possible price per share, consistent with a successful issue. They agreed that if a company had too much debt, investors would apply a low rating to the shares, because of the financial risk. However, the government and Kleinworts felt that this would happen only at very high debt ratios, well above the level they were proposing. Inded, they argued that, up to a point, debt was attractive to shareholders, since it increased earnings per share. Furthermore, the government argued strongly that BT's characteristics as a utility meant that it had below-average business risk. They viewed the quality of earnings as considerably higher than for any other UK company, because of the 'base level' of telephone calls that would be maintained even in the severest recession. This reinforced their view that BT could tolerate an above-average level of financial gearing and a below-average coverage ratio. Certainly, US telephone companies typically had debt ratios in the 50–70 per cent range (see Exhibit 5). And even within the United Kingdom, coverage ratios above 5 were viewed as extremely safe, while ratios of around 3 were still acceptable, and not uncommon (see Exhibit 4).

Towards an agreement

At this point, therefore, there was still a significant difference between the government and BT on capital structure. However, the government wanted agreement by Easter, to avoid any slippage in the flotation timetable, and they therefore set about seeking ways of closing the gap between BT and themselves. One option they considered, which moved some way towards BT's position, was to reduce BT's debt by £540 million. This would be achieved by replacing BT's existing debt of £2790 million to the National Loans Fund, together with the £1250 million pension fund liability, with a total of £3500 millon in new unsecured loans from the government.

In accounting terms, the balance of £540 million would be treated as a conversion of debt into equity. However, mindful that many would view this as a write-off of debt, and a cost to the Exchequer, government officials attempted to estimate the true cost of this move. Their conclusions were summarized by Sir Brian Hayes, Permanent Secretary at the DTI, who explained,

This loss of net present value (NPV) of the debt is attributable to the conversion of debt into equity. The effect of this in turn would be to make investors attach a rather higher value to the equity since the company was not so burdened with debt. There is no way of working out the extent to which that increased value offsets the reduction in the NPV of debt, but on a highly theoretical basis the increase in the value of BT's equity can be shown to cover two thirds or more of the loss of NPV in debt.

This, however, was before considering taxes. Throughout the negotiations, the government had been careful to focus on the agreed objective of giving BT a capital structure appropriate for the private sector, and had not been wearing its hat as tax collector. However, for the purposes of this exercise, the government did look at the impact of tax. Sir Brian concluded that if you also took into account 'the likely increase in BT's tax bill, because of the lower debt charge on its profits, that would bring the government very close to a break-even outcome'.

The government therefore decided to put the revised proposal to BT. To make the package appear more attractive, they also clarified their position over the timing of BT's first dividend. Privately, BT had feared that the government might declare a public dividend prior to the flotation. The government indicated that they would not, and that BT would need to pay only a single (final) dividend in the year 1984–85 (the flotation would take place more than half way through BT's financial year). It was thus made clear to BT that, meanwhile, they could retain their internally generated funds, which would further lower the debt ratio. The government's revised proposals therefore implied a debt ratio of 76 per cent as at 31 March 1984 (see Exhibit 3). However, by the end of 1984–85, assuming an additional £1 billion of retentions, the debt ratio would have fallen to 63 per cent. The government estimated that BT's cash flow would also be sufficient to repay its foreign debt over this period, and this meant the ratio could be as low as 56 per cent by 31 March 1985.

Looking further ahead, the debt ratio was expected to continue to fall, even though BT would start paying taxes and dividends. This was the conclusion reached in the prepublication version of a major report on BT prepared by de Zoete and Bevan, one of the government's stockbrokers to the sale. In this report (which later became the standard prequotation reference work on BT), de Zoete and Bevan provided a 5 year forecast for BT (Exhibit 6). On the assumption that BT's profits would grow at a real rate of 6 per cent up until 1988, then the debt ratio was expected to decline steadily throughout this period.

By the end of April 1984, it was becoming clear to BT management that they would have to agree to a higher debt ratio than they had initially been seeking. They would still not accept, however, the government's proposal of £3.5 billion of unsecured loan stock. As a final compromise, therefore, the government suggested that, to improve BT's debt ratio, £750 million of the loan stock be replaced by preference shares (for the full proposed balance sheet, see the final column of Exhibit 3).

Under this proposal, the preference shares would be held by the government, would carry a coupon of 11.95 per cent, and would be redeemable at par on 3 months notice at any time at the company's option, or in any event after 35

Exhibit 6: *Five year financial forecast*[1]

	1984[2]	1985	1986	1987	1988
			£ million		
Revenue					
Inland network	4135	4450	4750	5050	5380
International	1275	1450	1660	1900	2150
Apparatus	900	1000	1050	1100	1150
Services	640	750	900	1050	1200
Total revenue	6950	7650	8360	9100	9880
Costs					
Wage	2390	2540	2700	2890	3100
Bought	2190	2470	2775	3065	3340
Depreciation	855	980	1115	1255	1400
Interest	510	355	290	295	310
Total costs	5945	6345	6880	7505	8150
Pretax profit	1005	1305	1480	1595	1730
Tax	—	155	592	558	605
Preference dividends	—	46	62	62	62
Attributable profit	1005	1104	826	975	1063
Ordinary dividends	—	210	371	393	417
Retentions	1005	894	455	582	646
Pretax profit	1005	1305	1480	1595	1730
Add: depreciation	855	980	1115	1255	1400
Total sources of funds	1860	2285	2595	2850	3130
Additions to fixed assets	1600	1800	2000	2100	2150
Increase in working capital	—	—	—	—	—
Tax payable	—	20	182	506	705
Dividends payable	—	46	412	441	464
Repayment of loan capital	122	56	95	110	125
Reduction in net liquid funds	138	363	(94)	(307)	(314)
Total uses of funds	1860	2285	2595	2850	3130
Net fixed assets[3]	8896	9716	10601	11446	12196
Net current assets	305	680	589	339	320
Net assets	9201	10396	11190	11785	12516
Government loans	2750	2706	2645	2592	2569
Foreign loans and leases	461	461	430	430	400
Tax and dividends payable	—	345	776	842	980
Redeemable preference shares	750	750	750	750	750
Ordinary shareholders funds	5240	6134	6589	7171	7817
Capital employed	9201	10396	11190	11785	12516

Notes
1. Forecast prepared by Jack Summerscale and Chris Wells of de Zoete and Bevan.
2. Forecast figures, since the full year results for 1984 were not yet available at this time.
3. Balance sheet figures estimated from de Zoete forecasts.

years. Although the preference shares would represent a prior charge to the shareholders, the preference dividends could nevertheless be passed in times of financial distress, without precipitating insolvency, although this seemed an unlikely scenario in the case of BT. Nevertheless, this feature of preference shares did mean that financial analysts were somewhat split in the way they calculated debt ratios. Kleinworts advised that many commentators would probably treat the preference shares as debt in calculating gearing and coverage ratios, but that there was sufficient division and ambiguity here to be exploited. The government's view was summed up by Sir Gordon Downey, the Comptroller and Auditor General, who said,

> the government considered that the preference shares would be regarded as shareholders' funds and so would reduce the debt ratio while guaranteeing the government a prior claim to a fixed level of dividend comparable to a return on debt. These shares would not add to the market value of equity, which had to be restricted if 51 per cent of it was to be marketed successfully.

The government had already made one additional concession, namely that the new, fixed interest rate, unsecured loan stock 'portfolio' would be somewhat 'longer' in terms of maturity than BT's existing debt (see Exhibit 7 for a summary of the proposed amounts, coupons, and maturity dates for the new loan stocks). Furthermore, the government had agreed that BT would be able to 'roll over' any of the loans maturing between 1985 and 1989, and exchange them for any of the stocks with redemption dates between 1990 and 2006. This was to ensure that BT was not faced with massive debt repayments during its period of heavy capital expenditure. When these loans did become repayable, they would need to be refinanced with sterling debt, given that BT's earnings came almost entirely from the United Kingdom. The largely dormant domestic corporate fixed interest market meant that BT would have to rely heavily on the medium-term bank loan market. This had raised doubts about the amount of debt that could be refinanced in the London market at any one time. The old NLF loans had a very 'lumpy' repayment schedule, and to avoid aggravating the refinancing problem, the government had agreed that the new maturity schedule would be 'smoothed out' over time (see Exhibit 7).

However, there was to be no concession on interest rates. As the new loan stocks would be private-sector, unsecured debt, the government made it clear that they would carry commercial coupon rates, ranging from 12.75 per cent for the shorter-dated loans, to 12.25 per cent for the longer-dated stocks (see Exhibit 7). The government was able to borrow at lower rates than this, and the corresponding yields on high coupon gilts at the time were 11.1 per cent for shorts and 10.6 per cent for longs. This helped to reduce the economic value of the debt write-off, according to government documents outlining the 'cost to the Exchequer' of the government's latest proposal. Thus although the proposed balance sheet value of unsecured loans was £2750 million, the government estimated that the 'NPV' was actually £3092 million. This was calculated by

Exhibit 7: *Proposed structure of long-term loans*

(a) Details of proposed unsecured loan stocks

Interest rate (per cent)	Maturity date	Amount (£ million)	Interest rate (per cent)	Maturity date	Amount (£ million)
12.75	1985	44	12.50	1997	130
	1986	61		1998	130
	1987	53		1999	140
	1988	23		2000	150
	1989	85	12.25	2001	160
12.50	1990	92		2002	170
	1991	100		2003	180
	1992	106		2004	190
	1993	113		2005	210
	1994	124		2006	229
	1995	130	Total		2750
	1996	130			

(b) Breakdown of long-term loans by maturity date

Maturity dates	Original NLF loans		Proposed new unsecured loans		Long-term foreign loans[1]	
	Amount (£ million)	Per cent of total	Amount (£ million)	Per cent of total	Amount (£ million)	Per cent of total
Within 5 years	341	12	266	10	198	63
In 5–10 years	804	29	535	19	115	37
In 10–15 years	1130	41	660	24	—	—
In 15–20 years	401	14	850	31	—	—
After 20 years	114	4	439	16	—	—
Total	2790	100	2750	100	313	100

Note
1. The revised balance sheet would involve no change in foreign loans.

discounting the cash flows from the debt at the government's borrowing rate. Similar calculations were carried out for the proposed preference shares, and the original NLF loans and pension fund liability. These showed that, although the revised proposals involved writing off £540 million of debt in book value terms, the reduction in NPV was only £369 million (see Exhibit 8).

BT senior management met to consider the government's debt and preference shares proposal. The government claimed that this package went a long way towards meeting BT's concerns, and corresponded to a debt ratio of only 45–50

Exhibit 8: *Book value and NPV of debt under the proposed new capital structure*

Before/after changes	Security	Value at 31 March 1984 (£ million) Book value	NPV
Before changes	NLF loans	2790	2747
	Pension fund liability	1250	1525
	Total	4040	4272
After changes	Unsecured loans	2750	3092
	Preference shares	750	811
	Total	3500	3903
Difference	Reduction in debt	540	369

Source: Report by the Comptroller and Auditor General, HC 495, 1984–85

per cent (excluding preference, and as at 31 March 1985). BT management would still have preferred a lower level of debt. Furthermore, preference shares, with their tax inefficiency and hybrid nature, were not securities which BT would have chosen, although BT did appreciate the presentational arguments. They were acutely aware, however, that this issue had to be resolved quickly if they were to meet their privatization deadline. If they could agree on capital structure, they could then move on to the key remaining questions, namely dividend policy, and the pricing and marketing of the shares.

17. Williams (Hot Stampers) (A)

For some time the directors of Caversham Holdings had been concerned about the performance of one of their main subsidiary companies, Williams (Hot Stampers) Ltd. Williams manufactured brass stampings and associated non-ferrous products. Roughly half of its sales represented jobbing contracts to an established customer base, with no customer representing more than 4 per cent of total company sales. The other half of sales consisted of standard products such as stopcocks, gate valves and compression fittings for brass water fittings sold to the plumbing/heating trade. These activities were split between two manufacturing sites. The standard products were concentrated in a small factory in Birmingham, and the special contracts were handled by a second factory in Redditch. A combined total of just over a hundred people were employed on the two sites.

The processes involved in hot stamping production are as follows. Once a design and price have been agreed, dies and tools are made. Brass or copper rod is cut into small billets, which are heated to the correct temperature and then stamped to shape in presses capable of exerting forces of up to 900 tons. The excess material around the stampings is clipped away once they are cold. Other drilling, burnishing, and machining processes follow, depending on the nature of the item. Valves and stopcocks are assembled from components manufactured in this way. A final inspection stage precedes the despatch of the finished product.

In their promotional material, Williams (Hot Stampers) declared they provided

A service for non-ferrous components for use within industry. The company undertakes jobbing contracts for top quality hot stampings, unmachined or machined plus cold turned parts and fully assembled products. The work embraces industrial and

This case was written by Stewart Hodges, as a basis for class discussion, rather than to illustrate either effective or ineffective handling of an administrative situation. We are grateful to David White for material, suggestions and permission to publish the case.

domestic work for the water, refrigeration, gas, oil and automative industries, plus fancy and decorative goods. These high value purchases require careful study to find the right supplier, and it is important to consider the capability offered. . . [Williams are] capable of meeting the requirements of modern industry with standards compatible to BS 5750. Supplier assessment, continuous production and quality control throughout all stages of manufacture ensure customer quality requirements are met in full.

The process advantages of hot stamping were claimed to be low cost; high volume; freedom from tool charges in quantity; dimensional accuracy and complicated shapes in one operation; reduction of machining to a minimum; reduction in waste and inspection; freedom from porosity; good surface finish; favourable mechanical properties; resistance to corrosion and wear; long life; and good electrical and thermal conductivity.

The industry contained numerous small capacity brass stampers, and some larger group operations which had benefited from investment in new technology. The market was becoming increasingly competitive, particularly on the standard lines, where cheap Italian imports were rather threatening. Williams' existing management was old and traditional and new leadership was required to adapt to this challenge. A new managing director, David White, was appointed in March 1980. Prior to joining Williams he had held posts progressing from Team Engineer Group Leader and Projects Manager, to Engineering Manager, embracing trouble-shooting engineering and full commercial activity in an international business organization.

As luck would have it, the market for Williams' products collapsed almost immediately after White was appointed. Monthly sales of standard products fell by about 60 per cent in 2 months and sales of specials declined by 40 per cent in the same period. This was due to an industry wide destocking and affected all companies in the industry. Throughout the summer of 1980 there was no improvement in the standard parts business, while the special products showed a further decline. By September it had become evident that the company would have excess capacity for a considerable period and that the split site operation was a major handicap. It was therefore decided to consolidate all production to the Redditch site which would be capable of meeting the requirements of the entire existing customer base. The 1980 accounts, which cover the year to 31 December, reflect the state of the company immediately after the closure of the Birmingham factory but before the facilities were entirely consolidated at Redditch in the first quarter of 1981 (Exhibits 1, 2 and 3). These accounts also reflect substantial expenditure which had been made on dies and tools needed to develop a new product range and on plant refurbishment to ensure confident production plans.

The move entailed a number of redundancies reducing the numbers employed to little more than a third of their original size. Key staff were retained and it was expected that this should secure the customer base if prices, service and quality could be maintained. The success of this would depend on

Exhibit 1: *Williams (Hot Stampers) balance sheet as at 31 December (£)*

Fixed assets	*1980*		*1979*	
Leasehold property		3 026		3 554
Plant and machinery		241 442		207 438
Fixtures and fittings		24 504		9 595
Motor vehicles		26 220		15 804
		295 192		236 391
Current assets				
Stock and work in progress	480 113		426 362	
Due from holding company	0		9 425	
Sundry debtors	303 259		426 591	
Cash in hand	512		355	
	783 883		862 733	
Less: Current liabilities				
Sundry creditors	509 600		621 705	
Bank overdraft secured	15 918		310 727	
Amount due to holding company	978 089		0	
	1 503 608		932 432	
Net current liabilities		(719 725)		(69 698)
		(424 533)		166 693
Loan repayable within 5 years (secured)	44 660		88 220	
Less: Deferred taxation	0		16 360	
		44 660		104 580
		(469 193)		62 113
Financed by				
Share capital	74 030		74 030	
(Deficiency)/surplus on profit and loss account		(543 223)		(11 917)
		(469 193)		62 113

recovery. The rapid fall in market size had left a glut of standard products on the market and the buying emphasis was on price. Despite the rationalization of the manufacturing facilities business was rather desperate throughout the

Exhibit 2: *Williams (Hot Stampers) manufacturing trading and profit and loss account (£)*

	1980		1979	
Sales		1 464 312		1 854 861
Less: Cost of materials used	970 988		1 150 328	
Wages and national insurance	300 400		394 965	
Power	32 971		33 942	
Sundry works expenses	8 821		16 187	
Consumable tools	13 459		16 104	
Dies and tools	41 491		44 789	
Plant and die repairs	36 299		5 355	
	1 404 428		1 661 669	
Gross profit		59 884		193 192
Less: Establishment charges				
Management charge	2 200		3 696	
Rent, rates and water	27 665		24 143	
Lighting and heating	1 735		1 786	
Telephone	7 315		5 555	
Salaries	65 512		68 027	
Stationery and postage	4 596		5 580	
Insurance	14 311		13 247	
Pension scheme contributions	10 088		9 435	
Sundries	1 931		4 700	
		135 352		136 170
Selling and distribution charges				
Discount allowed	1 181		11 157	
Advertising	7 730		2 751	
Carriage and packing	20 882		26 931	
Travel and entertaining	17 383		14 423	
Provision for doubtful debts	1 341		2 771	
Sales commission	10 690		7 847	
		59 208		65 881
Other charges				
Professional charges	1 076		2 713	
Repairs and maintenance	14 077		1 997	
Bank charges	0		282	
Engineering training board levy	0		2 639	
		15 153		7 630
Total charges		209 712		209 681
Trading (loss) profit for the year		(149 828)		(16 489)

Exhibit 3: *Williams (Hot Stampers) profit and loss account for year ended 31 December (£)*

		1980		1979
Turnover (based on sales less returns adjusted for movement in work in progress)		1 464 312		1 854 861
Trading (loss)/profit for the year		(149 828)		(16 489)
Auditors remuneration	4 318		3 501	
Interest	114 964		28 865	
Leasing	4 257		12 125	
Directors remuneration[1]	41 509		15 257	
Depreciation	57 487		25 506	
		(222 534)		(85 254)
Net (loss)/profit for the year		(372 362)		(101 743)
Taxation		16 360		(16 130)
Net (loss)/profit after taxation		(356 002)		(117 874)
Extraordinary items[2]		(175 304)		0
Net (loss)/profit after taxation and extraordinary items		(531 306)		(117 874)
Balance brought forward		(11 917)		105 956
Balance carried forward		(543 223)		(11 917)

Notes
1. Directors remuneration for 1980 includes compensation for loss of office.
2. Extraordinary items consist of redundancy payments net of government rebate, £52 736; removal and setting up of plant, £24 075; and stock reduction following reorganization, £98 493.

integration with the workers moved from the Birmingham site. At the beginning of 1981 the market remained unstable with no clear indication of summer of 1981. Accordingly it came as little surprise to David White to be told in September by the Chairman of Caversham that 'We have decided that the best thing to do is to sell Williams.' However, he was surprised when the Chairman continued, 'We have decided to sell it to you.'

Caversham Holdings was engaged in factoring metal products, but did not need Williams to manufacture them. The annual turnover of Caversham was about £20 million, excluding Williams, with little dependence on intercompany work. Caversham's management could not see a very optimistic future for retaining Williams within the group. Equally, the alternative of simply closing Williams down was unattractive as there were lease obligations on the Redditch site extending to 1997 and amounting to about £20 000 a year. In addition, rates on the property would amount to roughly £13 000 a year. There was no real prospect of a third party sale, even though in careful hands, it was felt that there

Exhibit 4: *Williams (Brass Products) cash flow forecasts as at October 1981 (£000)*

Cash flows	November –December 1981	January– March 1982	April– June 1982	July– September 1982	October– December 1982	Total 1981–2
Receipts	—	169	249	231	241	890
Less Payments:						
Suppliers	9	126	187	162	182	666
Caversham	—	9	13	13	13	48
Payroll/overhead	30	48	53	58	58	247
Capital expenditure	10	—	—	—	—	10
Bank interest	—	—	3	—	3	6
Total payments	49	183	256	233	256	977
Quarterly surplus	(49)	(14)	(7)	(2)	(15)	(87)
Cumulative surplus	(49)	(63)	(70)	(72)	(87)	(87)

Cash flows	January– March 1983	April– June 1983	July– September 1983	October– December 1983	Total 1983
Receipts	256	288	252	272	1068
Less Payments:					
Suppliers	145	206	192	210	753
Caversham	13	13	13	14	53
Payroll/overhead	57	60	63	65	245
Bank interest	—	4	—	3	7
Total payments	215	283	268	292	1058
Quarterly surplus	41	5	(16)	(20)	10
Cumulative surplus	(46)	(41)	(57)	(77)	(77)

could still be a viable business. This was the reasoning which had led them to suggest a management buyout.

After a little work, the following terms for the buyout emerged. The Redditch premises would be taken over by a new company, which would be called Williams (Brass Products) Limited, in November 1981. The parent company would continue to pay the full property rental for the first 2 years, and thereafter it would pay reducing amounts over the next 2 years. By 1986 the new company would have taken over the full payments. Similarly, the responsibility for the rates would be transferred over a 2 year period. For the use of plant, fixtures

Exhibit 5: *Williams (Brass Products) projected accounts as at October 1981 (£000)*

Projected accounts	14 months to December 1982		12 months to December 1983	
Profit and loss account				
Sales		1120		1093
Materials		817		795
Gross profit		303		298
Less				
Payroll	176		166	
Rent of plant	6		6	
Overheads	83		79	
Bank interest	6	271	7	258
Net profit before tax		32		40
Projected balance sheet at end of accounting period				
Fixed assets				
Motor vehicles		10		10
Current assets				
Stock	103		106	
Trade debtors	230		255	
Cash	—		—	
	333		361	
Current liabilities				
Creditors	167		213	
Caversham	57		9	
	224		222	
Net current assets		109		139
		119		149
Presented by				
Needed funds		87		77
Retained surplus		32		72
		119		149

and fittings, the new company would pay a rental of £6000 per annum, with an option to purchase in December 1984 or to renegotiate a fresh rental arrangement. In order to commence business the new company would require about £110 000 worth of stock of finished goods and work in progress, and it

Exhibit 6: *The prospects for Williams (Brass Products) as at October 1981*

The trade recession in 1980 affected all brass-based operations and threatened the continued existence of the company. The solution was to combine production into the Redditch site in the first quarter of 1981. Key staff were retained though necessary redundancies took place. The market remained depressed through 1981.

The holding company, Caversham, had decided to terminate involvement and it is proposed that the established customer base with existing goodwill will ensure viable ongoing trading by a new company, Williams (Brass Products) Ltd.

Product base
Service activity for hot brass/copper stampings to contracts specification. Work secured by direct orders and current order book value *circa* £220 000.

Also supplies standard plumbing/heating products. Competitive national market penetration through full-time sales representatives and sales agents. Manufactured items supplemented by factoring activity of cheaper imports.

Background
Established over 50 years with monthly peak activity of £195 000 in 1980, and has an excellent name for quality and service. No business was lost by the consolidation to the Wolverhampton site. Market for standard products eroded by cheaper imports. Diversification into new lines of fittings in 1980 supplemented activity and now increasingly recognized.

The viability of the business is supported by the following:

Contract work
1. Sales margin improved by better manufacturing methods:
   gas fired furnaces (newly established);
   automatic feed;
   subcontract machining.
2. A broadly diversified customer base of 'blue chip' customers, and a good trading name.
3. Strong inhouse expertise retained. Personnel with 10 or more years experience for major functions of estimation, inspection, stamping, clipping, distribution and management.

Standard lines
1. New product range is better established.
2. Cheaper material and import sources established.
3. Subassembly purchase has potential to significantly improve margin for increased sales.
4. Good trading name.

D. White, October 1981

was agreed that this could be paid for by monthly payments of £4400. When business commenced, a mixed ledger would be maintained so that outstanding receivables could be collected while new sales were being obtained. Caversham would also sell the existing motor vehicles to the new company for £10 000. No other significant financial considerations were involved.

The only remaining obstacle was to obtain suitable financing for the new company. The managers concerned had less than £10 000 to contribute as equity, and although some property was available to back personal guarantees, this would fall short of the level of borrowing contemplated. Two banks were approached, Caversham Holdings' bank and another bank. Caversham already had a considerable amount of bank borrowing (almost £2 million). Given this level of gearing, Caversham's bank was quite interested in arranging for Williams to be spun off. In order to determine the amount and type of financing that was required and to assist the banks to appraise the situation, a set of financial projections was prepared for the following 2 years on the basis of the assumptions outlined above. These are appended as Exhibits 4 and 5, together with a brief statement of the main issues affecting Williams' business prospects (Exhibit 6).

PART F

VALUATION OF CORPORATE LIABILITIES

18. Redland

In March 1985, Gareth Jones, Redland's Treasurer, looked out beyond the tiled roofs of surburban Reigate at the rolling Surrey countryside in the distance, and thought about the telex he had just received from Morgan Stanley.

Some months had now passed since the 1984 Finance Act had introduced new tax rules for zero-coupon sterling corporate bonds. The new legislation had created an asymmetry whereby although borrowers/issuers obtained an annual tax deduction for the 'interest' element, bond holders/investors did not incur any tax liability until the bond was either sold or redeemed.

Despite the apparent tax attractions, there had been little interest to date, and no zeros had been issued by UK companies. However, in March 1985, the government announced that legislation would be introduced to end gilt 'bond washing' (see below). Within days, Gareth had received a telex from Morgan Stanley offering to lead manage a zero-coupon issue on Redland's behalf.

Background and history

Redland began business in 1920 as a manufacturer of concrete roof tiles. Today, roof tiles still remain the company's most important product, and Redland is the world's largest manufacturer. The company has also expanded into clay and slate roof cladding materials, clay bricks and into building aggregates where, in the United Kingdom, it is one of the half-dozen largest producers, owning the largest hardrock quarry in Europe. The company's recent performance is summarized in Exhibit 1.

In May 1982, Redland made a major acquisition by purchasing Cawoods, for the equivalent of £118 million (by the issue of 73 million Redland shares, implying a bid premium of 37 per cent for Cawoods). Cawoods was engaged in UK coal and oil distribution, as well as aggregates, ready mixed concrete, and a

This case was written by Mike Staunton under the supervision of Paul Marsh as a basis for class discussion rather than to illustrate either effective or ineffective handling of an administrative situation.

Exhibit 1: *Redland 10 year financial summary for year ending 31 March (£ million)[1]*

	1976	1977	1978	1979	1980	1981	1982	1983	1984	1985[4]
UK sales	95.9	102.8	114.1	129.7	160.8	163.6	454.5	492.8	555.3	560
Overseas sales	89.2	131.2	156.4	175.8	236.1	226.4	263.8	306.3	345.0	390
Share of associates	55.5	75.3	89.0	91.5	98.1	125.2	219.6	260.3	283.9	290
Total sales	240.6	309.3	359.5	397.0	495.0	515.2	937.9	1059.4	1184.2	1240
UK profit	14.0	14.2	15.4	17.6	20.2	18.9	33.7	41.7	50.7	50
Overseas profit	10.2	14.3	16.6	18.8	32.4	22.6	17.0	16.2	29.8	40
Share of associates	4.6	7.5	9.3	10.9	10.7	10.9	12.9	14.3	20.1	25
Operating profit	28.8	36.0	41.3	47.3	63.3	52.4	63.6	72.2	100.6	115
Net interest payable	(2.1)	(1.4)	(1.4)	(2.1)	(6.0)	(5.6)	(3.8)	(5.9)	(6.8)	(10)
Pretax profit	26.7	34.6	39.9	45.2	57.3	46.8	59.8	66.3	93.8	105
Tax	(12.4)	(15.3)	(16.0)	(16.2)	(23.0)	(21.5)	(24.6)	(26.2)	(34.7)	(35)
Minority interests	(2.8)	(3.9)	(4.8)	(5.6)	(9.1)	(5.8)	(4.6)	(5.0)	(7.6)	(10)
Attributable profit	11.5	15.4	19.1	23.4	25.2	19.5	30.6	35.1	51.5	60
Net assets	1a3.0	147.9	170.9	194.3	223.4	229.0	328.6	419.5	438.3	505
Return on capital[2]										
historic cost	24.7	26.7	25.8	24.8	28.9	23.1	22.2	21.0	23.9	25
current cost	12.7	13.1	13.7	14.0	15.8	11.4	12.0	12.9	17.0	19
Ordinary shares										
issued (millions)	90.8	91.4	95.0	96.0	121.6	122.2	196.6	209.4	209.7	214
Earnings per share[3]	10.6	13.5	16.3	19.6	20.9	15.9	15.7	17.5	24.6	28
Dividends per share[3]	4.2	4.6	5.1	7.6	9.5	10.5	10.5	11.5	13.6	14
Assets per share[3]	61.9	73.7	85.2	95.1	100.3	110.3	100.9	116.9	125.4	130
Price per share[3]	103	99	140	194	151	185	184	248	300	288

Notes
1. Redland plc merged with Cawoods Holdings Limited in May 1982. Sales and profits for 1981–82 onwards include the results for Cawoods for the whole of these years, computed in accordance with the principles of merger accounting.
2. The return on capital employed is calculated as the ratio of profit before tax plus interest paid to average total assets less current liabilities plus bank overdrafts. It is expressed as a percentage.
3. Earnings, gross dividends and assets per share and the share price are all in pence and are all adjusted to reflect the rights issue in 1975–76 (1 for 7 at 67p per share) and the capitalization issue in 1979–80 (1 for 4).
4. In 1984–85 the accounting policy for the translation of overseas profits and losses was changed to the average rate method and figures for 1984–85 and 1983–84 reflect this change. Profits and losses for earlier years are based on the closing rate method and have not been restated. The figures for 1984–85 were estimated as at 27 March 1985.

number of peripheral activities which were subsequently sold. The acquisition of Cawoods provided a diversification into fuel distribution, as well as the integration of complementary aggregates and ready mixed concrete businesses. In addition, it brought tax advantages for Redland which, with two-thirds of its profits earned overseas, had unrelieved advanced corporation tax. Since the acquisition, half of Redland's sales and profits had been in the United Kingdom, with fuel distribution now accounting for 25 per cent of turnover and 7 per cent of total operating costs. The remaining 75 per cent of Redland's turnover was in building materials, split approximately 70 per cent in tiles and bricks, and 30 per cent in aggregates. Roof tiles accounted for approximately 55 per cent of current profits, with aggregates contributing 26 per cent.

Over the years, Redland had also expanded its operations overseas to over 30 countries, with licenses in a further 20 countries. Overseas subsidiaries now accounted for half the group's profits and sales, and nearly two-thirds of its assets. The largest contributors to overseas earnings were Continental Europe (56 per cent), North America (20 per cent) and Australia and the Far East (14 per cent). In Continental Europe, Redland had a 56 per cent stake in Braas, a building materials manufacturer and supplier, which ranked as the largest producer of concrete roof tiles in Germany. It also jointly owned RBB Europa, the largest producer of building materials in the Netherlands. In 1983, Redland extended its North American interests by acquiring McDonough Brothers (now renamed Redland Worth Corporation), which owned and operated one of the ten largest crushed stone quarries in America, located in Texas.

The treasurer's role

For a group with nearly 12 000 employees, Redland had a very lean head office administration. The UK management board had only five members (including the Finance Director), and was supported by nine small corporate functions. Three of these, Treasury, Accounting and Taxation, were concerned with financial decision-making.

The Treasury Department was responsible for financial planning, financing decisions, banking relationships, cash management, and foreign exchange exposure. Despite this impressive array of responsibilities, Gareth Jones described his prime role quite simply as being 'to ensure that Redland doesn't run out of money, and that all parts of the group are well supplied with cash when needed'.

Cash and liabilities were managed and monitored in a number of ways. Weekly borrowing figures were supplemented by the provision of monthly cash flow forecasts and management accounts to the board. Gareth Jones was a firm believer in the importance of cash generation ('the only thing you can't cheat on') as an indicator of business performance, and felt he had a clear notion of the relationship between cash generation and profits growth. Liability management policy was reviewed at a monthly meeting, involving the Finance Director, Gareth Jones and an outside merchant bank adviser.

Another important responsibility was the management of the group's foreign exchange exposure, both in terms of transaction and translation exposure. Transaction exposure arises in the normal course of international trade because of the exchange rate fluctuations which can occur during the interval between signing contracts or delivering goods, and the date of payment. Translation exposure, on the other hand, arises from the uncertainty about the exchange rates at which the financial statements of foreign subsidiaries, and any corporate liabilities denoted in foreign currency, will be translated into sterling for consolidation purposes. While the treasury management of overseas subsidiaries was centralized within Redland, there was very little transaction exposure, given the minimal cross-border trade. Gareth's major focus, therefore, was on translation exposure.

Cash planning and budgeting was carried out on a rolling, 12 months ahead basis. Gareth was dubious about the benefits of extending this beyond a 1 year horizon, given the cyclicality of Redland's business, and general economic uncertainty. He argued that the current system provided considerable flexibility, allowing Redland to adjust budgets and capital expenditure plans depending on the economic outcome.

One of Gareth's most important functions in planning financial requirements was not only to anticipate cash needs, but also to select the cheapest and most appropriate forms of funding to meet these cash requirements.

Financing costs and borrowing policy

Gareth Jones argued:

> People have been slow to realize that the cost of debt is cheaper than the cost of equity at present levels of interest rates. For instance, with long term sterling interest rates of 11 per cent, the after tax cost of debt (based on an average tax rate of 33 per cent) would be 7.4 per cent. Whereas with Redland's current earnings per share (e.p.s.) of 28p and share price of 288p, the cost of equity would be 9.7 per cent ($28/288 \times 100$ per cent) for this year and, if e.p.s. rose to 31p, the cost of equity would be nearly 11 per cent next year. Since debt is significantly cheaper than equity, it is therefore possible to increase e.p.s. by borrowing, in addition to benefiting from the greater flexibility of debt.

Partly because of this, Redland had not had a rights issue since 1975. Commenting on this, Gareth argued that 'rights issues for general corporate purposes are not a good idea, since without the promise of additional earnings, all they do is dilute shareholders' equity. In contrast, when we finance a specific acquisition with equity, we are saying to shareholders that we see an opportunity to increase earnings by buying assets.' He felt that one of the problems with issuing equity was that it made sense only if market conditions were right. Thus depending on the level and recent performance of both

Redland's own share price, and also the Stock Market as a whole, there would be times when equity would simply be ruled out. He added:

> Around the time of the McDonough acquisition, we wouldn't like to have issued equity had we not believed that our shares were fairly valued then. We are reluctant to issue equity at times when we believe our shares are undervalued (for example, if the current share price is 230p but the price half a year ago was 300p). Equity is also, by its nature, only available to Redland in sterling.

However, as part of his prime responsibility, Gareth had to ensure that the equity market would always be available should, for instance, Redland seek to fund an acquisition with shares. Hence, over time, the growth in real terms of the dividend per share was viewed as an important objective for Redland. He was also conscious that the level of dividend increase was viewed by the Stock Market as a management signal about future prospects. Gareth argued that Redland would be reluctant to see the dividend cover fall below two and, if the financial stability of Redland was seriously threatened, he would be prompted to recommend a cut in the dividend. He was, however, aware that such a fall could cut off equity as a source of finance.

Redland's 'gearing' (net debt/book equity) ratio rose rapidly prior to 1982, reaching 42 per cent in March 1982. However, the all-equity financed acquisition of Cawoods (involving an increase of 60 per cent in Redland's share capital) reduced gearing to under 25 per cent, in which range it had remained (Exhibit 2). While there had been no rights issues, the two recent major acquisitions of McDonough (in January 1983) and Rosemary Brick and Tile (in October 1984) were financed mainly by equity (the former with 12 million shares and £22 million cash, the latter with 4.5 million shares and £4 million cash). This increase in equity had been counterbalanced by the use of US debt to fund capital expenditure for Redland Worth.

Redland did have a target gearing ratio, although Gareth saw little purpose in making the actual figure public, since this could make Redland a hostage to fortune. In addition, Redland considered net interest cover and cash flow cover measures to be important. Gareth argued that with post-depreciation annual cash flows of £40 million you could quite easily afford £120 million of debt, since you could pay it all back in 3 years. In the past he admitted to being more circumspect about increasing debt, given its sensitivity to interest rate movements, but he was now more tolerant about higher gearing.

In January 1984 Redland obtained an A1/P1 credit rating (the highest normally given to a non-US company) which enabled it to issue up to US$75 million of commercial paper in New York. The company expected to issue paper to replace more expensive bank borrowings in the US, thereby saving ½ per cent per annum in interest costs. Robert Napier, the Finance Director, commented 'the issue of commercial paper is an important step towards gaining greater recognition for Redland by the US investment community. Later we

245

Exhibit 2: *Summary of Redland's financing*

(a) Gearing movements for year ending 31 March

	1981	1982	1983	1984	1985
Gross debt (£ million)	49.9	73.6	97.2	89.2	118.5
Net debt (£ million) OUTSTANDING	31.3	68.8	59.6	52.3	64.9
Gross funds from operations (£ million)	63.0	58.8	92.9	115.6	129.0
Equity, book value (£ million)	134.8	163.3	244.7	263.0	285.5
Exchange rates:					
US dollar/£	2.23	1.79	1.46	1.44	1.24
DM/£	4.71	4.28	3.53	3.74	3.81

(b) Borrowing

(i) Gross borrowing by currency (£ million)

	1984	1985
Sterling	(16.8)	9.5
Dollar	99.1	101.2
Other	6.9	7.8
Total	89.2	118.5

(ii) Proportion of borrowings at fixed rather than floating rates

March 1983:	30 per cent
January 1984:	over 75 per cent
March 1985:	66 per cent

(c) Prices of quoted Redland loan stocks

Loan stock	Price quotes	Last trade	Maturity dates	Interest payments
6.25 per cent Debenture stock 1980–85	£93–£98	£94.5 (9/84)	October 85	April and October
6.25 per cent Debenture stock 1988–93	£69–£74	£67.5 (8/84)	April 93	April and October
7.5 per cent Debenture stock 1990–95	£73–£78	£75.25 (3/85)	March 95	March and September

Source: Stock Exchange Daily Official List, 27 March 1985

(d) Risk measures for Redland shares*

Beta	1.14
Variability	28 per cent
Specific risk	20 per cent

*Source:** London Business School *Risk Measurement Service* 31 March 1985

may want to raise long-term debt or even get our shares quoted in the US. We are very keen on the US where 30 per cent of our capital is employed.'

Gareth preferred borrowing to be fixed rate, in order to bring an element of certainty into matters. Also in January 1984 therefore, Redland signed a number of interest rate swap agreements, with the result that two-thirds of its dollar debt was at fixed rates of interest. David Lyon, Redland's Managing Director, commented at the time:

> What we achieve by the swaps is that we fix our interest cost at around 11½ per cent. If US interest rates are below 11½ per cent, then the construction industry demand is strong and we are earning profits to pay the premium. We are protecting ourselves against the possibility — or the probability — that during the next 8 years interest rates may go substantially above present levels.

Exhibit 2 gives a breakdown of Redland's borrowing by currencies, as well as the proportions of fixed and floating rate debt. Gareth explained that the build up of US dollar debt had coincided with capital expenditure funding needs for Redland Worth at a time when Redland took the view that the dollar would not continue to strengthen. He stressed that he would always want such dollar debt to be more than covered by US assets.

The zero-coupon issue

A zero-coupon bond consists of an obligation by the issuer to repay the nominal (or face) amount at some fixed future date. No interest payments are involved and the return to the holder comes in the form of the uplift from the discounted initial price to the nominal value. This means, for example, that a 7 year zero-coupon bond sold to yield 10 per cent per annum would sell for $100/(1+0.10)^7$ or 51.32 per cent.

Approximately US$19 billion (nominal amount) of zeros have been issued since 1981, roughly half being purchased by Japanese investors, who until recently could realize tax-free capital gains. German private investors also derive a tax deferment advantage by holding zero-coupon debt. Following the virtual evaporation of the US domestic corporate zero market after the passing of US legislation in 1982, most zero-coupon bonds had been issued in the euromarkets (for a description of these, see below, pp. 249–50) with volume rising from $470 million in 1983 to $1650 million in 1984. While neither the zero coupon nor the eurosterling markets were large in relation to total euromarket issues (Exhibit 3), Gareth Jones believed there would be a reasonable prospect of being able to issue a eurosterling zero, particularly given the potential tax attractions to UK investors.

There had been no prior issues of this kind, perhaps because UK investors had previously preferred other forms of tax-efficient investment. One popular vehicle had been offshore roll-up funds which effectively turned interest income

Exhibit 3: *Capital market volumes*

(a) UK Corporate issue markets (UK and foreign company issues)

(i) Average annual amounts (£ million)

Period	Debt	Equity	Total	Debt (per cent)	Private bank borrowing
1961–64	207	252	459	45	na
1965–68	397	163	560	71	373
1969–72	348	308	656	53	1365
1973–76	98	680	778	13	2951
1977–80	95	806	901	11	4275
1981–84	1142	1975	3117	37	5256

(ii) Recent annual levels (£ million)

	1981	1982	1983	1984
UK companies				
Equity	2224	1198	2451	2026
Publicly quoted debt	375	931	420	447
Overseas subsidiaries of UK companies (eurosterling) debt	—	85	106	715
Foreign companies debt (eurosterling and bulldog)	65	100	233	1092
Total	2664	2314	3210	4280
Bank borrowing (for comparison)	5847	6568	1445	7162

Source: Midland Bank Review

(b) Euromarkets (total value of issues) in US $ million*

	1981	1982	1983	1984
International bonds	52 985	78 042	76 329	107 411
of which:				
Sterling eurobonds	501	748	1 947	3 997
Sterling foreign bonds	746	1 214	811	1 292

Source: * Morgan Guaranty Trust Co. of New York.

into capital gains, but legislation to curb this loophole had been announced in September 1983. An alternative mechanism was so-called gilt bond washing. This was the practice whereby investors reduced their income tax burden by buying a gilt-edged stock just after the dividend had been paid, and selling just before a subsequent dividend was due, when the price had risen to reflect the forthcoming payout.

Shortly after the government announced new legislation to end bond washing in February 1985, Morgan Stanley telexed three of their coporate contacts known to be interested in the zero-coupon concept, and Redland was the most positive respondent. The invitation was tempting, as a zero-coupon issue appeared, to Gareth, to be a cheap means of funding as well as an opportunity to re-establish Redland's name in the euromarkets. Gareth was also concerned about Redland's high proportion of dollar debt. A sterling zero-coupon issue could be used to repay floating-rate US debt. Finally, Gareth felt that this would be a cheap issue to manage. To switch currencies would involve only one foreign exchange contract, and the paying agent costs should be low as there were no coupon payments and just one final payment on maturity.

An equity issue was not contemplated, as there was no specific acquisition in mind and also because equity was regarded as more expensive than debt. While a domestic bond issue was considered, Gareth believed that the novelty of the zero-coupon feature could involve Redland in unnecessarily demanding conditions — either security might have been required, or alternatively, inflexible covenants might have been imposed.

As shown in Exhibit 3, the domestic corporate bond market had been an important source of funds throughout the 1960s (accounting for approximately 60 per cent of total new issues by companies), particularly following the introduction of Corporation Tax in 1965. However, the 1970s saw the decline of the corporate bond market to a mere 1 per cent of total new issues in 1978, as companies were reluctant to raise fixed interest loans. The subsequent revival had been due mainly to large domestic issues by the financial sector in 1982, and to substantial growth in eurosterling and bulldog issues following the lifting of exchange controls in 1979 (corporate euroissues totalled £1.8 billion in 1984). The UK domestic corporate bond market had been dull by comparison, with 34 issues raising £447 million in 1984, mainly from the financial sector and property companies. Bond issues had also declined in relative importance as a source of funds for companies — bank borrowing had risen from about 50 per cent of gross cumulative corporate debt in 1966 to over 80 per cent by 1984.

Gareth perceived, however, that the attitudes of corporate treasurers to long-term debt were changing. Recent management buyouts had demonstrated the value of gearing-up, and he believed that it was safer to do so at fixed rather than floating interest rates. He also strongly believed that a deep and freely accessible sterling corporate debt market was a fundamental element in the long-term success of British industry. While he felt that the government had given only limited encouragement to the corporate debt market, he nevertheless argued that it was encumbent on industry to try to respond to such initiatives.

Redland decided to make an issue in the euromarkets. The euromarkets trade in bonds denominated in the currency of one country but issued in some other country (for example a eurosterling issue is a sterling bond initially offered for sale outside Britain, and a eurodollar issue is a dollar bond offered for sale outside the United States). The same secondary euromarkets also trade in foreign bonds, which, in principle, are sold primarily in the domestic capital market of the currency of issue. An example would be a sterling bond issued by say a US company for initial sale in Britain (colloquially known as a bulldog issue). In practice, however, foreign bond issues are also taken up in large part outside the country in whose currency they are denominated. There are generally two main differences between domestic markets and euromarkets, so far as international investors are concerned. Domestic markets can be restricted by the application of inward exchange controls on foreign investors, and interest payments on domestic bonds are usually made to foreign holders net of withholding tax. An important consideration then is that the euromarkets remain less susceptible to the effects of government regulation of the domestic capital markets.

Gareth Jones felt that Redland would not obtain the best result in the eurodollar market. This was partly because of name recognition, and partly because the eurodollar bond market was accustomed to handling transaction sizes in excess of $100 million, and Redland did not wish to borrow this much. The euro-DM market was a possibility, but Redland did not need the issue proceeds in DM, nor did it wish to increase its DM liabilities. Proceeds from a euro-DM issue would therefore have to be converted into a sterling liability through a swap (effectively, a forward purchase of DM). Thus the eurosterling market with its lack of timing constraints (compared to the domestic bond and equity markets), simple risk-free issuance procedures and tolerant covenants for the company remained the market of Redland's choice (see Exhibit 4 for details of recent eurosterling bond issues). Simon Fraser, who was to handle the issue within Morgan Stanley, explained,

> it is important for euromarket investors to be familiar with the issuer's name, as well as believing that an issue will be traded actively in the future to ensure liquidity. The euromarkets are driven by the degree of international interest, and the level of interest in the eurosterling market is influenced by investors' views on the relative strength of sterling against other European currencies, as well as the absolute level of sterling interest rates.

Once Redland decided to go ahead with the eurosterling issue, Morgan Grenfell were quickly brought in as co-lead manager with Morgan Stanley. Morgan Grenfell had acted on Redland's behalf in the offer for Cawoods, and anyway it was a Bank of England requirement that sterling issues should have at least one UK institution as a co-lead manager. Later it was decided to add Barings (another of Redland's merchant bank advisors) and Warburgs (for their expertise in the eurosterling market). The objective was to form a very strong lead management group (each of the four co-lead managers bought £10 million face value of the issue) and so help ensure the successful market debut of the new instrument.

Redland were thinking in terms of raising about £25 million, which Morgan Stanley felt to be the lower limit for market liquidity. Morgan Stanley would have preferred a larger issue but Redland did not want to have to repay, say, £150 million in 7 years time, and the company eventually decided that the issue

Exhibit 4: *Eurosterling bond issues and yields (as at 27 March 1985)*

Issue year	Issuer	Amount (£ million)	Price (£)	Yield (per cent)
1982	Allied Lyons 12.625 per cent guaranteed bonds 1992	30	102.50	12.1
	Investors in Industry 12.25 per cent guaranteed notes 1988	30	102.00	11.5
	Reed International 16.75 per cent guaranteed bonds 1989	25	105.125	14.9
1983	Investors in Industry 10.50 per cent guaranteed notes 1990 10.75 per cent guaranteed bonds 1993	56	98.125 97.125	11.0 11.3
	BOC 11.75 per cent guaranteed bonds 1991	50	102.875	11.1
1984	Lloyds Bank guaranteed floating rate notes 1996	200	99.875	*
	BAT Industries 10.75 per cent guaranteed notes 1991	100	99.375	10.9
	ICI 8.50 per cent guaranteed convertible bonds 1999	100	110.75	7.3
	Investors in Industry floating rate notes 1994	75	99.375	*
	Yorkshire Bank guaranteed floating rate notes 1994	75	99.875	*
	Grand Metropolitan 10.875 per cent guaranteed notes 1990	50	96.625	11.7
	Four other issuers	115		

*Not given, as current yield to maturity depends on future interest rate movements.
Source: Association of International Bond Dealers

Exhibit 5: *Interest rates (on 27 March 1985)*

BRITISH FUNDS

1984-85 High	Low	Stock	Price £	+ or –	Yield Int.	Yield Red.
		"Shorts" (Lives up to Five Years)				
98 11/32	93 5/16	Treas 3pc 1985	98 15/32	+1/32	3.05	13.55
102 5/8	99 3/16	Treas 11½pc 1985	99 1/2	+1/16	11.56	13.10
99 3/4	96 9/16	Treas 8¾pcCnv '85	98 3/8	+1/16	8.89	12.53
104 3/16	99 5/16	Exch. 12¼pc 1985	99 15/16	+1/8	12.26	12.23
103 13/16	99 1/16	Exch. 11¾pc '86	99 13/16	+1/16	11.77	11.92
102 5/16	96 1/16	Treas. 10pcCnv 1986	98 5/16 xd	......	10.17	11.80
94 1/16	88 1/4	Treas 3pc 1986	93 5/8	+1/8	3.20	8.98
102	96 3/4	Exch. 10½pc Cv '86	98 1/2	+1/16	10.66	11.92
104 3/16	99 1/16	Treas 12pc 1986	100	+1/8	12.00	11.94
98 3/4	93 1/2	Treas 8½pc 1984-86‡‡	96 7/16	+1/4	8.81	11.54
108 13/16	102 7/16	Exch. 14pc 1986	103 1/16 xd	+1/16	13.58	11.87
89 3/4	85	Exch. 2½pc 1986	88 7/8	+1/8	2.81	9.95
107 11/16	100 13/16	Exch. 13¼pc 1987	102 5/16	+1/16	12.95	11.75
100 7/8	94 1/2	Treas 10¼pcCv '87	97 1/2	+3/16	10.51	11.74
87 3/4	83 1/8	Exch 2½pc 1987	87 3/8	+1/16	2.86	9.90
101 3/16	94 1/2	Exch. 10½pc 1987	97 15/16 xd	+3/16	10.72	11.68
92 3/4	87	Funding 6½pc '85-87‡‡	91 1/4 xd	......	7.12	11.34
99 5/8	92 7/8	Treas. 10pc 1987	96 5/8	+3/16	10.35	11.75
86 3/4	81 9/16	Treas 3pc 1987	86 1/8	......	3.48	9.89
105	97 1/4	Treas. 12pc 1987	100 1/2 xd	+7/16	11.94	11.79
94 7/8	87 9/16	Treas 7¾pc 1985-88‡‡	92	+1/4	8.42	11.10
100 3/8	92 11/16	Exch 10½pc '88	96 15/16	+3/16	10.83	11.70
98 7/16	89 15/16	Treas 9¾pc Cv '88	94 11/16	+3/16	10.30	11.76
83 1/2	77	Transport 3pc '78-88	83	+1/8	3.61	9.14
96 15/16	88 5/16	Treas. 9½pc '88	93 1/2 xd	+1/4	10.16	11.80
106 3/4	94 11/16	Treas 11½pc 1989	99 1/2	+1/4	11.56	11.65
96 11/16	87 11/16	Treas 9½pc Cnv. '89	93 5/16 xd	+3/16	10.18	11.63
99 5/8	90 11/16	Treas 10½pc 1989	95 7/8	+1/4	10.95	11.75
100 3/16	88 7/8	Exch.10pc 1989	94 5/16	+3/16	10.60	11.70
101 1/16	94 3/4	Exch 11pc 1989	97 5/16 xd	+1/16	11.29	11.74
85 1/8	77 1/2	Treas 5pc 1986-89	81 3/4 xd	+3/16	6.12	10.10
114 1/8	100 1/8	Treas 13pc 1990‡‡	105 1/4	+3/16	12.35	11.53
97 15/16	96 11/16	Exch 11pc 1990‡‡●	97 3/8	+3/16	11.30	11.70
110 7/8	100 3/4	Exch. 12½pc 1990	103 5/16	+1/4	12.10	11.60
		Five to Fifteen Years				
94 1/8	84 7/8	Treas 8¼pc 1987-90‡‡	91 7/8	+1/4	9.21	10.92
98 15/16	90 5/8	Treas. 10pcCv 1990	92 1/2 xd	+1/4	10.72	11.69
108 1/4	94 3/4	Treas 11¾pc 1991	102 1/2	+3/8	11.75	11.73
84 1/8	75 5/8	Funding 5¾pc '87-91‡‡	82 xd	+1/4	7.00	9.74
105 3/4	93 7/8	Exch. 11pc 1991	96 1/8 xd	+1/8	11.34	11.68
113 3/4	98 7/8	Treas 12¾pc 1992‡‡	107 3/4	+3/8	12.09	11.55
100 5/8	86	Treas 10pc 1992	94 1/4	+1/2	10.72	11.42
101	94 1/16	Treas 10½pc Cv 1992‡‡	100 3/4	+3/8	11.04	11.51
111 1/8	95 1/8	Exch. 12¼pc '92	104 1/8	+3/8	11.88	11.62
117 1/2	104 5/8	Exch 13½pc 1992	108 7/8 xd	+1/2	12.42	11.72
113 5/8	98 1/8	Treas 12½pc 1993‡‡	107 1/4	+3/8	11.93	11.59
79 3/4	71 1/8	Funding 6pc 1993‡‡	78 1/8	+1/4	7.70	9.88
121 3/4	106 3/4	Treas 13¾pc 1993‡‡	115 3/4	+3/8	12.38	11.67
126 3/4	108 1/4	Treas 14½pc 1994‡‡	117 1/8	+3/8	12.49	11.56
120 5/8	106	Exch 13½pc 1994	108 7/8 xd	+3/8	12.27	11.70
114 1/8	96 3/4	Exch. 12½pc 1994	106 1/8	+3/8	11.91	11.62
94 1/2	82 7/8	Treas 9pc 1994‡‡	91	+1/4	10.25	11.09
110 3/8	94 7/8	Treas 12pc 1995	104 3/8	+3/8	11.73	11.58
68 1/8	58 3/4	Gas 3pc '90-95	67 xd	+1/8	4.46	7.73
100 1/4	86	Exch. 10¼pc 1995	94 7/3	+3/8	11.02	11.41
117 7/8	102 5/8	Treas 12¾pc 1995‡‡	112 1/2	+1/2	11.82	11.44
124 1/4	106 7/8	Treas. 14pc '96	117 1/8	+5/8	12.21	11.58
94 3/8	83 1/2	Treas 9pc 1992-96‡‡	87 3/8	+1/4	10.34	11.06
134 7/8	118 1/4	Treas 15¼pc 1996‡‡	121 3/4 xd	+3/4	12.37	11.50
122 1/8	106 1/2	Exch 13¼pc 1996‡‡	116 7/8	+1/2	11.83	11.32
73 1/2	63 1/4	Redemption 3pc 1986-96	73 1/2 xd	......	4.08	6.26
121 3/8	104 1/2	Treas 13¼pc 1997‡‡	114 3/4	+3/4	11.79	11.31
104 1/2	87 3/8	Exch 10½pc 1997	96 1/4	+3/8	11.02	11.23
92 1/2	77 1/2	Treas 8¾pc 1997‡‡	85 1/4	+1/4	10.34	11.05
134 5/8	118 1/8	Exch. 15pc 1997	122 1/2 xd	+5/8	12.22	11.54
98 1/4	84 1/2	Exch. 9¾pc 1998	92 3/4	+1/2	10.72	11.08
94 7/16	88 5/8	Exch. 9¾pc 1998 'A'	93 5/8	+1/2	10.73	11.08
78	68	Treas 6¾pc 1995-98‡‡	72 1/4 xd	+3/8	9.26	10.64
138 5/8	122 5/8	Treas. 15½pc '98‡‡	127 5/8 xd	+3/4	12.14	11.42
115	100 1/8	Exch. 12pc 1998	109 7/8	+5/8	11.36	11.17
97 1/8	83 7/8	Treas 9½pc 1999‡‡	91 3/4	+3/8	10.57	10.93
116 3/4	103 5/8	Exch. 12¼pc 1999	107 7/8	+5/8	11.36	11.44
104 1/2	91	Treas. 10½pc 1999	99 7/8	+3/8	10.92	11.04
102 1/2	89 1/4	Conversion 10¼pc 1999	97 7/8	+3/8	10.87	11.03
		Over Fifteen Years				
123 1/8	106 3/8	Treas. 13pc 2000	116 3/8	+5/8	11.43	11.10
128 1/2	112 3/8	Treas. 14pc '98-01	122 5/8	+5/8	11.89	11.36
93 7/8	92 5/8	Conversion 9¾pc 2001	93 7/8	+5/8	10.52	10.71
114 7/8	98 5/8	Exch. 12pc '99-02	108 1/2	+5/8	11.28	11.08
100 3/8	90	Conversion 10pc 2002	94 1/8 xd	+3/8	10.58	10.71
128 3/4	110 3/4	Treas. 13¾pc 2000-03	121 1/4	+3/4	11.56	11.15
114 7/8	101 3/8	Treas. 11½pc 2001-04	105 5/8	+3/8	10.92	10.79
51 1/8	43 3/4	Funding 3½pc '99-04	49 1/8	......	7.23	9.30
101 1/2	95 5/8	Exch.10½pc 2005	101 1/2	+1/2	10.50	10.49
123 5/8	107 3/4	Treas. 12½pc 2003-05	118 1/4	+1/2	10.97	10.77
87 1/8	76 7/8	Treas. 8pc 2002-06‡‡	80 1/2 xd	+3/8	9.92	10.24
117 1/8	100	Treas. 11¾pc 2003-07	110 1/8	+5/8	10.88	10.72
132 1/8	117 1/2	Treas. 13½pc '04-08	122 1/8	+5/8	11.06	10.75
64 7/8	56 1/8	Treas. 5½pc 2008-12‡‡	59 1/2	+1/4	9.29	9.80
85 1/4	72 3/4	Treas. 7¾pc 2012-15‡‡	79 7/8	+3/8	9.86	10.02
124 5/8	108 7/8	Exch. 12pc '13-'17	118 3/4	+5/8	10.41	10.32

Undated

41 1/2	35 7/8	Consols 4pc	39 3/8	+1/8	10.32	
37 3/8	32 1/2	War Loan 3½pc‡‡	35 5/8	+1/4	10.14	—
44 7/8	40 1/2	Conv. 3½pc '61 Aft.	42 5/8 xd	......	8.20	—
31 5/8	27 3/4	Treas. 3pc '66 Aft.	28 3/4	......	10.41	—
25 3/4	22 3/4	Consols 2½pc	24 3/8 xd	......	10.23	—
26	23	Treas. 2½pc	24 1/4 xd	......	10.30	—

Abbreviations: xd ex dividend

● "Tap Stock".

‡‡ Tax-free to non-residents on application.

Exhibit 5 *(cont)*

FT-ACTUARIES INDICES

FIXED INTEREST

PRICE INDICES	Wed March 27	Day's change %	Tues March 26	xd adj. today	xd adj. 1985 to date
British Government					
1 5 years..............	116.17	+0.19	116.29	0.35	2.94
2 5-15 years	128.11	+0.44	127.81	0.26	3.29
3 Over 15 years......	135.70	+0.50	135.02	—	2.03
4 Irredeemables.....	148.01	+0.47	147.31	—	1.62
5 All stocks............	126.82	+0.36	126.63	0.26	3.00
6 Debentures & Loans ..	109.00	+0.25	108.73	—	2.39
7 Preference..........	76.86	+0.03	76.84	—	2.15

BRITISH GOVERNMENT INDEX–LINKED STOCKS

	Wed March 27	Day's change %	Tues March 26	xd adj. today	xd adj. 1985 to date
8 All stocks............	109.65	−0.68	110.40	—	0.78

†Flat yield.

AVERAGE GROSS REDEMPTION YIELDS

			Wed March 27	Tues March 26	Year ago (approx.)
	British Government				
1	Low	5 years............	10.84	10.89	9.95
2	Coupons	15 years............	10.65	10.71	10.04
3		25 years.............	10.20	10.26	9.66
4	Medium	5 years............	11.72	11.79	10.53
5	Coupons	15 years............	10.99	11.05	10.51
6		25 years............	10.42	10.49	9.98
7	High	5 years............	11.79	11.85	10.66
8	Coupons	15 years............	11.13	11.21	10.65
9		25 years............	10.53	10.59	10.05
10	Irredeemables ....†		10.05	10.09	9.62
11	Debs &	5 years............	12.16	12.25	11.32
12	Loans	- 15 years............	11.78	11.79	11.32
13		25 years............	11.64	11.69	11.33
14	Preference...........................†		12.76	12.77	12.70
15	Inflation rate	5%..........	3.40	3.35	3.35
16		10%..........	3.21	3.16	3.16

EURO-CURRENCY INTEREST RATES

(Market closing rates)

Mar. 27	Sterling	U.S. Dollar
Short-term...........	$14\frac{1}{8}$-$14\frac{5}{8}$	$7\frac{3}{4}$-$7\frac{7}{8}$
7 day's notice	$14\frac{1}{8}$-$14\frac{5}{8}$	$8\frac{5}{8}$-$8\frac{3}{4}$
Month	$13\frac{3}{4}$-$13\frac{7}{8}$	$8\frac{1}{16}$-$8\frac{1}{16}$
Three months.......	$13\frac{5}{16}$-$13\frac{7}{16}$	$9\frac{1}{16}$-$9\frac{3}{16}$
Six months...........	$12\frac{7}{16}$-$12\frac{9}{16}$	$9\frac{5}{8}$-$9\frac{3}{4}$
One year	$12\frac{3}{16}$-$12\frac{5}{16}$	$10\frac{1}{16}$-$10\frac{3}{16}$

LONDON MONEY RATES

Mar. 27 1985	Sterling Certificate of deposit	Interbank	Local Authority deposits	Company Deposits	Market Deposits	Treasury (Buy)	Treasury (Sell)
Overnight........	—	10-$14\frac{3}{4}$	$14\frac{1}{8}$-$14\frac{5}{8}$	$12\frac{1}{2}$-$14\frac{1}{2}$	10-$14\frac{3}{4}$	—	—
2 days notice ..	—	—	$14\frac{1}{4}$-$14\frac{5}{8}$	—	—	—	—
7 days or........	—	—	—	—	—	—	—
7 days notice ..	—	$14\frac{1}{8}$-$14\frac{5}{8}$	$14\frac{1}{8}$-$14\frac{5}{8}$	$14\frac{1}{2}$	$13\frac{1}{2}$-$13\frac{3}{4}$	—	—
One month......	$13\frac{7}{8}$-$13\frac{1}{8}$	$13\frac{3}{4}$-$13\frac{1}{16}$	$13\frac{7}{8}$	$14\frac{1}{8}$-$14\frac{7}{8}$	$13\frac{1}{4}$	$13\frac{5}{16}$	$13\frac{1}{8}$
Two months....	$13\frac{1}{2}$-$13\frac{5}{8}$	$13\frac{5}{8}$-$13\frac{5}{8}$	$13\frac{5}{8}$	$13\frac{3}{4}$	13	$13\frac{1}{16}$	$12\frac{7}{8}$
Three months..	$13\frac{1}{4}$-$13\frac{1}{16}$	$13\frac{5}{16}$-$13\frac{1}{2}$	$13\frac{5}{8}$	$13\frac{5}{8}$	$12\frac{3}{4}$	$12\frac{3}{4}$	$12\frac{5}{8}$
Six months......	$12\frac{7}{16}$-$12\frac{5}{16}$	$12\frac{7}{16}$-$12\frac{5}{8}$	$12\frac{1}{2}$	—	—	—	—
Nine months ...	$12\frac{5}{16}$-$12\frac{3}{16}$	$12\frac{1}{4}$-$12\frac{5}{8}$	—	—	—	—	—
One year........	$12\frac{1}{16}$-$11\frac{15}{16}$	$12\frac{1}{8}$-$12\frac{1}{4}$	$12\frac{1}{8}$	—	—	—	—

Source: The Financial Times

Exhibit 6: *Summary of draft prospectus dated 12 April 1985*

£60 000 000
Redland Finance plc
Zero-coupon notes due 1992

Redland Finance plc The company is an intermediate holding company and is a wholly owned subsidiary of Redland plc (the 'guarantor').

Use of proceeds It is intended to apply the net proceeds of the issue to repay certain of the floating rate borrowings of the Group.

Description of the notes The issue of £60 000 000 zero-coupon notes due 1992 (the 'notes') will be constituted by a trust deed incorporating:

(1) *Form and denomination* The notes will initially be represented by a single temporary global note with a common depositary for the Euroclear System and Cedel S.A. The temporary global note will be exchangeable for definitive notes either in bearer or in registered form.
(2) *Status* The notes, which do not bear interest, will be direct, unconditional and unsecured obligations of the company.
(3) *Guarantee* The guarantor will unconditionally and irrevocably guarantee all payments in respect of the *Notes*.
(4) *Negative pledge* So long as any of the notes remains outstanding neither the company nor the guarantor will create or have outstanding any mortgage or charge upon its assets to secure any international indebtedness.
(5) *Redemption and purchase* (a) Redemption at maturity: unless previously redeemed or purchased and cancelled, the notes will be redeemed at 100 per cent of their principal amount on the 7th anniversary of the date of issue. (b) Redemption for taxation reasons: the amount payable shall be equal to the sum of (i) the initial issue price; and (ii) the aggregate amortization of the original issue discount from the date of issue to the date of such redemption.
(6) *Taxation* All payments will be made without withholding or deduction for taxes imposed by the United Kingdom.
(7) *Repayment in event of default* This will be limited to repayment of the issue price plus accrued interest.
(8) *Governing law* The notes shall be construed in accordance with English law.

Business of Redland plc A brief review of the principal activities of the Group, together with a 10 year financial history.

Financial statements of Redland plc Audited consolidated accounts for the years ended 31 March 1984 and 26 March 1983, together with the unaudited interim statement of Redland which was published on 19 November 1984.

Subscription and sale The managers have agreed to subscribe for the notes and the company has agreed to pay a management commission of 1.25 per cent of the principal amount of the notes. The managers have invited certain banks, brokers and dealers (the 'selling group') to purchase the notes at the issue price less a selling concession of 0.75 per cent of the principal amount. The notes have not been and will not be registered under the United States Securities Act of 1933.

United Kingdom Taxation The notes will be deep discount securities for the purpose of Section 36 of the Finance Act 1984. Thus, for United Kingdom tax purposes, on a disposal or redemption of a note the holder may be chargeable to tax on an amount representing the accrued discount attributable to the period between his acquisition and disposal or redemption of the note as income. The discount will not be assessed to United Kingdom tax in the hands of holders who are not residents of the United Kingdom.

was to be £60 million nominal value. However, to avoid unnecessary use of debt capacity it was essential to limit the amount of debt stated in the balance sheet to the original issue proceeds (for example, £60 million × issue price) plus accumulated interest. The auditors' agreement to this was achieved by ensuring that the terms of the issue reflected the desired accounting treatment. Without such clauses in the issue terms, a default in a zero-coupon issue could theoretically result in the full nominal amount becoming repayable on any default.

There was a debate among the lead managers about the term of the proposed issue: 5 years was viewed as too short in that it would not provide enough price volatility to interest European investors; 10 years, however, was considered too long by Redland, and also introduced worries about the price risk, given the greater volatility of zero-coupon relative to ordinary bonds. In the end, a 7 year maturity was agreed upon as being attractive and easier to sell.

Another major technical difficulty was taxation. To obtain the tax deduction for a full year's interest in the way envisaged by the legislation would entail a launch of the issue at least 4 weeks prior to the end of an accounting period (Redland's year end was 30 March). Otherwise the deferral, by a year, of the tax relief would make the issue uneconomic (adding 1–2 per cent to the cost of funds, on Gareth Jones' estimates) versus the alternatives. The use of Redland Finance plc as the issuer, with its April year end, solved this possible problem.

Negotiations were not routine given the absence of a similar issue to use as a reference point. Gareth Jones was the chief proponent of the issue within Redland, and although he had confidence in Morgan Stanley, privately, Morgan Stanley acknowledged a high degree of uncertainty, given the innovative nature of the issue. Furthermore, viewpoints among the lead managers differed depending on whom they considered their most likely investor base — including such distinct categories as UK institutions, contrasted to European, and possibly Japanese investors.

In their initial pricing analysis, Morgan Stanley had calculated the internal rate of return which would ensure that a particular type of investor would be indifferent between a high-coupon gilt and the zero-coupon issue (see Exhibit 5 for data on gilt prices and interest rates at this time). The calculations were based on the 1985–92 period, assuming a corporation with a tax-rate declining from 40 per cent in 1985 to 35 per cent by 1986 (in line with the 1984 UK Budget changes), and an individual with a tax rate falling from 40 per cent to 35 per cent over the same period. While the latter class of investors would find the zero-coupon issue an attractive investment opportunity, Morgan Stanley believed that targeting the bond towards institutions would be more efficient for selling purposes. Following this initial pricing suggestion, which showed a saving over the equivalent gilt yield, discussions between the managers were based on their particular views of where the issue would trade in the market. Conscious of their dual role of underwriting, Simon Fraser of Morgan Stanley commented that 'deals are priced to sell and yet ensure the lowest possible cost of borrowing to the issuer. In this case, it was very difficult to quantify the downside risk, given the lack of a suitable reference point.'

There was very little discussion about the level of fees, given the precedents from the US market and previous euromarket deals (for comparison, a conventional 7 year issue would have cost 1.875 per cent (of the amount raised) in fees). There was considerable discussion, however, about the tax treatment of the issue expenses. Normally, the latter would consist of a management fee and a selling concession. As there is no contractual relationship between the issuer and the selling group, the selling concession of ½ per cent (of face value) would not be tax deductible under UK law, although the management fee of 0.75 per cent would be. The additional tax loss of £120 000 was unacceptable to Redland, and so the managers were able to agree to a management fee of 1.25 per cent (of face value) and no selling concession. The managers do have a contractual relationship with the selling group, and hence have an acceptable tax treatment if they allow a selling concession.

By 27 March 1985 all the terms of the proposed issue except the price had been agreed. These terms and conditions are summarized in the draft prospectus in Exhibit 6. At this point, however, the price had to be finalized. Both Redland and the lead managers had their own views on what this should be, and the time had now come for them to complete their negotiations.

19. Oasis Lines

Each of two shipping companies, Oasis Lines and Aegean Enterprises, is negotiating leasing arrangements for a small fleet of ships. The total cost of each fleet is approximately £10 million, and the average cost per ship if £1 million. The two companies wish to lease because neither expects to be in a tax-paying position in the foreseeable future.

They have each approached three lessors, Liverpool Leasing, Marine Credit and O'Ryan Finance, requesting tenders for a lease period of at least ten years. Lease rentals are normally set in relation to current rates for high coupon gilts and corporate debentures prevailing at the time of purchase. The lessors' quotations are to be based on annual rental payments, payable in advance. Provision is to be made for the division of the proceeds of the sale of the vessel at the end of the primary period and for the level of any secondary period payments. However, the net sale proceeds for salvage of this type of vessel in 10 years time is expected to be only 3 per cent of its current cost.

The lessors have been asked to respond with sealed tenders which state their terms and the time at which these terms expire. A copy of a typical lessor's standard form for quoting lease terms is shown in Exhibit 1. All three lessors are currently considering whether they should submit tenders for a 10 year, or for a longer lease. Since interest rates are currently quite volatile, they also wish to estimate by how much the lease rental terms would need to be adjusted for plausible changes in interest rates.

All three lessors currently have sufficient taxable capacity to cover at least two of the proposed deals. They are all subject to corporation tax at 35 per cent, payable with a one year's delay. On purchasing the ships, the lessors will enjoy capital allowances of 25 per cent per annum on a declining balance basis.

Meanwhile, both Oasis Lines and Aegean Enterprises are estimating what sort of terms they can expect to be offered. When they receive a tender, they know that they will either have to accept it, or make a verbal or written counter-offer.

This case was written by Stewart Hodges for use as a financial negotiating exercise.

Exhibit 1: *Standard form of letter for leasing agreement*

Date...............................

Dear...............................

Following our recent meeting, I am pleased to set out below the rentals which would currently apply to the lease of the vessel(s) which you are considering acquiring. I understand that the vessel(s) will cost approximately £.......... million and will be operable in the month of .... 19.........

1. Annual rental payable in advance would be £........... per £1000 of expenditure over a .... year primary period. Quotations for other rental frequencies and primary periods will be supplied on request.

2. At the end of the primary period there would be an option to renew the lease at an annual rental, payable in advance, of .... per cent of the total cost of the vessel. Should the vessel be sold at the end of the primary period or at any time during the secondary period, we would be prepared to pay to the lessee .... per cent of the net sale proceeds as a rebate of rentals.

3. Any value added tax payable would be added to the rentals.

4. The rentals quoted assume that we would be entitled to 25 per cent per annum capital allowances on a declining balance basis on the full amount of our expenditure. Should this prove not to be the case or should there be a change in the basis of taxation or allowances (a change in the rate of corporation tax is not a change in the basis of taxation for this purpose) the primary period rentals would be subject to review. The rentals would also be subject to renegotiation should rates vary prior to our incurring the necessary expenditure by more than .... per cent from the following indicator of interest rates: ....

If these terms are of interest to you we would be very happy to explore with you the possibility of our providing a facility for the vessel(s). In this connection I should be grateful if you would let us have a copy of your latest accounts. Please let me know if you would like any additional information on our terms.

Yours sincerely,

---

20. ICL

On 19 March 1981, the British government announced that it would assist the troubled British computer manufacturer, ICL (International Computers Ltd). The assistance was to take the form of guaranteeing £200 million of new borrowing by the company for 2 years. Some observers felt that the government was doing too little, while others argued that it was doing too much. These criticisms, however, were just the latest salvo in a longstanding debate, since this was not the first time that a British government had intervened in support of the UK computer industry.

The background

International Computers Ltd (ICL) was formed in 1968 following a series of mergers which brought together the computer interests of a variety of UK electrical and engineering firms. The government had keenly supported ICL's creation. It believed that only by combining national resources could a company be created which was strong enough to compete on the international scene.

After a rather unpromising start — a further £40 million of government cash had to be injected in 1972 — things went well. Sales grew from £150 million in 1971 to over £700 million in 1980. ICL benefited from the government's policy of buying British, although its growth was not simply due to UK government purchasing policy. By 1980, only 5 per cent of ICL's turnover was from the government and over 40 per cent was from outside the United Kingdom. On the technical side, ICL could lay claim to a number of significant advances in mainframe computers.

The world computer industry then, as now, was dominated by IBM. In the mid-1970s, IBM's turnover of $15 billion per year exceeded the aggregate turnover of its seven nearest rivals. IBM and its competitors became known as Snow-White and the Seven Dwarfs; ICL was the only dwarf which was not

This case was written by Anthony Neuberger as a basis for class discussion rather than to illustrate either effective or ineffective handling of an administrative situation.

American. Outside Japan and North America, it was the second largest mainframe computer supplier after IBM.

IBM's domination of the market in many ways helped ICL. Under what some commentators called IBM's 'benign leadership', price competition was never intense. From 1970 to 1978, IBM kept its gross profit margin at a high and stable level, within the range 23.7–25.7 per cent. Its competitors tended to have lower and more variable profit margins, ICL's varying between 4.7 and 10.2 per cent. But demand was growing, and competitive pressures were muted.

However, towards the end of the 1970s a number of changes occurred in the mainframe computer market which were highly unfavourable to ICL.

First, new players entered the computer industry. A collaborative venture by Fujitsu and Hitachi was seen as the start of a serious attack by the Japanese on what had been a largely American preserve. A still more significant indicator of forthcoming change was the challenge by Digital Equipment Corporation (DEC) coming from the minicomputer market, which hitherto had been seen as separate from the mainframe market. Further ahead, there were indications that the mainframe computer field would increasingly converge with the tele-communications sector. With new competitors either coming in or threatening to enter the industry, IBM could no longer afford to hold up her umbrella and shelter the 'dwarfs'. In 1979, IBM started price cutting heavily, particularly at the top end of its range.

Second, sterling strengthened rapidly against the dollar. This, together with the high rate of inflation in the United Kingdom, led to a serious loss of competitiveness for ICL which was competing in a global market. Over the 2 years to the beginning of 1981, the United Kingdom's international competitiveness worsened by nearly 50 per cent (as measured by the IMF index of relative unit labour costs).

Third, under international agreement, the UK government was unable to offer ICL preference in computer purchase as from the beginning of 1981.

ICL did not find it easy to adjust to the structural changes in the industry. It was trying to compete against IBM across the board by offering a product range almost as wide as that of IBM when its entire turnover was less than IBM's R & D budget. Yet the alternative strategy, followed by the other 'dwarfs', of specializing on the needs of particular sectors such as banks or military applications, depended on the existence of a very large home market, which ICL lacked.

The crisis

When the crisis came for ICL, it came fast. In September 1980, the shares were standing at an all-time high of 196p. By the end of February 1981 they were around 35p. The immediate cause of alarm was the outflow of cash in 1980.

A superficial reading of the 1980 accounts (published in January 1981, and summarized in Exhibits 1, 2 and 3) shows a net increase in debt of £47 million over the year. But the true figure was much higher. First, allowing for the increase in export credits (see Exhibit 2), the net increase in debt was £69 million. More significant, however, was the fact that ICL, in an attempt to maintain sales volume in a difficult market, had greatly increased the proportion of computers which it leased to its customers rather than sold outright. To avoid burdening its own balance sheet with the financing needed to support the leases, ICL had set up two associated companies which were jointly owned with banks to handle the leasing deals. When an ICL machine was leased to a customer, ICL sold the machine to one of the leasing companies and the leasing company

Exhibit 1: *ICL Balance sheet (£ million)*

	As at 30 September	
Balance sheet	1980	1979
Fixed assets		
Fixed assets	128.8	142.6
Investments	17.3	15.6
Deferred assets	16.0	14.4
Total fixed assets	162.1	172.6
Current assets		
Stocks	172.7	133.1
Debtors	155.5	129.4
Cash	34.4	31.5
Total current assets	362.6	294.0
Current liabilities		
Creditors	156.1	128.2
Provisions	1.3	—
Taxation	4.5	7.3
Bank overdraft and short-term loans	44.9	15.4
Dividend	2.7	2.8
Total current liabilities	209.5	153.7
Total net assets	315.2	312.9
Long-term liabilities		
Share capital (25p ordinary shares)	33.4	33.4
Reserves	108.0	113.4
Minority interests	2.1	2.2
Medium and long-term loans	116.8	99.0
Leasing provision	29.5	21.4
Other deferred liabilities	25.4	43.5
Capital employed	315.2	312.9

Exhibit 2: *ICL profit and loss account and sources and uses of funds (£ millions)*

Profits and funding	Year ending 30 September 1980	1979	
Turnover	715.8	624.1	
Dividends from leasing companies	4.9	5.8	
	720.7	629.9	
Less: Bought-in materials and services	279.9	234.8	
Less: Employee costs	341.4	293.1	
Less: Depreciation	39.9	40.1	*Profit*
Less: Lease purchase provision	8.1	(1.8)	
Trading profit	51.4	63.7	*and*
Less: Interest	26.3	17.2	
Profit before tax	25.1	46.5	*loss*
Less: Tax	7.4	11.2	
Profit after tax	17.7	35.3	*account*
Less: Minorities	0.0	.2	
Less: Extraordinary items	7.7	0.0	
Profit attributable to shareholders	10.0	35.1	
Less: Dividends	4.0	4.0	
Net profit retained	6.0	31.1	
Funds from trading	65.7	73.6	
Increase in medium and long-term loans	19.1	14.5	
Increase in overdrafts and short term loans	29.5	4.7	
Increase in export credits	21.9	1.5	
Total sources of funds	136.2	94.3	*Sources*
Expenditure (net) on fixed assets and investments	27.8	62.2	*and*
Differences from exchange rate movements	11.6	9.2	*uses*
Extraordinary item	7.7	0.0	
Repayment of loans	1.3	3.4	*of*
Dividends paid	4.1	3.0	
Increase in net current/deferred assets	80.9	18.7	*funds*
Increase in cash at bank	2.9	(2.4)	
Other uses of funds (net)	(.1)	.2	
Total uses of funds	136.2	94.3	

*Funds from trading = profit after tax plus depreciation plus lease purchase provision

Exhibit 3: *Details of ICL's borrowings (£ million)*

(a) Analysis of ICL's loans

		1980	1979
Short-term loans	Bank overdrafts and loans: secured	16.2	7.8
	Bank overdrafts and loans: unsecured	26.6	4.8
	Other short-term loans	2.1	2.8
	Total short term loans	44.9	15.4
Medium and long-term loans	*Secured*		
	4.25 per cent Debenture stock 1975–80	—	0.6
	6.00 per cent Debenture stock 1975–80	—	1.5
	5.50 per cent Debenture stock 1979–84	4.0	4.0
	6.25 per cent Debenture stock 1981–86	5.0	5.0
	6.00 per cent Debenture stock 1983–88	5.5	5.5
	8.50 per cent Mortgage 1994	1.0	1.0
	Foreign currency loans (average coupon = 12 per cent)	1.4	1.6
	Unsecured		
	Foreign currency loans (average coupon = 11.2 per cent)	9.1	—
	Export credits repayable by instalment	90.8	79.8
	Total medium and long-term loans	116.8	99.0

(b) Analysis of repayment dates for medium- and long-term loans

	Bank		Other		Total	
	1980	1979	1980	1979	1980	1979
On demand/within 1 year	28.3	24.9	.1	.1	28.4	25.0
Within 1–2 years	26.6	21.0	—	2.2	26.6	23.2
Within 2–5 years	43.5	34.8	4.2	.2	47.7	35.0
After 5 years	2.4	.1	11.7	15.7	14.1	15.8
Total medium and long-term loans	100.8	80.8	16.0	18.2	116.8	99.0

(c) Analysis of total interest paid and received

	1980	1979
Bank overdrafts and loans	10.0	5.2
Other loans wholly payable in 5 years	1.1	1.0
Loans not wholly payable in 5 years	17.0	13.3
Total interest payable	28.1	19.5
Interest receivable	1.8	2.3
Net interest payable	26.3	17.2

then borrowed on its own account to finance the lease. Since the leasing companies were only associate companies, ICL did not have to consolidate their borrowings with its own, and the financing of the lease deals was off ICL's balance sheet. But whatever the formal position in the accounts, the fact remained that the computers were leased, not sold outright. If the customer chose to terminate the lease prematurely, the leasing company had the right to sell back the machine to ICL at book value. To obtain a true picture of ICL's cash position, it therefore makes more sense to look at the position of ICL jointly with its associated leasing companies.

According to press accounts, a report prepared for the government by accountants Touche Ross put the total cash outflow from the company (including its leasing associates) in 1980 at £150 million. That level of outflow for a company of ICL's size was clearly unsustainable. Other analysts estimated that ICL's total debt (overdrafts plus short, medium, and long-term loans, but excluding leasing associates) had increased to £190 million by early March 1981. The financial position, combined with underlying worries about ICL's strategic posture, and also with concern about ICL's unwillingness to give detailed financial information to the market, gave strong impetus to the slide in the share price.

At the Annual General Meeting on 3 February 1981, the Chairman gave some indication of a change in strategic emphasis — slimming the range of products, heavier emphasis on smaller machines and software — but continued to avoid the immediate issue. As the *Guardian* newspaper put it, 'The question of ICL's financing begged answering before the meeting. It has not been answered.'

The government's position

The government was in a dilemma. On the one hand, ICL was the largest European computer manufacturer. It was in a key, high technology sector. It employed 24 000 people in the United kingdom. It had supplied the UK government with £300 million of computers. On the other hand, the Conservative government had been elected less than 2 years previously on a platform strongly opposed to state intervention in industry.

The government tried to persuade others to act — first British companies, then foreign ones. BP, Shell, GEC, Burroughs, Sperry-Univac were names mentioned. But they were not interesed in taking ICL over on the terms the government stipulated. By March 1981, the position was becoming difficult. The company's bankers were pressing for a financial recovery plan. The share price was so low that somebody might have successfully taken over ICL to dismember it. The government felt it had to act.

So on 19 March 1981, the Industry Secretary, Sir Keith Joseph, told the House of Commons that he was going to intervene to the extent of guaranteeing a new loan of up to £200 million from the company's bankers. He emphasized, in the face of some disbelief, that the sole reason for taking this action was to safeguard the £300 million of ICL computers that the government had purchased; it did not presage a more interventionist government role in industry generally.

The terms of the guarantee

The guarantee agreement was regarded as confidential between the government, ICL and its bankers, and was not published. But the main provisions were fairly clear. At the time the guarantee was given, ICL had bank loans and overdrafts amounting to £70 million. These were secured by a floating charge on ICL's assets. Under the terms of the guarantee, the banks would undertake not to foreclose on these facilities for 2 years. They would further make available sums up to a maximum of £200 million which would be unsecured.

At the end of 2 years, the banks would be free to withdraw their finance. If ICL were unable to repay (either from its own funds or by raising new loans), and the banks lost some of the £200 million they had advanced to the company, the government would reimburse them. But the government would not reimburse the banks for any loss they suffered on the secured loans of £70 million.

Valuation of the guarantee

The government was much happier to support ICL by guaranteeing bank loans rather than by lending the money to ICL direct. A direct loan to ICL would have counted as public expenditure and the government was, as always, keen to keep public expenditure totals down. The government played down the potential cost of the guarantee to public funds. They hoped that within the 2 years, ICL would have solved its problems by merging with a stronger company or by putting its own affairs in order. The Minister concerned, Sir Keith Joseph, argued in Parliament that the guarantee would not lead to any public expenditure unless it was called. He said that he did not expect this to happen.

This view of the package, as a virtually costless means of keeping a company of national importance afloat, was hotly contested at the time. The *Guardian*, for example, argued that the £200 million was '£200 million not available for investing in other projects or for reducing taxation'.

But if most analysts agreed that the guarantee was not cost-free for the government, there was little agreement on how it should be valued. Some claimed that the cost could only be identified after the event — if the guarantee was not called, then it would indeed have cost the government nothing. Others argued that, in the absence of a guarantee, the company would probably have been forced into liquidation. On the assumption that the creditors would not be paid off in full, they would have lost money and the shareholders would have been left with nothing. By stepping in, the government safeguarded ICL's creditors and ensured that the shares had some value. This gain to the shareholders and creditors, it was argued, represented the true value of the guarantee to the company. Even more importantly, the strategic gain to the nation of securing the long-term future of the computer industry was of inestimable value.

One consultant who examined the situation attempted a more sophisticated analysis of the company's situation, in order to calculate the likelihood of ICL going into liquidation in the 2 years covered by the guarantee. He pointed out that, at the time, the average annual rate of failure of quoted companies was running at around 1 in 150. ICL was clearly in a weaker state than average, and a better estimate of the probability of their getting into financial difficulties could be made by taking on board their current financial health as portrayed in their annual accounts. Analysis of the accounts of many troubled companies had shown that bankruptcy was normally preceded by a deterioration in certain key financial ratios over a number of years. By combining these ratios in a formula, it was possible to derive a 'Z-score' for a company that could be used to predict the risk of bankruptcy. A number of financial information services provided data on company Z-scores using their own particular models. Exhibit 4 shows Z-scores for ICL, together with the distribution of Z-scores for other UK companies, as provided by Datastream.

Yet another approach was suggested in April 1981 by a financial analyst who specialized in valuing financial claims. He argued that the guarantee could be seen as a rather complicated financial option. He summarized his views as follows:

> Before the guarantee was given, the company was worth £240 million, represented by £50 million of equity and £190 million of debt. After the guarantee was given, the company was able to raise another £200 million. If at the end of 2 years, the company was worth more than £390 million, the government could escape without losing a penny, since even if ICL went into liquidation, all the debt could be paid off from the company's own assets. If the company were worth less than £390 million, the government would have to make good the shortfall, up to a limit of £200 million.
>
> ICL's equity can thus be viewed as a call option on its assets. Option theory can therefore be used to derive the value and volatility of ICL's assets before the guarantee was given, from the value and volatility of its equity (for example, from the estimates provided in Exhibit 5). By making suitable assumptions about the value and volatility of the assets acquired by ICL with its new guaranteed finance, the value and volatility of ICL's assets after the guarantee can then be estimated. Option theory can then be used to value the claims of the various stakeholders in ICL, and hence to value the government's guarantee.

A final commentator observed that, while the options approach provided a chance to demonstrate considerable technical virtuosity, it singularly missed the point. To understand the true nature of the guarantee, all that was required was a sense of history, and an understanding of politics. He argued that an impartial

Exhibit 4: *Z-scores for ICL and for other UK companies*

(a) Z-score for ICL and average Z-score for all quoted industrials

	Estimated Z-scores for	
Year ending September	ICL	All industrials
1974	3.0	2.6
1975	4.0	2.2
1976	2.9	1.9
1977	2.0	1.9
1978	2.1	2.4
1979	2.6	2.6
1980	0.6	2.2

(b) Distribution of Z-scores for failed and non-failed companies*

		Failed group	
Statistic	Non-failed group	2 years before failure	1 year before failure
Mean	2.5	−1.6	−2.8
Standard deviation	2.4	1.6	1.8
Upper decile	0	−3.7	−4.7
Upper quartile	0.5	−1.9	−3.5
Median	1.9	−1.2	−2.5
Lower quartile	4.0	−0.8	−1.5
Lower decile	7.0	0	−1.0

*Based on a survey of some 100 companies, approximately half of which subsequently failed. Note that the figures in the table indicate that 25 per cent of failed companies had a Z-score of worse than −1.9, 2 years before failure; 10 per cent of failed companies had a Z-score of better than −1.0, one year before failure.

Source: Datastream

survey of past instances of support for 'lame ducks' (like ICL) by British (or indeed any other) governments, would reveal a clear pattern. Such companies seldom recovered rapidly, although this was always claimed to be the 'expectation' before the event. Instead, governments typically got sucked into providing ever greater levels of support.

If the lame ducks eventually did recover, it was only after many years, and massive injections of public funding. The latter was typically orders of magnitude greater than the original commitment, and could very seldom have been justified commercially *ex ante*. The true cost of the ICL guarantee needed to be seen in these terms. Worse still for the nation, the ICL guarantee marked a watershed in government policy, and heralded further such costly 'rescue' operations in the future.

Exhibit 5: *ICL share price and implied volatility, January to April 1981*

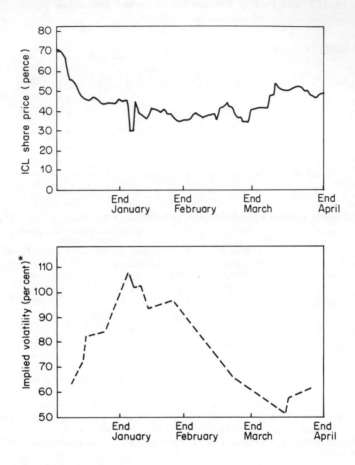

*These implied volatility figures were calculated by a stockbroker from the prices of 3 month, at-the-money, negotiated ICL call options, using the Black-Scholes option valuation formula. The risk-free rate used in these calculations was the yield on 3 month Treasury Bills. As at 19 March 1981, the 3 month Treasury Bill yield was 11.3 per cent, while the gross redemption yields on 1 and 2 year gilts were 11.7 and 12.1 per cent respectively.

21. National Westminster Bank

In 1968, the National Westminster Bank was created as a result of the merger of the National Provincial and Westminster Banks, which were originally established in the 1830s and which traced their history back to the 17th century. The resulting group was one of the two largest UK banks and one of the largest in the world, with assets of some £30 billion. It had about 100 area offices, over 3000 branches, and numerous related companies providing a full range of domestic and international banking services. It also had major interests in merchant banking, insurance broking, leasing and factoring, investment management, computer services and other banking related facilities.

The scheme of arrangement, which became effective in July 1968, gave former National Provincial and Westminster shareholders a roughly equal stake in the new company: 47 ordinary shares plus ten 7 per cent cumulative preference shares in the Bank were exchanged for every 40 National Provincial shares held; 49 ordinary shares and nine preference shares were exchanged for 40 Westminster 'B' shares and four Westminster 'A' shares respectively. The ordinary shares opened in the stock market at 395p and the preference shares started trading at 95p. From this modest mix of ordinary and preference shares, National Westminster Bank set off to construct an interesting and instructive balance sheet.

During the 1970s, the Bank's financing policy turned out to include not only merger issues of ordinary and preference shares. It also raised equity capital from the public by means of a rights issue, set up share option and share purchase schemes for its employees, and sold warrants to the public. Its debt financing included unsecured loans, eurobonds, floating rate notes, debentures, and the usual sources of short-term banking finance. In a short space of time, the Bank had provided examples of most of the important methods used by listed companies for raising finance. Summary balance sheet and profit and loss accounts are shown in Exhibits 1 and 2.

This case was written by Elroy Dimson as a basis for class discussion rather than to illustrate either effective or ineffective handling of an administrative situation.

Exhibit 1: *National Westminster Bank profit and loss accounts*

P and L Account	£ million for the year ending 31 December					
	1969	1971	1973	1975	1977	1979
Group profit before taxation and extraordinary items	63.7	83.8	189.5	104.4	227.6	441.5
Taxation	−29.4	−34.0	−90.7	−56.6	−117.6	−112.3
Extraordinary items and minority interests	−1.0	−1.2	−1.0	5.6	−3.8	0.9
Group profit attributable to shareholders	33.3	48.7	97.8	53.5	106.5	330.1
Ordinary dividends	13.2	16.4	13.6	15.7	25.8	40.8
Retained profit	20.1	32.3	84.2	37.8	80.7	289.3
Basic earnings per share						
Earnings	33.3	48.7	97.8	46.4	108.1	327.0
Weighted average shares in issue (millions)	91.0	91.0	183.3	183.5	223.6	230.6
Earnings per share (pence)	36.6[1]	53.5[1]	53.4	25.3	48.4[2]	141.8
Fully diluted earnings per share						
Adjusted earnings[3]	33.3	48.7	98.6	48.0	109.5	327.0
Shares issued or issuable (millions)	91.0	97.5	195.0	200.8	239.0	239.9
Earnings per share (pence)	36.6[1]	49.9[1]	50.6	23.9	45.8	136.3

Notes
1. Not adjusted for one-for-one scrip issue in 1972.
2. Earnings per share in 1977 would have been 77.3 pence under the accounting policies used for 1979, with a similar adjustment for fully diluted earnings per share.
3. The fully diluted earnings take account of the fact that, after conversion into ordinary shares, former warrant holders miss one dividend payment. They also lose title to interest paid after exercise of their warrants on any loan stock they have converted.

Warrants and loan stock

In January 1970, National Westminster Bank announced that it was making an unconditional offer for the ordinary shares of Lombard Banking Ltd. The consideration was to be in the form of 9 per cent loan stock 1993 with 12 warrants attached to each £100 stock unit.

The issue of warrants was the largest ever made in the United Kingdom, and it attracted considerable comment. The fact that the warrants were to be traded separately from the loan stock highlighted the general problems of valuing

Exhibit 2: *National Westminster Bank balance sheets as at 31 December (£ million)*

Balance sheet	1969	1971	1973	1975	1977	1979
Liquid assets, special deposits, CDs	1 579	1 290	3 436	3 777	4 857	7 256
Investments	365	602	428	653	788	1 079
Money lent	2 335	2 007	7 359	9 423	12 591	19 745
Premises, equipment, other assets	155	302	625	806	952	867
	4 434	4 200	11 850	14 659	19 188	28 947
Share capital and reserves	345	356	798	859	1 026	1 554
Loan capital	0	47	103	134	163	323
Money lodged	4 038	3 771	10 766	13 239	17 603	26 542
Other liabilities and provisions	50	26	183	427	397	528
	4 434	4 200	11 850	14 659	19 188	28 947
Details of loan capital						
9 pc sub unsec loan 1993[1]	—	38	37	37	31	21
8¾ pc sub unsec loan 1980	—	9	9	9	9	9
8 pc DM bearer bonds 1979–88	—	—	16	19	25	23
9 pc US$ capital bonds 1980–96	—	—	—	—	26	22
9 pc US$ 'B' capital bonds 1983–86	—	—	—	—	—	34
US$ floating (min 5½ pc) 1982–90	—	—	—	—	—	67
US$ floating (min 5¼ pc) 1983–94	—	—	—	—	—	45
3⅝ pc SF sub loan 1987	—	—	—	—	—	7
3¹¹⁄₁₆ pc SF sub loan 1987	—	—	—	—	—	7
US$ floating (min 6 pc) 1981–84[2]	—	—	—	—	63	54
US$ floating (min 4¾ pc) 1990[2]	—	—	—	—	—	8
Misc. debentures over 5 years[2]	—	1	41	69	9	26

1. Abbreviations used here are pc = per cent, sub = subordinated and unsec = unsecured.
2. Subsidiaries' loan capital.

warrants and convertible loan stocks. Prior to trading, there was much disagreement about what the market value of the National Westminster warrants would be. Exhibit 3, for example, shows how far the stockbrokers Hoare and Co. were prepared to depart from general beliefs in their attempts to value the warrants.

The loan stock of Lombard Banking was acquired 6 months later in exchange for 8¾ per cent loan stock 1980 with warrants attached. The loan stock was to rank *pari passu* with the 9 per cent stock. Interest in the new stock was to be payable at the end of March and September each year. Both stocks were redeemable at par on their maturity, or could be repurchased by National Westminster 'in the market or by tender at any price or by private treaty at or below 110 per cent'. The warrants, too, could be repurchased in the market or by tender available to all.

Exhibit 3: *The terms of the warrant issue in January 1970*

In a privately circulated memorandum to clients in January 1970, the research department at Hoare and Co. reviewed the terms of the warrants and loan stock. The following is extracted from their memorandum:

Warrants. Each warrant will enable a holder to subscribe for one National Westminster ordinary share at £3.10 on 1 October 1970, or 1 April or 1 October in the years 1971–79 inclusive.

Loan stock. The coupon is 9 per cent and interest dates are 30 June and 31 December. The first payment of interest is £4.50 on 30 June 1970. Final redemption is on 31 December 1993 at par plus accrued interest.

Rights to cash in against warrants. The loan stock may be used to subscribe for any shares to which the holder is entitled as a warrant holder. For this purpose the stock value will be deemed to be par.

Mr Bailey, of Hoare and Co., advised the firm's clients that

The market are expecting the National Westminster 9 per cent loan stock with warrants attached to start at around 100, valuing the warrants at 71p after taking the loan stock element out at 91.45 for a gross redemption yield of 10 per cent. With the equity at present standing at around £3.00 we would expect a price of £1.60 for the warrants giving a price of 110¾ for the loan stock and warrants combined. At a price of 100 we consider the stock undervalued and should be bought.

The method for adjusting the terms of the warrants for an issue of ordinary shares is to multiply the subscription price by an adjustment factor. The factor is equal to $(A \times B) + (C \times D)$ divided by $(A + C) \times B$, where the letters have the following meanings: A is the number of shares in issue prior to the rights offering. B is the share price two days before the offer price is announced. C is the number of shares offered by way of rights. D is the offer price.

Share issues

In April 1972, the Bank made a one-for-one capitalization issue of shares. In accordance with the method described in Exhibit 3, the subscription price of the warrants was adjusted from £3.10 to £1.55. Thus, the ex-capitalization prices of the ordinary shares and of the warrants were at half their earlier levels.

On 27 July 1976, the Bank announced a £65 million rights issue of 36.8 million shares in the proportion of one new share for every five already held. The offer was at £1.83 per share, a discount of 19 per cent below the price ruling 2 days before the announcement. The terms of the offering are summarized in Exhibit 4.

After the offer expired on 19 August 1976, the Bank was able to announce that the issue had been successful. Acceptances were received for nearly all shares offered, and the remainder were disposed of for the benefit of the shareholders. As a result of the rights issue, the subscription price of the warrants was changed to £1.50 per ordinary share. It remained at this level throughout the remaining life of the warrants. The price history of the warrants, and that of the shares and loan stocks, is presented in Exhibit 5.

Exhibit 4: *The terms of the rights issue in 1976*

Rights issue of 36 838 264 new ordinary shares of £1 each at £1.83 per share. The interim results of National Westminster Bank Limited ('the Bank') and its subsidiaries ('the Group') for the 6 months ended 30 June 1976 and the proposed rights issue were announced on 27 July 1976 . . .

Reasons for the issue. Shareholders will already know that the Group is engaged in a major programme of long-term capital investment . . . Your board considers this an appropriate time to augment the capital of the Group. Shareholders may have seen that the Board recently raised $50 million in the eurodollar bond market to be employed in its international business and your Board now proposes to raise approximately £65.6 million by way of the present rights issue for the Group's domestic business.

Terms of the issue. The 36 838 264 new ordinary shares offered by way of rights have been provisionally allotted . . . in the following proportions:

> *For every FIVE ordinary shares of £1 each ONE new ordinary share of £1 (and pro rata for other holdings) at £1.83 per share payable in full on acceptance.*

The new ordinary shares, when fully paid . . . will not rank for the interim dividend of 4.6955p per ordinary share declared on 27 July 1976 in respect of the year ending 31 December 1976. Dealings in the new ordinary shares (nil paid) are expected to commence on 30 July 1976.

Acceptance and payment. If you wish to subscribe for the new ordinary shares to which you are entitled, the enclosed provisional allotment letter, together with a remittance for the full amount of the subscription monies, must be lodged . . . with National Westminster Bank . . . not later than 3 pm on Thursday 19 August 1976, when the offer expires . . .

Current trading and dividends . . . Barring unforeseen circumstances, the directors would expect to be able to declare a final dividend for 1976 of 5.5663p per share on the ordinary shares making a total of 10.2618p per share for the year which, together with the related tax credit, is equivalent to 15.7874p per share. This would represent an increase of 20 per cent compared with the rate of 13.1561p per share for 1975; in the context of the rights issue, HM Treasury has confirmed that the necessary consent for this increase will be forthcoming under present regulations. . . .

Material conracts. Dated 27 July 1976 between the Bank and R. Nivison and Co. and J. and A. Scrimgeour Ltd ('the Broker') being the agreement for the underwriting of the issue for a commission of 1½ per cent payable to the brokers, out of which they will pay a subunderwriting commission of 1¼ per cent, in both cases calculated by reference to the gross proceeds of the issue.

Source: National Westminster Bank, 29 July 1976

Exhibit 5: *National Westminster Bank: warrant and stock price histories*

End of quarter	Ordinary shares (pence)	Dividends (pence)	Warrants (pence)	9 per cent stock £	8¾ per cent stock £	Bank shares	All shares	Treasury bill rate (per cent)
			National Westminster Bank Limited			FTA Indexes		
1962 : 3	402[1]	4[1]	..	..	..	87.3	90.1	3.7
4	412	..	..	..	..	90.0	94.5	3.8
1963 : 1	378	7	..	..	..	84.2	98.2	3.8
2	345	..	..	..	..	80.0	98.1	3.7
3	355	7	..	..	..	80.0	103.8	3.7
4	358	..	..	..	..	80.1	106.9	3.8
1964 : 1	330	7	..	..	..	74.1	104.6	4.3
2	257	11sr	..	..	..	69.6	105.8	4.5
3	293	7	..	..	..	78.4	109.3	4.7
4	284	..	..	..	..	79.3	98.0	6.7
1965 : 1	306	8	..	..	..	78.5	98.2	6.7
2	308	..	..	..	..	80.3	93.4	5.6
3	325	7	..	..	..	83.1	100.0	5.6
4	356	..	..	..	..	93.9	103.7	5.6
1966 : 1	354	10	..	..	..	93.2	104.8	5.7
2	367	..	..	..	..	94.9	111.3	5.8
3	325	5	..	..	..	84.1	93.1	6.9
4	330	..	..	..	..	87.1	94.1	6.6
1967 : 1	307	7	..	..	..	81.5	98.0	5.7
2	329	..	..	..	..	88.3	106.4	5.3
3	362	7	..	..	..	96.9	114.7	5.6
4	379	..	..	..	..	109.2	121.1	7.6
1968 : 1	416	7	..	..	..	115.4	139.4	7.2
2	438	8	..	..	..	120.6	154.5	7.4
3	353[1]	..[1]	..	..	..	117.5	160.7	6.7
4	396	..	..	..	..	127.0	173.7	6.9
1969 : 1	353	7	..	..	..	116.0	164.0	7.9
2	300	..	..	..	..	99.8	142.0	8.0
3	300	7	..	..	..	109.7	139.5	8.0
4	306	..	..	..	..	104.4	147.3	7.8
1970 : 1	310	8	97[2]	93	..	96.8	144.0	7.3
2	291	..	71	87	..	93.8	125.7	7.0
3	341	7	112	93	91	107.2	138.7	7.0
4	325	..	102	88	94	102.2	136.3	6.9

Exhibit 5 *(Cont)*

| End of quarter | National Westminster Bank Limited | | | | | FTA Indexes | | Treasury bill rate |
	Ordinary shares *(pence)*	Dividends *(pence)*	Warrants *(pence)*	9 per cent stock £	8¾ per cent stock £	Bank shares	All shares	*(per cent)*
1971 : 1	436	8	192	96	94	137.4	142.7	6.7
2	490	..	248	94	98	153.3	168.0	5.7
3	561	8	264	101	99	174.3	181.3	4.8
4	601	..	313	102	105	187.9	193.4	4.5
1972 : 1	858	10	539	101	99	262.8	217.7	4.4
2	442xc[3]	..	277[2]	95	99	258.5	206.4	5.7
3	388	5	225	96	97	231.6	199.0	6.7
4	460	..	302	93	98	265.4	218.2	8.5
1973 : 1	377	5	225	89	91	217.2	189.6	8.1
2	377	..	231	88	97	222.0	191.9	7.1
3	357	4	229	81	86	203.0	181.4	11.2
4	301	..	175	73	82	186.0	149.8	12.8
1974 : 1	223	4	144	67	76	139.9	118.3	12.3
2	205	..	102	60	66	125.7	105.4	11.6
3	122	4	43	57	72	79.7	76.9	11.3
4	98	..	31	51	72	69.0	66.9	11.3
1975 : 1	192	6	95	68	85	125.6	118.3	9.6
2	200	..	112	60	84	135.3	128.2	9.7
3	230	7	133	68	81	155.5	144.7	10.8
4	250	..	141	62	81	165.6	158.1	10.9
1976 : 1	232	4	126	66	86	155.4	164.6	8.6
2	210	..	109	66	88	151.7	155.4	11.3
3	200	7+5sr[4]	98[2]	67	86	130.4	135.0	12.7
4	223	..	113	65	84	144.8	150.3	14.0
1977 : 1	236	9	117	74	91	156.3	176.5	9.3
2	230	..	114	72	91	157.4	190.7	7.5
3	295	8	156	86	96	196.8	224.5	5.3
4	287	..	150	83	100	196.0	214.5	6.3
1978 : 1	277	10	138	80	95	188.8	205.3	5.8
2	255	..	128	76	95	179.8	210.7	9.3
3	263	9	141	79	94	181.9	228.4	9.2
4	285	..	152	75	94	195.5	222.2	11.6
1979 : 1	360	11	222	82	95	245.0	266.3	11.4
2	343	..	215	78	96	227.1	247.9	13.3
3	348	11	216	77	94	228.4	254.7	13.4

Notes
1. Average of National Provincial Bank and Westminster Bank 'B' prior to July 1968. No adjustments have been made for capital changes.
2. Subscription price was £3.10 until 1972:1, £1.55 during 1972:2 to 1976:2, and £1.50 from 1976:3. Warrant prices are expressed as price of the right to buy one share.
3. xc After one-for-one capitalization issue.
4. sr Cash payment from sale of rights.

Share option scheme

In April 1974 a share incentive scheme was set up for all established members of staff — see Exhibit 6. This scheme was a savings-related share option scheme linked to a 5–7 year save-as-you-earn (SAYE) contract. It granted options to purchase National Westminster shares at a price which was 10 per cent below the market price at the time the option was granted. The option was usually exercisable between 5 and 7½ years after being granted. The maximum sum which could be subscribed to the scheme was initially £20 per month, which matured to a tax-free sum of £1480 (after 5 years) or £1760 (after 7 years). The 'small consideration' required by the Bank in exchange for the option was £1 regardless of the number of shares under option.

National Westminster Bank's option scheme was taken up in large volume by its staff. The Bank noted that existing options, exercisable up to 7 years beyond the year end, could give rise to some 6 or 7 million new shares. In addition, exercise of options during the 1970s had already increased the issued share

Exhibit 6: *The main features of the savings-related share option scheme*

In a letter to shareholders, dated 8 March 1974, the Bank proposed a savings-related share option scheme with the following main features:

1. The scheme is designed to entitle all full-time UK employees (including full-time directors) . . . to apply for options to purchase ordinary shares in the Bank. . . .
2. In order to join the scheme an employee must enter into an SAYE contract under which an agreed sum is deducted each week or month from his salary. . . . At present the maximum permissible deduction is £20.00. After 5 or 7 years the accumulated sums . . . will be used to pay for the shares in respect of which an option has been granted should the employee decide to exercise his option.
3. The maximum number of ordinary shares in respect of which options under the scheme may be granted is 5 per cent of the Bank's present issued ordinary share capital . . . but there is provision for this figure to be adjusted by the auditors in the event of future alterations in the ordinary share capital of the Bank.
4. Employees will pay a small consideration for the grant of an option and the subscription price for the shares under option shall be not less than the higher of 90 per cent of the middle market quotation . . . and the nominal value of the shares.
5. . . . No employee may be granted an option or options over shares which would result in the total subscription price . . . exceeding the maximum . . . proceeds of his SAYE contract . . .
6. . . . Options may be granted within 30 days after the preliminary announcement of the consolidated results of the Bank. . . .
7. An option will usually be exercisable only while the employee remains in the employment of the Bank and within 6 months of the date on which the SAYE contract on the strength of which the option was granted matures. . . .

Exhibit 7: *Sale of shares through exercise of warrants and options (all figures in millions)*

	National Westminster warrants			National Westminster share options			Ordinary shares
	Number exercised	Consideration (£)	Number outstanding	Number exercised	Consideration (£)	Number outstanding	Issued and fully paid
1971	.1[1]	.2	12.6[1]	—	—	—	182.3[1]
1972	.7[1]	1.1	11.9	—	—	—	183.0
1973	.4	.7	11.5	—	—	—	183.5
1974	.0	.0	11.5	.0	.0	5.2	183.5
1975	.0	.0	11.5	.0	.0	5.8	183.5
1976	1.7	2.6	9.8	.0	.0	6.4	222.1[2]
1977	2.7	4.1	7.1	.0	.0	6.9	224.8
1978	2.6	4.0	4.5	.1	.1	7.2	227.5
1979	4.5	6.7	—	2.4	4.3	5.5	234.4

Notes
1. Adjusted for one-for-one capitalization issue
2. After one-for-five rights issue

capital of the bank by over 10 per cent (see Exhibit 7). By the time the warrants matured, share options issued through the savings related scheme were as numerous as the warrants they, in some ways, replaced.

Warrant exercise

Two days before their ultimate expiry date, 1 October 1979, the National Westminster warrants were the subject of a final comment in the Lex column of the *Financial Times*:

Unless they look sharp, some 1800 holders of National Westminster Bank warrants stand to lose around £4 million next week. They have until next Monday at the very latest to subscribe for National Westminster shares, and at the moment it looks as if they have forgotten the fact despite reminders from the Bank's registrar's department.

Right now the warrants are trading around 222p. For every warrant plus either £1.50 of cash or £1.50 nominal of loan stock, investors can subscribe for one NatWest share — currently worth 351p. The best way to exercise the right at the moment is via the NatWest 9 per cent unsecured loan stock 1993 which is trading at 76⅜. This values the warrant at 157½p to the investor. The second best way is via the 8¾ per cent loan stock 1980 and finally, if the investor has neither of these loan stocks, he can chip in £1.50 of cash. Either way the warrant should be exercised by next Monday or it becomes worthless.

In the end, most investors holding the warrants exercised their rights. As Exhibit 7 shows, virtually all of National Westminster Bank's warrants were eventually converted — in many cases, at the eleventh hour.

Several other companies in the financial sector had issued warrants, including merchant bank Hill Samuel, First National Finance Corporation, and a number of investment trusts. However, the NatWest warrant issue dwarfed these others in terms of size, and in the earlier years, accounted for as much as two-thirds of the capitalization of the entire warrant market. Furthermore, a warrant issue was a most unusual step for a clearing bank, and was regarded by some commentators as somewhat 'spivvy' and hence out of character. The expiry of the NatWest warrants thus closed an interesting chapter in the bank's financing history.

Postscript

Throughout this case, NatWest warrant prices are expressed as the right to buy one share. In fact, during most of the 1970s, National Westminster warrants entitled the holder to purchase two-thirds of a share (for a consideration of £1 from August 1976 to 1979), and the warrants were traded at two-thirds of the price shown in Exhibit 5 and in the text.

PART G

INTERNATIONAL FINANCE

22. Svenska Neuhaus

On the morning of 8 January 1985, Rolf Lindorn, the chief executive of Svenska Neuhaus, heard that the company had just won a bid to install a fibro-optical control system for a UK chemical plant. This new system was developed entirely by Svenska Neuhaus and was the only one capable of competing with similar products offered by American and Japanese firms. Svenska Neuhaus had been awarded the 1984 prize for 'Storsta Svenska Exportframgang' for this invention, and everyone still remembers how pleased Rolf Lindorn looked when he walked onto the stage to receive the award from the Prime Minister.

The following day (January 9), Rolf Lindorn and Ulf Ericson, the chief financial officer of Svenska Neuhaus, met with Ove Holbeck of Enskilda Banken to discuss financial issues related to the contract. Neuhaus' bid amounted to £4.4 million (Exhibit 1) and 9 per cent of this had already been paid by the UK firm that morning as a deposit. The balance was due when installation was completed. Neuhaus' chief engineer was pretty confident that this would be within the next 90 days (the completion date in the contract was 10 April 1985).

Exhibit 1: *Details of the Svenska Neuhaus bid made on 12 December 1984*

	Swedish Krona *million*	£ *million*
Materials	25.0	2.4
Direct labour costs	9.6	0.9
Direct overhead costs	6.9	0.6
Total costs	41.5	3.9
Profit factor	5.1	0.5
Total	46.6	4.4*

*Converted at the closing exchange rate for the day (10.58 Swedish krona/£)

This case was prepared by Evi Kaplanis and Antonio Mello as a basis for class discussion rather than to illustrate either effective or ineffective handling of an administrative situation.

The meeting focused on the exchange risk related to the outstanding amount of £4 million. Ove Holbeck was concerned about the value of the pound. He was worried that it might depreciate against the other major currencies and consequently against the Swedish krona which was pegged to a trade weighted basket of currencies (Exhibit 2).

Mr Holbeck explained to Rolf Lindorn and Ulf Ericson that they had several options. First, they could do nothing. This would leave Svenska Neuhaus exposed to fluctuations in the Swedish krona/British pound exchange rate. Thus if sterling appreciated against the Swedish krona, there would be a currency gain, while if it depreciated, there would be a currency loss.

Alternatively, they could hedge their exchange exposure. Mr Holbeck explained that if Svenska Neuhaus wished to hedge using the forward market, it would have to sell sterling forward. He told Lindorn and Ericson that Enskilda Banken was prepared to buy sterling at the 90 day forward quotation of Swedish krona 10.33/£.

To hedge using the money market, Svenska Neuhaus would have to borrow pounds in London now, convert them into kroner at the current spot rate (Exhibit 3), invest the proceeds in Sweden, and repay the pound loan in 3 months with the proceeds of the contract. Mr Holbeck suggested that a sterling loan could be arranged at 0.5 per cent above the prime lending rate (Exhibit 4) and Enskilda was prepared to pay 11.00 per cent on a 3 month Swedish krona deposit account.

Finally, Mr Holbeck suggested that hedging could be achieved through the Deutschmark (DM) — in other words, the DM could be used as a proxy for the Swedish krona, since the movements of these two currencies are largely correlated (Exhibit 5). Three alternatives were available to Neuhaus if they decided to hedge through the DM. First they could hedge using the money market. Second, they could hedge using currency options (Exhibit 6). Mr Holbeck explained that although options were expensive, they provided the company not only with insurance against adverse exchange rate movements, but also offered a potential gain when exchange rates moved favourably. Third, they could hedge using the futures contract (Exhibit 7). Mr Holbeck provided Mr Ericson with information on interest rates, forward rates and industrial exchange rates (Exhibits 2 to 8).

Ericson and Lindorn realized that 'no action' implied that they accepted the exchange risk. On the other hand, they recognized that hedging was costly.

Exhibit 2: *Weights used in trade weighted currency index for Swedish Krona**

Currency	1984 weightings	1983 weightings
US dollar	19.1	18.1
Deutschmark	16.2	16.6
£ sterling	13.2	13.0
Norwegian krone	9.4	9.3
Danish krone	8.2	8.5
Finnish markka	7.2	7.4
French franc	5.5	5.6
Dutch guilder	5.1	5.2
Belgian franc	3.8	3.7
Italian lira	3.6	3.7
Japanese yen	2.7	2.7
Swiss franc	2.2	2.3
Austrian schilling	1.5	1.6
Spanish peseta	1.2	1.2
Canadian dollar	1.1	1.1

*The Swedish krona was pegged to the European currency snake between 1973 and 1977 since when it has been tied to a trade-weighted currency index. The weights of the currencies in the basket are revised each year at the end of March and are calculated as a proportion of each country's average share in Sweden's foreign trade over the previous 5 years, with double weighting attached to the US dollar. The percentage weightings from April 1984 (and the prior year weightings) are as shown in the table.

Source: Riksbanken

Exhibit 3: *Spot and forward exchange rates and eurocurrency interest rates*

(a) The pound spot and forward exchange rates (9 January 1985)

	Close	3 months forward
Sweden	10.31–10.32 (Kr/£)	3.5–4.125 ore discount
Germany	3.6025–3.6125 (DM/£)	3.875–3.625 pfennig premium
United States	1.1415–1.4225 ($/£)	0.46–0.42 cents premium

(b) Eurocurrency interest rates (market closing rates, 9 January 1985)

	Sterling	US dollar	DM
3 Months	9.9375–10.0625	8.25–8.375	5.5625–5.6875

Source: *Financial Times* (10 January 1985)

Exhibit 4: *Comparison of money supply and interest rate figures*

	Money supply per cent rise on year ago		Money market		Commercial banks		Bond yields		Eurocurrency	
	Narrow (M1)	Broad*	Over-night	3 month	Prime lending	3 month deposit	Govern-ment longs	corp-orates	3 month deposit	bonds
Australia	10.2	11.4	10.50	14.20	13.50	13.80	13.70	14.70	12.57	12.87
Belgium	4.3	10.1	8.40	10.75	14.00	10.40	11.65	11.48	10.75	na
Canada	−2.6	3.9	10.25	9.70	11.25	9.75	11.92	11.85	9.85	11.91
France	5.6	7.8	10.75	10.75	11.50	10.75	11.83	12.94	10.63	11.67
Germany	2.5	4.0	5.50	5.75	8.00	5.23	7.20	7.08	5.57	7.48
Holland	4.6	7.3	5.88	5.88	7.50	5.88	7.60	7.79	5.88	7.54
Italy	10.4	11.5	15.88	16.00	17.00	11.50	13.10	13.25	14.38	na
Japan	3.4	7.7	6.19	6.29	5.50	3.50	6.55	7.10	6.22	7.16
Sweden	na	3.4	13.50	11.55	14.50	11.25	12.04	12.50	11.75	na
Switzerland	1.9	7.7	2.94	4.88	7.50	4.25	4.77	5.07	4.75	5.52
UK	18.7	11.1	5.25	10.19	10.50	9.94	11.03	12.76	10.06	11.36
US	5.0	9.9	8.38	7.95	10.75	7.85	11.84	12.70	8.38	11.48

Interest rate per cent per annum (8 January 1985, except bonds which are 4 January 1985)

Other rates in London: 3 month Treasury bills 9.2 per cent; 7 day Interbank 9.1 per cent; clearing banks 7 day notice 6.1 per cent. Eurodollar rates (Libor): 3 months 8.4 per cent; 6 months 9.0 per cent.

*M2 except Australia, Canada, Switzerland, United States, West Germany. M3, Japan. M2 + certificates of deposit, UK £M3. Definitions of interest rates quoted available on request.
Sources: Chase Manhattan, Chase Econometrics, Banque de Commerce (Belgium), Nederlandse Credietbank, Credit Lyonnais, Svenska Handelsbanken, ANZ Bank, Credit Suisse First Boston. These rates are indicative only and cannot be construed as offers by these banks.

Commentary: On both measures of West Germany's money supply, the 12 month rate of monetary growth picked up in November — while in Holland, both measures slowed in October. French banks cut their prime lending rates by half a point to 11.50 per cent; Italian banks cut theirs by a full point, to 17 per cent.

Source: The Economist

Exhibit 5: *Historical monthly spot exchange rates*

Date (end of month)		DM/$	SwKr/$	£/$
1982	January	2.3085	5.6510	0.5309
	February	2.3860	5.7910	0.5508
	March	2.4142	5.9510	0.5613
	April	2.3327	5.8120	0.5591
	May	2.3452	5.8595	0.5583
	June	2.4598	6.0920	0.5753
	July	2.4545	6.0910	0.5747
	August	2.4972	6.1685	0.5812
	September	2.5276	6.2905	0.5908
	October	2.5668	7.4340	0.5976
	November	2.4872	7.4610	0.6203
	December	2.3765	7.2945	0.6194
1983	January	2.4475	7.4520	0.6532
	February	2.4212	7.4395	0.6574
	March	2.4265	7.5090	0.6761
	April	2.4581	7.4930	0.6404
	May	2.4871	7.5531	0.6491
	June	2.5419	7.6425	0.6534
	July	2.6435	7.7470	0.6575
	August	2.6867	7.9080	0.6657
	September	2.6391	7.8220	0.6686
	October	2.6264	7.8170	0.6688
	November	2.6970	7.9600	0.6827
	December	2.7238	8.0010	0.6894
1984	January	2.8139	8.1800	0.7125
	February	2.6058	7.7890	0.6716
	March	2.5900	7.7160	0.6932
	April	2.7174	7.9975	0.7161
	May	2.7333	8.0710	0.7219
	June	2.7842	8.1840	0.7393
	July	2.8964	8.3960	0.7657
	August	2.8870	8.4563	0.7630
	September	3.0253	8.5750	0.8013
	October	3.0296	8.6194	0.8214
	November	3.0963	8.8025	0.8339
	December	3.1480	8.9895	0.8647

Source: *International Financial Statistics*

Exhibit 6: *Currency option prices on 9 January 1985*

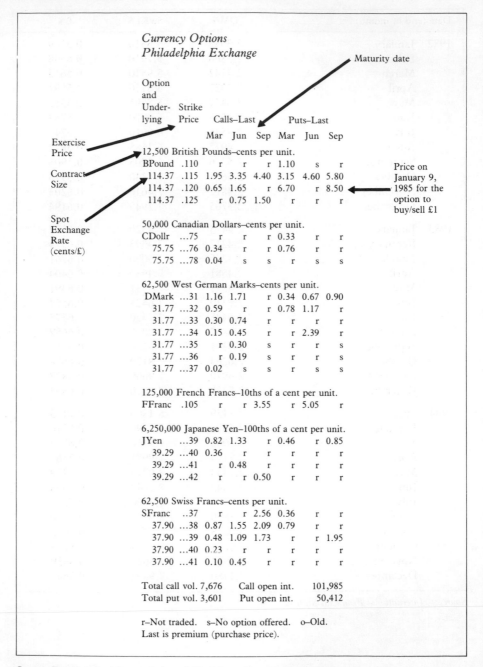

Currency Options
Philadelphia Exchange

Maturity date

Option and Underlying	Strike Price	Calls–Last			Puts–Last		
		Mar	Jun	Sep	Mar	Jun	Sep

12,500 British Pounds–cents per unit.

		Mar	Jun	Sep	Mar	Jun	Sep
BPound	.110	r	r	r	1.10	s	r
114.37	.115	1.95	3.35	4.40	3.15	4.60	5.80
114.37	.120	0.65	1.65	r	6.70	r	8.50
114.37	.125	r	0.75	1.50	r	r	r

Exercise Price

Contract Size

Spot Exchange Rate (cents/£)

Price on January 9, 1985 for the option to buy/sell £1

50,000 Canadian Dollars–cents per unit.

		Mar	Jun	Sep	Mar	Jun	Sep
CDollr	...75	r	r	r	0.33	r	r
75.75	...76	0.34	r	r	0.76	r	r
75.75	...78	0.04	s	s	r	s	s

62,500 West German Marks–cents per unit.

		Mar	Jun	Sep	Mar	Jun	Sep
DMark	...31	1.16	1.71	r	0.34	0.67	0.90
31.77	...32	0.59	r	r	0.78	1.17	r
31.77	...33	0.30	0.74	r	r	r	r
31.77	...34	0.15	0.45	r	r	2.39	r
31.77	...35	r	0.30	s	r	r	s
31.77	...36	r	0.19	s	r	r	s
31.77	...37	0.02	s	s	r	s	s

125,000 French Francs–10ths of a cent per unit.

		Mar	Jun	Sep	Mar	Jun	Sep
FFranc	.105	r	r	3.55	r	5.05	r

6,250,000 Japanese Yen–100ths of a cent per unit.

		Mar	Jun	Sep	Mar	Jun	Sep
JYen	...39	0.82	1.33	r	0.46	r	0.85
39.29	...40	0.36	r	r	r	r	r
39.29	...41	r	0.48	r	r	r	r
39.29	...42	r	r	0.50	r	r	r

62,500 Swiss Francs–cents per unit.

		Mar	Jun	Sep	Mar	Jun	Sep
SFranc	..37	r	r	2.56	0.36	r	r
37.90	...38	0.87	1.55	2.09	0.79	r	r
37.90	...39	0.48	1.09	1.73	r	r	1.95
37.90	...40	0.23	r	r	r	r	r
37.90	...41	0.10	0.45	r	r	r	r

Total call vol. 7,676	Call open int.	101,985
Total put vol. 3,601	Put open int.	50,412

r–Not traded. s–No option offered. o–Old.
Last is premium (purchase price).

Source: Reprinted with permission of *Wall Street Journal.* © Dow Jones and Company, Inc. (10 January 1985). All rights reserved

Exhibit 7: *Currency futures prices on 9 January 1985*

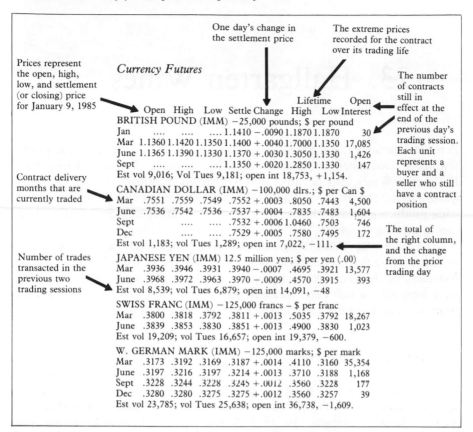

Prices represent the open, high, low, and settlement (or closing) price for January 9, 1985

One day's change in the settlement price

The extreme prices recorded for the contract over its trading life

Currency Futures

The number of contracts still in effect at the end of the previous day's trading session. Each unit represents a buyer and a seller who still have a contract position

Contract delivery months that are currently traded

Number of trades transacted in the previous two trading sessions

The total of the right column, and the change from the prior trading day

```
                                          Lifetime      Open
       Open   High   Low  Settle Change  High   Low  Interest
BRITISH POUND (IMM) −25,000 pounds; $ per pound
Jan    ....   ....   .... 1.1410 −.0090 1.1870 1.1870     30
Mar  1.1360 1.1420 1.1350 1.1400 +.0040 1.7000 1.1350 17,085
June 1.1365 1.1390 1.1330 1.1370 +.0030 1.3050 1.1330  1,426
Sept   ....   ....   .... 1.1350 +.0020 1.2850 1.1330    147
Est vol 9,016; Vol Tues 9,181; open int 18,753, +1,154.
CANADIAN DOLLAR (IMM) −100,000 dlrs.; $ per Can $
Mar   .7551  .7559  .7549  .7552 +.0003  .8050  .7443  4,500
June  .7536  .7542  .7536  .7537 +.0004  .7835  .7483  1,604
Sept   ....   ....   .... .7532 +.0006 1.0460  .7503    746
Dec    ....   ....   .... .7529 +.0005  .7580  .7495    172
Est vol 1,183; vol Tues 1,289; open int 7,022, −111.
JAPANESE YEN (IMM) 12.5 million yen; $ per yen (.00)
Mar   .3936  .3946  .3931  .3940 −.0007  .4695  .3921 13,577
June  .3968  .3972  .3963  .3970 −.0009  .4570  .3915    393
Est vol 8,539; vol Tues 6,879; open int 14,091, −48
SWISS FRANC (IMM) −125,000 francs − $ per franc
Mar   .3800  .3818  .3792  .3811 +.0013  .5035  .3792 18,267
June  .3839  .3853  .3830  .3851 +.0013  .4900  .3830  1,023
Est vol 19,209; vol Tues 16,657; open int 19,379, −600.
W. GERMAN MARK (IMM) −125,000 marks; $ per mark
Mar   .3173  .3192  .3169  .3187 +.0014  .4110  .3160 35,354
June  .3197  .3216  .3197  .3214 +.0013  .3710  .3188  1,168
Sept  .3228  .3244  .3228  .3245 +.0012  .3560  .3228    177
Dec   .3280  .3280  .3275  .3275 +.0012  .3560  .3257     39
Est vol 23,785; vol Tues 25,638; open int 36,738, −1,609.
```

Source: As Exhibit 6

Exhibit 8: *Daily exchange rates — Swedish krona to £1 sterling*

Week commencing	Monday	Tuesday	Wednesday	Thursday	Friday
12 November 1984	10.735	10.750	10.740	10.740	10.705
19 November 1984	10.725	10.642	10.610	10.570	10.557
26 November 1984	10.495	10.545	10.570	10.557	10.563
3 December 1984	10.560	10.600	10.625	10.560	10.592
10 December 1984	10.610	10.560	10.580	10.525	10.565
17 December 1984	10.530	10.477	10.430	10.395	10.465
24 December 1984	10.452	na*	na	10.430	10.430
31 December 1984	10.405	na	10.385	10.405	10.400
7 January 1985	10.380	10.365	10.315		

*na indicates not available, since a public holiday

23. Hallgarten Wines

Peter Hallgarten's travel schedule is inflexible: it can be varied by, at most, a few days. December in particular is a busy month. As Chief Executive of Hallgarten Wines Ltd he must travel throughout Europe to determine the quality of the new harvest. There is always pressure to visit a large number of wine-producing areas, while making sure that sufficient time is set aside for seeing existing suppliers.

In October 1986, Peter Hallgarten therefore assigned several days for working at home to review his current business plans. A factor which caused him considerable concern was the variability of exchange rates. Volatile currencies were a problem which Peter had learned to live with, but recently a number of proposals had been put to him which required consideration.

The House of Hallgarten

Peter Hallgarten's family have a longstanding involvement in the German wine industry, and in 1898 Peter's grandfather, Arthur Hallgarten, started his own wine brokerage company. In 1933 Arthur's son Fritz sought refuge from Germany and established Hallgarten Wines Limited as the London importer for German wines. He specialized in estate bottled wines with original labels, and also a generic range of German wines. Peter, the son of Fritz Hallgarten, initially studied for a career in chemistry but in 1958 joined the family wine company.

Peter and his company are well known and highly respected in the wine and spirit industry. Hallgarten Wines is operated, however, with a small and tightly knit workforce. There is a Sales Director reporting to Peter, as Chairman; and in 1986 the company employed 30 sales, warehouse, delivery and administrative staff. The company imports around two million (70 cl) bottles per year. Its

This case was written by Elroy Dimson with the assistance of Cecilia Reyes and Mike Staunton as a basis for class discussion, rather than to illustrate either effective or ineffective handling of an administrative situation. We are grateful to Peter Hallgarten for his help, and to Shanta Acharya for research assistance on our earlier draft. Some items of internal company data have been disguised to preserve confidentiality.

Exhibit 1: *Consolidated accounts for Hallgarten Wines Ltd*

Balance sheet	£'000 for year ending 31 December				
	1985	1984	1983	1982	1981
Tangible assets	105	100	111	80	83
Investments	20	20	20	30	28
Fixed assets	125	120	131	110	111
Stocks	493	633	573	519	521
Trade debtors	1139	1227	1077	960	1007
Other current assets	50	50	50	175	35
Current assets	1682	1910	1700	1654	1563
Total assets	1807	2030	1831	1764	1674
Current liabilities	876	1134	997	1005	935
Net assets	931	896	834	759	739
Shareholders funds	925	874	818	756	735
Other long-term liabilities	6	22	16	3	4
Capital employed	931	896	834	759	739

Profit and loss account					
Sales	4448	4433	4213	3863	3790
Trading profit	120	136	105	105	137
Depreciation	32	31	25	24	24
Operating profit	88	105	80	81	113
Investment income	9	22	11	7	0
Profit before interest	97	127	91	88	113
Interest paid	7	1	2	8	8
Net profit before tax	91	126	89	80	105
Tax	39	69	26	58	na
Profit after tax	52	57	63	22	na
Dividends	1	1	1	1	na
Retained earnings	51	56	62	21	na

turnover is over £4 million, and the firm has a capital employed of around £1 million. Exhibit 1 provides summary financial data on the company.

The UK wine market

In recent years UK wine consumption per head has increased marginally (from 8 litres in 1978 to some 9 litres today) but is still minimal compared to France's per capita consumption of 89 litres and the European average of 45 litres per person (down from 50 litres in 1978).

World wine production is dominated by Europe, with approximately 80 per cent, led by France with 22 per cent. West Germany accounts for 8 per cent of world production, and in 1983, its exports of 240 million litres (about 15 per cent of its total production) went primarily to the United Kingdom (98 million litres) and the United States (57 million litres). The total UK table wine market, including still and sparkling wine, both imported and UK produced, amounted to 380 million litres, accounting for some £2 billion of consumers' expenditure. The bulk of the UK wine market is made up of imported still wines. In 1983, they accounted for 92 per cent of the market by volume and 88 per cent by value.

Germany ousted Spain from its position as third largest supplier to the UK market in 1978 and overtook Italy in 1980. In 1983 Germany accounted for 27 per cent of total imported still wine clearances compared to French wines which accounted for 46 per cent by value (but only 38 per cent by volume). Trade estimates suggest that the shares for off-licence (supermarkets and specialist retailers) and on-licence (pubs and restaurants) sales are respectively 65 per cent and 35 per cent by volume. Within the off-licence trade, the approximate split between supermarkets and specialist retailers is in the ratio 60:40.

The structure of trade in wine importing and wholesaling has changed radically over the past decade. Many of the functions of broker, shipper, agent, importer and wholesaler have now been integrated vertically, sometimes with that of the grower, in other cases with the retailer's function. There is a variety of routes by which wine reaches the consumer. Another feature has been the growth of own labels which predominate in the supermarket trade, and it has been estimated that 'own labels' now account for over 55 per cent of all supermarket wine sales. Indeed, the Sainsbury group claims to be the largest wine retailer, with up to a 15 per cent share of the table wine market.

In the United Kingdom, there are two components in the tax applied to wine: customs duty and value added tax (VAT). Duty is independent of the value of wine, but is applied according to the alcohol content. A typical wine with less than 15 per cent alcohol will incur duty of £0.98 per litre. VAT (currently 15 per cent) is applied to wine after the addition of duty.

Wine prices

Sales of German wines were reported by a prominent German wine house (Deinhard) in early 1984 to fall in the following prices brackets: under £2 per bottle, 20 per cent; £2–£3 per bottle, 66 per cent; over £3 per bottle, 14 per cent. Interestingly, prices appear not to have increased since then; a store check at the end of 1986 at supermarkets and specialist shops in London revealed prices such as the following: Goldener Oktober £2.69, Johannisberger Erntebringer 1981–2

Exhibit 2: *Domestic wine prices in the United Kingdom, Germany and France, 1980–85**

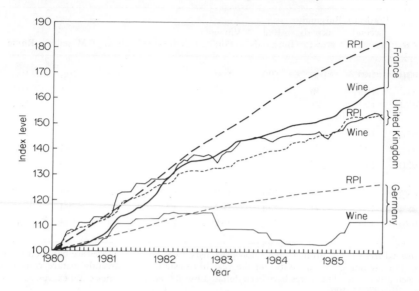

*This exhibit displays the monthly levels of domestic wine prices and the corresponding retail price index (RPI) levels for the United Kingdom, Germany and France, rebased to 100 as at 31 December 1979. The annual percentage inflation rates for the three countries were as follows:

	1980	1981	1982	1983	1984	1985	1986
United Kingdom	18.1	11.9	8.7	4.6	5.0	6.1	3.5e
Germany	5.5	6.0	5.3	3.0	2.5	2.2	0.1e
France	13.5	13.3	12.0	9.5	7.7	5.8	2.8e

Sources: Datastream, Bulletin Mensuel de Statistique and *Preise und Preisindizes für die Ein und Ausfuhr.*

£3.69, Crown of Crowns £2.45, Black Tower £2.25, Blue Nun £2.99, Bereich Nierstein 1984 £1.99, and Deinhard Green Label £3.95. Own label and Euroblend products were available at significantly lower prices than these. These prices have in the recent past increased by less than the general rate of inflation, currently around 3 per cent per annum.

The lower the quality of wine, the more its price will also reflect the supply of competing wines from other producing countries. For example, prices have been affected on occasions when unexpectedly large quantities of Italian or Californian wine have been dumped on the market. Exhibit 2 shows that domestic wine prices, in both the United Kingdom, Germany and France, have been considerably more volatile than the general level of retail prices.

The prices of the best wines, since they are distinctive, fluctuate according to the quality of the vintage and the quantity produced in each category. Most producers of these best wines retain a certain proportion of each harvest for subsequent sales and, in addition, there are regular auctions of wine, such as

Exhibit 3: *Retail wine prices in the United Kingdom adjusted for inflation 1970–86**

Year	Bordeaux second growth	Burgundy second growth	Red Burgundy	Vintage Port	Champagne	Alsace	Moselle	Rhine
1970	100	100	100	100	100	100	100	100
1972	103	136	134	108	118	112	225	195
1974	172	171	172	188	166	181	127	144
1976	107	167	150	141	107	80	83	80
1978	142	277	183	145	136	119	95	70
1980	178	273	257	130	157	122	130	65
1982	152	373	203	132	137	96	114	52
1984	137	271	274	163	134	126	84	53
1986	145	223	238	188	155	98	103	68

*Compiled from Berry Brothers and Rudd price lists 1970–86. The figures are based on the retail price (but excluding customs duty) for the year in question for a currently mature vintage for a representative wine. The prices have been deflated by the retail price index and expressed in index form with 1970 = 100.

those held by Christies in London. Over the longer term, prices also seem to vary with the business cycle, but there still remain considerable differences between the price movements of individual wines, even those produced in the same region. Finally, the prices at which importing firms can sell their inventories more or less parallel the fluctuations in the price of the current crop. These effects can be seen clearly in Exhibit 3, which records the retail prices (adjusted for inflation) of several representative types of wine.

Products and prices

Unlike France, where the grading of quality wines is largely geographical, in Germany exactly the same vineyards that produce quality wine (QmP, the top quality, and QbA, a middle level) can also produce table wine (Tafelwein) and Landwein (a superior German Tafelwein, from one of 15 specified districts). Although Liebfraumilch (a QbA) is the most widely exported, Germany also produces many fine wines, virtually all from the late-ripening Riesling grape. The House of Hallgarten is best known for its Liebfraumilch, Niersteiner, Piesporter, sparkling Schloss and other German wines, where good quality and reliability are important to both the trade buyer and consumer. In addition, there are recently introduced lines such as Hallgarten's new top quality QmP branded range, Kabinett, Spätlese and Auslese.

The House of Hallgarten in fact offers a full list of German and French wines, as well as a range of liqueurs and fine spirits. German wine accounts for some 70 per cent of the company's turnover, while French wine now represents nearly 30 per cent. This proportion has increased over recent years as a result of Peter's

Exhibit 4: *The House of Hallgarten price list, December 1986**

Category	Number of varieties	Price range (£)
French table wines and vin de pays	9	1.73–2.16
Bordeaux red wines	22	2.08–43.00
Bordeaux white wines	7	1.95–4.17
Loire wines	6	1.88–4.66
Chablis	5	5.50–6.83
Burgundy-Côte d'Or/Maconnais	32	2.68–10.42
Beaujolais/Midi/Provence	12	2.15–7.00
Rhône Valley wines	22	2.20–10.66
Chateauneuf-du-Pape wines	9	4.66–6.08
Vin Doux Naturel	2	5.16–5.66
Alsatian Rhine wines	5	2.32–4.33
Champagne/sparkling wines	5	2.33–7.67
Euroblend/Tafelwein/Landwein	3	1.60–2.42
Liebfraumilch/Own Label Qba	6	1.63–1.92
Moselle	16	1.82–3.64
Rheinhessen	10	1.97–2.70
Rheingau/Nahe/Palatinate	7	1.96–2.50
Palatinate/Nahe Estate Bottled	11	2.30–4.83
Rheinhessen/Franconia/Baden Estate Bottled	12	2.45–4.17
Rheingau Estate Bottled	1	2.57–4.25
Moselle Estate Bottled	15	2.23–4.89
Saar Estate Bottled	11	2.42–4.42
Ruwer Estate Bottled	11	2.25–7.25
Beerenauslesen	11	6.75–11.25
Trockenbeerenauslese	5	14.33–33.50
Eiswein	4	9.33–13.50
Connoisseur selection	7	3.58–5.42
Portuguese wines	5	3.33–6.42
English wines	1	2.33–2.33
Grenadine/Cooler	2	1.17–1.90
Liqueurs and fine spirits	8	3.08–8.83

*This exhibit summarizes a glossy 20 page price list. All prices are in £ per bottle (approximately 70 cl), and includes customs duty but not VAT.

continuing policy of diversification away from German wines, a policy which has also taken him into selling small quantities of Portuguese, Israeli and English (Isle of Wight) wines. In August 1986, Hallgarten Wines disposed of the distribution rights for the range of Royal Liqueurs invented by Peter during the 1970s and early 1980s, which had previously accounted for 3–5 per cent of the firm's turnover. Consequently, by late 1986 about 99 per cent of Hallgarten's sales revenue was attributable to its wine business.

The firm sells 300–400 different lines, and promotes them with a 20-page lavish, colour illustrated price list, summarized in Exhibit 4. A typical print run

Exhibit 5: *Illustrative production and selling timetable for European wines*

Standard White Wines
(such as Liebfraumilch)

Typical list price (excluding VAT)	£1.70–£2.50
Annual quantity (bottles)	0.5 million
Harvest month	October 1986
Quantity and price agreed *	November 1986–February 1987
Bottling period	February–December 1987
Arrival in United Kingdom	February 1987–March 1988
Sales period	March 1987–May 1988

Better White Wines
(such as Moselle)

Typical list price (excluding VAT)	£2.50–£3.50
Annual quantity (bottles)	0.7 million
Harvest month	October 1986
Quantity and price agreed*	November 1986–February 1987
Bottling period	February–December 1987
Arrival in United Kingdom	February 1987–March 1988
Sales period	March 1987–May 1988

Standard Red Wines
(French)

Typical list price (excluding VAT)	£2.50–£3.50
Annual quantity (bottles)	0.4 million
Harvest month	September–October 1986
Quantity and price agreed*	June 1987
Bottling period	June 1987 onwards
Arrival in United Kingdom	August 1987–July 1988
Sales period	September 1987–December 1988

*The dates shown for agreeing quantity and price apply to the major contract buyers, for example, of standard white wines. Whereas these buyers tend to purchase forward, smaller importers currently tend to buy on a 'spot' basis from producers throughout the calendar year.

for the price list is about 5000 copies, with a cost which depends on artwork requirements, but which might be £4000–5000 per revision, plus distribution expenses.

Trade buyers, such as restaurant proprietors, set their own prices on the basis of the wholesale costs they expect to incur. Consequently, if Hallgarten pays more than expected for a particular wine the costs cannot easily be passed on down the trading chain, for this would impose the expense of reprinting menus and wine lists on the trade buyer. It is equally difficult to withdraw a product which appears on the current Hallgarten list. If the goodwill of customers is to be fostered, Hallgarten can adjust prices only when the price list is reprinted. As with most other wine suppliers, this occurs once a year. On-licence buyers (such as restaurants and hotels) account for around 35 per cent of Hallgarten's sales by volume.

The difficulty of recovering cost increases is a problem not only with the less expensive wines that are mostly enjoyed when young and for which up to a year's inventory may be held. It is also a problem with the fine wines, for which Hallgarten's stock would also have to be replenished at a higher price. Thus, with his price list fixed for up to a year in advance, Peter Hallgarten's margins are obviously eroded by adverse movements in wine prices.

The German grape harvest usually takes place over a period of 2 months from mid-September onwards. Most everyday wine is made to be drunk within 2 years of the harvest, though Riesling QbA and the highest quality (QmP) wines may not reach their peak for 5 or 7 years. This gives rise to varying timescales

Exhibit 6: *Seasonal breakdown of Hallgarten sales*

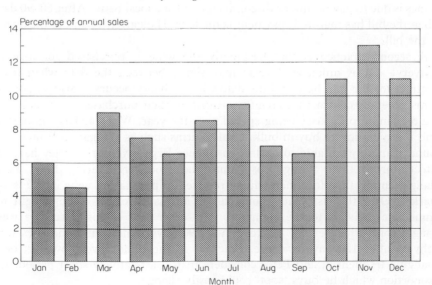

for the production of different qualities of wine. Exhibit 5 indicates these timescales and shows that Hallgarten can be exposed to adverse wine price fluctuations for a protracted period. Partly because of this, Peter has recently increased the proportion of his stock which he buys in the 'spot' market, rather than for forward delivery (see below).

Wine sales tend to peak in anticipation of the Christmas and New Year period, and final-quarter sales are higher than in the rest of the year. There are, in addition, month-to-month fluctuations in demand, most notably the surge which precedes the spring Budget when an increase in tax on wines and spirits is often expected. Exhibit 6 provides a sales breakdown for Hallgarten Wines over the 12 months of the year.

Terms of trade

When an importer such as Hallgarten Wines seeks to buy wine, there are various practices which are standardized in the industry. One is that wine transactions are denominated in the currency of the exporting country. In Hallgarten's case, the producer usually invoices Hallgarten Wines before the goods leave Germany. The German wine exporter sends a bill of exchange to Hallgarten with the shipping documents. The bill requires Hallgarten to pay for the goods on terms agreed with the producer. By adding the word 'accepted' and his signature, Peter Hallgarten 'accepts' the debt indicated on the bill of exchange, and typically 1 week after they have left Germany, the goods arrive in the United Kingdom. The accepted bill of exchange is sent to the German supplier. The supplier either waits 2–3 months until Hallgarten Wines is due to pay in full, or discounts the bill at a local bank. After 60–90 days when the bill has matured, payment is made by Hallgarten's bank to the owner of the bill.

A second practice is that frequently the wine is purchased for forward delivery, and as much as 2 years may elapse between the date when firms contract for the purchase and the date when delivery occurs. Large importing firms generally contract for about two-thirds of their purchases in late autumn, the remaining purchases being spread over the year. Whereas large importers find it economical to buy in bulk, smaller firms such as Hallgarten Wines have found it more profitable to decline to finance large inventories: they have, in effect, forced their storage costs onto the producer. During 1986, Peter Hallgarten has therefore increasingly resorted to purchasing wine in the 'spot' market. Over the last year, about half of all his purchases were bought for immediate delivery to the company. The other half of his purchases were bought forward, often for delivery in 60–90 days' time, but sometimes with delivery after 120 days or more. Practices in the trade have, however, been changing frequently, and Peter considers that in a relatively short period, the proportion which he buys 'spot' could easily change.

A third practice is that payments to the wine exporter by the importer are often timed to occur at the end of the month in which the wine clears the customs houses. Since customs duty is not paid until the wine is released, the imported wine may then remain in the importing firm's bonded warehouse for up to a year.

Finally, the discount and credit arrangements extended by importers to their customers tends to be fairly standardized. A rule of thumb is that an average gross sales margin of 18–20 per cent is required for a wine importer to break even (Hallgarten Wines achieves 20 per cent). However, for very large customers the margin is trimmed to 10–12 per cent, while for direct sales (or 'brokerage') business a margin of 5 per cent is regarded as acceptable. The margins which Hallgarten negotiates, as well as the company's standard credit terms (1/30, EOM, net 60), are thus typical of their competitors.

Currency exposure

Peter Hallgarten insists that his company is primarily a wine importer and wholesaler, and not a commodity or currency trader. However, there are

Exhibit 7: *Volatility of the deutschmark/£ and franc/£ exchange rates**

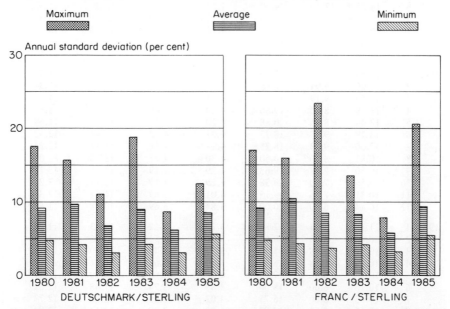

*This exhibit is based on a series of volatilities (annualized standard deviations) for changes in the DM/£ and Ffr/£ exchange rates. Volatilities were estimated from daily data within each month, starting in January 1980. For each calendar year, the exhibit plots the mean of the 12 monthly volatilities and the highest and lowest of these twelve estimates. The mean of all the volatilities is: DM/£ 8.3 per cent and Ffr/£ 8.7 per cent. The correlation between daily percentage changes in the DM/£ and Ffr/£ exchange rates over this period is 0.49.

Exhibit 8: *Month-end £, DM and Ffr interest and exchange rates, 1980–86*

Year and month	12-month percentage Eurointerest rate			DM/£ exchange rate		FFR/£ exchange rate	
	UK	Germany	France	Spot rate	12-Month forward	Spot rate	12-Month forward
1980: 1	16.00	8.63	13.50	3.93	3.68	9.21	9.01
2	17.13	9.44	15.00	4.04	3.77	9.49	9.32
3	17.69	10.25	15.00	4.19	3.93	9.67	9.45
4	14.75	8.69	13.25	4.08	3.87	9.53	9.41
5	15.00	8.56	12.88	4.17	3.94	9.70	9.52
6	14.25	8.19	12.63	4.14	3.92	9.62	9.48
7	13.44	7.88	11.88	4.19	3.98	9.69	9.55
8	15.25	8.19	12.63	4.28	4.02	9.96	9.73
9	14.44	8.75	13.31	4.33	4.12	10.05	9.95
10	14.94	8.62	12.69	4.65	4.40	10.71	10.50
11	14.00	9.44	13.00	4.54	4.36	10.54	10.45
12	14.19	9.06	12.69	4.68	4.47	10.85	10.71
1981: 1	13.13	9.38	12.75	5.03	4.86	11.58	11.54
2	12.13	12.75	13.38	4.73	4.75	11.10	11.23
3	12.38	11.56	13.13	4.71	4.68	11.12	11.19
4	12.63	12.13	13.88	4.74	4.72	11.22	11.35
5	13.00	12.81	17.00	4.81	4.80	11.44	11.85
6	13.38	12.44	20.00	4.65	4.61	11.09	11.74
7	14.63	12.50	20.13	4.58	4.50	10.86	11.39
8	14.25	12.50	24.00	4.53	4.46	10.89	11.82
9	16.13	11.75	23.50	4.15	4.00	9.97	10.61
10	16.00	11.44	19.00	4.16	4.00	10.44	10.71
11	14.44	9.69	18.13	4.33	4.15	10.90	11.25
12	15.88	10.38	18.63	4.30	4.10	10.90	11.16
1982: 1	14.69	10.31	17.19	4.35	4.18	11.06	11.30
2	14.00	9.94	16.88	4.34	4.19	11.06	11.34
3	13.63	9.19	19.50	4.31	4.14	11.13	11.71
4	13.69	8.50	19.88	4.19	4.00	10.93	11.53
5	13.44	8.56	20.88	4.20	4.02	10.96	11.68
6	13.19	9.38	18.75	4.27	4.12	11.84	12.42
7	12.00	9.13	18.25	4.27	4.16	11.87	12.53
8	10.81	8.50	20.50	4.30	4.21	12.02	13.07
9	10.50	7.94	19.63	4.29	4.19	12.11	13.11
10	9.56	7.00	19.38	4.29	4.19	12.11	13.20
11	10.31	7.06	19.75	4.01	3.89	11.34	12.31
12	10.44	6.00	20.00	3.84	3.69	10.88	11.83
1983: 1	11.38	5.94	17.88	3.75	3.57	10.63	11.25
2	10.81	5.63	18.63	3.69	3.51	10.46	11.19
3	10.69	5.38	15.13	3.57	3.40	10.70	11.12
4	10.13	5.38	16.50	3.84	3.67	11.51	12.17
5	10.38	6.00	17.25	4.06	3.90	12.19	12.95
6	10.13	6.00	18.00	3.89	3.74	11.68	12.52
7	10.63	6.00	16.75	4.02	3.85	12.06	12.73
8	10.56	6.50	17.00	4.03	3.89	12.14	12.84
9	9.88	6.31	16.25	3.94	3.82	11.97	12.66
10	9.75	6.19	15.00	3.93	3.80	11.95	12.52
11	9.63	6.50	16.75	3.95	3.84	12.03	12.81
12	9.88	6.44	14.50	3.95	3.82	12.08	12.59

Exhibit 8 (continued)

1984:	1	9.94	6.44	14.38	3.96	3.83	12.11	12.59
	2	9.50	6.25	16.75	3.88	3.77	11.96	12.75
	3	9.38	6.13	15.88	3.73	3.62	11.51	12.19
	4	9.44	6.25	14.13	3.79	3.68	11.63	12.12
	5	10.88	6.81	15.00	3.79	3.65	11.62	12.05
	6	10.69	6.81	14.50	3.76	3.63	11.54	11.94
	7	12.38	6.63	13.81	3.78	3.59	11.60	11.75
	8	10.81	6.25	12.88	3.79	3.63	11.62	11.84
	9	10.81	6.06	12.13	3.77	3.61	11.58	11.72
	10	10.63	5.94	12.13	3.68	3.53	11.29	11.44
	11	10.00	5.69	11.75	3.70	3.56	11.34	11.52
	12	10.25	5.63	11.50	3.66	3.50	11.19	11.32
1985:	1	12.19	6.19	11.50	3.57	3.38	10.92	10.85
	2	12.63	6.56	11.88	3.63	3.43	11.05	10.98
	3	11.94	6.25	11.88	3.85	3.66	11.77	11.76
	4	12.13	6.13	11.25	3.83	3.63	11.69	11.59
	5	12.19	5.69	10.25	3.94	3.71	11.99	11.78
	6	12.06	5.69	11.50	3.96	3.73	12.07	12.01
	7	10.81	5.00	11.88	3.99	3.78	12.16	12.28
	8	11.06	4.75	11.88	3.89	3.67	11.90	11.99
	9	11.00	4.75	11.50	3.75	3.54	11.44	11.49
	10	11.31	5.19	11.13	3.77	3.56	11.50	11.48
	11	11.19	4.75	10.19	3.74	3.52	11.40	11.30
	12	11.75	4.88	12.50	3.54	3.32	10.84	10.91
1986:	1	12.69	4.69	13.00	3.38	3.14	10.33	10.36
	2	11.75	4.44	11.00	3.23	3.02	9.93	9.86
	3	10.31	4.50	10.13	3.45	3.25	10.62	10.60
	4	9.56	4.50	7.50	3.36	3.20	10.69	10.49
	5	9.50	4.81	7.56	3.43	3.28	10.91	10.71
	6	9.63	4.69	7.38	3.37	3.22	10.75	10.53
	7	9.97	4.69	7.38	3.12	2.97	10.15	9.91
	8	9.63	4.38	7.44	3.03	2.88	9.93	9.73

occasions when he has bought and then resold wine in an overseas market, without taking physical delivery of the product. These opportunistic transactions have generally been profitable. Similarly, he periodically seeks an opinion from his bank manager on the strength of sterling, relative to the Deutschmark or French franc, before deciding whether to buy the appropriate quantity of foreign currency in the forward market.

The bank manager will usually supplement his opinion with a quotation for forward purchase of his chosen currency. If Peter accepts the quotation, the resulting contract commits Hallgarten and the bank to exchange sterling for another currency at the agreed rate of exchange, and on the date specified in the contract. Peter also uses rates published in the *Financial Times* as a guide to the cost of forward cover, though these quotations are in fact the rates for commercial contracts, ie in amounts of £25 000 or more, and with only a limited range of maturity dates (see Exhibit 10a below for specimen quotations).

When Peter makes a forward purchase of foreign currency, he normally enters into a negotiated contract with his bank, where the amount and delivery date are specified to suit the company's needs. Though some banks have indicated that a commission would be payable, Hallgarten's bank does not charge a fee for arranging forward cover. However, Peter has noticed that the buy–sell spread tends to be wider for his negotiated contracts than that quoted in the press.

If forward purchase is cheaper than buying foreign exchange in the spot market and/or if he expects the foreign currency to appreciate, then Peter will consider hedging at least part of his exposure. He therefore finds that it is a normal part of his business for him to speculate on the sterling/Deutschmark and sterling/franc exchange rates. He sees this as inevitable for an importer in the position of Hallgarten Wines. Moreover, he points out that if he can trade in currencies more shrewdly than his competitors, then the firm's trading income will be enhanced.

Recently currencies have been very volatile (see Exhibits 7–8), and the performance of Peter's bank manager in predicting exchange rate movements has been, to say the least, disappointing. As an alternative, Peter has considered whether to use a specialist firm to provide forecasts of the relevant exchange rates. However, he is not certain how he would choose between the many forecasting services which are available.

Hedging alternatives

Another avenue would be to hedge exchange rate exposure using currency futures or options contracts. Peter had previously rejected these instruments as being too sophisticated for a firm the size of Hallgarten, but recently Barclays Bank had launched its BERO (bearer exchange rate option) certificates (Exhibit 9). A sterling put BERO (giving Peter the right, throughout the next 6 months, to buy Deutschmarks at the current exchange rate) would cost about £250 for £5000–worth of cover. The BERO certificate could be purchased and sold over the counter at the local bank (see Exhibit 10b for specimen quotations).

Peter was quite interested in the BERO concept, since this constituted a 100 per cent guarantee of protection against adverse currency fluctuations, while Hallgarten would still benefit from any favourable movement in the exchange rate. But he was doubtful whether the BERO was the best way to hedge his exposure. He therefore decided to examine other approaches to managing the foreign exchange risk of the company. The most obvious alternative was to use currency futures.

Currency futures are essentially forward contracts which are bought and sold in a specialized marketplace. The futures contract, like a forward contract, is an agreement to exchange one currency for another; but unlike the forward contract, the maturity dates and the value of the contract are standardized. This

Exhibit 9: *Specimen premiums for a £5000 currency option certificate as at 28 February 1986*

Barclays BERO Certificate

SPECIMEN PREMIUMS — DM/STERLING BEROs

Premiums for BEROs (which represent the total cost for the rights under the certificates) are based like other currency options on the following:

option (strike) price in relation to the current exchange rate
period of the option (or time left to expiry date)
prevailing exchange rate volatility
prevailing forward margins (which themselves are a function of interest rate differentials).

The table below gives examples of typical sale and repurchase premiums in £ sterling of one £5000 sterling put (DM call) and sterling call (DM put) BERO certificate, at different exchange rates. It is based on strike prices of sterling puts at 3.15 and 3.20 and Sterling calls at 3.30 and 3.35 with a 6 month expiry date.

CURRENT RATE: *3.10*

	Puts			Calls	
Strike	Sale	Repur	Strike	Sale	Repur
3.15	354	329	3.30	52	33
3.20	411	389	3.35	40	23

CURRENT RATE: *3.15*

	Puts			Calls	
Strike	Sale	Repur	Strike	Sale	Repur
3.15	298	272	3.30	69	47
3.20	353	328	3.35	52	34

CURRENT RATE: *3.20*

	Puts			Calls	
Strike	Sale	Repur	Strike	Sale	Repur
3.15	252	224	3.30	89	65
3.20	298	272	3.35	70	48

CURRENT RATE: *3.25*

	Puts			Calls	
Strike	Sale	Repur	Strike	Sale	Repur
3.15	208	181	3.30	114	88
3.20	253	225	3.35	90	66

CURRENT RATE: *3.30*

	Puts			Calls	
Strike	Sale	Repur	Strike	Sale	Repur
3.15	173	144	3.30	142	116
3.20	209	182	3.35	115	89

CURRENT RATE: *3.35*

	Puts			Calls	
Strike	Sale	Repur	Strike	Sale	Repur
3.15	140	114	3.30	177	150
3.20	175	146	3.35	142	116

CURRENT RATE: *3.40*

	Puts			Calls	
Strike	Sale	Repur	Strike	Sale	Repur
3.15	114	87	3.30	214	190
3.20	142	116	3.35	176	149

CURRENT RATE: *3.45*

	Puts			Calls	
Strike	Sale	Repur	Strike	Sale	Repur
3.15	90	68	3.30	258	237
3.20	116	89	3.35	213	189

Source: Barclays Bank

makes it cheaper and easier to close out a position in a currency. In London, currency futures contracts are traded on the London International Financial Futures Exchange (LIFFE). Unfortunately, though contracts are available in Deutschmark and sterling, these (and other) currencies are traded on LIFFE

Exhibit 10: *Forward, futures and options quotations as at 8 September 1986*

Contract	Bid and offer quotations for various contract maturities				
(a) Forward contracts	*Spot Rate*	*1 month*	*3 month*	*6 month*	*12 months*
DM/£ Forward	3.064–78	3.047–67*	3.020–40	2.984–04	2.912–35
Ffr/£ Forward	10.041–71	10.033–71	10.029–70	10.025–66	10.015–57
(b) BERO certificates	*October 17*	*November 17*	*December 17*	*March 17*	*June 17*
£/DM Call @ 3.10	—	—	57–72*	76–95	—
@ 3.15	—	—	33–45	52–70	—
@ 3.35	—	5–15	—	—	—
@ 3.40	—	5–15	—	—	—
£/DM Put @ 2.95	—	—	43–58	96–115	—
@ 3.00	—	—	72–87	133–155	—
@ 3.30	—	416–426	—	—	—
@ 3.35	—	495–505	—	—	—
(c) Futures contracts	*Spot Rate*	*3 month*	*6 month*	*9 month*	*12 month*
$DM/Futures	0.4837–39	0.4840–44*	0.4857–62	—	—
$/£ Futures	1.4868–75	1.4860–75	1.4715–30	—	—
(d) Traded options	*October*	*November*	*December*	*March*	*June*
$/DM Call @ 0.48	0.95–07*	1.33–44	1.63–75	2.25–38	2.70–88
@ 0.49	0.48–57	0.85–95	1.14–25	1.75–88	2.22–38
@ 0.50	0.18–26	0.50–60	0.76–87	1.35–47	1.82–95
$/DM Put @ 0.48	0.45–55	0.80–90	1.03–15	1.50–65	1.85–00
@ 0.49	0.95–06	1.30–45	1.53–65	2.00–15	2.35–50
@ 0.50	1.67–78	1.95–10	2.15–27	2.60–75	2.92–07
$/£ Call @ 1.40	8.40–90	8.55–85	8.80–30	9.30–80	9.95–25
@ 1.45	4.00–25	4.70–05	5.20–50	6.10–50	6.80–30
@ 1.50	1.30–60	2.10–45	2.70–05	3.80–25	4.50–00
@ 1.55	0.20–45	0.75–05	1.30–60	2.25–60	2.95–35
@ 1.60	—	—	0.55–75	1.25–55	1.85–15
$/£ Put @ 1.40	0.05–30	0.60–90	1.20–50	2.80–10	4.10–60
@ 1.45	0.80–10	1.90–20	2.75–15	4.75–15	6.30–80
@ 1.50	3.00–30	4.40–75	5.35–75	7.50–95	9.10–60
@ 1.55	6.75–25	8.00–30	8.85–20	10.85–35	12.40–90
@ 1.60	—	—	13.00–45	14.70–20	16.15–75

*Quotations are given with the lower value first, as illustrated here. A forward rate quotation of 3.047–67 means that the bank sells at the commercial rate (that is, over £25 000-worth of currency) of 3.047, buying at 3.067. A BERO price of 57–72 means that the bank buys a £5000 face value certificate with a maturity of 1 month and strike of 3.10 for £57, selling at £72. The futures quotations, which are for units of DM 125 000 and £25 000 respectively, have a similar interpretation to the forward rates. Finally the traded options, which have units of trading of DM 62 500 and £12 500 respectively, are quoted in US cents per DM or £: thus, the quotation of 0.95–07 means that the broker buys an October $/DM call with a strike of 0.48 for 0.95 cents and sells for 1.07 cents per Deutschmark.

against the dollar, while it is necessary to use the Philadelphia Stock Exchange to buy futures on the French franc (also traded against the dollar).

Peter was aware that trading in the currency futures market involves commission payments which are negotiated between the individual client and the broker or member of the exchange, and that margin payments are also required. An attraction for Hallgarten Wines was that, unlike forward contracts, use of the futures market would not automatically consume lines of credit. However, Peter was doubtful about whether this was a real benefit, since the company would have to ensure that it could adequately meet margin calls. Exhibit 10c provides specimen quotations for futures on the Deutschmark and sterling.

Peter's other alternative was to buy foreign exchange protection by means of a currency option, not necessarily a BERO. In exchange for paying the appropriate premium, Hallgarten would have the right, but not the obligation, to buy or sell a set amount of one currency against another at a fixed rate on or before a specified date. As the option holder, Hallgarten would benefit from a favourable movement in the exchange rate while being protected from any adverse movement. Traded options on the $/£ and $/DM exchange rates (only) are traded on LIFFE and the London Stock Exchange, while other currencies are traded in Philadelphia, Chicago and elsewhere (see Exhibit 10d for specimen quotations). Over-the-counter currency options are also available in many banks for most currencies, though their face values would normally be much larger than that of the BERO.

Peter Hallgarten had also read about other forms of currency protection. Salomon Brothers, for example, offer a 'range forward' contract, while Citicorp Investment Bank's 'cylinder options' are similar. Those contracts specify a range of exchange rates between two currencies which will apply when the contract matures, but the exchange rate is guaranteed not to exceed or fall short of the limits which are stated in the contract. These types of contract are available in various currencies; but at present the contracts are all against the dollar, so Peter thought it would require some ingenuity to use this approach to hedging exchange rate exposure.

Given the hedging methods that were available to him, Peter started work on developing a strategy for Hallgarten Wines Limited. He was particularly keen that his policy for dealing with the exchange risks and other international financial risks encountered by the company should be practical and easy to implement.

24. Cadbury Schweppes

In March 1985, Cadbury Schweppes (CS) announced their full year results for the year ended 29 December 1984, and at the same time, revealed that they would be raising $80 million through the issue of a convertible eurobond. The terms of the issue had yet to be finalized. This issue formed part of a sequence of financing operations which the group had undertaken throughout the early 1980s to support its expansion programme, particularly overseas.

Background and history

Cadbury Schweppes was a major international group, engaged in the manufacture and marketing of chocolate confectionery, soft drinks, tea, coffee and a wide range of food products. The company marketed most of its major products under the 'Cadbury' and 'Schweppes' names. Principal brands included Cadbury's Dairy Milk, Cadbury's Fruit and Nut, Cadbury's Creme Eggs, Schweppes' Tonic Water, Ginger Ale and Club Soda, Rose's Lime Juice, Typhoo Tea, Kenco Coffee, Cadbury's Bournvita cocoa drink, Chivers and Hartley jams and jellies, and Cadbury chocolate biscuits.

The company was formed in 1969 through the merger of Cadbury Group and Schweppes, which had been in business for more than 150 and 200 years, respectively. The company employed over 35 000 people, and had operations in 22 countries. Its products were sold in more than 90 countries, and its principal markets were the United Kingdom, North America, Europe and Australia.

In 1984, company sales and profits reached their highest ever levels (see Exhibit 1). Over the period 1980–84, CS had achieved compound annual growth rates in sales and trading profits of 16.7 and 17.7 per cent, respectively. Over the same period, the proportion of sales and trading profits generated outside the United Kingdom increased significantly. By 1984, overseas sales were 54 per cent of the Company's total, while overseas profits accounted for 60 per cent of total group trading profits (Exhibit 2).

This case was written by Paul Marsh as a basis for class discussion rather than to illustrate either effective or ineffective handling of an administrative situation. We are grateful to Pam Pocock and Ian Cooper for help in preparing an earlier draft of this case.

Exhibit 1: *Cadbury Schweppes' financial results: 5 year summary (£ million)*

	1984	1983	1982	1981	1980*
Consolidated profit and loss accounts					
Sales	2016.2	1702.8	1494.2	1228.7	1086.4
Trading profit	154.4	125.6	104.8	89.5	80.5
Interest payable less investment income	(37.6)	(25.4)	(21.1)	(13.5)	(22.4)
Associated companies	7.2	6.7	6.0	4.6	3.2
Profit before taxation	124.0	106.9	89.7	80.6	61.3
Taxation	(42.1)	(38.5)	(34.8)	(29.8)	(12.8)
Profit attributable to minorities	(9.4)	(7.8)	(6.0)	(3.7)	(2.6)
Extraordinary items	(7.4)	(18.2)	(9.6)	(12.8)	(4.8)
Profit attributable to shareholders	65.1	42.4	39.3	34.3	41.1
Dividends	(28.9)	(24.2)	(21.9)	(20.6)	(15.3)
Profit retained	36.2	18.2	17.4	13.7	25.8
Increase/(decrease) in borrowings net of cash	(17.9)	55.2	147.1	(64.3)	(5.4)
Summarized consolidated balance sheets†					
Assets employed					
Stock	316.6	266.9	265.7	187.5	178.8
Debtors	357.5	294.9	245.6	193.3	158.2
Cash, loans and deposits	36.6	48.3	82.7	136.8	48.7
	710.7	610.1	594.0	517.6	385.7
Short-term borrowings	(64.5)	(104.7)	(100.4)	(53.2)	(46.9)
Other creditors and provisions	(507.7)	(406.2)	(355.2)	(263.9)	(189.5)
	138.5	99.2	138.4	200.5	149.3
Fixed assets	627.5	530.5	460.7	339.0	273.7
	766.0	629.7	599.1	539.5	423.0
Financed by:					
Capital of Cadbury Schweppes	129.5	114.4	114.4	114.3	95.7
Reserves	389.2	285.5	275.2	269.9	196.3
Long term loans	198.5	187.9	171.4	125.6	108.1
Minority interests	48.8	41.9	38.1	29.7	22.9
	766.0	629.7	599.1	539.5	423.0
Borrowings net of cash	226.4	244.3	189.1	42.0	106.3

*Financial year 1980 comprised 53 weeks
†The amounts for debtors, creditors and minority interests in 1981 and 1980 are not strictly comparable because of the revised presentation requirements of the Companies Act 1981.

Exhibit 2: *Cadbury Schweppes: sales, profits and assets by region (£ million)*

	Total	United Kingdom	Europe	North America	Australia	Africa, Asia and New Zealand
1984						
Sales						
Confectionery	858.0	346.2	45.9	270.5	120.1	75.3
Drinks	742.5	234.8	154.2	215.5	121.0	17.0
Beverages and foods	352.5	276.6	32.0	—	19.1	24.8
Health and hygiene	63.2	63.2	—	—	—	—
	2016.2	920.8	232.1	486.0	260.2	117.1
Trading profit						
Confectionery	86.2	37.0	4.6	20.4	14.1	10.1
Drinks	53.8	15.2	10.8	16.5	9.9	1.4
Beverages and foods	13.6	9.3	1.1	—	1.0	2.2
Health and hygiene	0.8	.8	—	—	—	—
	154.4	62.3	16.5	36.9	25.0	13.7
Operating assets						
Confectionery	408.9	157.0	21.1	161.6	34.0	35.2
Drinks	285.7	102.8	45.1	88.1	41.5	8.2
Beverages and foods	120.4	86.5	5.4	—	17.6	10.9
Health and hygiene	18.2	18.2	—	—	—	—
	833.2	364.5	71.6	249.7[2]	93.1	54.3
1983						
Sales						
Confectionery	721.5	307.7	38.0	201.2	91.8	82.8
Drinks	647.6	229.8	129.1	173.6	96.9	18.2
Beverages and foods	274.9	228.0	28.7	—	—	18.2
Health and hygiene	58.8	58.4	.4	—	—	—
	1702.8	823.9	196.2	374.8	188.7	119.2
Trading profit						
Confectionery	69.9	33.8	3.0	12.3	10.0	10.8
Drinks	41.8	12.1	6.5	14.6	7.5	1.1
Beverages and foods	12.0	9.5	1.1	—	—	1.4
Health and hygiene	1.9	1.9	—	—	—	—
	125.6	57.3	10.6	26.9	17.5	13.3
Operating assets						
Confectionery	358.9	154.9	23.2	116.1	25.3	39.4
Drinks	254.5	103.4	32.0	72.0	35.5	11.6
Beverages and foods	85.0	72.7	6.4	—	—	5.9
Health and hygiene	17.5	17.5	—	—	—	—
	715.9	348.5	61.6	188.1	60.8	56.9
Trading profit to operating assets (per cent)						
1984	18.5	17.1	23.0	14.8	26.9	25.2
1983	17.5	16.4	17.2	14.3	28.8	23.4
Gross capital expenditure (£ million)						
1984	131.4	40.0	14.0	48.5	22.1	6.8
1983	122.0	60.4	13.5	28.8	10.7	8.6

1. The geographical analysis is based on the location of the operating companies. Operating assets represent tangible fixed assets, stock, debtors and creditors after excluding borrowings, taxation and dividends.
2. Includes approximately £50 million Canadian assets.

In 1984, 44 per cent of the sales and 40 per cent of the trading profits generated outside the United Kingdom were from North America (see Exhibit 2). Growth in this region had been rapid, and had been achieved through exports, capital investments, and by acquisition. In 1978 Cadbury Schweppes (CS) bought Peter Paul, the third largest US chocolate maker, for $58 million. And 4 years later the company made another two acquisitions in the States: Duffy-Mott, a producer of apple juice, apple sauce and vegetable juice, bought from American Brands for $60 million, and Holland House, a manufacturer of non-alcoholic cocktail mixes, acquired from National Distillers and Chemical Company for $8.8 million. During this period, the company had also been investing in its other markets. Annual capital expenditure was running at £120–£130 million worldwide (Exhibit 3), with over 50 per cent being spent in the United Kingdom on rationalization and redundancy costs.

Financing the expansion

Cadbury Schweppes had been profitable throughout this period, but not sufficiently profitable to fund its expansion internally (see Exhibit 3). The acquisition of Peter Paul had been financed by US dollar borrowings, and in 1981 CS issued 73.9 million shares via a 1 for 5 rights issue at 77p to raise £55.1 million after issue expenses. Sir Adrian Cadbury, the Chairman commented 'we must endeavour to expand and develop the group's overseas interests. We would be prepared to identify the right sort of acquisition. The top priority is still North America. Pending any such overseas investment, the proceeds of the issue will be available for the Group's short term cash requirements.' The rights issue was not particularly well received by the market, and the shares fell 8p to 85p on the news. This, however, was against the background of a general fall of some 2 per cent in the All Share Index.

During 1982, when the company bought both Duffy-Mott and Holland House, long and medium-term borrowings increased by £46 million. Overall, the company's gearing (net borrowings to shareholders funds) increased from 10.9 per cent in 1981 (an unusually low level for the company) to 48.5 per cent in 1982. Over this period, Cadbury Schweppes continued to focus on the huge potential of the North American market. Profit from the region had grown by 37 per cent in 1983 and had tripled over the previous 3 years. But the expansion had pushed up the company's borrowing levels, and during the course of 1983, CS sought to minimize the cost of its borrowings. One move made by the group was to raise a proportion of its borrowing requirements for working capital from the US commercial paper market*.

---

*Commercial paper is an unsecured IOU, issued by a corporation on a discount basis, promising to pay the holder full face value at redemption. Commercial paper has a variety of different maturities, closely paralleling Treasury bills, normally between 30 and 90 days, and not exceeding 270 days.

Exhibit 3: *Cadbury Schweppes: sources and uses of funds*

Sources and uses	1982	1983	1984
Sources of funds			
Operations:			
Income before taxes, minority interests and extraordinary items	89.7	106.9	124.0
Less: equity in earnings of associated companies, net of dividends	4.4	5.3	5.0
	85.3	101.6	119.0
Depreciation	39.5	45.0	55.9
Total generated from operations	124.8	146.6	174.9
Other sources:			
Disposal of fixed assets	11.6	12.3	19.6
Ordinary shares issued for cash to shareholders and minorities	0.4	0.1	74.6
Total sources	136.8	159.0	269.1
Application of funds			
Dividends paid to shareholders and minorities	29.4	25.5	28.2
Tax paid	22.2	33.0	29.0
Purchase of fixed assets and investments	104.6	126.1	133.4
Acquisitions of subsidiaries	60.2	—	20.1
Additional shares acquired in associates	2.1	1.1	—
Extraordinary items	9.4	16.8	18.6
	227.9	202.5	229.3
Increase in working capital			
Accounts receivable	34.0	46.6	56.0
Inventories	43.9	1.2	43.5
Liabilities (excluding borrowings)	(26.0)	(42.7)	(89.9)
Exchange restatement of working capital (excluding net borrowings)	(8.5)	(9.3)	(20.1)
	43.4	(4.2)	(10.5)
Total applications	271.3	198.3	218.8
Net outflow (inflow) of funds	134.5	39.3	(50.3)
Net borrowings			
At beginning of year	42.0	189.1	244.3
Exchange restatement	12.6	15.9	32.4
Net outflow (inflow) of funds	134.5	39.3	(50.3)
At end of year	189.1	244.3	226.4

In order to do this, CS had to gain a credit rating in the United States. This in itself involved more than a man-year of effort. Jeremy Howarth, who was to run the commercial paper programme for CS, explained

> we had to bare our soul to the rating agencies (Moody's and Standard and Poor's). Their investigators leave no stone unturned. They are unimpressed by exciting profit forecasts or expansion plans. What they want to know is whether a company can redeem its paper in 7 or 90 days. Conservative financial ratios and careful risk management are the qualities they are looking for. Company strategy on debt ratios, dividends, capital spending, acquisitions and divestiture plans were all covered exhaustively in the grilling given to CS.

These efforts proved worthwhile, however, and CS was rated A1 by Standard and Poor's and Prime 1, or P1, by Moody's. CS therefore gained the highest credit rating normally afforded to a non-US private-sector company, and hence could offer the lowest interest rates on its short-term debt. At that time, interest rates on commercial paper were some three-quarters of a per cent lower than the alternative dollar LIBOR rate. The Company attributed this to the elimination of the bank's spread, combined with the rating and guaranteed liquidity afforded by commercial paper.

Using the commercial paper market, CS raised US $34 million as short-term debt and an additional $33 million, which it classified as long-term debt because it was backed by long-term committed bank lines of credit. In the same year, the Group took a close look at the structure of its longer-term debt, took advantage of lower interest rates and through a number of swap transactions, restructured the maturities of its debt. The *Financial Times* commented on 20 March 1983, 'Fixed rate sterling liabilities have been assumed against equivalent amounts of variable rate deposits, which have been financed with US commercial paper. By arranging corresponding long-term back-up credit lines, Cadbury has effectively been able to borrow the fixed rate sterling at rates showing appreciable savings over more conventional alternatives'.

The American quotation and its rationale

A year later, in March 1984, the group announced it was seeking a listing, and raising up to $100 million in new equity in the American over-the-counter (OTC) market via American Depository Receipts (ADRs)*. There were a

---

*ADRs are a quick and convenient mechanism for transferring ownership, receiving dividends, and taking care of other routine transactions in foreign securities. They work in the same way as warehouse receipts for commodities. A US bank acts as depository and issues ADRs representing a specified number of underlying shares. The bank then acts as US transfer agent for the ADRs, distributing dividends in dollars, and disseminating information about the company. ADR transactions are recorded on the books of the US depository bank, and this minimizes the impact of foreign taxes and exchange control laws.

number of motives for this move. First, CS had been investing heavily in North America, which was their fastest growing region. Nevertheless, with about 8 per cent of the US confectionery market, and a smaller share in soft drinks, Sir Adrian felt that they still lacked the necessary 'clout'. He believed there were big opportunities in the United States, particularly in confectionery, and wanted to see the US contribution rise from a quarter to a third of group profits. North American investment was therefore a priority, and the issue proceeds would be used 'for capital expenditures in connection with the expansion and improvement of the North American manufacturing facilities, principally in confectionery, and for further development of the company's brands in North America'.

Sir Adrian saw the involvement of North American investors as part of the company's commitment to, and strategy of seeking a higher profile in the United States. The listing would be helped by the 'American consumers' increasing awareness of our products in the market place', and in turn, 'the issue should help to make Cadbury chocolate and Schweppes drinks better known'. John Hepburn, London Managing Director of Morgan Stanley, the US bank which was to lead manage the issue, supported this view: 'If your business strategy is to sell more product in the United States, selling your company's stock in the United States makes sense. Its a prestigious form of advertising.'

Second, the equity issue would reduce the company's gearing. At the year end, gearing stood at 61 per cent (Exhibit 4); in March, when the ADR issue was announced, it was closer to 70 per cent; and on current estimates, it could reach nearly 80 per cent by the mid-year results in June. Most of the increase came from US commercial paper which CS was using like a dollar overdraft. By June, it was estimated that outstanding commercial paper could reach £200 million. The increase in debt was primarily attributable to working capital requirements as a result of normal seasonal trends and increased sales, although it also reflected the capital expenditure programme, and exchange rate fluctuations.

The gearing level, and the cash hungry nature of the business was causing concern both inside the company and amongst external analysts. Virtually all financial press coverage at the time made some reference to this question. For example, the *Investors Chronicle* (16 March 1984) commented: 'At the end of 1982, investors first started to pay above average attention to CS' gearing. . . . On the one hand, there is the company's undoubted success on the trading front, and on the other, a balance sheet leaking cash and showing every sign of continuing to do so this year.' Clearly, the new equity from the ADR issue would lower gearing 'at a stroke', particularly since CS stated that it would be used 'to reduce short-term debt, principally through the repayment of outstanding commercial paper', pending its longer term use in the company's investment programme.

Third, CS felt that the ADR issue gave them considerable future flexibility. As Hugh Collum, the Finance Director explained, 'the United States is the

Exhibit 4: *Cadbury Schweppes: 5 year summary of financial ratios*

Ratio	defined as	units	1984	1983	1982	1981	1980
Profitability							
Margin	$\dfrac{\text{Trading profit}}{\text{Sales}}$	per cent	7.7	7.4	7.0	7.3	7.4
Return on assets	$\dfrac{\text{Trading profit}}{\text{Operating assets}^*}$	per cent	18.5	17.5	16.1	18.3	18.2
Interest and dividend cover							
Interest cover	$\dfrac{\text{Trading profit}}{\text{Net finance charges}}$	times	4.1	4.9	5.0	6.6	3.6
Dividend cover	$\dfrac{\text{Earnings per ordinary share}}{\text{Dividend per ordinary share}}$	times	2.7	2.5	2.2	2.5	3.0
Debt to equity ratios							
	$\dfrac{\text{Net borrowings}}{\text{Shareholders funds}}$	per cent	43.6	61.1	48.5	10.9	36.4
	$\dfrac{\text{Net borrowings}}{\text{Shareholders funds plus minority interests}}$	per cent	39.9	55.3	44.2	10.1	33.8
Liquidity ratios							
Quick ratio	$\dfrac{\text{Current assets less stock}}{\text{Current liabilities}}$	per cent	74.2	73.2	78.7	114.0	93.5
Current ratio	$\dfrac{\text{Current assets}}{\text{Current liabilities}}$	per cent	133.8	130.2	142.3	178.9	174.6
Asset ratios							
Operating asset turnover	$\dfrac{\text{Sales}}{\text{Operating assets}^*}$	times	2.4	2.4	2.3	2.5	2.5
Working capital turnover	$\dfrac{\text{Sales}}{\text{Working capital}}$	times	8.6	8.0	7.0	7.4	6.2
Per share							
Earnings per share {	pretax basis	pence	23.62	21.25	17.96	17.72	15.06
	net basis	pence	15.65	13.60	10.98	11.32	12.18
	net of extraordinary items	pence	14.05	9.52	8.82	8.24	10.91
Dividends per share		pence	5.90	5.40	4.90	4.60	4.10
Net assets per share		pence	102.1	89.22	86.95	85.79	78.11

*Operating assets represent tangible fixed assets, stock, debtors and creditors after excluding borrowings, taxation and dividends

greatest capital market in the world, and this move increases both our flexibility and visibility. It should stimulate US investments.' Sir Adrian added 'If the shares become better known on Wall Street, CS will be able to raise more money there in the future on good terms.' Furthermore, although there were no immediate plans for further US takeovers, the ADRs could nevertheless be used as paper for future acquisitions, or for stock option compensation programmes for US managers.

Finally, the ADR issue was favoured on cost grounds. As Hugh Collum pointed out 'an issue in the US will be at full market price, as opposed to the 15 per cent or so discount on a rights issue in the United Kingdom. This should give no cause for discontent among existing British shareholders. We're not giving anything away for nothing'. He also pointed out that 'existing shareholders will see their earnings diluted by less than 5 per cent in the coming year'. Hugh Collum was persuaded that a rights issue would not have been well received, and the financial press seemed to agree. The *Daily Telegraph* (9 March 1984) stated that 'shareholders in CS can afford a smile for it looks as if (instead of a rights issue), the Americans are going to finance the next stage in the company's growth'. Similarly, the *Financial Times* (10 April 1984) commented 'Meanwhile the shares might be expected to benefit from the removal of the rights issue cloud which has hung over them . . . and there is now the juicy prospect, of course, of an onset of US buying'.

Issuing the ADRs

CS aimed to complete the extensive preparations required for a US quotation — the registration statement for the Securities and Exchange Commission (SEC), a second set of accounts based on US accounting standards, the issue prospectus, the ADR facility, and the OTC listing agreement — by mid-May. They then planned to offer the shares 'when the market looks good'. As Hugh Collum explained, 'we'll wait until the day to decide how many shares to issue. It'll depend on market conditions'. The issue was to be underwritten by a syndicate managed by Morgan Stanley, Lehman Brothers and Kleinwort Benson. The ADRs would be quoted on the OTC NASDAQ system rather than on the New York Stock Exchange since a listing on the latter would have required CS to switch over to quarterly earnings statements.

The issue was backed up by extensive investor relations work. In mid-May, this culminated in a US 'roadshow' by Sir Adrian Cadbury, Dominic Cadbury (the Chief Executive), and Hugh Collum. They visited all the major financial centres (New York, Boston, San Francisco, Los Angeles and Chicago), expounding the merits of the group's shares to institutional investors. However, at the last moment, in late May, the issue was postponed. The markets had been unsettled by the Continental Illinois affair and banking collapse rumours, and although the Dow Jones Index had fallen by only 3 per cent during May, the CS share price had fallen by 6 per cent. CS announced that 'the issue will proceed when the financial markets are more settled'.

In the event, the issue took place in September, shortly after CS announced its half-year results (a week earlier and slightly better than the market had expected). The company in fact issued 6 million ADRs each representing 10 CS shares. The price was set at $17, which was equal to the middle market closing CS share price in London on 10 September, converted into dollars at the market closing exchange rate. Out of the gross proceeds of $102 million, CS paid $4.8 million to the underwriters for underwriting discounts and commissions, and a further $2.2 million for other issue expenses, leaving net proceeds of $95 million. The offering was completed on 11 September. William Kneisel, Managing Director of Morgan Stanley in New York declared the issue 'a tremendous success . . . there has been very strong demand from both the major and small institutions, despite the outlook for sterling'.

This verdict was echoed by Hugh Collum who commented, 'The group has now consolidated its presence on a second major capital market'. He added 'A comparable rights issue would have been at a discount from current market prices. With ADRs, the company was able to sell its shares at the current market price. By issuing equity in the US rather than in its domestic market, the company saved more than $12 million'.

Treasury management

Hugh Collum had joined the CS Board as Finance Director in September 1983. Before then, he had been Deputy Finance Director with responsibility for treasury management. Given the increasing importance of the treasury function within CS, Hugh Collum decided to create the new position of Director of Treasury. Martin Bralsford was therefore recruited from the Rank Organisation to fill this slot. Amongst Martin Bralsford's new responsibilities were: financing policy; new issues; debt management; cash budgeting, planning and management; foreign exchange exposure management; tax planning; leasing; credit management; capital budgeting procedures; and capital market and bank relations.

Treasury management in UK companies had in recent years been experiencing something little short of a revolution. As the *Financial Times* commented in a special feature on 18 June 1985,

> Ten years ago, the profession hardly existed; today corporate treasury is perhaps the fastest growing sector of industrial management. The impetus came in the early 1970s with the introduction of floating exchange rates . . . when companies realised that the swings on currency markets could wipe out commercial profits if exchange rate exposure was not constantly managed. And in recent years, the volatility of interest rates . . . has provided an additional boost.
>
> Today, most large or medium-sized firms regard a corporate treasurer as an essential part of the senior management team; and treasury management is beginning

to rival accountancy as the natural route to a seat on the Board as finance director. Many of the multinationals have set up what are in effect small banks, with active dealing in currency and deposit markets regarded as an integral part of the business. Treasurers have also learnt that it is often cheaper to finance UK investments in other currencies by, say, raising dollars on the US commercial paper market and translating the funds into sterling. Interest rate swaps have provided the opportunity for different companies to share their respective strengths on world credit markets and minimize their weaknesses. . . . The increasingly international nature of financial markets, and the constant addition of new instruments such as futures, currency options, and future rate agreements have put pressure on the treasurer to take a more active role.

It was against this general background that Martin Bralsford took over the Treasurer's seat at Cadbury Schweppes. Martin was already well known within the profession as a progressive thinker, and as an active Council Member of the Association of Corporate Treasurers. This fitted well with Hugh Collum, who had a reputation as an innovative and forward-thinking Finance Director. Both individuals seemed ideally suited to CS, with its increasing focus on overseas growth, currency exposure management, and the use of international financial markets. The *Financial Times* summed this up by concluding 'nowhere is the Group balanced more delicately on the threshold of change than in its financial department'.

Financial objectives

Within Cadbury Schweppes, a major exercise was in progress to develop a summary of group objectives which would be used to guide management plans and shape corporate strategy. These objectives were to be announced with the 1984 annual results, and a formal statement of group objectives would then appear for the first time in the 1984 Annual Report.

Broadly, these objectives stated that the group would concentrate on its principal business areas of confectionery, soft drinks, beverages and food products, and maximize the use of existing assets, rather than diversifying into unrelated areas. In particular, in confectionery and soft drinks, CS aimed to increase its share of the world market and progressively to improve its ranking in the international league of chocolate manufacturers and non-cola carbonated soft drinks companies. This was to be achieved through a decentralized organization structure 'based on product streams to encourage the maximum use of our assets on a worldwide basis through product sourcing and effective planning of capital expenditure'.

Cadbury Schweppes also wished to develop a statement of their financial objectives which would then be published alongside the business objectives in the Annual Report. These were to take the form of target values for various financial ratios. The ratios which the Company currently calculated and published are shown in Exhibit 4. One of the new financial team's early priorities therefore was to look at financial policies, and to help decide which ratios the company should publish targets for, and what these targets should be. This involved making judgements on how the group's operating and financial policies gelled together, and linked in with, say, the dividend policy.

In the late 1970s, the CS board had agreed on two targets for internal planning purposes. The first was a 25 per cent return on net assets, and the second was that earnings per share should grow by at least 5 per cent per annum in real terms. It was not immediately clear, however, how these targets meshed together and with the criteria used for capital budgeting.

The group currently estimated its overall after-tax cost of capital as 14.5 per cent. It was felt that new investments which returned more than this would generally add to shareholder wealth. This figure had been carefully computed, taking into account the risk level of CS shares, and the company's gearing level. This was a DCF rate of return applicable to new investment, however, and it was important to establish how it translated into return on net asset targets.

To establish this, use was made of the group's 5 year financial planning model. This took the various divisions' forward business projections and investment plans, and under alternative assumptions, allowed the group to project future profit and loss, balance sheet and funds flow statements, together with the accompanying financial ratios. Taking these forward projections into account, and also the 14.5 per cent cost of capital cutoff rate, the finance team concluded that the group's 25 per cent return on assets, and 5 per cent real growth in earnings per share targets were broadly consistent.

Hugh Collum and Martin Bralsford also considered how these targets would mesh with dividend policy. The group had an extensive capital expenditure programme, although the emphasis had now switched to increasing capacity rather than modernization and rationalization. Gross capital expenditure in 1984 was expected to exceed £130 million, and the 1985 figure would be equivalent in real terms. The company therefore remained cash hungry, and since it was still highly geared, there was a strong argument for avoiding excessive dividends.

An even stronger argument was felt to be that dividend payments were tax inefficient. Because of the geographical spread of profits outside the United Kingdom, stock relief, and high levels of UK capital expenditure, the Group had accumulated surplus advance corporation tax (ACT) of over £30 million. The group would not to be able to fully utilize this against its tax charge on UK profits until the end of the decade. A switch to less 'generous' dividends would reduce this problem and be more tax efficient.

The finance team recognized, however, that dividends per share had shown steady growth of 9–10 per cent per annum over the last 5 years, and that there would be severe inhibitions about any moves to a lower growth path. Nevertheless, to retain some flexibility here, it was felt appropriate to phrase the dividend policy target in terms of dividend cover. It was finally agreed that the group's objective should be that 'earnings will cover dividends up to three times'.

Exhibit 5: *Cadbury Schweppes: borrowings by maturity and type of loan*

Borrowings

The elements of borrowings are included in various balance sheet items under the format prescribed by the Companies Act 1981. The total and net borrowings are made up as follows.

	Consolidated	
	1984	1983
	£m	£m
Creditors due within one year		
Loans and overdrafts repayable within one year or on demand	46.0	85.2
Acceptance credits	0.4	4.8
Finance leases	18.1	14.7
Creditors due after more than one year		
Loans repayable between one and two years	4.5	11.9
Loans repayable between two and five years	74.6	75.1
Loans repayable after five years	54.4	42.0
Finance leases	65.0	58.9
Total borrowings	263.0	292.6
Investments—short term loans and deposits	(13.9)	(30.3)
Cash at bank and in hand	(22.7)	(18.0)
Net borrowings	226.4	244.3

Creditors: amounts falling due within one year

	Consolidated	
	1984	1983
	£m	£m
Secured loans		
United Kingdom companies:		
9 per cent First mortgage debenture stock 1988–93	—	0.1
Overseas companies:		
Various loans	1.0	3.1
Bank overdrafts	0.4	0.6
Unsecured loans		
United Kingdom companies		
Bank loans:		
£25m 1983–86	—	25.0
US$50m 1983–88	—	6.9
Other foreign currencies	3.2	1.9
Bank overdrafts	17.1	3.3
Overseas companies:		
Commercial paper US$1m	0.8	23.6
Bank loans	1.7	2.2
Bank overdrafts	21.8	18.5
	46.0	85.2
Payments received on account including deposits on returnable containers	27.1	26.0
Trade creditors	208.2	147.2

Creditors: amounts falling due after more than one year

	1984		1983	
	Payable after 1 year but within 5 years	Payable after 5 years	Payable after 1 year but within 5 years	Payable after 5 years
	£m	£m	£m	£m
Group				
Secured loans				
United Kingdom companies				
9 per cent First mortgage debenture stock 1988–93	0.5	3.6	0.5	3.7
8¼ per cent First mortgage debenture stock 1994–2004	—	3.0	—	3.0
Overseas companies:				
Other loans	2.6	6.8	1.8	3.6
Unsecured loans				
United Kingdom companies:				
7¾ per cent Guaranteed bonds 1990 (US$18m)	12.0	3.4	6.8	5.5
Bank loans				
US $50m 1983–88	—	—	27.6	—
US $52m 1987	44.8	—	35.9	—
Other foreign currencies	4.2	—	6.5	—
Overseas companies				
Commercial paper US $49m (see below)	—	36.6	—	22.8
Bank loans	14.5	0.7	7.2	3.0

Borrowings include amounts which are secured by means of:

	Consolidated	
	1984 £m	1983 £m
Mortgage debentures on property in the United Kingdom	7.1	7.3
Fixed charges on property of overseas subsidiaries	10.8	6.6
Debentures in the form of fixed and floating charges in respect of overseas subsidiaries	—	2.6
	17.9	16.5

Borrowings analysis by currency

	1984 £m	1983 At 1984 Exchange Rates £m	1983 Actual Rates £m
Sterling	73.5	87.2	87.2
US$	120.9	208.8	167.0
A$	12.8	(21.9)	(19.0)
Other	19.2	7.4	9.1
	226.4	281.5	244.3

	1984	1983
Bills of exchange payable	10.1	6.8
Acceptance credits	0.4	4.8
Owed to subsidiaries	—	—
Tax on profit	19.6	16.9
Advance corporation tax	12.4	10.3
Other taxes and social security costs	45.0	37.8
Current obligation under finance leases	9.1	6.9
Advances by leasing companies pending completion of finance leases	9.0	7.8
Other creditors	35.2	25.6
Accruals and deferred income	85.4	74.3
Dividend payable to minority shareholders	1.9	1.6
Proposed dividend to shareholders of Cadbury Schweppes plc	21.8	17.4
	531.2	468.6

Net interest expense by currency

	1984 £m	1983 At 1984 Exchange Rates £m	1983 Actual Rates £m
Sterling	10.8	9.0	9.0
US$	22.5	19.0	15.2
A$	(1.3)	(2.5)	(2.2)
Other	5.6	4.2	3.4
	37.6	29.7	25.4

Other loans	0.5	0.3	0.7	0.4
	79.1	54.4	87.0	42.0
Non-current obligations under finance leases	37.7	27.3	31.6	27.3
Tax on profit	12.8	0.5	10.7	—
Other creditors	3.2	—	2.7	0.3
	132.8	82.2	132.0	69.6
	215.0		201.6	

Interest on bank loans and finance leases is at variable rates.

The commercial paper represents short term notes issued in the United States for which maturities are normally between thirty and ninety days. As indicated above, US$49 m of these notes have been classified as long term debt because of the group's intention to refinance these borrowings on a continuing basis and committed 10 year facilities of this amount have been arranged with banks specifically to back up the issue of commercial paper.

Borrowings analysis by interest expense

	1984 £m	1983 £m
Fixed interest rate borrowings	101.4	44.8
Lease loan	83.1	73.8
Variable interest rate borrowings	78.5	174.0
Gross borrowings	263.0	292.6
Cash	(36.6)	(48.3)
Net borrowings	226.4	244.3

Gearing and debt policy

Finally, Hugh Collum and Martin Bralsford turned their attention to what they currently saw as the most troublesome financial target, namely gearing. At the end of 1983, gearing, as measured by net borrowings to shareholders funds was 61 per cent. Prior to the ADR issue in September, gearing had, as predicted internally, reached nearly 80 per cent. The general feeling in the Group was that such borrowing levels were far too high, and that unless gearing was kept within reasonable bounds, this could threaten the group's prime credit status (the group's rating for commercial paper was reviewed each year). This, in turn, would affect the interest rates at which CS could borrow, and hence its cost of capital. It was felt that loss of prime status could also damage the Group's ability to respond to investment opportunities and to meet the corresponding funding requirements.

The New York ADR issue, and the equity so raised had relieved some of the pressure, particularly since the proceeds had been used to repay short-term dollar debt. This, combined with careful debt management, meant that the 1984 year end gearing was likely to be down to around 44 per cent. However, it was felt that the American issue could have other implications for gearing. In particular, their new exposure to the North American markets could imply less flexibility over future gearing levels. The CS finance team felt that there was greater awareness of gearing in the United States than in the United Kingdom, and that the American markets tended to think that UK blue chip companies were generally too highly geared.

Taking all of these various considerations into account, it was decided that the group's formal gearing objective should be to keep the ratio of debt to equity below 50 per cent. The corresponding target for income gearing (cover) was that trading profit should be at least five times greater than interest charges. In setting these targets for gearing and coverage, CS were careful to include all forms of borrowing, including leasing. CS had made significant use of financial leases (Exhibit 5), mainly in the United Kingdom, since they felt these had provided a cost-effective means of financing their capital expenditure programme.

Leasing was, in fact, just one example of the many different forms of borrowing which lay behind the overall gearing figures. CS had also issued fixed and variable rate loans, secured and unsecured loans, quoted and unquoted loan stock, embracing a wide variety of different currencies and maturities (see Exhibit 5). This reflected a deliberate policy of ensuring that the company's sources of funding were well diversified, with no one market dominating. CS felt this gave them access to a wide variety of funds, and the flexibility at any point in time to borrow where funds were cheapest, an important facility, given that interest rates were currently volatile and difficult to predict.

The group did, however, take the view that the majority of its long-term borrowing requirements should be funded at fixed rates, maturing at regular intervals, so as to reduce unforeseen variations in interest expense. Thus, while they borrowed where it was cheapest (currently US commercial paper, which was still some 30–40 basis points cheaper than the dollar LIBOR rate), they continued to enter into interest rate guarantee and swap arrangements to convert floating into fixed rate debt, and also, to alter the term and currency of their debt as they felt appropriate. In 1984, for example, they had entered into interest rate guarantee arrangements in respect of $46.5 million of floating rate debt 'to restrict the adverse impact of increases in interest rates, whilst retaining the benefit of lower rates'. In early 1984, CS had also completed a further swap from US dollars into a £10 million fixed interest rate loan which, in addition to the two similar transactions in 1983, now made a total of £30 million of 10 year fixed rate sterling debt. US$6 million was also swapped into fixed rate pesetas 900 million, and US$21 million into fixed rate Australian $25 million.

The currency switching aspect of these swaps was intended to reduce the group's exposure to foreign exchange fluctuations. In spite of these transactions, however, the finance team recognized that foreign exchange fluctuations were still having a significant effect on both the gearing ratio and interest cover. They therefore turned their attention to reviewing the group's policies on foreign exchange exposure.

The management of foreign exchange exposure

1984 was a time of considerable volatility in currency movements when, even more than usual, the international focus was on the dollar. The dollar had been strong for about 3 years, and at the end of July stood at $1.30/£, a rise of 20 cents since the turn of the year (Exhibits 6 and 7).

CS distinguished between two forms of currency risk; transaction exposure and translation exposure. Transaction exposure arose in the normal course of CS's international business transactions because of lags between the dates contracts were signed or goods delivered, and the dates of payment. The risk here was that the exchange rate would fluctuate before the transaction was completed, thereby changing the amount of domestic currency paid or received.

The operating divisions within CS were allowed to take whatever (notional) positions they liked in currencies. They could thus choose to cover exchange exposure, or leave it open. The sole constraint was that the only 'bank' with which they could deal was the CS Treasury group. All the operating divisions' currency transactions and forward cover operations were then cleared at current market prices with the Treasurer's Department. This was to encourage divisional awareness of currency movements and their implications for the different businesses. However, while these currency transactions were fully taken into account in measuring divisional performance, they had no direct bearing on group exposure.

The way in which transaction exposure was monitored and measured at group

Exhibit 6: *Cadbury Schweppes share price and the dollar/pound exchange rate*

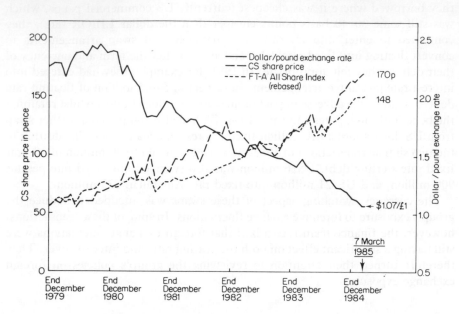

level was through a central cash management system and currency book maintained by the Treasurer's Department. Working on the basis of a set of 18 month rolling forecasts of all anticipated currency transactions throughout the group, Treasurer's first estimated the company's net currency exposure. This net position was established after taking account of any naturally occurring offsetting transactions, such as dollar interest payments being partly offset by dollar receipts for confectionery exports.

Treasurer's Department then decided whether to cover or leave open the various net currency positions, depending on their view on exchange rates and the cost of cover. They never speculated, however, in the sense of deliberately creating open positions in order to capitalize on anticipated exchange rate movements. Indeed, even the extent of their naturally occurring open positions was subject to a board override, and there were also a set of clearly specified exposure limits (for example, unless they had prior board level approval they could not exceed a $15 million long or short position in US dollars).

Translation exposure, on the other hand, brought a different set of problems. Translation exposure occurred because of the need to translate the financial statements of foreign subsidiaries, and any corporate liabilities denominated in foreign currency into their sterling equivalent for consolidation purposes. Thus this form of exposure arose not from the exchange of cash or other assets, but instead as a direct result of the financial accounting and reporting process.

CS accounting policies dictated that foreign currency borrowings, together with the net assets of overseas group companies, should be translated into

Exhibit 7: *Monthly percentage returns and risk measures: CS shares and the $/£ exchange rate**

Month	CS share return (in £)	$/£ Exchange rate	CS share return (in $)	Month	CS share return (in £)	$/£ Exchange rate	CS share return (in $)
1980 Jan	9.1	2.4	11.8	1983 Jan	1.7	−7.0	−5.4
Feb	−3.3	−.3	−3.6	Feb	.0	−.4	−.4
Mar	8.6	−5.0	3.2	Mar	−4.2	−1.3	−5.5
Apr	3.2	5.0	8.4	Apr	.0	5.8	5.8
May	−5.9	4.2	−2.0	May	−1.8	.8	−1.0
June	5.3	.1	5.4	June	3.7	−3.5	.0
July	.0	−1.3	−1.3	July	−2.7	1.1	−3.8
Aug	.0	3.4	3.4	Aug	−1.9	−1.3	−3.1
Sept	13.3	−.8	12.5	Sept	−3.6	−.3	−3.9
Oct	−1.5	1.8	.3	Oct	5.0	.0	5.0
Nov	5.5	−3.1	2.3	Nov	9.5	−2.5	6.8
Dec	2.9	1.1	4.1	Dec	2.6	−1.1	1.5
1981 Jan	4.2	−.7	3.5	1984 Jan	2.5	−2.4	.0
Feb	5.4	−8.2	−3.2	Feb	5.0	5.5	10.7
Mar	10.3	3.4	14.0	Mar	.8	−2.9	−2.1
Apr	14.0	−4.8	8.5	Apr	10.6	−3.2	7.0
May	−11.8	−2.8	−14.3	May	−12.5	−.1	−12.6
June	8.6	−7.7	.3	June	5.9	−3.2	2.5
July	−3.4	−4.9	−8.1	July	−4.0	−3.5	−7.4
Aug	17.6	.9	18.7	Aug	13.2	.6	13.9
Sept	−21.0	−1.2	−22.0	Sept	3.1	−5.9	−3.0
Oct	3.8	3.2	7.1	Oct	10.8	−.9	9.8
Nov	9.6	4.6	14.6	Nov	2.6	−2.3	.3
Dec	−2.3	−1.6	−3.8	Dec	3.2	−3.5	−.4
1982 Jan	10.5	−3.0	7.2	1985 Jan	−1.2	−1.9	−3.1
Feb	−2.1	−3.4	−5.4	Feb	3.7	−4.3	−.7
Mar	11.8	−1.4	10.2				
Apr	−1.0	1.2	.1	Mean	2.66	−1.11	1.52
May	2.6	−.3	2.2	Standard			
June	−8.9	−3.8	−12.3	deviation	7.10	3.02	7.67
July	14.1	1.1	15.4				
Aug	11.4	−1.9	9.3				
Sept	4.3	−1.2	3.1				
Oct	−2.5	−1.0	−3.5				
Nov	7.7	−2.6	4.9				
Dec	−7.1	−.3	−7.4				

*Cadbury Schweppes Risk Measures are reported in the London Business School *Risk Measurement Service* (first quarter, 1985) as follows: annualized standard deviation of returns ('total risk') = 24 per cent; beta ('systematic' or 'market risk') = 1.01 (standard error = 0.12); residual standard deviation ('specific risk') = 18 per cent; and R-Squared ('diversification') = 46 per cent. These figures are based on a 5 year monthly returns history.

sterling at the middle market rates ruling at the end of the financial year. As a result, unrealized exchange differences arose when the new values were compared with the prior-year figures, based on prior-year exchange rates. The resulting exchange gains or losses were dealt with as a movement on reserves.

Hugh Collum and Martin Bralsford were particularly concerned that exchange rate fluctuations, and particularly the strength of the dollar, were having a significant 'windfall' impact on the company's gearing ratio. The key issue here was the matching of foreign exchange borrowings and overseas assets, since changes in the sterling equivalent of currency debt were compensated by an offsetting increase in the sterling equivalent of currency assets. To mitigate the worst effects of translation exposure, CS therefore adopted a 'policy of proportionately matching borrowings to the currencies of the assets they support, which in turn limits the impact of currency fluctuations on shareholders' funds and earnings when stated in sterling'.

This target implied that if, for example, CS had 30 per cent of its net assets in the United States, then it would aim to have 30 per cent of its borrowings denominated in US dollars. It was felt that this would minimize the impact of currency movements on the gearing ratio, and enable the company to better manage this key variable.

Achieving and maintaining such a 'matched' position was not easy, however, particularly given the volatility of exchange rates, and the significant short-term and seasonal fluctuations in borrowings. By the year end, the company was still not fully 'matched' (see Exhibits 2 and 5), and this situation, combined with the continuing strength of the dollar, was giving rise to particular concern in the early weeks of 1985.

The situation in early 1985

By the end of December 1984, the dollar had risen to $1.16/£, and seemed to be reaching fever pitch. By the end of January, it stood at $1.13/£ (see Exhibits 6 and 7). Meanwhile, CS short-term dollar borrowings had increased somewhat since the year end, partly because of seasonal factors (CS cash balances tend to be relatively high at the year end as a result of seasonal movements in working capital). Total dollar borrowings (including short-term receivable financing) were now $195 million or nearly 75 per cent of total dollar net operating assets, compared with the CS target of 33 per cent (see Exhibits 2 and 5). Relative to target, CS had some $100 million excess US dollar borrowings.

As in the boardroom of many British multinationals at that time, the CS directors were expressing considerable anxiety about the impact of the rise in the dollar. There was a general concern amongst the business community that the dollar would continue to go up, and that it could end up as high as 80 cents to the pound. The debate focused on the group's dollar debt of $200 million. The general consensus was that this was crippling the company, and playing havoc with the gearing ratio. Dominic Cadbury, the Chief Executive, became persuaded that some action was required.

Hugh Collum was away at the time in the United States, and Martin Bralsford was therefore asked to look again, with some urgency, at the structure of the group's finances. While Martin agreed that there was a need to contain the gearing, he took a rather different view on both the impact of, and prospects for the $/£ exchange rate. First, he argued that, in transaction terms, the dollar's strength was not hurting the company. CS was generating cash in the United States, and the UK companies were exporting products to the States. On balance, it seemed that the dollar's strength was rather beneficial in this respect.

Second, he argued that it was important not to look at the dollar borrowings in isolation, but instead, to recognize that there would be a corresponding gain in the sterling book value of the dollar assets. Clearly, even when one looked at both sides of the balance sheet, gearing had still risen. Overall, however, he was still not clear that the net effect of the dollar's strength was necessarily bad for the group. He noted, in fact, that the sterling price of CS shares had risen, but that there had been almost no movement in the dollar price of the ADRs (see Exhibits 6 and 7).

Martin nevertheless recognized that the board expected some action, and so he rapidly began thinking through the various alternatives. He identified three possible courses of action. First, CS could effect an immediate shift from dollar to sterling borrowings. While this would rebalance the dollar to sterling liabilities, it would also lead to an increase in the interest charge, since sterling interest rates were currently 2.25 per cent above US rates. More seriously, however, this strategy would involve crystalizing the position, and the resultant exchange losses at a particularly bad time. Martin personally felt that the dollar was now overvalued against the pound. However, the alternative of waiting until specified exchange rates were hit carried significant risks, since the target rates might never be achieved. Overall, therefore, Martin did not feel that CS should be switching from dollar to sterling borrowings, given the current level of, and uncertainty surrounding, the exchange rate.

The second alternative involved purchasing currency options to protect the downside risk. A 6 month option to purchase US dollars at the current spot rate would cost 4.2 per cent. Thus CS could protect themselves against the effect of further dollar strength on their excess dollar borrowings of $100 million for the next 6 months at a cost of $4.2 million. However, Martin argued that unless they were to run the options continuously, they would be of value only if CS believed that the exchange rate uncertainty would be resolved over the life of the option. Otherwise, CS would be facing the same dilemma again in 6 months time.

The third alternative was to issue a convertible eurobond, denominated in US dollars, but convertible into CS equity. Martin felt that the advantage of this was that 'it would be deferred equity, and further equity is needed'. Furthermore, he felt that a convertible issue of this kind would find a ready market in Europe, since European investors currently favoured UK securities, but not the UK currency. A convertible issue would also be tax-efficient. Compared with an equity issue, it would avoid adding to the cumulated ACT surplus (and hence delaying the date when this would be exhausted), at least until the bonds were converted, and dividend payments commenced. Meanwhile, the interest on the convertible would be tax-deductible, and would lead to a future tax saving once cumulated surplus ACT had been exhausted. Prior to conversion, the issue would provide low cost debt.

Since the proceeds of the convertible issue would be used to repay straight dollar debt, Martin felt that the issue would have a beneficial impact on gearing, and at the same time, reduce the group's dollar exposure. He argued that it would also provide

> a double option, both on the equity (in sterling) and on the dollar. Thus a rise in the dollar will be offset by a fall in the value of the conversion feature, and vice versa. Given that our share price is likely to increase as the US dollar strengthens, given our substantial US dollar assets and earnings, the conversion of the bonds remains likely even if the US dollar strengthens. If it weakens, then our share price may not grow at the same rate, but even if the debt were not converted, the ultimate liability to repay US dollars would be less onerous. Also the interest rate over the life of the bond would be lower than a straight fixed rate issue.

In a memo to Hugh Collum outlining these alternatives, Martin therefore strongly advocated the convertible bond issue.

Hugh Collum was also attracted to this idea. CS had not been in the eurobond market since 1973, and there was certainly not a surfeit of their paper around. Furthermore, following the success of their US issue, CS had received a number of indications that there would be demand for their shares in Europe, and perhaps the Far East, particularly Japan. The Schweppes name was already well known on the Continent, particularly in Switzerland (Jacob Schweppes, the founder of Schweppes, was Swiss). The issue would help to further spread the CS name, and provide investor support to back the company's commercial presence and brands in Europe.

Hugh Collum also saw the issue as a way of placing quasi-equity without having to make a rights issue. He felt that the obligation under company law and the Stock Exchange listing agreement to issue new equity by way of rights made equity unnecessarily expensive, because of the issue discount, as well as the underwriting and administrative costs. In contrast, he viewed the convertible issue as a method of placing deferred equity at a price above the current market price, in a way which was administratively very cheap (that is, simply a 2.5 per cent placing fee). The euroconvertible would also allow CS to expand and internationalize their shareholder base rather than simply offering new shares to existing holders. He therefore felt comfortable in proposing the convertible issue to the board.

The convertible issue

The CS board agreed to the general notion of a convertible issue, targeted to be converted into equity within 4–5 years. They did not take the view that they were selling the shares in any sense cheaply. CS had achieved good results, the share price had been performing well, and there was no feeling that the shares were overvalued or undervalued.

Having obtained board approval in principle, the CS finance team needed to move swiftly. The Chief Executive wanted to announce the issue with the full year results on 7 March. Since it was now the end of January, they had just 6 weeks to complete all the necessary work. During this period, they would also have to organize an Extraordinary General Meeting of shareholders to approve the issue, since the convertible would clearly not be issued by way of rights.

At an early stage, CS sought the involvement of Kleinwort Benson, one of its two merchant banks. Robert Henderson, the non-executive Deputy Chairman of CS was the Chairman of Kleinwort Benson Lonsdale. Kleinworts knew CS extremely well, and since this was particularly important given the timescale, Kleinworts were the obvious choice for lead manager. Kleinworts provided confirmation that a convertible issue was an appropriate move. Viscount Chandos, who was to handle the issue for CS, commented

A US dollar convertible does present a subtle and cost effective way to alter the currency balance of Cadbury's liabilities, at the same time as providing additional long-term capital and giving the opportunity to achieve in Europe and the Far East the same successful promotion of Cadbury Schweppes' name as was achieved last autumn in the United States.

Kleinwort's subsequent role centred around managing, underwriting and marketing the issue, and in providing advice on the terms and pricing, with particular emphasis on what would be acceptable in the market place. They were lead managers in a syndicate which included Morgan Stanley, Credit Suisse First Boston, Swiss Bank Corporation, and other European, North American and Japanese banks.

Initially, CS had thought in terms of a $60 million issue. Both Hugh Collum and Kleinworts favoured a larger issue and felt $100 million was feasible. They finally settled on an $80 million issue, since this represented the balance of advice, and market soundings indicated that they could safely raise this amount. At this stage, it was anticipated that the bonds would have a ten year term.

One alternative which was seriously considered was to issue dollar bonds with warrants attached. However, CS wanted an instrument which, on conversion, would automatically cancel the dollar debt. They proposed a semidetached warrant, which on exercise, required the holder to surrender the bond in return for a dollar payment. This alternative was rejected, however, since the banks argued that there were different clienteles for debt, equity and warrants, and that they would not be able to market this particular package. They also cautioned that the euromarkets were far less receptive to unusual or exotic instruments then, say, the New York market. Instead, they preferred conventional issues by well-known names.

Very early on, Martin Bralsford, who was handling the details of the issue, formed a general view on the appropriate terms. He estimated that CS could issue straight dollar debt, with a 10–15 year term, on a yield of 12 per cent. Kleinworts advised him that there were essentially two categories of convertibles. The first was the 'low coupon/low conversion premium' issue, at say a coupon of 4 per cent below that on straight bonds, and a conversion premium (that is, the price of the bond, relative to the value it would have if converted immediately) of about 10 per cent. The second was the 'high coupon/ high conversion premium' variant, at say a coupon of 1 per cent below straights, but with a conversion premium of 20–25 per cent.

Of these two alternatives, Martin judged that an 8 per cent coupon combined with a 10 per cent conversion premium would be the more appropriate package, given that CS wanted to be as certain as possible that the bond would eventually be converted. Kleinworts concurred with this, especially given that this was a eurobond issue. As Viscount Chandos explained,

> Traditionally, the eurobond market has not welcomed issues with premia of 15 per cent or higher, such as are commonly available in both the US and, to a lesser extent, the UK markets. The classic conversion premium therefore has been 10 per cent over the prevailing market price, although recent Japanese issues have offered conversion premia as low as 5 per cent.

To double check this figure, and to establish a 'walkaway price', Martin carried out some approximate forward projections. Assuming a 14.5 per cent after tax cost of capital, and a 4.3 per cent net dividend yield, he estimated that the CS share price was expected to rise by 10 per cent per annum. He then discounted the future cash flows from the bond, together with the terminal value of the shares on conversion (assuming different conversion dates) back to present value at 14.5 per cent. With an 8 per cent coupon and a 10 per cent conversion premium, it seemed that the bonds should be issued at par.

On this basis, Martin estimated that these terms would encourage conversion in 4–5 years time, although the optimal timing would depend on the difference between the bond coupon and the yield on the shares. Hugh Collum was concerned about the dilution effect of early conversion, and CS therefore insisted on a grace period with no conversion permitted prior to 15 January 1986, to prevent any dilution during the current financial year. This condition met with considerable resistance from the bankers, especially the Swiss. However, when CS later wanted to change the maturity of the bonds from 10 to 15 years 'to make doubly sure the issue converted', there was ready agreement to this request. With a 15 year maturity, CS estimated that there was something like a 90 per cent probability of conversion.

There was also some discussion about the call provision, registration and rating. For flexibility, CS wanted a provision which allowed them to buy in and remarket the bonds, rather than simply to call and cancel them. The banks were against this, since they did not want CS to act as another market maker, particularly during distribution. They insisted on a 2 year grace period, during which any bought-in bonds would be cancelled. It was decided that the bonds would be in bearer form only, and would not be registered. This was because CS did not want the bonds marketed in the United States, since this could involve competition with their ADRs. Since the United States was not the target market, CS decided not to apply for a bond rating. They wanted to hold fire on this until they could be sure of getting and keeping a double-A rating. In any event, they felt that it was name recognition rather than ratings which mattered in Europe.

Finalizing the terms

CS announced their full year results on 7 March (see Exhibits 1–4). In an accompanying statement, Sir Adrian Cadbury, the Chairman, said:

> Since the board has clear and positive plans for the continued development of the group overseas, particularly in North America, we consider it is prudent to raise further long term capital on a dollar basis. An opportunity to achieve this objective is now available in the international capital markets. Accordingly, we are today announcing our intention to issue $80 million of 15 year bonds convertible into ordinary shares, conditional on shareholders' approval. The immediate impact of this issue will be to enable the company to move forward with its plans for overseas investment and growth, by putting in place a further tranche of long-term capital. It will also reduce the group's interest expense and short-term debt.

This announcement brought an enthusiastic reception from the *Financial Times* which, on 8 March 1985, commented:

> Cadbury is confident that the convertible bond will broaden its European shareholder base. The strategy of backing up product marketing by generating interest in the company's capital clearly has its attractions. However the new bond also reflects the attention that Cadbury has been paying to its debt portfolio, which has been hit by exchange rates in recent months. There has been some currency switching and the ADR issue allowed the company to reduce dollar debts by $100 million. The bond increases the fixed debt proportion of the loan portfolio and conversion will be from dollar debt into sterling equity.

At this stage, no firm announcement was made about the terms of the issue, since these had not yet been finalized. A draft offer document had, however, been prepared and this is summarized, together with the proposed issue terms, in Exhibit 8.

Hugh Collum and Martin Bralsford felt comfortable with these proposed terms. However, they recognized that the pricing of convertibles was a fine art and reputations can be affected. So, just to be sure that the calculations stood up to a rigorous test, they sought the opinion of an expert in options pricing.

CADBURY SCHWEPPES
Public Limited Company
(incorporated in England with limited liability)
US $80 000 000
8 per cent Convertible Bonds 2000
Issue price 100 per cent

The US $80,000,000 8 per cent Convertible Bonds 2000 (the 'Bonds') of Cadbury Schweppes Public Limited Company (the 'Company' or 'Cadbury Schweppes') will be in bearer form in the denomination of US £5000 each, and will rank as direct, unsecured obligations of the Company. The Bonds will mature on 15 December 2000 unless previously converted, redeemed or purchased as described in 'Description of the Bonds'.

Unless previously redeemed or purchased, Bonds will at the holders' option be convertible, at any time on or after 15 January 1986 until and including 8 December 2000, into Ordinary Shares of the Company (the 'Ordinary Shares') credited as fully paid. The initial conversion price of US $1.97 per Ordinary Share, which is subject to adjustment, would give rise to 2538 Ordinary Shares for each Bond converted, (equivalent to a price of £1.82 per Ordinary Share at the fixed rate of exchange of US $1.0810 to £1 applicable throughout the life of the Bonds).

Interest on the Bonds will be payable on 15 December 1985 and annually in arrears thereafter on 15 December in each year.

The issue of the Bonds is conditional, *inter alia*, upon the approval of the Ordinary Shareholders of the Company (see 'Subscription, Underwriting and Sale').

Application has been made to the Council of The Stock Exchange in London for the Bonds to be admitted to the Official List. A copy of this document, which comprises approved listing particulars with regard to the Company in accordance with The Stock Exchange (Listing) Regulations 1984, has been delivered to the Registrar of Companies for registration in accordance with those Regulations.

Offers and sales of Bonds and the distribution of this document, including in the United States of America or to or for the benefit of United States persons, are restricted as mentioned in 'Subscription, Underwriting and Sale'.

The Bonds will be represented initially by a temporary global bond, without interest coupons, which will be deposited with a common depositary for Cedel S.A. ('Cedel') and the Euroclear System ('Euroclear') at the closing on or about 3 April 1985 and which will become exchangeable for definitive bonds, with interest coupons attached, after the last day (the 'Exchange Date') of the period of 90 days following completion of the distribution of the Bonds, as determined by Kleinwort, Benson Limited, and after the certification of non-United States beneficial ownership.

Kleinwort, Benson Limited	Credit Suisse First Boston Limited
Morgan Stanley international	Swiss Bank Corporation International Limited
Algemene Bank Nederland N.V.	Banque Nationale de Paris
Crédit Lyonnais	Deutsche Bank Aktiengesellschaft
Lehman Brothers International, Inc.	Samuel Montagu and Co. Limited
Morgan Guaranty Ltd	Nomura International Limited
Orion Royal Bank Limited	Union Bank of Switzerland (Securities) Limited

Other Details of the Bonds

1. *Negative Pledge:* The company cannot secure additional debt without giving equal treatment to the existing unsecured bonds.

2. *Interest:* The first interest payment will be $280 per bond, representing the period from 3 April to 15 December 1985.

3. *Conversion:* The initial conversion price will be adjusted for any scrip issues, rights issues or other capital changes. Shares arising from conversion will rank equally with existing shares, but there will be no entitlement to dividends for any financial period ended on or prior to such conversion date.

4. *Redemption at the Option of the company:* From 16 December 1987 onwards, the company can redeem some or all of the bonds by giving at least 45 and not more than 90 days notice. If the bonds are redeemed during the year ending 15 December 1988, the redemption price will be 104 per cent of the principal amount. This price will fall by 0.5 per cent per annum until it reaches par in 1996. Thereafter, redemption will be at par. Bonds may not be so redeemed prior to 15 December 1989 unless (i) the average middle market price of the shares over the 30 day period ending on the fourteenth day prior to the date on which notice is given shall have been at least 130 per cent of the average of the conversion prices in effect on each such dealing day or (ii) at least 95 per cent of the bonds have already been converted, redeemed or purchased and cancelled. In the case of a partial redemption of bonds, the bonds to be redeemed shall be selected individually by lot.

5. *Purchases:* The Company may at any time purchase bonds provided that, so long as the bonds are listed on The Stock Exchange, (i) the price shall not, in the case of purchases made through The Stock Exchange or by tender, exceed the average of the middle market quotations for the 10 dealing days before the purchase is made or (if the market price of the bonds is not more than 5 per cent, above such average), in the case of a purchase made through The Stock Exchange, such market price and (ii) if purchases are made by tender, tenders are made available to all bondholders alike. In addition, the company may at any time purchase bonds by private treaty at any price not exceeding 250 per cent of their principal amount.

6. *Cancellation:* All bonds purchased prior to 16 December 1987 or redeemed or converted as aforesaid shall be cancelled forthwith, together with all Coupons surrendered therewith, and may not be reissued or resold.

7. *Taxation:* All payments will be made without withholding or deduction for taxes imposed by the United Kingdom.

8. *Repayment in Event of Default:* If the standard conditions including the normal cross-default clauses are not met, then the bonds become immediately repayable at their full face value.

9. *Subscription, Underwriting and Sale:* The 'managers' have agreed to subscribe or procure subscribers for the total principal amount of the bonds at the issue price less a selling concession of 1.5 per cent of their principal amount. The Company has agreed to pay to the managers commissions of 0.5 per cent (plus VAT where applicable) for their services as managers to the issue, and a further 0.5 per cent for underwriting commissions. The company has agreed to pay all costs incurred by it in connection with the issue.

10. *Stabilizing Activities:* In connection with the offer, the managers may (as agents for the underwriters and in accordance with applicable law) over-allot and/or effect transactions with a view to stabilizing or maintaining the market price of the bonds at levels other than those which might otherwise prevail in the open market. Such transactions, if commenced, may be discontinued at any time.

PART H

FINANCIAL PLANNING

25. Precision Engineering (A)

Precision Engineering Co. Ltd (PE) is a long-established, medium/heavy precision engineering company undertaking subcontract work for the metal processing industries. In 1982–83 the company's principal customer was the Davy Corporation, which accounted for 61 per cent of that period's sales revenue.

In April 1982, losses for the second year in succession were announced. Sales were £2 million, with a breakeven of £2.2 million. The company was acquired by new owners. The order book at the time of acquisition was down to £450 000, and the company was characterized by no selling effort, inadequate control systems, low morale at all levels in the organization, inefficiency in plant layout and factory organization, and lack of investment. PE's financial position was deteriorating rapidly. Monthly losses had increased to approximately £30 000 and the company had an accumulated deficit of £606 000 (Exhibit 1 (a) shows the profit and loss account at the time of acquisition, and Exhibit 2 shows the balance sheet.)

The new owners imposed tight financial and production control systems and undertook a major effort to increase orders. By October 1982, the order book had been increased to £1.2 million, of which £550 000 was a single order for the Davy McKee (Poole) Division of the Davy Corporation. The increased volume was expected to ensure PE's profitability for the 6 months October 1982–April 1983, and to re-establish its position in the marketplace.

Traditionally, orders of this size had been financed by large progress payments, but the current recession forced Davy to accept the order from its customer (Kaiser Steel, USA), without the 'standard' level of progress payments. As a result, PE faced a short-term cash flow problem from December 1982 through to May 1983, peaking in March 1983 at £218 000 in excess of its bank borrowing limit of £500 000. Borrowing requirements in the other months were, however, in all cases no more than £67 000 above the limit. In November 1982, the board sought £250 000 from the Industrial and Commercial Finance Corporation (ICFC). This would provide it with the short-term financing to see

This case was written by Stuart St P. Slatter, as a basis for class discussion rather than to illustrate either effective or ineffective handling of an administrative situation.

Exhibit 1: *PE: profit and loss account for year ending 30 April (£000)*

	1982	1981
(a): Pre-acquisition profit and loss		
Sales from continuing operations	2073	3056
Less: Cost of sales and operating expenses	2147	3070
Operating loss from continuing operations	(74)	(14)
Less: Interest expense, net	34	137
Plus: Operating profit (loss) of subsidiaries transferred	413	(118)
Profit (loss) before taxation	304	(270)
Less taxation charge/(credit)	184	(139)
Profit (loss) before extraordinary items	120	(131)
Less: Extraordinary items		
Loss on transfer of subsidiaries	499	—
Rationalization costs	69	53
Goodwill written off	—	107
Net profit (loss)	(448)	(291)
Retained earnings (accumulated deficit)		
Beginning of year		
As previously reported	(7)	53
Less: Goodwill and deferred contract expenses		
written off	212	25
As restated	(219)	28
Transfer from surplus on revaluation		
of property, plant and equipment	61	44
Accumulated deficit (year end)	(606)	(219)

(b): Turnover by business activity (continuing businesses only)

	1982–83 (est)	1981–82	1980–81	1979–80
Subcontract engineering	1702	806	1110	1389
Mechanical handling	Nil	914	1147	81
Plastics	178	353	830	749
Total	1880	2073	3087	2219

it through the cash requirements of the Davy McKee order. (Davy was willing to certify the work-in-progress.) Longer term, it would permit the balance sheet restructuring needed to allow PE to grow in an economic environment where large progress payments could no longer be expected. The board believed that

Exhibit 2: *PE: Pre-acquisition balance sheet as at 30 April 1982 (£000)*

Current assets	
Stocks and contract work-in-progress	404
Debtors and prepayments	363
Cash	1
	768
Current liabilities	
Creditors and accrued liabilities	472
Advance payments in excess of contract work-in-progress	87
Due under hire-purchase agreements	9
Bank overdraft	284
	852
Net current liabilities	(84)
Non current-debtors	36
Property, plant and equipment, net	439
Due from (to) former parent company	(50)
Non-current portion of amount due under hire-purchase agreements	(5)
	336
Representing	
Share capital	813
Surplus on revaluation of property, plant and equipment	129
Accumulated deficit	(606)
	336

an injection of £250 000 of long-term funds would be adequate to restore liquidity and provide prudent gearing.

Background

Precision Engineering (PE) was founded in 1857 to build textile machinery under a patent awarded to the founders. It was family-controlled until 1969, when it was sold to merchant bankers, Grindlay Brandts. The bank operated PE as part of its industrial holding company (purchasing the Plastics Machinery Division in 1971 from receivership), until 1978, when it sold the holding company to the directors. PE was poorly managed during the 1970s, at which time it lost customers and made an unacceptable return on capital employed. In 1978, a £2.8 million contract was signed with Davy McKee of Sheffield to design and manufacture a steel coil handling system for Yugoslavia. No selling effort was made while the contract was being undertaken, with the result that there was virtually no order book by the end of 1980. It was at this time that Grindlay Brandts' management decided to divest themselves of PE.

In April 1981, PE was purchased by Nostra Holdings, a company owned 51 per cent by the Mayfair Group of Australia (a waste disposal group) and 49 per cent by two PE directors. The company's attraction to its new owners was its subsidiary, Blue Circle Equipment Ltd, which supplied equipment to the solid waste disposal industry. A second subsidiary, Wastedrum Ltd, was established to provide waste collection and disposal services for public authorities. Management allocated all its time to the subsidiary companies and took immediate steps to divest itself of the PE engineering business. On 16 April 1982, Nostra Holdings sold PE for £1 to a group of investors who had a successful track record in turning around small engineering companies.

Activities and product lines

PE undertook medium/heavy precision engineering for the steel plant industry and the Ministry of Defence (MoD), and marketed a range of injection moulding machine tools for the plastics industry. The three principal activities of the company were subcontract engineering, mechanical handling and plastics.

Subcontract engineering involved PE in medium/heavy precision engineering work for manufacturers of steel and aluminium plant. The principal products engineered were mandrels (cylindrical rods round which metal is forged or shaped), edge trimmers, laying heads and underbodies. PE had special expertise in the manufacture of hydraulic equipment. This was a very specialist area with few competitors and high value contracts, but subject to considerable fluctuations in the level of activity.

PE also carried out subcontract light and medium high precision engineering for the Ministry of Defence. In addition, it undertook other subcontract engineering work, such as crank cases for marine engines, and work for steel fabricators.

In the field of mechanical handling, PE designed and manufactured heavy material handling equipment such as coil handling systems, walking beams, chain conveyors, turntables, upenders, downenders and cooling conveyors.

Finally, PE supplied injection moulding equipment for the plastics industry. These products were smaller and lighter and included machines designed and manufactured by PE, and machines imported from Poland. PE's own machines consisted of two principal products, both of which were vertical machines, used mainly by in-house moulders in the electronics, automotive and domestic appliance industries. The machines were technically excellent. They were from 10 to 70 tons, with a shot weight from approximately 1–27 oz (28–765 g), selling at between £12 000 and £35 000 each. The imported machines consisted of a range of horizontal moulding machines. Electrical cabinets and safety guarding to PE's own design and manufacture were fitted to these machines to make them acceptable to the UK market. The machines were from 80 to 420 tons locking force. They sold on price and terms at between £19 000 and £60 000.

Sales in 1982 were primarily from subcontract engineering work for the steel industry, although, over the previous 3 years the sales mix had fluctuated widely (see Exhibit 1(b)).

The market

PE's principal market was the steel industry, which had been in recession since 1980. The worldwide market for steel, measured in terms of crude steel output, had declined from a peak of 747 millon tonnes in 1979 by 14 per cent, to 645 million tonnes in 1982. The industrialized countries had shown the largest decline — the 1982 output of 337 million tonnes was down by 23 per cent on 1979 output. Prices were depressed due to surplus capacity, especially in the EEC and Japan, and export prices continued to be undermined by low-priced deals from the Eastern Bloc. M. T. Lawrence, writing in the *Mining Annual Review* (1982), estimated that it would take 7–8 years at 3 per cent per annum demand growth before the Western World surplus was reduced sufficiently to allow prices to rise. Between 1979 and 1982, cumulative inflation was about 40 per cent in the United Kingdom.

Although the much-heralded recovery in steel had failed to appear, certain segments of the market had been growing and were expected to grow in the short and medium-term future, despite the recession. Developing countries had been continuing to expand crude steel production capacity to meet the increasing demand in their own markets. The increase, however, was unevenly distributed (South Korea, China, Qatar and Venezuela accounting for much of the increase, whilst other areas, notably Africa, had made little progress). Industrialized countries in the west, while contracting crude capacity, had been investing in production capacity of more specialized, higher quality steels, and in improving productive efficiency. In 1980, the International Iron and Steel Institute (IISI) member countries' capital expenditure was US$16.4 billion, compared with $12.9 billion in 1977 (representing a constant level of investment measured in 1972 prices).

In the industrialized countries, the most rapidly growing segment of the market had been in continuous casting ('concast'), the energy-efficient and labour-saving method of producing steel slabs in one operation instead of first pouring the steel into ingots, and then reheating to make slabs. This process accounted for 10 per cent of western crude steel output in 1972, rose to 30 per cent in 1979, and continued to increase its market share of crude production. The majority of PE deliveries to the steel industry were for concast production. PE saw its future in the more sophisticated ends of the market, including concast.

PE also manufactured equipment for the aluminium market. While this industry had been hard hit by the recession, certain segments continued to grow, principally turnkey aluminium plant for developing countries, and recycling and packaging plant in developed countries. PE produced equipment for these growth sectors.

In terms of PE's plastics industry business, the UK market for injection moulding machines and related equipment was expected to be between £20 million and £25 million in 1982. Under normal conditions, the growth was 10 per cent per annum, but as it was directly related to the economy, sales were depressed and were not expected to improve until end-user markets improved. The two clear ends of the market were divided into trade moulders and specialist (in-plant) moulders.

Trade moulders were concerned with the production and sale of plastic mouldings for subsequent utilization or marketing by others. Production runs were often short and unpredictable, making production planning, and hence full machine utilization difficult to achieve. Trade moulders often bought a new machine to fulfil a specific order, so the machine had to be immediately available and at reasonably low cost, so as to amortize itself rapidly. Trade moulders required reliable, flexible, low-cost machines on quick delivery. Very high speed operation and sophisticated control equipment were not essential.

Specialist (in-plant) moulding was found within the operations of most manufacturers of consumer goods. It involved the production of specific parts which were components of the end product. Production runs were long and closely controlled. Specialist moulders required sophisticated machines with product consistency and repeatability over long runs to achieve quality and economy. Machines were often made to customer design and frequently included closed-loop hydraulic and microprocessor systems. Design suitability and productivity were important. Delivery time and capital cost were not usually a constraint on the purchase decision. Indeed, a high price was often seen as a confirmation of quality. PE's range was targeted at the specialist moulders.

Customers

PE's principal customer was the Davy Corporation, the world leader in the engineering and construction of rolling mill, forging, extrusion and metal process industries. During 1980–82, 95 per cent of PE's work was for Davy McKee of Sheffield, and in the 1982–83 financial year, Davy was expected to account for approximately 61 per cent of PE's sales revenues. In 1982, the steel rolling business was relatively buoyant in the United Kingdom, with five major mills in the late stages of design/early stages of manufacture, and several recent orders of aluminium mills. However, there was nothing in the long term.

As subcontractor to Davy, PE's volume was heavily dependent on Davy's success. Exhibit 3 shows details of Davy's turnover and profit before tax for the

Exhibit 3: *Davy Corporation: financial performance (£ million)*

(a) Financial summary

Year to 31 March	Annual Turnover	Pretax profit	Gross dividend*	Dividend cover*	Order book 30 June	Forward load
1978	387	25.4	8.25	3.1	1240	750
1979	611	26.1	9.57	3.4	1688	1006
1980	752	15.9	9.57	1.7	1810	1073
1981	671	18.7	9.57	2.1	1910	1036
1982	877	22.9	10.53	2.0	2107	1042

(b) Profit before tax

	1981–82	1980–81
Engineering and construction		
United Kingdom	13.1	16.9
United States, German and other	15.1	12.1
German legal settlement added back	2.4	—
Engineering and manufacturing	.6	−1.3
Central charges	−8.3	−9.0
	22.9	18.7

(c) Analysis of turnover

	1982	1981
By destination		
United Kingdom	116	108
Rest of EEC	16	16
Rest of western Europe	12	13
Eastern Europe, including USSR	93	103
Near and Middle East	19	12
Indian subcontinent	9	4
Far East	53	52
Africa	66	36
North America	393	241
Central and South America	74	74
Australasia	26	12
	877	671
By source		
UK companies home	116	106
export	185	199
Non-UK companies	576	366
	877	671

*Dividend is pence per share; dividend cover is number of times covered by earnings.

339

PHILLIPS & DREW

AGM 6 October 1982

EQUITY BOOK SERVICE

Bill Seward   **5.01**

Davy Corporation   Hold

The shares have been a weak market over the last six months, reflecting very depressed US demand for plant coupled with the probable loss of the large Indian steelworks contract. Earnings will fall significantly this year, whilst the recovery in 1983/84 may be relatively modest. Nevertheless, the group is a world-scale competitor in an industry that still seems to have good longer term growth prospects and this, together with the good yield, seems to fully support the shares at this level.

Price: 110   **FTA: 383**   **25 October 1982**

Year to 31 March	1982 actual	1983 forecast	1984 forecast
Published earnings p	16.0	11.5	13.3
P&D earnings p	15.2	10.8	12.5
P/E ratio (P&D)	7.2	10.2	8.8
P/E rel (range 70-140)	46	74	76
Gross dividend	10.5	10.5	11.0
Cover (P&D)	2.1	1.4	1.6
Current cost cover	1.7	1.1	
Yield %	9.5	9.5	10.0
Yield rel (range 185-90)	186	172	162

Issued Capital 94 million ordinary 25p shares.
Equity Market Capitalisation £103m (0.09 per cent of FTA).

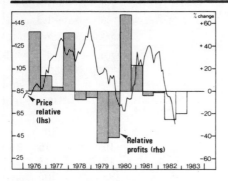

Price relative (lhs)
Relative profits (rhs)

1982/83

AGM statement: 'Taking into account US market conditions and state of world economy, short term prospects for profits are not favourable and earnings for current year are likely to be lower.'

UK contracting: Order books for the UK-based companies are 'reasonably good' (notwithstanding the probable loss of the big Indian steel plant order) although conditions remain 'highly competitive'. Interest receivable is an important contributor to UK contracting profits, and given the decline in interest rates, overall profits may only be maintained.

Engineering and Manufacturing: 1981/82 saw a £2m turnround into overall profits, notwithstanding combined losses in heavy fabrication at Teeside and in forgings and foundries of about £2m. The loss of the Indian steel plant order is a blow here, and the AGM statement noted there was 'no upturn' here. Hence only a modest further recovery seems likely.

Overseas contracting: The sharp drop in the forward load for the overseas companies was concentrated in the USA, since the German company retains a 'reasonable' order book; Davy is now speeding up its US rationalisation plan. The absence of last year's £2½m legal settlement in Germany will help, but profits could nevertheless still fall sharply overall.

Central costs: will fall, reflecting the repayment of US loans.

1983/84

Recovery in activity levels should begin, probably in second half of year as world moves slowly out of recession.

HALF YEARLY FIGURES

£m	1980/81 H1	H2	1981/82 H1	H2	1982/83 H1	H2
	actual				forecast	
Turnover	323	348	388	489		
% change	−15	−6	+20	+40		
Pre-tax profits	6.1	12.6	6.6	13.8	5.7	12.3
% change	+36	+12	+8	+10	−14	−11

MEDIUM TERM FORECASTS

£m	1981/82 actual	1982/83 forecast	1983/84 forecast
UK contracting	13.1	13.0	14.5
Overseas contracting	15.1	11.0	12.0
Total contracting	28.2	24.0	26.5
Engineering & manufacturing	0.6	1.0	1.5
Central costs (mainly finance)	(8.4)	(7.0)	(7.0)
Pre-tax profits	20.4	18.0	21.0
Of which interest receivable	13.0	10.0	9.0
Tax %	38	40	40
Published earnings	12.7	10.8	12.6
Deferred tax etc	(0.6)	(0.6)	(0.7)
Fully taxed earnings	12.1	10.2	11.9
Shares ranking (m)	79.3	94.4	94.4
Pub earnings per share p	16.0	11.5	13.3
Fully taxed earnings per share p	15.2	10.8	12.5
Gross dividend per share p	10.5	10.5	11.0

Estimated pre-tax profit breakdown

%	Home	Export	Overseas
1981/82	10	40	50
1982/83	15	35	50

Our Buy, Sell and Hold recommendations are based on the likely movement of the share price relative to the FTA All-Share Index.

years 1978–82, and gives details of the sources of Davy's income. Exhibit 4 gives a stockbroker's analysis of the company. Despite the recession, the Davy Corporation sales had increased by 31 per cent from 1981 to 1982, with a profit before tax of £22.9 million, and a turnover of £877 million.

Davy (founded 150 years ago) was originally a Sheffield-based manufacturing company, serving mainly the domestic market. After a financial disaster in the late 1960s it had been reconstructed. Between 1968 and 1982, Davy had grown rapidly through growth in the international contracting market and the rapid expansion of industries using process plant. Davy acquired the German company of Zimmer, serving the fibres industry, and the US company of McKee (in 1978 for £55 million), and transformed itself into a multinational corporation with three centres in the United Kingdom, United States and Germany. Its principal competitors in the metal process industry market were Sack, SMS Schloeman Siemag, and Mannesman Demag (Germany), IMI, Mitsubishi and Sumitomo (Japan), Clecim (France), and Mesta (United States).

Davy's strength lay in managing large turnkey projects. They provided large, sophisticated components for rolling mills and specialized plants, and sub-contracted the more commonplace. As of October 1982, PE was a subcontractor to Davy McKee (Sheffield) — the mechanical project and construction company — and Davy McKee (Sheffield and Poole) — the equipment designer and manufacturer, on four projects: the Kaiser Aluminium Foil Mill, California, expected to be worth £550 000 to PE; an extension contract on the Acominas integrated iron and steel works in Brazil (worth £7.7 million to Davy and £1 million to PE); the Sicartsa Steel Plate Mill, Mexico, worth £350 million to Davy McKee, Sheffield, for delivery mid-1983 to autumn 1984; and a turnkey aluminium semifabricating plant, Yugoslavia, worth $40 million to Davy McKee, Poole, and £300 000 to PE, for delivery in May 1982.

PE also sold direct to end users, such as British Steel Corporation (BSC), particularly where the market was a replacement market for 'standard' products, or where PE was providing significant design input, as in mechanical handling systems. In November 1982, PE had made a joint tender with Davy for mechanical handling equipment worth £4.5 million to PE, for the proposed Port Talbot £100 million development. The expected decision date was December 1982.

Finally, PE sold injection moulding machinery to a large number of customers in a variety of industries. Some of the organizations currently using PE equipment were: Ferranti, GEC, General Motors, GKN, Joseph Lucas, Plessey and Smiths Industries. However, there was little or no demand for PE's machines in 1982.

Competition

The major competitive weapons used in the subcontract medium/heavy precision engineering market were price, delivery and quality. Price was important, since orders were obtained almost exclusively through competitive tendering. The 1980–82 recession had made price the most important aspect of competition, and competitors were taking work at less than full overhead recovery. A key factor for success was a firm's ability to determine competitors' prices and, as a well-established, reputable firm, PE's customers sometimes provided indications of the price level required for success.

Historically, PE's delivery performance had been poor, but the new Board had introduced a production control system which was expected to improve delivery times significantly. On the other hand, PE was well known among its customers (especially the larger steel plant contractors) for its quality. This was the major reason why PE received enquiries and indications of tendering levels. However, there were a number of competitors capable of similar quality work, and PE could not rely solely on its quality image for marketplace success.

The introduction of computer-controlled machine tools, which offered flexibility to the job shop manufacturer (as well as to the batch manufacturer), posed the major competitive threat to PE. This was seen to be the principal reason why PE needed to invest in new plant and equipment.

PE's competitors in general engineering were subcontractors with turnovers generally less than £5 million per annum. In the steel industry segment, market shares were difficult to obtain, but management estimated that PE had one-quarter to one-third of the UK market for mandrels. The competitors in this segment, in order of competitive strength, were Windrush Engineering, who had up-to-date plant and machinery, a full design and project management capability, but were generally more expensive than PE; Eastface Engineering, who had a fully computerized production control system, were very price competitive on mandrels, but manufactured equipment only in the lightest end of PE's range; John Case Engineering, who had no specific competitive advantage; Bordale, who were competitive in mandrels; and Foss Engineering, a subsidiary of British Leyland, who had computer numerically controlled (CNC) machinery centres and lathes, were MoD classified, and were very competitive in batch work, but only for the MoD.

The principal competitors in heavy materials handling (again in order of competitive strength) were: FTN, who designed equipment for coiling, as well as handling equipment, but did not manufacture; Windrush, who were price competitive on chain, design coiling equipment, but otherwise comparable to PE; John Case, who were price competitive on roller tables, but not the heavier end of the market; and Sack GmbH and Hansmann GmbH. In the hydraulics market, PE's only customer was Davy. There were four suppliers to Davy in this segment, and Davy was interested in keeping all four, so work tended to be equally distributed, but erratic.

Finally, the market for plastics injection moulding machines was highly fragmented, with many continental suppliers whose prices, particularly on the smaller machines, were as much as 33 per cent lower than PE's. PE concentrated in the segment of the market where design was more important than price: specialist trade moulders, particularly for ceramic moulding and insert moulding.

Economics of the business

Medium/heavy precision engineering was characterized by relatively high overhead costs. The overhead costs incurred were those required by the MoD to maintain engineering and inspection facilities to Defence Standard 05–24. Significant personnel reductions had been made by Nostra Holdings, but fixed costs continued to decline during 1982 as the result of the transfer of plastics machinery production from East Works (sold to Nostra Holdings at the time of purchase) to Atlas Works, the transfer of the drawing office at Watford to Warrington, and capital expenditure (of £23 000) on the new heating system.

Fixed costs were higher in the 6 months April–November 1982 than volume normally dictated, because the new Board decided to maintain indirect labour levels in order to ensure that PE was capable of obtaining and executing the same type of work it had had in the past. It was considered unlikely that PE would have received the large order from Davy McKee (Poole) for the edge trimmer, if indirect costs had been reduced further. The increase in volume brought about by the Davy McKee (Poole) order, and the increase in direct labour required to complete the order on time, was expected to improve the ratio of direct to indirect labour. The overhead recovery rate was very sensitive to the ratio of direct to indirect labour, which meant that, as volume increased, the required overhead recovery rates declined dramatically. When this occurred, PE became more price competitive. A 10 per cent increase in volume led to a reduction in the overhead recovery rate on a 'typical job' of 12 per cent, or a total cost reduction in the estimate of approximately 5 per cent. Variations in competitors' overhead recovery rates were seen to be the single biggest difference in costs between PE and its competitors.

Profits, therefore, were extremely sensitive to volume. Assuming the historic 50:50 split between materials and labour costs (both direct and indirect), PE's breakeven sales volume was £2.2 million.

Management and organization

PE was controlled by a board of directors consisting of the three principal shareholders, the Managing Director and the Engineering Director. The principal shareholders held 22, 44 and 25 per cent respectively of each class of the issued share capital, and were partners in a firm specializing in the management of distressed companies. When PE was acquired in April 1982, the new owners appointed a business graduate (who was also a qualified chartered accountant) to undertake the initial phase of the turnaround. He resigned in

Exhibit 5: *Precision Engineering: organization chart and management profiles*

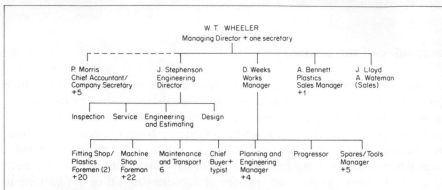

(plus six part-time fitters (plastics); two school apprentices; two part-time canteen staff)

Management profiles

William Wheeler (Managing Director): Joined PE as Works Director in May 1980, appointed General Manager in February 1981, and Managing Director in November 1982. Previously worked for 26 years for John Jones and Sons (Salford) Ltd., manufacturers of hydraulic presses. After starting in the drawing office, he became Works Manager in 1968 and Works Director in 1974. Aged 44.

John Stephenson, CEng, MIMechE (Engineering Director): Joined PE as Engineering Director in 1975. Previously worked for 19 years in various project engineering jobs. Aged 58.

Peter Morris (Chief Accountant/Company Secretary): Joined PE in 1970 as a cost accountant and after a series of promotions became Chief Accountant in 1980. Prior to joining PE, he had worked in several accounting functions.

David Weeks (Works Manager): Joined PE as Production Engineer in February 1980, responsible for production planning and monitoring of production performance. Promoted to present position in 1981. Previous experience as an estimator for an injection moulding company, and as a production engineer for Tenneco Walker (UK) Ltd. Possesses Higher National Diploma in Production Engineering. Aged 29.

Alan Bennett (Plastics Sales Manager): Returned to PE in 1980 after 5 years in sales and service engineering positions with other injection moulding equipment manufacturers. Previously employed by PE for 5 years as a service engineer. Aged 35.

Joe Lloyd (Design Manager): Joined PE in 1976 as Senior Project Engineer and subsequently became Divisional Manager in charge of heavy mechanical handling equipment. Previously Chief Designer of the Planet Corporation (1973–76) and for 15 years was a designer and R and D engineer for GEC. Aged 46.

Murray Westcroft (Buyer): Joined PE in 1972 having previously worked for 12 years in an engineering firm as stores manager, materials controller and production manager. Aged 61.

October 1982, claiming that he had developed an ulcer, and joined a consultancy company. The General Manager/Works Director, William ('Bill') Wheeler, was appointed Managing Director as from 1 November 1982.

The shareholders continued to provide the overall direction and control of the company through weekly visits and direct reporting from Peter Morris the Chief

Accountant, who they considered to be a capable individual, able to exercise tight cash flow management (Exhibit 5).

The day-to-day management of the company was under the control of a management team led by Bill Wheeler (see the organization chart in Exhibit 5). The team had extensive engineering industry experience and was well known and respected by the principal customers. Bill Wheeler, in particular, was considered to have both the leadership skills necessary to turn the company around, and the management skills necessary to improve the poor morale that had developed in the company as the result of declining volume; he was good at communicating with the shop floor. Details of the other members of the management team are given in Exhibit 5.

The organization chart in Exhibit 5 shows the number of employees by department. The company employed 94 people in November 1982, many of whom were highly skilled. Management planned to add six additional operatives over the months November 1982 to April 1983, to meet the requirements of the large Davy McKee (Poole) order.

The company had only one union, the AUEW, with whom industrial relations were good. There had been no demarcation disputes and labour worked wherever was necessary in the plant, although morale was poor. The union wage agreement was expected to last until 31 March 1983. The hourly shopfloor rates paid in 1982 were £2.78 (Grade A), £2.70 (Grade B), £2.59 (Grade C) and £1.99 (for labourers).

PE had two salesman based in Warrington: one dealt with the North, covering Davy McKee, BSC in the North-east, Vickers in the North-west, West Yorkshire, Lancashire and Greater Manchester; and the other dealt with the South (West Midlands and South Wales).

Manufacturing operations

PE operated from an 84 000 ft^2 (7800 m^2) site in the middle of Warrington (see the photographs in Exhibit 6). Half of the site was freehold, while the remainder was held on a 999-year lease which was granted in 1857. The ground rent was £40 per annum. The site contained a 50 000 ft^2 (4600 m^2) factory and adjoining offices. The overall state of repair of the factory was satisfactory, and no substantial capital expenditure was foreseen on this in the near future.

In terms of plant and equipment, PE's machine tools were versatile, but old. PE had been starved of capital investment in recent years and some new capital expenditure was foreseen in the near future to ensure that PE remained competitive on costs. In some instances, consistent quality was achieved only by the skill of the machine operators.

The engineering function at PE was involved in design, project work and estimating. The design work was mainly in heavy mechanical handling, plastic injection moulding machinery and hydraulic systems, but was extended to other

Exhibit 6: *Precision Engineering's works. (a) One of PE's two Elga Mills. (b) A general view of one of the fitting and assembly shops. (c) A close-up of the Marwin Maxi Mill, a numerically controlled Machining Centre. (d) Boko F63-10 Universal Boring and Drilling Machine. (e) A Granor heavy-duty centre lathe at work on a large roll.*

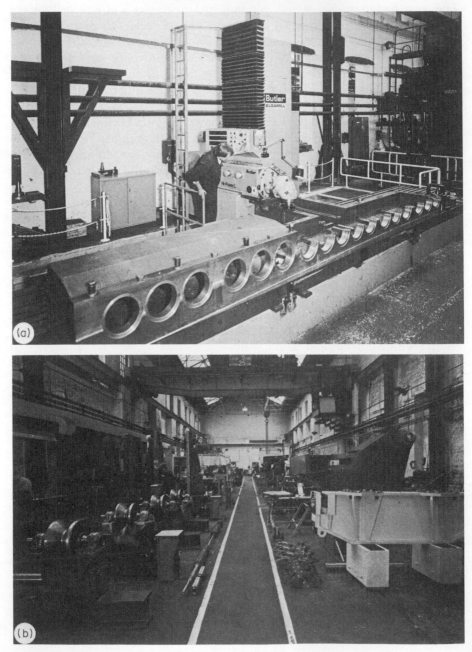

special equipment when necessary. Project work started at the order stage and involved preparing drawings, specifications etc. for production, issuing critical material requisitions to the purchasing department, checking technical details, investigating technical problems, liaising with customers where necessary, assisting production planning in the preparation of project timetables, and producing and maintaining contract files. The estimating work began with the preparation of separate material and labour estimates, which were then brought together into a single estimate for approval by the Managing Director and other directors before a tender was submitted to a customer.

The quality assurance function included a standards room maintained at a constant temperature, in which were stored the inspection standard and inspection measuring equipment, such as micrometers, comparators, electronic three-dimensional measuring machine, hardness tester, etc. All inspection aids were regularly checked against the standards, and record cards were kept for each instrument. Adjacent to the standards room was the main inspection area containing three calibrated cast iron tables on which work pieces were set for inspecting. All aspects of work inspection were carried out and included magnetic particle inspection for detecting cracks in welds or base material. Inspection was also carried out at production machine locations.

The quality assurance department worked closely with customers' inspectors, and supplied all necessary quality control documentation. PE was Ministry of Defence Approved to Defence Standard 05–24. This approval was renewed in August 1982 for a further period of 3 years. PE was also an approved supplier to the National Coal Board, British Steel Corporation, British Rail and British Nuclear Fuels. Private sector firms that had given specific quality approval to PE included: the Davy Group, Michelin Tyre Company, Vickers Engineering, and Salem Herr Boss. PE also maintained a service engineer and spare parts operation for the plastics machinery business at the Warrington plant.

In terms of systems, PE rented a Nixdorf 8870 computer on which it ran its financial accounts, sales ledger, purchase ledger and payroll. The removal of the former subsidiary companies vacated space on the disc. Some elements of the new production control system were in the process of being computerized. The production control system was designed to monitor project performance and both labour and machine efficiency. The Chief Accountant produced profit and loss, liquidity statements and balance sheets on a monthly basis.

Recent performance

The management claimed a number of achievements in the 6 month period following the April 1982 acquisition. First, an increased selling effort by management had helped PE to regain some of its old customers, notably Davy McKee (Poole), BSC, Ashlow Steel and the Ministry of Defence, resulting in the order book increasing from £450 000 to £1.2 million and the expansion of the customer base. Employee morale had improved with the order book. Second, new management control systems were implemented. Third, there had been a general improvement in manufacturing efficiency which had ensured the renewal of the MoD Defence Standard 05-24, after an in-depth systems audit by MoD personnel. Fourth, there had been the various overhead reductions already referred to. And finally, initial contacts had been made with new customers not previously served by PE.

The lead time required to obtain and execute work meant that a turnaround to profits in a company like PE could not be achieved in the first 6 months. The new owners had been aware of this on acquisition, and budgeted for continued losses for the first 6 months of operation. Actual losses incurred since the beginning of the financial year are shown in Exhibit 7. Although the

Exhibit 7: *Actual and forecast profit and loss statement for 1982–83 (£000)*

P and L account	Actual					Forecast							
	May 1982	June	July	Aug	Sept	Oct	Nov	Dec	Jan 1983	Feb	Mar	Apr	Total
Sales	81	78	43	112	103	55	168	161	69	461	394	154	1880
Less: Cost of sales:													
Labour and overheads	51	55	16	74	64	27	97	81	38	224	191	77	996
Materials	30	23	21	72	38	27	69	75	28	214	184	70	851
Gross margins	—	—	6	(34)	1	1	2	5	3	23	19	7	33
Less: Actual overheads	67	64	68	71	60	64	66	72	68	69	73	63	807
Less: Depreciation	6	6	6	6	6	6	6	6	6	6	6	6	72
Less: Interest	4	3	5	4	4	4	4	5	5	6	7	6	58
Plus: Overheads recovered to inventory	54	43	50	44	46	40	80	79	75	83	74	77	747
Profit before exceptional items	(23)	(30)	(23)	(71)	(23)	(33)	6	1	(1)	25	7	9	(157)
Less: Exceptional items	—	2	3	(25)	(3)	—	—	—	—	—	—	—	(23)
Profit before tax	(23)	(32)	(26)	(46)	(20)	(33)	6	1	(1)	25	7	9	(133)

accumulated deficit for 1982–83 stood at £125 000 after 6 months, by the end of the year the deficit was expected to be down to £20 000.

The ICFC proposal: future plans

In their proposal to the ICFC, the directors outlined their future plans and expected financial performance. In terms of marketing strategy, the directors saw PE's short-term strategy as continuing in the design and manufacture of those types of products which it had historically made for both existing and former customers. The expansion of the order book in the past 6 months had been from this area. It was also the company's short-term objective to find new customers for its engineering skills, and sales calls had already been made on some customers in industries other than steel and aluminium (for example, British Gas at Morecambe Bay, the Off-Shore Supplies Office, etc.).

In the longer term, PE planned to develop new customers *and* to provide additional products/services to existing customers. While realizing the problem of overdependence on the Davy Corporation, the directors thought significant opportunities existed in Davy's non-metal activities (such as chemicals, pharmaceuticals, synthetic fibres, coal, water treatment, pollution control, etc.) for PE to diversify its product base to other industries, and eventually other customers. The board saw this strategy as the most effective means of achieving its long-term goal of product/customer diversification. PE was to undertake a

Exhibit 8: *Capital expenditure budget 1982–85 (£000)*

Capital expenditure item	1982–83	1983–84	1984–85
Redecoration of plant and office	5	10	10
CNC machine (Miller)	100*		
Engineering director's car	8*		
Butler Elgamill bedplates		15	
Digital readout to Elgamill	6		
Horizontal borer no. 4 (replace no. 3)		80*	
New building to yard area			35**
Horizontal borer no. 5 (replace Craven)			120
Refurbish 6ft (1.8m) vertical boring machine		15	
Metric measurement and tooling		6	6
Replace lorry		12*	
Replacement cars		14*	15*
Factory lighting and wiring		3	5
Factory roofs and floors		5	5
Printing machine and microfilm			8
Total	119	160	204

* Hire purchase
**Mortgage

marketing study to determine which industry segments provided PE with the most profitable growth opportunities.

The lack of appropriate capital investment over the last 10 years could not be cured immediately, but the board believed that future prospects from current products for existing customers alone were likely to support a capital investment programme amounting to £483 000 over the next 2½ years; £300 000 of this amount was for three major machines — a CNC machine and two new horizontal borers — items Bill Wheeler considered to be urgently needed. Exhibit 8 summarizes the capital expenditure budget.

PE's financial and market performance would, of course, have to improve as planned if the full amount of expenditure was to be justified. However, the board believed that the immediate acquisition of an Oerlikon CNC FB2H horizontal milling machine to replace the Butler Lathe and the Marwin machine was justified. The CNC could achieve tolerances to .0005 in (.0127 mm) compared with .0015 in (.038 mm) currently; cutting speeds were twice those achieved on current machines. More significantly, the CNC machine allowed four faces to be accurately and speedily machined at a single setting, utilizing the indexing table. These advantages were maximized in batch production since the machine's memory allowed it to repeat precisely on subsequent items the dimensions achieved on the first item of the batch.

The net cost of the CNC machine to PE was estimated to be £100 000, after taking account of the grant payable under the Small Engineering Firms Investment Subsidy Scheme.

The ICFC proposal: expected financial performance

Detailed sales budgets by customer were prepared for the 18 months November 1982–April 1984 (for the balance of the 1982–83 financial year and the 1983–84 financial year). These are shown in Exhibits 9 and 10. The sales forecasts were regarded as being extremely conservative, since most of the sales for November 1982–April 1983 were firm orders and indicated as such by job numbers. Moreover, those jobs which had been quoted (an 'E' prefix in the Exhibits) but for which no firm orders had been received, had only been included where management believed the likelihood of an order was extremely high. Finally, unquoted jobs which had been included such as the Sicartsa (Mexico) and Sibernik (Yugoslavia) projects for Davy McKee, had been conservatively forecast using Davy McKee's most pessimistic assumptions. It had been assumed that the £100 million BSC Port Talbot project to modernize plant would not go ahead. PE had already given BSC a provisional £4.4 million quotation for the design and manufacture of mechanical handling equipment. It was expected that if the project did go ahead, PE would get at least part of the work, either directly or as a subcontractor. The forecasts assumed no orders from new products for existing customers. The 18 month forecast was, therefore, no more than a 'momentum' forecast, and assumed no additional sales from new marketing efforts. In 1984–85, a 15 per cent growth in volume was expected.

Exhibit 7 shows the (unaudited) monthly profit and loss for PE for the 5 months ending 30 September 1982, and the budgeted profit and loss for the next 7 months. PE was expected to show a profit of £46 000 on sales of £1.4 million from November 1982 to April 1983. In 1983–84, profits were forecast at only £80 000, or 3.3 per cent of sales, due to the conservative sales assumption. This level of profitability was the same as that made by PE under poor management in the 1976–77 financial year, further indicating how conservative the assumptions were. Profits were forecast to reach £195 000 on sales of £2.76 million in 1984–85, thus showing the sensitivity of profits to volume growth.

Exhibits 11 and 12 show a detailed cash flow forecast for 7 months (November 1982–April 1983). PE's cash borrowing requirements peaked at £718 000 in March 1983, due to the large order for Davy McKee (Poole). Exhibits 13 and 14 show a detailed cash flow forecast that was prepared to show the cash flow directly connected with this order.

PE had an overdraft arrangement with the Warrington branch of Williams and Glyn's Bank. This was secured by a fixed and floating charge over the assets of the company. Since this overdraft limit was set at only £500 000, PE needed additional borrowing facilities for the period December 1982 to May 1983, at which time PE was expected to return to a cash position well within its overdraft facilities. Exhibit 15 shows a monthly cash flow forecast for the 1983–84 financial year, which again shows a bank borrowing requirement in excess of £500 000 was needed for the period July–September 1983.

Exhibit 9: *Sales budget by invoice date, October 1982–April 1983 (£000)*

Number	Client and description	Oct 1982	Nov	Dec	Jan 1983	Feb	Mar	Apr	Total
1. 37/249	Davy McKee (Sheffield) Laying heads		74.0						
2. 92/2260	Distington Lifting beam		2.0						
3. 90/207	Davy McKee (Poole) Spare chain	0.6							
4. 92/2421	B.R. Eng. M/c Fire plugs	1.5							
5. 99/214	MoD Chilwell Rope assembly		0.4						
6. 92/2426	L. Gardner Crank cases	4.1	4.3	4.3	4.3	4.3	4.3	4.3	
7. 37/255	Davy McKee (S) 2 guide rings	4.8							
8. 37/250	Davy McKee (S) Spare laying head		32.7						
9. 92/2360	BSC Pantey Coiler drum		40.4						
10. 92/2428	Wellman Cranes Spares		4.8						
11. 92/2430	Distington Spares		.6						
12. 92/2432	BSC Cumbria Mod's side plates		.6						
13. 92/2365	BSC Lackenby Underbogies			101.2					
14. 92/2420	Davy McKee (P) Cut to length line			47.0					
15. 99/212	MoD Chilwell Towing bracket				6.4				
16. 99/213	MoD Chilwell Towing brackets				13.1				
17. 99/215	MoD Axle arms				6.1	18.3	24.4	·24.4	
18. 97/257	Davy McKee (S) Line shafts				11.5				
19. 92/2403	Davy McKee (P) 2 Entry shear					289.0*			
20. 97/256	Davy McKee (S) Line shafts					22.6			
21. 97/258	Davy McKee (S) Line shafts					97.4			
22. 92/2403	Davy McKee (P) Edge trimmer						277.0*		
23. 99/216	MoD Chilwell Towing bars							10.3	
24. E5670	Davy McKee (P) CTL spares				9.9				
25. E5668	Davy McKee (P) CTL spares					3.0			
26. E5653	Ashlow Crop 'n cobble shear						25.0		
27. E5647/9	Davy McKee (P) Kaiser spares					8.0			
28. E5634	Davy Head Wrightson spares						2.5		
29. E5580	Davy McKee (P) Mandrel spares							7.8	
30. E5679	Techniwell Tubes						17.3		
31. E5661	BSC Ebbw Vale Piston							2.1	
32. E5671	MoD Shock absorber links							12.0	
33.	General engineering work	5.0	5.0	5.0	5.0	5.0	5.0	5.0	
34.	Davy McKee (S) Sicartsa							50.0	
35.	Plastics machines	36.0			10.3	10.3	35.0	35.0	
36.	Plastics spares	3.0	3.0	3.0	3.0	3.0	3.0	3.0	
	Total	55.0	167.9	160.6	69.8	461.0	394.0	154.0	1462.3

*Items 19 and 22 together comprise the large Davy McKee edge trimmer contract. The figures shown are the original August 1982 estimates (see Exhibit 14) plus £16 000 of extras in addition to the basic order.

Exhibit 10: *Sales budget by invoice date, May 1983–April 1984 (£000)*

Number	Client and description	May 1983	June	July	Aug	Sept	Oct	Nov	Dec	Jan 1984	Feb	Mar	Apr
1. 99/215	MoD Axle arms	17.7											
2. E5666	Davy McKee (S) chocks			40.0									
3. E5629	BSC Shepcote Lane (Whet brush m/c)				55.6								
4. E5614	Speed Seal (rig tackle)		30.0										
5. E5584	Davy Head Wrightson spares			13.7									
6. E5576	Davy McKee (P) Processor head					65.7							
7. E5532	Centri-Tech (Pipe machinery)								200.0				
8. E5518	Davy McKee (P) Reel head					37.9							
9. E5492	BAC Falkirk chocks							37.5					
10. E5681	Davy McKee (P) Upcut shear			83.0									
11. E5674	Davy McKee (P) Mandrel				18.3								
12. E5671	MoD Shock absorber links	12.0	12.0	14.0									
13.	General engineering work	5.0	5.0	5.0	5.0	5.0	5.0	5.0	5.0	5.0	5.0	5.0	5.0
14.	Davy McKee (S) Hydraulics	25.0	25.0	25.0	25.0	25.0	25.0			15.0	10.0	15.0	10.0
15.	Davy McKee (S) Sicartsa	50.0	50.0	50.0	50.0								
16.	Davy McKee (P) Sibenik				60.0	60.0	60.0	60.0	60.0				
17.	L. Gardner Crank cases	4.3	4.3	4.3	4.3	4.3	4.3	4.3	4.3	4.3	4.3	4.3	4.3
18.	Plastics machines	18.5	10.3	38.0	38.0	11.5	18.5	38.0			10.3	18.5	18.5
19.	Plastics spares	3.0	3.0	3.0	3.0	3.0	3.0	3.0	3.0	3.0	3.0	3.0	3.0
20.	Salem Herr Voss						14.0			20.0			15.0
21.	MoD various FV spares			8.0	12.0	12.0	12.0	12.0	12.0	8.0		8.0	12.0
22.	Mechanical Handling, various		12.0			12.0			12.0			12.0	
23.	Mechanical handling major job (½ million)				40.0	50.0	50.0	60.0	70.0	70.0	70.0	45.0	45.0
	Total*	135.5	151.7	284.0	311.3	286.5	191.8	219.9	366.3	125.3	102.7	110.8	112.8

*Total annual sales for May 1983–April 1984 are 2399. These are broken down as follows: general engineering 1394, hydraulics 200, mechanical handling 548, and plastics 256.

Exhibit 16 shows forecast year-end balance sheets for 1983, 1984 and 1985. Assuming that the additional borrowing requirements were financed by either additional short-term borrowings or longer-term debt, total borrowings as a percentage of shareholders' funds were forecast to fall from 176 per cent at year-end 1982–83 to 51 per cent by year-end 1983–84, and 50 per cent at year-end 1984–85.

Exhibit 11: *Cash flow forecast November 1982–April 1983 (£000)*

	1982 November	December	1983 January	February	March	April
Cash inflow						
Receipts from customers	204	60	124	179	105	381
Sale of machine	—	—	—	20	—	—
Total	204	60	124	199	105	381
Cash outflow						
Wages and salaries	32	37	32	32	37	32
Creditors	73	73	103	113	193	123
Petty cash	1	1	1	1	1	1
HP and pension scheme	6	6	6	6	6	6
Capital expenditure	—	—	22*	2	2	7
Inland Revenue	41	41	15	15	15	15
VAT	—	20	—	—	15	—
Bank interest	—	13	—	—	17	—
Total	153	191	179	169	286	184
Net cash inflow/outflow	51	(131)	(55)	30	(181)	197
Month end borrowing requirements	381	512	567	537	718	521

*VAT on purchase of CNC machine

Exhibit 12: *Cash receipts by customer, November 1982–May 1983 (£000)*

November 1982		January 1983		April 1983	
B and R	5	Loewy Robertson* (p.p.)	33	Loewy Robertson*	233
BSC Cumbria	4	Davy McKee (Sheffield)	12	Davy McKee	93
Fielding and Platt	9	Panteg	46	MOD	20
Gardener	5	Wellman	5	Davy retentions	18
Kemson	1	Spares and others	18	Others	18
MEC	1	Davy retentions	10		381
Pendle	4		124		
Polieserv	1				
Salem	16				
White Cross	3	February 1983		May 1983	
Int. Ceramics	16	BSC Lackenby	116	Distington	8
Davy-Loewy	10	Loewy Robertson*	38	Loewy Robertson*	239
Loewy Robertson*	121	Gardener	5	MoD	28
Others	8	Others	18	Others	18
	204	Loewy Retention	2		293
			179		
December 1982		March 1983			
Davy McKee (Sheffield)	10	COD Chilwell	22		
Davy McKee (Sheffield)	29	MoD	7		
Distington	2	Davy McKee	13		
B and R	2	Others	18		
Gardener	5	Davy McKee	45		
Spares etc.	12		105		
	60				

*Loewy Robertson now renamed Davy McKee (Poole). Note that p.p. denotes progress payment.

These financial projections, together with full information about the directors' future plans and strategy for PE were sent to ICFC. Later that month, ICFC were due to make a full day visit to the company. The aim of the PE directors was to convince ICFC that the company had a future, and to persuade them to lend PE £250 000.

Exhibit 13: *Cash effects of Davy McKee (Poole) edge trimmer contract (prepared October 1982) (£000)*

Cash flow item	1982 Oct	Nov	Dec	1983 Jan	Feb	Mar	Apr	May	June*
Scheduled materials receipts	25	109	61	83	47				
Cash effect:									
October deliveries			12	12					
November deliveries				9	9	91			
December deliveries					19	42			
January deliveries						19	64		
February deliveries								47	
			12	21	28	152	64	47	0
Add: VAT where applicable			2	3	4	23	9	3	
			14	25	32	175	73	50	0
Add: Labour at £12.40 per hour	5	45	45	45	45	20			
Total cash outflow	5	45	59	69	77	195	73	50	0
Cash inflow									
(inclusive of VAT)	64	32		32			233	239	0
VAT payable/(reclaimable)			11			(26)			49
Cumulative net cash flow	59	46	(24)	(61)	(138)	(307)	(147)	42	(7)

*There is a 5 per cent retention due after 12 months on this contract.

Exhibit 14: *Davy McKee (Poole) Edge Trimmer contract (estimated August 1982) (£000)*

Contract number	Sales value	Material subcontract	Direct labour	Overhead recovery	Total cost	Profit estimate
0401, 1301 and 1302	185	108	12	46	166	19
0101	188	115	10	40	165	23
112 and 0102	108	60	8	32	100	8
0301, 0302 and 0303	37	25	1	7	33	4
0601	23	11	3	10	24	(1)
Miscellaneous	9	6	1	2	9	0
	550	325	35	137	497	53

*The order was calculated on the above basis but management has assumed only a 5 per cent profit in the profit and loss forecast.

Exhibit 15: *Cash flow forecast for 1983–84 financial year (£000)*

Cash flow item	1983 May	June	July	Aug	Sept	Oct	Nov	Dec	1984 Jan	Feb	Mar	Apr
Receipts from customers[1]	293	154	158[2]	152	284	311	287	192	220	366	125	103
Less: Payments:												
Labour and overheads[3]	173[4]	92	115	91	86	86	88	89	87	87	85	85
Direct materials[5]		67	130	143	131	86	102	171	55	45	49	50
Capital expenditure[6]	8	5	5	7	6	7	21	7	18	9	8	24
Net cash inflow/(outflow)	112	(10)	(92)	(89)	61	132	76	(75)	60	225	(17)	(56)
Month end borrowing requirement	409	419	511	600	539	407	331	406	346	121	138	194

Notes
1. Assumes debtors of 60 days from June onwards.
2. Includes £22 000 VAT repayment
3. Assumes all expenses paid in month they are incurred.
4. This figure incorporates both labour and overheads, and direct materials.
5. Assumes materials paid for in month when sales are invoiced.
6. Capital expenditure and HP payments.

Exhibit 16: *Forecast year-end balance sheets[1] for 1982–1985 (£'000)*

Balance sheet	September 1982	April 1983	April 1984	April 1985
Net assets				
Stock[2]	91	75	75	75
Work-in-progress (net of advances)	198	276	359	351
Total stock	289	351	434	426
Debtors and prepayments[3]	495	550	223	460
Petty cash	1	1	1	1
Current assets	785	902	658	887
Bank overdraft	(486)	(521)	(194)	(255)
Creditors and accruals[4]	(414)	(448)	(499)	(499)
Hire purchase	(14)	(102)	(152)	(203)
Bank loan	(8)	(11)	—	—
Mortgage	—	—	—	(35)
	(922)	(1082)	(845)	(992)
Net current liabilities	(137)	(180)	(187)	(105)
Fixed assets[5]	425	482	570	684
	288	302	383	579
Shareholders funds				
Share capital	813	813	813	813
Capital loans	100	100	100	100
Surplus on revaluation of fixed assets	129	129	129	129
Retained earnings	(754)	(740)	(659)	(463)
	288	302	383	579
Total borrowings as a percentage of shareholders funds	171	176	51	50

Notes
1. PE's balance sheet was completely restructured at the time of its acquisition by the present shareholders as a result of the former owners stripping out the assets relating to the two waste disposal businesses.
2. Major stock writeoffs were taken at the time of acquisition. Management was working towards reducing its inventory of plastic injection moulding machines.
3. Debtors fluctuated substantially from month to month, since contracts varied in length, size and progress payment terms. Analysis of debtors as at 31 October 1982 indicated debtors of £361 000, less bad debt reserves of £29 000 and retentions of £67 000, giving a balance of £265 000. Of this balance, £80 000 was due in less than 30 days, £98 000 in 30–60 days, and £87 000 in more than 60 days.
4. At the time of acquisition there was a significant backlog of PAYE and VAT payments, amounting to £120 000. The new Board reached agreement with the Inland Revenue and the Customs and Excise authorities to bring payments up to date by December 1982. PE was going to meet this commitment.
5. The land and buildings had been revalued in 1980, although plant and equipment had not been revalued for over 10 years.

26. Wallis Fashion Group

In July 1979, managing director Jeffrey Wallis and deputy managing director Harold Wallis were in the process of reviewing with their finance director a commitment to increase the dividends paid by their company. The commitment arose from a scrip issue which the company had announced a year earlier, and which had been (correctly) interpreted by the financial community as a statement of intent to raise the total annual dividend paid on the Wallis Fashion Group's ordinary shares.

Background and early history: 1923–48

The Wallis Fashion Group was a vertically integrated women's wear manufacturing and retailing business. Its stylish outlets were crammed with trendy womenswear and were located in prime shopping areas.

Its beginnings, however, were very modest. In 1923, Nat Wallis started a low-grade garment retailing business in Chapel Street, Islington. By the time the firm gained a Stock Exchange listing in 1936, it had 25 shops located in working-class, market trading areas of London such as Chapel Street and Brixton. When Nat Wallis's son Jeffrey entered the business in 1948, he developed a deep distaste for its methods and merchandise. As he described it, 'the shop ground floors consisted of long arcade windows with probably at least 60 garments in each window — if there was space in the window, they filled it up. Up and down the arcade prowled Damon Runyon-type characters with colourful names like Long Alf or Grimsby Jack with personalities to match, who were employed to chat up prospective customers in order to get them into the shop.'

Commercial metamorphosis: 1949–68

When his father died in 1948, Jeffrey Wallis, aged 24, gained control of the business. He was determined to upgrade the firm's merchandise and image, and

This case was written by Elroy Dimson and Paul Marsh as a basis for class discussion rather than to illustrate either effective or ineffective handling of an administrative situation.

turn it into 'the Marks and Spencer of the high fashion industry'. This was no mean task. To begin with, he tried to improve the quality by using better suppliers — but he had no success. 'They wouldn't be seen dead with their merchandise in our shops.' He came to two conclusions. First, Wallis would have to design and manufacture a higher proportion of its products itself. Second, the shops would have to be redesigned and moved to middle-class areas.

The main problem in achieving this was gaining access to designs. Wallis started making frequent trips to Paris and immersing himself in haute couture. At the time, the power of the French houses was in its zenith. They dictated to and regulated the world fashion industry, making vast sums from selling paper patterns to the top manufacturers. However, by imposing delays through press release dates, the French houses ensured that their patterns could not be used for the same season for which their collections were designed.

Jeffrey Wallis, however, managed to beat this system. As he explains, 'I paid my money, stuck to the official dates, but did everything very quickly in my own factory — other people could have done it too, but it was too much trouble for them.' He put together a design team, set up his own 'Pick of Paris' factory, and became famous for selling cheap and extremely accurate copies of couture clothes.

In the 1960s, when haute couture started to become old hat, Wallis adapted rapidly. Ironically, having made his mark as an imitator, he was the first to recognize the strength of British design. He became a strong supporter of British student design, and he regularly recruited outstanding graduates from the Royal College of Fashion and other leading colleges. The company rapidly became known as a prestigious training ground for fashion designers. A distinct and instantly recognizable 'Wallis look' began to emerge which was quintessentially English. With the advantage of running their own manufacturing operation, the company was able to translate these designs into popular, up-to-the-minute lines available from their branches throughout the country. During this period, however, profit took second place to aesthetic appeal and design.

Financial metamorphosis: 1968–73

Near the end of the decade, the company recruited an innovative financial controller. The Board were introduced to management accounting, and the directors realized just how many mistakes they had made and the scope for improvement. With its greater financial awareness, the company sold off outlets with poor sales potential and concentrated on building a chain of high street shops. Window displays were reduced to a minimum to increase selling space, stock turnover was increased and advance purchases of cloth closely monitored, markdowns were reduced, and margins maximized.

The new financial orientation produced small profits in 1969, a turnaround from the losses of the mid–late 1960s. Wallis celebrated its metamorphosis in 1970 by doubling its dividend, to restore it to the level it had in the more profitable early 1960s.

The year ending 31 January 1970 was the second year of profits, albeit £11 000 on a turnover of £2.6 million. This was followed in early 1971 by an unwelcome bid from the Burton Group, which had gradually built up its holding from 1960 onwards. Wallis was defended (by the merchant bank Brandts) with the claim that:'Wallis has now achieved an unrivalled ability to spot trends immediately and reflect them straight through to production'.

Despite being a public company, a large block of the shares were controlled by the Wallis family. Their 43 per cent holding in the company's equity enabled them to defeat Burton's takeover attempt.

Wallis's defeat of the bid was vindicated by a major enhancement of the company's reported profitability. The following year's results disclosed a 40 per cent rise in turnover, accompanied by a pretax profits rise to £224 000, more than three times the all-time peak of £63 000 in 1963–64. The dividend paid on the company's shares was again raised, this time six-fold. At the same time, a three-for-one scrip issue was announced. The stock market presented its accolade to the Wallis group. Its share price now stood at four times its 1970 level, and 20 per cent above Burton's bid price.

In 1972, the company succeeded in roughly maintaining its turnover and profit. In October, when the Burton group disposed of its 36 per cent stake in Wallis, the family further increased its holdings by acquiring half of these shares while the other half were sold to Wallis's bankers for placing. By the mid-1970s, the Wallis family controlled some 64 per cent of the company's equity.

Exhibit 1: *Wallis Fashion Group dividends, earnings and share prices, 1970–79*

Year	Turnover £ million	Pretax Profits £ million	Earnings per share* p	Dividend per share* p	Share price* p
1970†	2.6	.0	.1	.1	1.6
1971	3.6	.2	1.2	.4	6.8
1972	3.5	.2	.9	.4	14.0
1973	4.7	.5	2.7	.7	11.5
1974	5.1	.5	2.4	.6	5.5
1975	7.1	.7	3.1	.6	10.5
1976	8.9	.4	1.4	.6	8.8
1977	11.4	.7	2.1	.6	14.3
1978	15.2	1.0	7.5	1.0	77.0
1979	21.9	1.5	12.9		

*Adjusted for three-for-one scrip issues in August 1971 and August 1978. Dividends are net of standard rate income tax, after the introduction of the imputation tax system in 1973.
†All data except share prices are for the financial year ending 31 January. Share prices are as at the year-end.

By 1973, Wallis Fashion Group was in a position to announce a further dramatic improvement. Profits now stood at £474 000, and the annual dividend was raised by 60 per cent. The share price rose to more than double the figure which Burtons had offered (see Exhibit 1).

Expansion: 1973–77

As a close company, Wallis fell outside the dividend restraints imposed by the British Government during the 1970s. However, during the mid-1970s the company chose to limit its distributions. There were three reasons for this. First, there were moral pressures to conform to the broad terms of the restraints. Second, the Wallis brothers had no need for additional income; and indeed, from 1976 they elected to waive much of their dividend entitlement. Third, the company wished to conserve cash for expansion. There were no borrowings in the balance sheet, and the Wallis family had no desire to dilute their equity by making a rights issue.

By far the most important motive for maintaining a low payout ratio was the desire to expand the group. In 1973, the company's expansion was in full swing, and it was operating over 30 shops throughout the United Kingdom. Over three-quarters of its total range was manufactured within the company. New outlets were being opened, almost at the rate of one per month. By 1975, 2 years later, there were some 50 outlets, including eight in Germany and Switzerland. By 1977, 60 shops were being operated in the United Kingdom and Europe. This figure was to grow to about 80 by 1979, with plans for expansion to 90 by 1980 (see Exhibit 2).

Naturally, the rapid expansion imposed considerable stresses on the management team. Wallis, while very much the typical entrepreneur, was perhaps unusual in his willingness to seek outside advice. In 1976, he asked consultants to look at the company's structure and methods. The consultants' advice led to the creation of a new middle management stratum, including a number of new posts for a corporate planner, a marketing specialist and a business analyst. The aim was to attract a higher and more professional calibre of manager.

In spite of the changes, Wallis's own stamp and style were firmly imprinted on the group. Wallis, the man, and Wallis Fashion Group, the company, were inextricably linked. Over the years, Wallis had evolved his own particular philosophy for running a fashion business. Three principles were especially dear to him. First, what he describes as 'the philosophy of freshness'; second, careful and systematic range building; and third, an intelligent classification of his shops based on a statistical analysis of past performance.

In 1977, Wallis was introducing over 20 new styles into each store each week, to ensure 'freshness and change'. Markdowns and sales were used to eliminate slow moving lines and mistakes. Wallis's view was that 'if you can suck out of

Exhibit 2: *The Wallis Fashion Group's retail outlets, January 1979†*

London	Cambridge	*Wales*	*Belgium*
Bromley	Canterbury	Cardiff(2)*	Brussels
Brent Cross	Cheltenham	Swansea*	
Chelsea	Chester*		*West Germany*
Croydon	Coventry*	*Scotland*	Bremen*
Golders Green	Darlington*	Aberdeen(2)*	Cologne*
Kingston	Guildford	Dundee*	Darmstadt*
Knightsbridge	Hull*	Edinburgh (3)*	Dortmund*
Marble Arch	Leeds	Glasgow(2)*	Dusseldorf*
Oxford Circus	Liverpool*	Stirling*	Frankfurt*
Oxford Street	Manchester(3)*		Hamburg*
Richmond*	Middlesborough	*Northern Ireland*	Hanover*
South Molton Street	Newcastle(3)*	Belfast	Karlsruhe*
	Northampton		Munich*
Provinces	Nottingham	*Irish Republic*	Stuttgart*
Bath	Plymouth*	Dublin(2)*	West Berlin*
Birmingham(3)*	Oxford		Wiesbaden*
Bournemouth*	Sheffield	*Switzerland*	
Bradford*	Sunderland*	Basle*	*Sweden*
Brighton	Watford	Glatt*	Stockholm*
Bristol	Wolverhampton*	Zurich*	

*Including shops within a store.
†In addition, a further six British and five European outlets were scheduled for imminent opening.

the system a bad style which is selling at 20 weeks stock turn and replace it with a good style and a 3 week stock turn, by definition, you can almost afford to burn the bad style'. The range building policy was designed to ensure that each style was 'exposed sensibly across the shop chain to ensure fast accurate feedback of sales information'. The aim here was to ensure that the right garments went to the right stores in the right quantities. Important in achieving this aim was the shop categorization system which reduced the total number of shops to about five manageable groups. This system permitted rapid feedback on best selling lines allowing heavy repeats in time to hit the peak of the season.

Jeffrey Wallis was also acutely aware that minimizing risk in the volatile fashion industry required not only first-class marketing information, but also careful attention to financial budgeting and planning. Hence he set great store by his rolling corporate plan — based on departmental volume and value budgets for every year, and for each season, month, shop and shop department. This permitted factory loading requirements to be ordered well in advance; it also gave the designers ample time in which to match their ideas to budgetary constraints.

During this period, Wallis's shares, though thinly traded, attracted increasing attention from the financial press. But by mid-1977, the dividend yield on the company's shares looked embarassingly low, notwithstanding the cash demands arising from the continued expansion of the business. In August, the *Investors Chronicle* reported the year's results with the statement: 'Only the maintained dividend detracts from the good performance of Wallis Fashion', though it went on to assert that, nevertheless, 'A near three-and-a-half times covered yield of 7.7 per cent at 50p presents a sound picture' (26 August 1977).

Continued growth: 1977–78

By June 1978, any uncertainties that might have dissuaded Wallis's directors from increasing dividends had evaporated. The 30 per cent increase in turnover recorded in 1977 was repeated in 1978. The £300 000 increase in annual profits was also repeated in 1978. By any standard, the company was in a healthy position to increase its dividends again, the shares yielding an over four times covered 4 per cent.

On 14 July, the board announced a doubling of the final dividend payment, to be followed by a three-for-one scrip issue. This represented a 60 per cent increase in annual dividends, compared to earlier years.

Wallis Fashion's announcement had an immediate impact. By August, the shares stood at twice their June level, and the company had recaptured the imagination of many in the investment community. Through the remaining months of 1978, the company received a succession of favourable reports in the financial press (see Exhibit 3). Near the end of 1978, non-executive chairman Lord Mancroft reported on the unaudited half-year results:

> During the first half of the year the company was able to take advantage of improved trading conditions, and as a result we can report substantial increases in both turnover and profit. Since the half-year the trading situation has been less favourable due to unseasonable weather, but nevertheless we still expect to show a significant increase in profit for the year as a whole. Your directors have declared an interim dividend of 1p per share on the ordinary shares of the company. In declaring this dividend the company has taken account of its intention to pay a higher proportion of its total dividend as interim dividend. The dividend, together with its attributable tax credit, is equivalent to 1.49p per share. (Exhibit 4)

Wallis was not alone in remaining generally confident about future prospects. Other women's fashion companies shared in optimism about the future, despite minor irritants such as the transport strike and the unreliable summer weather. Indeed, it was clear that Lord Mancroft's note of caution was more a warning against reading too much into the explosive leap in first-half profits, than because the Wallis board was really worried.

Indeed, at this time, Jeffrey Wallis's principal concerns were all centred on how to facilitate further expansion. He summarized these as the 'three p's: property, production and people'. He conceded that of these, property was the least serious — although there was always a constant need to be on the lookout

Exhibit 3: *Press reports on Wallis Fashion Group, Autumn 1978*

In August, the *Observer* wrote:

Wallis Fashion's share price has more than quadrupled since I commended them to your attention in June 1977. . . . During the trading year to last January, Wallis achieved its ambition of becoming a member of the £1 million pretax profits club, thanks to reorganization and the countrywide popularity of their frock shops. . . . This year, chairman Lord Mancroft, and his directors will be taking a giant stride towards their next target, which is of course the even more exclusive £2 million profits club. How close will they get? Well, with the tills tinkling merrily throughout the group the word is that profits of not less than £1.6 million are on their way. (13 August 1978)

Two months later, the *Sunday Times* was even more enthusiastic:

The price of most stores' shares and consumer oriented stocks have caught up with expectations. But one share where market expectations have so far been pitched far too low, even though the shares have risen this year from 11½p to 80p, is Wallis Fashion. . . . Interim, pretax profits due in December will be good, but the second 6 months is Wallis's all-important trading period. Already it is clear that market estimates of pretax profits for the year to January, rising more than 50 per cent from £1.03 million to £1.6 million, will be too low. . . . If it holds last year's dividend on the capital increased by the recent scrip issue then the shares yield 7.5 per cent. Rarely do growth companies offer such good value and high return. (15 October 1978)

The *Sunday Telegraph* followed, in November with a favourable forecast:

Interim results due shortly from Wallis Fashion Group will not disappoint. A substantial advance over the previous pretax profits of £53 000 is expected and bulls anticipate 1978–79 pretax profits doubling to £2 million. (26 November 1978)

At the very end of November, Wallis published its interim results. The *Investors Chronicle*, for one, was not disappointed:

Wallis Fashion Group has announced profits for the 28 weeks to 12 August up from £53 000 to £356 000; sales were up from £6.4 million to £9.88 million. Demand for women's fashions has been very strong and Wallis has obviously got its merchandise policy right. The company is in a very strong growth phase. . . . The interim dividend has been quadrupled to reduce the disparity between the two payments. On last year's dividends the yield with the shares at 93p is only 1.6 per cent. But Wallis is a close company so there should be a useful overall dividend increase this year. The fully taxed prospective P/E is around 10. The rating is justified. (1 December 1978)

---

for new shop sites and ways of increasing warehouse, office and factory space. Production was a more serious issue. While 80 per cent of Wallis's goods were 'own made', only 25 per cent actually came from Wallis's own factories. The balance was produced by outworkers and it was becoming increasingly difficult

Exhibit 4: *Wallis Fashion Group, dividend and profit announcements, 1975–79*

(a) Dividends (in pence) and capital changes

Year	Distribution	Per share gross	net	Announced	Paid	Ex-date
1975	Interim dividend	1.49	1	3 December 1974	15 February 1975	9 December 1974
	Final dividend	2.31	1½	31 July 1975	10 October 1975	22 August 1975
1976	Interim dividend	1.54	1	19 December 1975	12 February 1976	28 December 1975
	Final dividend	2.31	1½	8 October 1976	19 November 1976	18 October 1976
1977	Interim dividend	1.54	1	22 December 1976	12 February 1977	4 January 1977
	Final dividend	2.27	1½	19 August 1977	18 November 1977	17 October 1977
1978	Interim dividend	1.52	1	22 December 1977	11 February 1978	3 January 1978
	Final dividend	4.48	3	14 July 1978	31 August 1978	24 July 1978
	3-for-1 scrip issue	—	—	14 July 1978	—	4 September 1978
1979	Interim dividend	1.49	1	29 November 1978	12 January 1979	11 December 1978

(b) Profits and turnover (£000)*

Announced	28 weeks ended	Turnover excluding VAT	Profit before tax	Net profit
19 December 1975	16 August 1975	3929	69	23
22 December 1976	14 August 1976	4747	80	27
22 December 1977	13 August 1977	6444	53	25
29 November 1978	12 August 1978	9884	356	171

*Unaudited, consolidated half-year results. For full-year results, see Exhibit 5.

to find good outworkers who were willing to manufacture to Wallis's price and quality standards. To achieve Wallis's high quality/low cost aim, greater control was required over production so that its organization could be improved and economies of scale be realized. In the longer run, the clear implication was that Wallis would need to forego the flexibility of using outworkers and instead acquire more factory space and become even more vertically integrated. As a first step in this direction, the company opened a new factory in Mold in North Wales in 1978.

Finally, Wallis was concerned about people. He recognized that the design team was the 'lifeblood of the company'. The problem here was that growth could easily lead to the designers taking on more administrative responsibilities. As Wallis put it, 'the danger with a designer is that the more you turn him into a manager, the less creative he becomes'. Also, 'the more his ideas incorporate past successes, the greater the risk of things getting too safe, and if this happens, the company is dead'. Wallis was also concerned that as the company grew, he was unable to spend as much time as he would have liked with his designers. 'One should never allow oneself to stray too far from the stove.' The company's final 'people' problem was management. Wallis knew that the pace of future expansion, particularly overseas, would be largely dictated by the speed with which the company was able to develop a strengthened and enlarged management team.

Setbacks: 1979

Unfortunately, a mild autumn in 1978 bit into the company's pre-Christmas business, and the weather during the January sales was appalling. Nevertheless, the results to 31 January 1979 showed turnover and pretax profits up by almost half, to £22 million and £1.5 million respectively (Exhibit 5). In addition, the surplus on directors' revaluation of properties rose from £4.2 to £5.0 million (Exhibit 6). The company's investment of £0.9 million in further shops and equipment also offered the prospect of additional profits (Exhibit 7).

However, between the end of the financial year and the publication date of the annual report, July 1979, the situation deteriorated. The spring and summer were desperately unseasonable. Although the sun shone, it failed to shine for

Exhibit 5: *Wallis Fashion Group consolidated profit and loss account*

| P and L Account | £'000 in years ending 31 January | | | | |
	1975	1976	1977	1978	1979
Turnover					
Sales (excluding VAT)	7 127	8 883	11 360	15 172	21 890
Rents and interest	38	34	83	113	101
Trading profit					
Profit before charges	900	721	1 168	1 520	2 144
Charges					
Depreciation etc.	131	180	243	267	346
Bank interest	26	96	103	104	55
Hire charges	—	—	40	68	155
Directors' emoluments	52	44	50	56	77
	209	320	436	495	633
Net profit before tax	691	401	732	1 025	1 511
Taxation					
UK corporation tax	233	—	—	134	(13)
Deferred tax	140	219	392	—	—
Overseas tax	11	5	47	109	177
	384	224	439	243	164
Net profit after tax	307	177	293	782	1347
Dividends					
Preference	3	3	3	3	3
Ordinary declared	65	64	65	103	208*
Ordinary waived	—	(10)	(16)	(25)	(38)
Total dividends	68	57	52	81	173
Profit retained	239	120	241	701	1 174

*Based on a final dividend payment for year to 31 January 1979 of 1p per share.

Exhibit 6: *Wallis Fashion Group consolidated balance sheets*

Balance sheet	£'000 as at 31 January				
	1975	1976	1977	1978	1979
Current assets					
Stocks	986	1 365	1 878	2 616	4 250
Debtors etc.	233	475	451	620	1 061
Cash	532	36	81	73	198
	1 751	1 876	2 410	3 309	5 509
Current liabilities					
Creditors etc.	1 292	1 485	1 630	1 887	3 237
Overdraft	—	467	520	257	358
Bills payable	—	100	—	—	—
Tax	356	129	216	532	704
Dividends	65	55	49	79	93
	1 713	2 236	2 415	2 755	4 392
Net current assets	38	(360)	(5)	554	1 117
Fixed assets					
Freehold property*	148	148	148	148	159
Leasehold property*	704	949	1 033	994	1 105
Plant, furniture, etc.**	622	1 181	1 303	1 327	1 719
ACT recoverable	38	29	57	40	134
Net assets	1 550	1 947	2 536	3 063	4 234
Represented by					
4.55 per cent cumulative preference shares of 50p	65	65	65	65	65
Ordinary shares of 10p	260	260	260	260	1 040
Profit and loss account	834	953	1 124	2 738	3 129 †
Deferred tax	391	669	1 087	—	—
Capital employed	1 550	1 947	2 536	3 063	4 234
*Directors valuation of properties	3 000	3 300	3 400	5 342	6 264
**Authorized capital expenditure	525	175	100	1 017	1 357

†Based on a final dividend payment for year to 31 January 1979 of 1p per share.

long enough to convince shoppers that summer had arrived. Betty Daulton, manageress of Wallis in London's Oxford Street, explained: 'The sun makes all the difference. People don't buy summer clothes in the rain. If it rains in the morning, they stay at home.'

Another problem was the change in the structure of the fashion industry. The fashion business had essentially been a conspiracy to persuade women to look alike. But the end of the 1970s witnessed a rebellion against following the

Exhibit 7: *Wallis Fashion Group source and application of funds*

Funds flow	£'000 in years ending 31 January			
	1976	1977	1978	1979
Sources of funds				
Profit before taxation	401	732	1 025	1 511
Depreciation and amortization	180	243	267	346
	581	975	1293	1857
Applications of funds				
Investment in shops, equipment, etc.	992	449	252	864
Taxation paid	158	32	84	86
Dividends paid*	68	58	52	158
	1 217	538	388	1 108
Addition to working capital	(636)	437	904	749
Applied as follows				
Increase in stock	379	514	734	1633
Increase in debtors (1977:decrease)	242	(24)	169	441
Increase in creditors	(293)	(45)	(257)	(1349)
	327	445	650	725
Movement in liquid funds				
Increase in overdraft (1978:decrease)	(467)	(53)	262	(101)
Increase in bank balances (1976+8:decrease)	(496)	45	(8)	125
	(963)	(8)	255	25
	(636)	437	904	749
*Dividends waived	—	10	16	53

dictates of Paris, London and Rome. Women chose to follow their own whims, wearing ethnic clothes and many other different styles. The skills of the Wallises in translating the current fashion idea into popular lines were of far less use, and the firm made serious misjudgements about the 'looks' which would sell.

Left with substantial stocks, Wallis's summer sales therefore opened with spring fashions still crowding the racks. These problems were compounded by the downturn in the tourist trade, especially in London, a result of the unusual strength of sterling.

The final setback was the rise in value added tax from 8 to 15 per cent. This prompted a pre-budget consumer spending spree, which pre-empted much of the summer sales' turnover. Retailers found that, even if it were adminstratively feasible, it was not possible to pass on the higher rate of VAT to customers, and margins consequently took the strain. Despite the £1 billion in tax rebates, which were supposed to offset the VAT increase, sufficient customers just could not be attracted into the Oxford Street or high street stores.

Without its expected level of turnover, Wallis's forward purchases of cloth now looked worrying. The company's vertically integrated structure meant that cloth must be purchased 6–9 months ahead of anticipated demand. There was now an excessive commitment to cloth which was either not needed yet or (worse still) not needed at all. These commitments werre financed by substantial borrowings at high rates of interest.

The borrowings were particularly worrying because — in addition to continued expansion at home and abroad, in Paris, Amsterdam, Brussels and Strasbourg — the company had committed itself to a large unit in the West One shopping scheme under development in Oxford Street. They were expected to pay fitting-out costs of almost £2 million for the store, and an initial annual rental of £450 000.

Most fashion retailers were experiencing difficulty, and the 1979 downturn was producing a spate of stories about impending takeovers and closures. Tootal's Van Allen chain was said to be in difficulties, while British Land was rumoured to be considering disposal of the Dorothy Perkins chain. The Bus Stop group of shops, it was suggested by trade sources, was on the verge of bankruptcy. The rumours were an additional source of worry for the Wallis directors. It was clear that the company would get by only if pre-Christmas trading conditions were a marked improvement on the recent past.

Though the company was still one of the stock market's star performers over the past year, in recent months the shares had performed worse than any other in the clothing sector (Exhibit 8). While much of their energies were being allocated to extricating the company from its difficulties, the directors of Wallis nevertheless had to decide on the dividend announcement that was to accompany the annual report.

At least three options were available to the company. At one extreme, they could leave the year's total dividend unchanged. At another extreme, they could leave the rate paid on nominal share capital unchanged. Finally, they could follow the declared intention of having the interim represent a higher proportion than hitherto of increased total dividends. Proofs of the annual report had already been returned to the printers, and a speedy decision would have to be made.

Exhibit 8: *Stock market information on the clothing industry, 30 June 1979**

Company name	Capitalization £ million	Dividend yield per cent	Dividend cover	Return on capital per cent	Beta	Specific risk per cent	Quarterly abnormal return per cent	Annual abnormal return per cent
Nottingham Manufacturers	67	4.0	4.0	25	1.0	31	−6	−8
Baird, William	27	9.1	3.2	25	1.0	31	−10	−12
Lee Cooper Group	23	1.6	12.4	35	.8	54	18	165
Selincourt	14	9.5	2.4	19	.7	34	−5	−2
Dewhirst, I.J.	13	1.7	3.9	22	.8	39	45	101
Corah	11	8.1	2.7	21	1.1	34	4	−5
Pullman, R and J	10	8.5	1.5	22	.6	26	−14	10
Campari International	8	2.4	5.4	20	1.0	45	−1	−23
Simpson, S.	8	5.0	3.3	21	.7	38	10	14
Amber Day	7	7.5	2.1	29	1.0	33	−1	6
Cope Sportswear	7	.5	7.3	20	.7	70	6	42
Ellis and Goldstein	6	10.9	1.6	17	.7	31	6	6
Wallis Fashion Group	6	4.2	3.7	35	1.0	54	−24	161
Miller, F. Textile	6	4.6	3.3	31	1.0	28	6	19
Forminster	5	2.9	4.7	49	.8	38	−6	35
Wearwell	5	1.3	na	10	.9	50	8	2
Hawtin	5	2.3	6.8	25	.8	51	−9	19
Martin, Albert	5	7.5	2.2	17	1.0	26	−8	−31
Boardman, K.O. International	4	6.7	.6	7	.8	40	−15	62
Strong and Fisher	4	9.2	1.2	11	.7	36	2	29
Casket, S.	4	3.9	5.5	28	.8	38	−4	164
Pawson, W.L.	4	4.0	2.2	10	.8	77	−4	37
House of Lerose	4	9.1	3.0	19	.7	26	3	28
Tricoville	4	2.9	5.2	39	1.0	40	14	72
Ladies Pride	3	5.1	3.9	22	.8	46	−7	−2
Sunbeam Wolsey	3	13.1	3.3	14	na	na	−7	na
Reliance Knitwear	3	4.3	2.0	11	.8	65	−1	−4
Pittard Group	3	10.4	1.2	14	1.0	26	−4	−33
Dixon David	3	4.5	2.9	20	.5	46	6	173
Gelfer, A and J	3	11.4	1.9	31	.7	28	−15	23
Kayser Bondor	2	7.8	3.0	15	.4	37	6	22
Booth (International Holdings)	2	11.5	1.7	11	.5	33	0	9
Lincroft Kilgour	2	11.6	3.0	17	.9	29	−3	−22
Steinberg Group	2	8.0	2.8	11	1.0	71	−13	23
Dewhurst Dent	2	4.1	2.6	7	.6	38	−17	−23
Spencer, George	2	11.6	1.4	8	.7	47	−5	−29
Macanie (London)	2	12.7	.8	10	.9	42	12	22
Towles	2	4.0	7.6	na	.6	40	30	48
Bolton Textile	2	4.2	1.1	13	.7	53	−5	77
Beales, John	2	9.3	2.2	9	.7	34	−9	−35
Montfort Mills	2	9.3	2.7	16	.7	32	−3	−11

Exhibit 8 *(continued)*

Company name	Capitali-zation £ million	Dividend yield per cent	Dividend cover	Return on capital per cent	Beta	Specific risk per cent	Quarterly abnormal return per cent	Annual abnormal return per cent
Atkins Hosiery	2	10.5	2.6	18	.5	39	29	17
Tern-Consulate	2	7.6	2.3	18	1.1	66	0	13
Davenport Knitwear	1	7.1	4.4	29	.3	34	16	80
Firmin	1	5.2	3.6	31	na	na	na	10
Ingram, Harold	1	5.1	2.5	8	.7	45	−9	0
Lawtex	1	7.3	3.9	13	.6	47	11	5
Goodman and Stockman	1	8.8	3.0	26	.6	39	−9	13
Ramar Textiles	1	4.3	2.0	11	.7	64	−12	29
Lowe, Robert H.	1	4.0	3.4	23	.5	35	3	11
Albion	1	7.6	4.4	13	.7	62	19	128
Stirling Knitwear	1	3.3	6.6	na	1.1	52	31	22
Equally weighted mean	4	7.2	2.5	20	.8	48	5	28
Capitalization weighted mean	na	6.0	2.8	24	.8	39	−1	11

*23 companies capitalized at less than £1 million omitted.
Source: London Business School *Risk Measurement Service* and Datastream.

27. Burmah Oil

Our case really begins on 26 May 1908, in an inhospitable area of the Persian desert known as the Mosque of Solomon. For 6 years, a team had been drilling for oil in the surrounding countryside. The enterprise was the brainchild of a Cornish gold millionaire, William Knox d'Arcy. D'Arcy's own investment of £225 000 had been exhausted by 1905, and since then exploration had been financed by the Burmah Oil Company, a well-established firm enjoying large cash inflows from its Burmese fields. By 1908, nearly £1 million had been invested in exploration with no tangible results. Even d'Arcy's confidence was waning.

In early May, Reynolds, the head of the drilling team, was told by London that no more funds were available and he was instructed to cease drilling. Reynolds ignored the telegram. It might, he rationalized, have been miscoded. He would continue exploration for about 4 weeks, until the confirming letter arrived.

At 4.30 on the morning of 26 May, Reynolds was awakened by excited shouting. He arose to see a 50 ft (15 m) column of oil. So was born the Anglo-Persian Oil Company, later renamed British Petroleum (BP), and so came about Burmah Oil's large shareholding in that company.

The second important year in the history of Burmah Oil was 1942, when the company's Burmese installations were largely destroyed by Burmah employees before they could fall into the hands of the Japanese enemy. The Burmese oil fields were subsequently nationalized and the company's trading operations were confined to India and Pakistan. Burmah Oil was later involved in a famous dispute with the British government, which in 1965 was to pass the War Damage Act retrospectively preventing the company from seeking to claim damages from the Crown in respect of the Burmese installations.

This case was written by Richard Brealey, Elroy Dimson and Julie Fedorko as a basis for class discussion rather than to illustrate either effective or ineffective handling of an administrative situation. Some extracts from this case were previously published in the Instructor's Manual to accompany *Principles of Corporate Finance* by R. Brealey and S. Myers, copyright © 1984 by McGraw Hill Inc.

Planning for Burmah's Future

A third phase in Burmah's development opened at the beginning of the 1960s. The company's operations continued in India and Pakistan; but Burmah's assets consisted primarily of its substantial investment in BP, worth £126 million at the end of 1961, and its smaller investment in Shell Transport and Trading, worth £23 million. As a minority shareholder in both BP and Shell, Burmah did not consolidate the earnings of either company. It simply recorded in its profit and loss account the dividends received from its two huge investments. In addition, Burmah did not pay tax on the BP and Shell dividends as long as it passed them straight on to its own shareholders in the form of a Burmah Oil dividend. Exhibit 1 shows the relative importance in 1961 of Burmah's trading operations and its investments in BP and Shell.

Burmah Oil in 1962 was a company worried about its future. It had been built up on the basis of its oil and gas operations on the Indian subcontinent. But by 1962 it was already clear that the company faced progressively stringent limitations on its business there, and increasing pressure to transfer its operations to local ownership. The March 1962 seizure of power in Burma by the Socialist Revolutionary Government accentuated the urgency of this problem.

The company was at a crossroads. Political instability in its area of operations and the possibility of nationalization loomed large. The company gloomily contemplated the prospect that a third of its profits might be lost by the end of the decade. Something had to be done.

In the Burmah boardroom a variety of ideas were aired. One member proposed that trading operations be allowed to run down and that the company should effectively turn itself into a closed-end investment trust whose principal holdings would be BP and Shell. This would not involve any great blow to Burmah's prestige as it had been known primarily as an investment trust for some time. In addition, the company was able to reap few benefits from its operations in the East as a result of foreign exchange controls on remittance to the United Kingdom.

Few of the board were in sympathy with this suggestion. One member expressed dissatisfaction at the notion that Burmah should be in the oil business 'by proxy'. Besides, it was widely agreed that Burmah had considerable expertise in the oil business and that it was foolish to throw away this valuable asset.

Several members of the board felt that the stockmarket was seriously undervaluing Burmah's trading operations. They presented some calculations which showed that the bulk of the market value of Burmah was accounted by the investment in BP and Shell. They suggested that the problem was the sheer size of the BP/Shell holding which obscured the importance of Burmah's own activities. It was, as one put it, a 'deadweight'. The solution advanced by these

Exhibit 1: *Financial status of Burmah Oil in 1961*

(a) Balance sheet at 31 December 1961	£ million	(b) Profit and loss account for 1961	£ million
Issued £1 ordinary shares	82	Operating income	4
Reserves*	88	Income from trade investments, etc	4
Ordinary shareholders' funds	170	Dividends on BP and Shell shares	12
Preference share capital	4	Profit before tax	20
Loan capital	4	Tax	9
Total liabilities	178	Profit after tax	11
Fixed assets	4	Ordinary dividends	9
Investments*	156	Retained profits for the year	2
Net current assets	18		
Total assets	178		

(c) Recent trading profits and dividends	1961	1960	1959	1958	1957
			£ million		
Trading profit (including dividends from trade investments)	8	7	9	8	7
Dividends on BP and Shell shares	12	11	9	8	9

*Including adjustment for revaluing BP/Shell shares at market value

members was to distribute the shares in BP and Shell to Burmah stockholders. This would immediately increase the value placed by investors on the trading operation. If Burmah could cut itself free from BP and Shell, it would automatically solve its other worries. As the third largest independent oil company in the United Kingdom, with widespread expertise in exploration and pipeline technology, the company would be a very attractive acquisition for several foreign oil companies.

The idea of a merger was also not generally popular. An important lobby pressed for expansion of Burmah's trading operations. Burmah had begun as an oil company and should remain one. In recent years, the income from Shell and BP had far exceeded profits on trading. This was the time to redress the imbalance.

The expansionists suggested that Burmah should counterbalance its investments on the Indian subcontinent by developing new resources of oil and gas in the western hemisphere. A head-on collision with BP and Shell was unthinkable. Therefore Burmah's strategy should be to develop a major position in high margin, low volume, specialty oils. The expansionists argued that Burmah should not only diversify geographically, it should also reduce its risk by diversifying out of the oil business. In particular, there were exciting opportunities in the fast-growing petrochemicals business and in a number of businesses supplying the motorist. These areas were logical extensions of Burmah's traditional business.

But this raised the question of finance. The company had insufficient internally generated funds to underwrite any expansion, nor could it look to the dividends from BP and Shell, as it had undertaken to pass these on to shareholders. But the expansionists were strongly opposed to distributing the BP/Shell shares to stockholders. They believed that these shares gave Burmah the necessary financial muscle to expand out of its difficulties. They analysed the BP/Shell holdings as follows:

> Burmah's lack of debt, and the large uncommitted backing afforded by its BP and Shell holdings, means that it can raise very large amounts of money at 'blue chip' rates in support of its growth strategy. However, the benefit of raising debt finance is reduced because the interest cannot be relieved against taxable earnings. Moreover, just as Burmah is denied enjoyment of the cash flows from its own overseas operations by fiscal and monetary constraints, so too it is denied the full benefit of the cash flows generated by its stakes in the equities of BP and Shell, receiving only dividends which it has undertaken to pass on in full to its stockholders.
>
> So long as most of Burmah's assets are tied up in companies over whose cash flows and dividend policies it can exercise no control, its growth will be restricted and its operational earnings will continue to be swamped by the sheer size of the dividends received from BP and Shell, even if the expected decline in earnings from the traditional areas does not occur. Moreover, should those dividends be seriously reduced, Burmah would have no adequate cushion in its operations for the protection of stockholders.
>
> On the other hand, Burmah's holdings in BP and Shell are so large that they can be used to obtain for its stockholders greater benefits than would be available to them as direct holders of these stocks.

Thus the expansionists suggested that the BP/Shell holdings should be used as backing to raise the necessary finance for expansion. A sensible target debt ratio (defined as debt to capital employed) would in their view be around 30 per cent. With this capital structure, Burmah's stake in BP would thereby benefit shareholders more than if they individually owned the BP shares.

A decade of expansion

In 1962 Burmah acquired Lobitos Oilfields. The decision was not only important in itself, it was a further sign that the expansionists had won the day. Burmah would keep its large BP/Shell holdings and use them as backing for its geographical and product diversification.

The company's next major opportunity came in 1966 when it became known that Castrol was looking for a merger partner. Castrol was a leading British producer of specialty lubricants. Although Castrol was a well-managed firm with a well-known product line, it faced a similar problem to Burmah. It was in danger of being squeezed out of one of its principal markets. The oil majors were anxious to promote their own oils, and with the development of tied petrol stations, Burmah felt Castrol was in an exposed position. Castrol fitted well with Burmah's intention to develop a specialty oil business in the western hemisphere.

At about the same time, the company had been considering a plan to expand the Ellesmere Port refinery. This plan took a new turn with the acquisition of Castrol. Because Castrol was largely dependent on competitors for supplies of base stocks, the decision was taken to extend the project to supply a large part of Castrol's needs. A new proposal along these lines suggested three other worthwhile modifications to the scheme. First, the much larger tonnage of products from the lighter fractions could most profitably be used by converting them into petrol. Second, as the company was separately studying the possibility of entering the petrochemicals field, it seemed sensible to build in some extra flexibility to increase the output of light fractions at Ellesmere Port. Third, the scale of the proposed development made it economical to concentrate all UK refining at Ellesmere Port and to close down the small Barton refinery.

The revised plan was finally approved in January 1969 at a cost of £30 million, more than double the cost of the initial scheme. Moreover, poor costing and site troubles soon revealed that this figure was an underestimate of the likely outcome. The final cost was to be £41 million, with no more than £9 million of the increase attributable to specification changes. To make matters worse, after abortive discussions with Laporte Chemicals and the emergence of severe overcapacity in the petrochemicals industry, Burmah decided to postpone indefinitely any plans to produce petrochemicals.

Diversification away from oil

The Ellesmere Port development led to several other acquisitions. First, Burmah bought Petrocarbon Developments, an engineering company with capabilities in the design and construction of petroleum and petrochemical plant. Second, the prospect of a five-fold increase in fuel and lubricants from Ellesmere Port led Burmah to expand its marketing and distribution operations to handle the additional output. During 1968 and 1969 it acquired several garage chains and oil distributors to safeguard outlets. Third, in 1970 Burmah acquired Halfords, the motorists' accessory chain. The Halfords deal not only linked Burmah with a 'household name', but was considered of strategic importance by the company since it afforded 'security of outlet to Castrol because of the increasing tendency for lubricants to be sold through the supermarket and the high street shop'.

While Burmah was consolidating its position in the oil industry, moves were also being made towards product diversification. With Lobitos, Burmah had inherited Dussek Brothers, manufacturers of electrical insulating compounds, and Campbell Technical Waxes, producers of industrial wax compounds. The Castrol acquisition had brought with it Expandite, which manufactured products for the building industry. Since Burmah saw little prospect of further acquisitions in the UK oil sector of the calibre of Castrol, it decided on a policy of 'acquiring market leaders in the fields into which Castrol and Lobitos had themselves diversified'. In 1968 this policy led to the purchase of Rawlplug, manufacturers of building products and masonry fixtures, which complemented the activities of Expandite.

In 1968 these non-oil industrial operations were organized into two major groups. The Burmah Industrial Products group was formed from the old Lobitos' subsidiaries, Campbell and Dussek, from the former Castrol subsidiaries, Atlas and Expandite, and from Rawlplug. The other group, Burmah Engineering, was composed of Flexibox (which manufactured mechanical seals), Dynaflex (which produced garage lubrication equipment), and Petrocarbon Developments.

Exhibit 2: *Financial status of Burmah Oil in 1969*

(a) Balance sheet at 31 December 1969	£ million	(b) Profit and loss account for 1969	£ million
Issued £1 ordinary shares	131	Operating income	14
Reserves*	466	Income from trade investments, etc	7
Ordinary shareholders' funds	597	Dividends on BP and Shell shares	19
Preference share capital	19		40
Minority interests	18	*Less:* Interest charges	3
Loan capital	102	Profit before tax	38†
Deferred tax, pensions, etc	6	Tax	8
Total liabilities	742	Profit after tax	30
Fixed assets	99	Minorities and preference dividends	4
Investments*	571	Profit for ordinary shareholders	26
Net current assets	72	Ordinary dividends	22
Total assets	742	Retained profits for the year	5

(c) Recent trading profits and dividends

	1969	1968	1967	1966	1965	1964	1963	1962	1961
					£ million				
Trading profit (including dividends from trade investments)	22	22	18	17	12	13	11	12	8
Dividends on BP and Shell shares	19	19	17	16	16	15	13	13	12

*Including surplus on revaluing BP/Shell shares at market value
†All figures are rounded in this and subsequent exhibits; hence totals may not agree

In reviewing Burmah's progress at a board meeting in 1970, the Managing Director was able to point with considerable satisfaction to developments since 1962. The nationalization of much of Burmah's Eastern business had come to pass but, despite this, profits from trading operations had expanded from £8 million in 1961 to £22 million in 1969. The company's plans envisaged that trading profits would be larger than the BP/Shell dividends within another 2 years.

The pattern of this expansion had broadly followed the plans laid down in 1962. The company had established itself in the western hemisphere as an important producer and distributor of specialty oils. At the same time, it had diversified into oil-related products in rapidly growing industries.

The non-oil business was now well organized in four distinct divisions: Edwin Cooper (Chemical Additives), Burmah Industrial Products, Halfords, and Burmah Engineering. Yet Burmah argued that these developments had been undertaken without putting excessive strains on the company's balance sheet. Bank advances totalled only £24 million as composed to short term investments of £57 million. As Exhibit 2 shows, the debt ratio remained within the company's self-imposed target of 30 per cent.

Planning for the 1970s

The managing director envisaged several tasks for the next 5 years. First, he pointed to the satisfactory rates of return on some of the firm's recent acquisitions (Exhibit 3a) and he argued that the company should look for further opportunities to buy well-established businesses serving the motorist. Second, the company was aware that it would never be a major force in the oil industry without larger reserves of crude. The company therefore planned to increase its exploration activity, particularly in the North Sea and in the Cooper Basin and North-west shelf of Australia. Third, with no effective presence in the world's largest market for oil, the United States, Burmah would be on the lookout for acquisition opportunities.

Finally, Burmah had to do something about Ellesmere Port. It was clear that the scheme incorporated a serious flaw: profitability was tied closely to transportation costs of the crude landed there. The cost of shipping crude to Ellesmere was written into the original concept at World Scale 85. World Scale is a complex formula for quoting tanker rates in both the long-term chartering and single voyage ('spot') markets. Provided World Scale (WS) rates remained at or below WS 85, then the Ellesmere Port project was profitable. But as spot rates climbed to a new high during 1970 (Exhibit 4a), the Ellesmere Port project began to look like a financial liability before it was even completed.

Burmah had no tanker fleet of its own. In marked contrast, most oil companies owned or chartered-in on a long-term basis about a third of their tanker requirements. The balance was chartered from a wide range of shipping

Exhibit 3: *Financial details of Castrol, Rawlplug and Halfords in their acquisition year*

	Castrol group 1966	Rawlplug group 1968	Halfords 1969
(a) Profitability of acquired companies			
Average capital employed (£ million)*	37.1	26.0	13.3
Net profit (before interest, tax and extraordinary items) (£ million)	5.0	1.5	1.3
Rate of return on average capital employed (per cent)*	13.5	5.8	9.8
Comparative distributable profit (£ million)	3.0	1.3	1.2
Number of Burmah ordinary shares issued (£ million)	6.4	4.9	3.4
Earnings per Burmah ordinary share issued (pence)	46.9	26.5	35.5
Burmah dividend per share (pence)	15.0	16.5	16.3
Dividend — times covered	3.1	1.6	2.2
Burmah group earnings per share (pence)	18.7	20.9	19.7
(b) Premium paid by Burmah to acquire companies			
Acquisition price (£ million)	27.5	24.5	13.8
Premium relative to market price before the announcement (per cent)	30	46	26

*Capital employed figures include goodwill.
Source: Burmah Oil, Special Report to Stockholders, 1973

Exhibit 4: *Spot Tanker rates, Persian Gulf to North-west Europe: weighted average monthly figures 1968–74.*

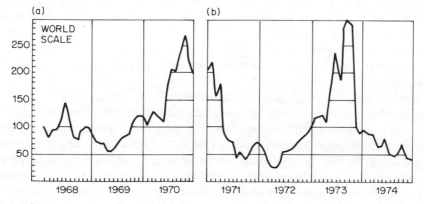

Source: *Investors Chronicle,* 24 January 1975

Exhibit 5: *Projections in 1972 of the US energy gap.*

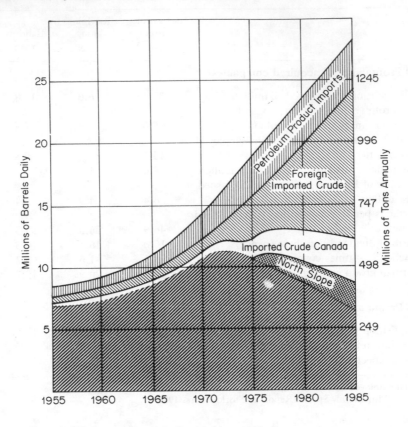

Source: Burmah Oil, Special Report to Stockholders, 1973

companies, quite a number of which owned only one vessel. Many of these ship owners, particularly the Greeks and Scandinavians, preferred to hire out their tankers on the short-term or spot market. The rate for single voyages was obviously much more volatile than for long charters, but historically, the average over time of the spot rates had not been too different from the average long rate.

Burmah had identified two important trends in the tanker industry. First, the low production costs of the Japanese shipyards and the improved operating efficiency of the large tankers was causing a progressive shift towards the larger vessels (very large crude carriers, or VLCCs). Tanker owners who were already capitalizing on this technological advantage were making handsome profits. Due to production leadtimes, however, there would continue to be a shortage of VLCC capacity for some time to come. Second, Burmah's projections suggested that there would be an increasing need for the United States (as well as Europe and Japan) to import petroleum products and crude (Exhibit 5). There would therefore be a chronic shortage of tankers for some years to come, with an estimated doubling in demand for tankers by 1980. Burmah felt that, with no fleet of its own, it was offering a hostage to fortune.

The board was, therefore, asked to consider a proposal that Burmah establish its own tanker fleet 'with the principal object of reducing, as far as possible, the effective cost of crude landed at the Ellesmere Port refinery'. In order to realize

Exhibit 6: *Burmah's principal acquisitions, 1966–74*

Year and acquisition	Nature of business	Country	Payment	Value
1966				
Castrol	Specialist lubricating oils	United Kingdom	Shares	£27.5 million
1968				
Rawlplug	Masonry fixtures	United Kingdom	Shares	£24.5 million
Curfew	Garage chain	United Kingdom	Cash	na*
Orion	Garage chain	Netherlands	Cash	na
Carey Oil	Fuel oil distributors	United Kingdom	Cash	na
Westoils	Fuel oil distributors	United Kingdom	Cash	na
Trading NV	Oil production/marketing	Belgium	Cash	na
AB Svenska	Oil marketing	Sweden	Cash	na
Petrocarbon Developments	Specialist plant construction	United Kingdom	Cash	na
1969				
Gem	Fuel distributors	United Kingdom	Cash	na
Whalen and Block	Oil blending	Sweden	Cash	na
Monsanto Additives	Oil additives	United States	Cash	na
Major	Petroleum products distribution	United Kingdom	Shares	£2.7 million
1970				
Halfords	Motorists' accessories retailer	United Kingdom	Shares	£13.8 million
1971				
Kleen-Fo	Car care products manufacture	Canada	Cash	na
Burg Services	Industrial chemical	United Kingdom	Cash	na
1972				
Tabbert	Caravan manufacturer	Germany	Cash	na
Quinton Hazell	Motor components supplier	United Kingdom	Shares	£56.0 million
1973				
Carruthers	Heavy cranes	United Kingdom	Cash	£2.1 million
Veedol	Lubricants manufacture/sale	Canada	Cash	£11.0 million
1974				
Signal Oil and Gas	Oil and gas producer	United States	Cash	$420.0 million

*Acquisition values not available for non-quoted acquirees

economies of scale on its tanker operations, Burmah would operate very large crude carriers (VLCCs) of over 250 000 tonnes. Inevitably, therefore, Burmah would have surplus carrying capacity. But directors regarded this as an advantage rather than a disadvantage; the long-term rates at which Burmah would charter-in tankers were well below spot rates, and therefore vessels could be chartered out again immediately at a profit on the spot market. In addition, therefore, to securing Burmah's transportation needs, the tanker operation was expected to be a good source of profit.

The discussion that followed was a wide-ranging one. Some members of the board were unhappy that Burmah might be perceived by investors as a conglomerate that always paid too much and got too little (see Exhibit 3b). The managing director strongly resisted such suggestions. Burmah's diversification strategy was carefully controlled. Acquisitions were concentrated in oil-related industries (Exhibit 6), and the company's new divisional structure ensured close control over its subsidiaries.

The debate on tankers centred on the merits of vertical integration. The benefits of the security of supplies were generally acknowledged, but there was some feeling that Burmah was being forced into tankers in order to recover some of the heavy costs of Ellesmere Port. However, other directors responded that the expenditure on Ellesmere Port was a sunk cost; the tanker investment must be viewed in the context of its impact on Burmah's entire portfolio of activities, and it was on this basis that it was worth pursuing.

There were also some questions about the financing needs for the tanker subsidiary. The Finance Director was able to give some assurances on this point. In accordance with general practice it was not Burmah's intention to own any vessels. They would be chartered on a long-term basis or leased (bareboat chartered). Thus there would be no net financing need, and the balance sheet would be unencumbered with any additional charge. The most that would be required is a minor note to the accounts, an example of which was subsequently distributed to members of the board (Exhibit 9). Furthermore, Burmah's strong asset backing would give it easy access to leasing finance. Since access to finance seemed to be the main requirement for entrance into the tanker industry, Burmah seemed particularly well placed.

Burmah Oil Tankers

Burmah's decision in 1970 to continue with its expansion and to operate its own fleet of tankers appeared to be well timed. Exhibit 6 shows how the company continued to diversify into oil-related businesses by buying a manufacturer of car components (Quinton Hazell), a German manufacturer of caravans (Tabbert), an industrial chemical cleaning business (Borg Services) and a heavy crane producer (Carruthers). (Exhibit 8 provides a record of the resulting share

Exhibit 7: *Financial status of Burmah Oil in 1973*

(a) Summary balance sheet as at 31 December 1973	£ million	(b) Profit and loss account for 1973	£ million
Issued £1 ordinary shares	144	Operating income	49
Reserves*	461	Income from trade investments, etc.	13
Ordinary shareholders' funds	605	Net dividends on BP and Shell shares	14
			76
Preference share capital	19		
Minority interests	42	*Less:* Interest charges	19
Loan capital	186	Profit before tax	57
Deferred tax, pensions, etc	53	Tax	10
Total liabilities	905	Profit after tax	47
Fixed assets	304	Minorities and preference dividends	2
Investments*	540		44
Net current assets	61	Ordinary dividends	17
Total assets	905	Retained profits for the year	27

(c) Recent trading profits and dividends

	1973	1972	1971	1970	1969
			£ million		
Trading profit (including dividends from trade investments)	62	35	30	25	22
Dividends on BP and Shell shares	20†	20	20	21	19

*Including surplus on revaluing BP/Shell shares at market value
†Including tax credit under the 1973 imputation tax system

issues.) And in addition, by the end of 1973, the company operated 30 vessels. Under the leadership of Elias Kulukundis, a former adviser to Aristotle Onassis, Burmah Oil Tankers had been successful at chartering-in at long-term rates which were below spot rates, and then using the vessels in the single voyage spot market. As a result, Burmah Oil Tankers contributed gross profits in 1973 of £18 million, almost one-third of the net operating profits of the whole group.

By 1973, Burmah had tripled the operating profits with which it had started the decade (see Exhibit 7). In that year's Special Report to Stockholders, the company compared its continuing plans for new investment up to the end of 1978 with the actual capital expenditure during the period 1969–71. It divided investment expenditure into 'on balance sheet' investment, expected to rise from £90 million to £313 million over the planning period (with 'no new acquisitions allowed for in these figures') and 'off balance sheet' expenditure.

Exhibit 8: *Burmah Oil share issues, 1962–80*

Year	Reason for share issue	Number issued (million)	Shares in issue (million)
1961	—	—	82.5
1962	Acquisition of Lobitos	11.6	94.1
1964	1 for 4 scrip issue	23.5	117.6
1966	Acquisition of Castrol	6.4*	123.9
1968	Acquisition of Rawlplug	4.9	128.8
1969	Acquisition of Major	.4	129.2
	Conversion of £5.9 million 7½ per cent Loan Stock 1981/86	1.8	131.0
1970	Acquisition of Halfords	3.4	134.4
1972	Acquisition of Quinton Hazell	9.3†	143.7
1972–74	Conversion of warrants	0.3	144.0
1974–80	—	—	144.0

*Plus £21.2 million partly convertible 7½ per loan stock 1981/86
†Plus £4.5 million 8½ per cent loan stock 1991/96

The latter was to consist of 'very considerable assets controlled by the company which will not be shown on the balance sheet. By far the greater part of these will be tankers which, though controlled by Burmah Oil Tankers, will be either leased or chartered.' Thus Burmah sought to continue expanding both the businesses it had acquired, and the refining and tanker businesses which it had developed internally.

During the previous year, Burmah had entered into an agreement with the Bahamas government to be the sole lessee of a transshipment terminal being built on the Grand Bahama Island. This terminal would take the largest crude carriers from the Middle East and transfer the oil to small tankers for shipment to US East Coast ports. (None of these ports were equipped to handle VLCCs.) Burmah intended to use its own vessels to service the Bahamas terminal and, therefore, increased its fleet in anticipation of the terminal becoming operational. Towards the end of 1973, Burmah signed a contract with Shell to transport oil to the United States through the terminal. The Shell contract committed 20 per cent of the terminal's capacity, but with tanker rates still rising, Burmah decided to wait before taking on any other customers.

Another important development for Burmah Oil Tankers was two contracts, to transport liquid natural gas (LNG). On the strength of these contracts Burmah arranged for eight LNG vessels to be built in the United States by General Dynamics. Burmah financed the construction of these ships by a $160 million construction loan to General Dynamics. On completion, they were to be owned by a consortium of US leasing companies and leased to Burmah on a leveraged lease (Exhibit 9).

Exhibit 9: *Burmah's financial commitments in respect of charter-in obligations*

Period in which payment is due	Oil tanker and LNG vessel commitments in £ million as at 31 December*			
	1971	1972	1973	1974
Payment during 1972	14	—	—	—
Payment during 1973	⎫	20	—	—
Payment during 1974		28	53	—
Payment during 1975		28	63	86
Payment during 1976		28	⎫	68
Payment during 1977		28		
Payment during 1978		28		
Payment during 1979	PV	28		
Payment during 1980	@ 0%	28		
Payment during 1981	= 204	28		
Payment during 1982		28		
Payment during 1983		⎫	PV	PV
Payment during 1984			@ 15%	@ 15%
Payment during 1985		PV	= 313	= 395
Payment during 1986		@ 0%		
Payment during 1987	⎭	= 215		
....	—	⎭		
....	—	—		
Payment during 2002	—	—		
Payment during 2003	—	—	⎭	
Payment during 2004	—	—	—	⎭
Payment during 2005	—	—	—	—

*Burmah Oil Tanker's charter-in commitments were not reported in Burmah's accounts prior to 1971. During 1971 and 1972, the (undiscounted) total commitments shown above were reported. From 1973 onwards, the first two annual payments were given explicitly, while later years' payments were reported as a present value ('PV') after discounting each year's cash flow at 15 per cent.

Oil exploration and development

Recognizing that it could not hope to be a major force in the oil industry without larger reserves of crude, Burmah stepped up its exploration of activities in the Gulf of Mexico, Canada, Australia and the North Sea.

Burmah's interest in the Gulf area of the United States dated back to 1959 when it participated in a partnership with Murphy Oil to explore tracts in Louisina and Texas. Later exploration was undertaken by Southdown Burmah, owned jointly by Burmah and the Southdown Oil Co., but when this company was disbanded some 3 years later in 1969, control passed to a new subsidiary, Burmah Oil Development. Between 1970 and 1973 alone the company reported the purchase of 30 leases in the Gulf area for a total cost of approximately $289 million. Numerous wells were drilled with a large measure of success.

In Canada, limited operations begun in 1959 were widened in 1963 with the acquisition of oil and gas properties from Colorado Oil and Gas. Burmah's involvement was further increased when it acquired a 67 per cent interest in the Great Plains Development Company, which brought large gas reserves and increased Burmah's potential for exploration. Through Great Plains, Burmah participated in exploration in western Canada, the Arctic Islands, and subsequently, Alaska.

In Australia, Burmah's involvement in its own right dated back to 1960, and the company's interests were also represented through a 54 per cent holding in Woodside-Burmah. Exploration in the early 1960s yielded gas but major success came only in the early 1970s with the discovery of large gas and condensate deposits in the North-west Shelf area.

Burmah's initial experience in the North Sea had not been encouraging. Though a Burmah-led consortium was the first to discover oil in the North Sea, in 1966, this was not in commercial quantities. The oil industry had little experience in drilling at depths of over 400 ft (120 m) and no experience of operating in seas where winds touch 130 mph (208 km/hour) and occasional 100 ft (30 m) waves roll by. After several years, Burmah only had two small gas fields. But in January 1974, there was a major discovery 100 miles (160 km) north-east of the Shetlands, on a block that gave Burmah a 20 per cent stake in the Ninian field. With over a billion barrels of estimated recoverable oil, Ninian was the third largest of the British North Sea oil fields. Thus, Burmah's crude reserves suddenly expanded; but at the same time, it was faced with the task of finding £240 million of development funds.

For some time, Burmah had been seeking to augment its oil production by acquisitions in the United States. It had discussions with Continental Oil Company of America in 1971, but the negotiations were terminated. Similar discussions with Ladd Petroleum broke down during 1973. In January 1974, however, the year appeared to get off to a promising start when Signal Oil, the US West Coast conglomerate, agreed to sell its oil interests to Burmah for $420 million in cash (at the start of 1974, £1.00 = $2.32), plus the write-off of $60 million of loans by Signal Oil to the parent company. Signal's domestic US production of some 45 000 barrels a day almost doubled Burmah's crude supplies. At the same time, Signal provided Burmah with a 19 per cent interest in the Thistle field, a medium-sized field in the British North Sea.

Burmah turned to the problem of raising $420 million. It approached the Chase Manhattan Bank and its international affiliate, the Orion Bank. They arranged a consortium to lend Burmah the entire $420 million, of which $150 million was in the form of eurodollars, with the remainder consisting of domestic dollars. The rate of interest on these loans was to vary according to general market conditions, but for 2 years, the rate on much of the domestic borrowing was to be kept below 8¾ per cent, which was also 2 percentage points lower than the rate prevailing in Britain.

When Burmah accepted the $420 million loan, it agreed that it would at all times ensure that its total debt would never exceed an agreed percentage of total capital. Restrictions such as this are commonly demanded by lenders, and Burmah's agreement did not cause alarm in the company. After Chase's dollar loan, the liabilities side of Burmah's balance sheet for the first time reached Burmah's target debt ratio of 30 per cent. In his year-end speech to stockholders (written in April 1974), the Chairman, Mr Lumsden, referred optimistically to recent developments, and said they 'should bring considerable benefit to the company in future years'.

A bad year for Burmah

Burmah appeared to enter 1974 in a fairly satisfactory state. Even before the discovery of oil in the Ninian field, and the acquisition of Signal Oil (both in January 1974), revenues, trading profits and earnings per share had been seen to increase rapidly since 1965 (Exhibit 10). Burmah had carried out its promise to finance the expansion largely out of debt, but long-term debt as a proportion of capital employed was still a fairly modest 25 per cent, below the company's target of 30 per cent. Even after the Chase loan, the debt ratio was only a little above the target, and the ratio could be expected to drop as profits were ploughed back into reserves. Since 1965, Burmah's shares had appreciated by 40 per cent, almost exactly in line with the British market. One optimistic brokerage report forecast a further sixfold growth in trading profits between 1972 and 1976, with the principal growth coming from the tanker business.

The year 1973 had not been a happy one for the world's stock markets. The *Financial Times* had described it as 'one of the worst Stock Exchange years in memory', with the FT Index down 32 per cent. But 1974 was to be much worse. The Arab oil embargo exacerbated both inflation and recession, and London stock prices experienced their sharpest decline since the great crash of 1929.

Exhibit 10: *Summary profit and loss accounts for Burmah Oil, 1965–73 (£ million)*

	1965	1966	1967	1968	1969	1970	1971	1972	1973
Revenue	na	120	126	167	182	236	273	349	496
Operating income	6	11	12	15	14	15	19	26	49
Investment income	22	22	23	27	28	30	29	26	24
Less: Interest paid	0	2	2	3	3	5	8	10	16
Profit before tax	28	32	34	39	40	40	40	42	57
Tax	4	7	7	9	10	10	9	9	10
Profit after tax	24	25	27	30	30	30	31	33	47
Earnings per ordinary share (pence)	18.5	19.8	20.2	20.9	19.7	20.6	20.9	21.4	30.7

*Net of interest received on short-term investments

Exhibit 11: *Indexed price movements of oil companies' shares, 1974–75*[*]

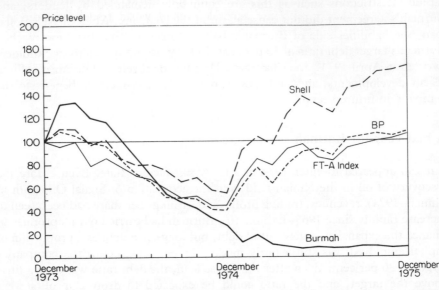

*Price and index levels are as at the month-end. Actual prices for 1973–75 were respectively; Burmah £3.70, £1.00 and £0.31; BP £5.37, £2.18 and £5.80; Shell £2.30, £1.27 and £3.78; and FT-Actuaries All Share Index 149.76, 66.89 and 158.08.

The oil stocks were not immune to the bear market. By the beginning of October, the prices of BP and Shell shares had fallen 49 and 55 per cent respectively from their levels at the end of 1973 (Exhibit 11). Thus, the huge borrowing power derived from Burmah's investment in BP and Shell suddenly disappeared. An important result of this fall in value was that Burmah had now exceeded the debt limits imposed in the Chase loan agreement.

Burmah had a choice. It could either ask its shareholders to put up more equity to support the debt, or it could offer Chase an inducement to relax the borrowing limits. Since the company's stock price had fallen by 52 per cent that year, Burmah was reluctant to issue more shares in October 1974. In exchange for a higher rate of interest, therefore, Chase agreed to value the BP shares at prices higher than actual market value, thereby satisfying the original loan covenant. At the same time, a new requirement was introduced which required interest charges to be covered at least one-and-a-half times by profits.

The renegotiation therefore shifted the focus from the value of the BP shares to the level of Burmah's profitability. Since £16 million, or 30 per cent of Burmah's previous year's trading profits, had been generated by the tanker subsidiary, the progress of that business was obviously crucial. But Burmah felt safe, since projections made in May 1974 indicated that total profits from tankers in 1974 would be similar to 1973, and a figure of £18 million was forecast.

Burmah Oil Tankers' success in 1973 had stemmed largely from its policy of hiring out a large proportion of its fleet on the spot market. In 1973 spot tanker rates had risen sharply with the general level of world trade and bouyant American demand for Middle East crude. Unfortunately, this position was dramatically reversed by the Arab oil embargo at the end of the year. Within the space of 9 months, tanker rates had declined by three-quarters (see Exhibit 4b on p. 379).

With the Bahamas terminal due on stream shortly, the company decided not only to keep three of its newly chartered VLCCs in the spot market in 1974, but also to sign long-term charters for three further VLCCs. Burmah intended to place these ships in the spot market also. However, not only was the Bahamas terminal behind schedule, but American demand for foreign crude was falling in response to a five-fold increase in crude oil prices. Burmah had accepted only one customer for the Bahamas terminal and the contracted shipment of 2 million tonnes of crude oil per year accounted for a bare 20 per cent of the terminal's capacity. By the end of 1974, there were 42 vessels in the Burmah fleet, of which three were laid up and idle and half the remainder were competing in the spot market, where charter rates had fallen drastically. Four months later, half the Burmah fleet was laid up.

The first public hint of difficulties was in December 1974, when *Business Week* drew attention to the renegotiation of the Chase loan and asserted that Burmah had run into a 'serious cash squeeze'. Burmah was now 'leveraged to the tune of 55 per cent of net assets. . . (and) the company might have to borrow as much as $116 million more to keep things rolling'. Burmah was quick to deny the charge. Its cash position, it announced, was 'certainly no worse than anyone else's. We are well aware of our future cash needs and facilities are available to meet them.'

The statement was not sufficient to stem the series of rumous that now began to flood the London Stock Exchange. Finally, on a dark and cheerless Christmas Eve, with most of the City having departed to celebrate the season of goodwill, the Chairman of Burmah revealed to the Bank of England that the tanker operations were now likely to show a substantial loss. In consequence, the group was forecasting only a small total profit for the year, and the company expected to be in default on its recently renegotiated Chase loan. Furthermore, the prolonged decline in the value of Burmah's BP holdings had also put Burmah in default on an earlier issue of long-term bonds.

Ambition's debt is paid

One week after the company's first approach to the Bank of England, Burmah Oil issued the following statement:

Following discussions with HM Government and the Bank of England, the following arrangements have been agreed between the company and the Bank of England to provide interim support to the company pending realization of certain major assets in continuation of a programme already in hand.

1. It is proposed that certain existing long-term dollar borrowings amounting to $650 million will be renegotiated as 12 month borrowings guaranteed by the Bank of England.
2. In addition, the Bank of England has offered certain assistance to enable the company to deal with its sterling borrowings.
3. Certain changes will be made in the management of the company.
4. Messrs Peat, Marwick, Mitchell and Co will be appointed to assist in the financial management of the group.
5. A full review of the tanker operations will be undertaken in the light of the independent investigation already commissioned by the company early in December.

As security for the assistance provided, the Company's unpledged holdings of shares of the British Petroleum Company Limited and the Shell Transport and Trading Company Limited will be made over to the Bank of England with the right of realization.

Thus the Bank of England provided loan guarantees and other assistance to tide Burmah over its difficult period. In return, Burmah also accepted the Labour government's principle of 51 per cent public participation in the Ninian and Thistle fields of the North Sea. While the Bank had the right of realization of the BP stock, a statement by Burmah the next day made it clear that the holding 'has not been taken over by the Government or the Bank of England'.

This prompt action by the Bank in guaranteeing Burmah's dollar obligations was sufficient to solve the company's most pressing problem. Unfortunately, as further discussions took place between Burmah, the Bank and government departments, it became increasingly obvious that the problem was much more than a technical default.

First, Burmah was under pressure from other lenders who were not covered by the Bank of England's guarantees. Some of these lenders pointed to fine print in the loan agreements which stated that Burmah would not discriminate against them by providing exclusive security to other lenders. If Burmah's BP and Shell holdings were to be used to provide security, these lenders wanted to be included.

Second, it became apparent that the tanker operation had lost roughly £30 million in 1974, with no immediate prospect of any improvement. Burmah was likely to show a loss, rather than the small profit expected only weeks earlier. Furthermore, the potential cash drain from tanker operations might continue for the foreseeable future. A confidential Chase Manhattan Bank calculation indicated that 'under pessimistic assumptions', Burmah could lose as much as $760 million from its tanker business by 1982 (Exhibit 12). The company had to find the time to reorganize its tanker liabilities.

Third, and most important, Burmah had urgent needs for fresh capital. It certainly could not issue more debt. With trading in its ordinary shares temporarily suspended, and with unofficial trades occurring at about one-tenth of the price a year earlier, a sale of equity was regarded as impossible. Without additional funds, the company would be obliged to cease operations and would immediately become liable for all future payments on its tanker charters. The Bank of England's initial help was not enough to save Burmah.

The Chairman of Burmah, Hamish Lumsden, felt bound by repeated assurances to Burmah stockholders that the BP stake would not be sold without the formal consent of shareholders at a general meeting. But it became clear to the Bank that it would have to insist on acquiring the BP shares outright. At that stage, Burmah and its advisers hoped that any sale of the BP holding would be at the then market value, and that Burmah would share in any profits on resale. Sir Jaspar Hollom, Deputy Governor of the Bank, told Burmah that 'a profit-sharing arrangement would be reasonable'.

On 22 January 1975, the bombshell burst. The Governor of the Bank, Gordon Richardson, and the Deputy Governor met Burmah and disclosed that the government had decided that the price for the BP shares would be £2.30 each. Moreover, the government was not prepared to accept any profit-sharing formula. The Governor and Deputy Governor continued to think profit-sharing was reasonable, and had done what they could to represent this view to the government. But the Paymaster General, Edmund Dell, who was handling matters for the government, made it clear that anything other than an outright sale of the BP stock would be unacceptable: 'If Burmah does not like the deal,' Mr Dell is alleged to have said, 'it can go elsewhere.' Faced with liquidation as the only alternative, Burmah had to accept the rescue package it was being offered.

Three weeks after the agreement with the Bank of England, therefore, Burmah announced a new support arrangement with the Bank — and a new chairman. Whereas the company had previously only pledged its BP holding as security, it now agreed to sell 78 million shares of BP to the Bank at a price of £2.30 per share. The Bank continued to guarantee Burmah's $650 million of American loans, and in addition, agreed to provide a standby facility of £75 million to aid the company in its short-term borrowings. As security for this assistance, the Bank was given a mortgage on Burmah's American assets. It also stipulated that the proceeds from the prospective sale of the Great Plains subsidiary should go towards repayment of the loans, and that the company should attempt to sell its American assets in order to repay the balance.

The new support agreement provided Burmah with two benefits. First, the sale of BP shares gave it the badly needed cash to continue operations. Second, the guarantees and the additional standby agreement gave Burmah the time that it needed to sell assets in order to repay some of the great load of debt. However, the link between Burmah and BP, which began in 1908 with the first discovery of oil in the Middle East, effectively ended in January 1975. For the Bank of England, the purchase of BP shares proved to be extremely profitable. Within a few months, the price of BP had doubled, and the Bank was soon to show a profit of more than 100 per cent.

Exhibit 12: *Chase Manhattan Bank's estimate of Burmah oil tanker commitments at end 1974*

Burmah interest	Type of charter	Number of ships	Deadweight tonnage (mm)	Cash flow item	Projected cash flow in $ millions								
					1975	1976	1977	1978	1979	1980	1981	1982	Total
Only a charter interest	Without employment	18	2.4	Charter-in obligations	85	70	72	68	65	70	28	18	476
				Lay-up savings	21	18	19	19	17	26	18	8	146
				Net cash flow*	**(64)**	**(52)**	**(54)**	**(53)**	**(50)**	**(44)**	**(9)**	**(10)**	**(336)**
	With employment	5	.8	Charter-in obligations	21	17	17	17	17	17	18	18	142
				Lay-up savings	30	27	27	27	27	28	28	28	222
				Net cash flow*	**10**	**10**	**11**	**11**	**11**	**11**	**11**	**11**	**86**
Owned: On time charter with hire purchase	Without employment	1	.1	Charter-in obligations	—	—	1	3	3	3	3	3	16
				Lay-up savings	—	—	1	2	2	2	2	2	11
				Net cash flow	—	—	**(1)**	**(1)**	**(1)**	**(1)**	**(1)**	**(1)**	**(6)**
	With employment	2	.3	Charter-in obligations	11	12	12	13	12	13	13	14	100
				Charter out	10	10	10	10	10	10	10	10	80
				Net cash flow	**(1)**	**(2)**	**(2)**	**(3)**	**(2)**	**(3)**	**(3)**	**(4)**	**(20)**
Owned: Bareboat charter with hire purchase	Without employment	10	.6	Charter-in obligations	13	13	12	13	14	12	9	9	95
				Lay-up cost	1	1	1	1	1	1	1	1	8
				Net cash flow	**(14)**	**(14)**	**(13)**	**(14)**	**(15)**	**(13)**	**(10)**	**(10)**	**(103)**
	With employment	9	.8	Charter-in obligations	43	27	24	21	22	23	23	24	207

Description	Ships	Value ($bn)									Total
Quasi-owned	4	1.8									
Charter-out			34	30	21	19	19	20	20	21	184
Net cash flow*			**(11)**	**1**	**(5)**	**(5)**	**(5)**	**(4)**	**(5)**	**(5)**	**(39)**
Without employment	2	.2									
Charter-in obligations			na	na	3	35	71	77	77	77	340
Charter-out			—	—	2	6	12	13	13	13	59
Net cash flow			**—**	**—**	**(1)**	**(29)**	**(59)**	**(64)**	**(64)**	**(64)**	**(281)**
Held within firms owned 50 per cent by Burmah Oil Tankers	2	.3									
Charter-in obligations			13	13	14	14	14	15	15	2	100
Charter-out			8	8	8	8	8	8	8	1	57
Net cash flow			**(5)**	**(6)**	**(6)**	**(6)**	**(7)**	**(7)**	**(7)**	**(1)**	**(44)**
Settlement of terminated charter	1	.3									
Net cash flow			**(6)**	**(1)**	**(1)**	**(1)**	**(1)**	**—**	**—**	**—**	**(10)**
Total commitments	52	7.3									
Charter-in obligations			186	152	155	183	218	228	185	164	1471
Net cash flow*			**(92)**	**(62)**	**(74)**	**(101)**	**(128)**	**(125)**	**(84)**	**(84)**	**(750)**

*These column totals are correct, although they may not always tally perfectly with prior rows due to rounding errors, and Burmah's 50 per cent interest in Burmast.

Source: Chase Manhattan Bank

The Shareholders' Action Group

Many shareholders were dissatisfied with the terms of the rescue operation. A group of them formed an action group to protest that the purchase price had been unfair. At the 1975 Annual General Meeting, the treasurer of the association declared:

> In all their communications, the various government departments have maintained that the price was a fair one for the shareholders. There are over 160 000 of them and I have neither met nor heard of a single one who agrees. ('Hear, hear'.) Is there anybody in this room who agrees? (Cries of 'No'.)
>
> The method employed for the valuation of BP stock indicates to me as one who is used to financial negotiations that those members of the government who seek to support the method employed in the valuation do not know a stock transfer from a poached egg! ('Hear, hear.')
>
> The average market price over one normal month was utterly irrelevant as a measure of the true value of the BP shares.

By the end of 1975, there were still 142 000 individual shareholders in Burmah who owned 66 million of the company's 144 million shares: their average holding of 464 shares was worth under £150. The Labour government supported the Bank's rescue; but Conservative Members of Parliament, then in Opposition, expressed considerable sympathy with the plight of small investors in Burmah. The Burmah Shareholders Action Group became convinced that, in the event of a Conservative victory in the next General Election, their claims would be dealt with sympathetically.

Meanwhile, the Action Group's relationship with the company's board of directors was strained. Burmah's new Chairman, Alastair Down, was recruited from British Petroleum in early 1975 and was not previously associated with Burmah. Yet in his address to stockholders in May 1976, he contrasted his contracts with the more anodyne Committee of Institutional Shareholders ('an established body whose views I have found it helpful to receive') with the Action Group:

> The Burmah Shareholders Action Group is an unofficial body representing a minority . . . of stockholders. I have thought it right to discuss with the officers of the Action Group such matters as they have wished to raise with me from time to time. We do not always see eye to eye, but I realize that we have similar objectives, although we may sometimes differ as to the best method of achieving them.

Burmah decided, however, to take legal action against the Bank of England. The company sought to overturn the Bank's acquisition of the BP shares, which had become public knowledge on 23 January 1975. It wanted the BP securities to be returned to Burmah in exchange for reimbursement of the original purchase price, less subsequent BP dividends. Burmah argued that the transfer of BP stock to the Bank was, in legal terminology, 'unconscionable, inequitable and unreasonable', and that the Bank had obtained improper advantage through its role as banker and mortgagee.

The hint of disagreement between the Bank of England and the government also suggested to Burmah that the Bank might have been overruled by the Treasury. The Treasury would have been involved at the time in proposals for introducing a Petroleum Revenue Tax (PRT) which, together with new North Sea participation arrangements, greatly improved the outlook for oil shares. The Bank thereby took advantage of Burmah 'in breach of its duty of fair dealing'. In February, the PRT proposals were in fact published; and by the month-end, less than 6 weeks after the transfer of the BP holding, the Bank was showing a profit of 80 per cent on its 'rescue'.

Exhibit 13: *Lobbying by the Burmah Shareholders Action Group*

Burmah: a Conservative disgrace

In Opposition

"...it is very much the concern of the House and of the Opposition to see that public bodies behave honourably and fairly."

"There is a deep sense of outrage that although the Bank is ready to recognize the harsh effect of what has happened the Government should forbid it to do anything about the situation."

"...the episode will have done lasting damage to the credibility and independence of the Bank of England as a lender of last resort."
The Rt Hon Patrick Jenkin MP for Wanstead and Woodford (now Secretary of State for Social Services), Hansard, 25 February 1975, at col. 313.

"...highway robbery under duress...the Government has now become the biggest asset stripper of the lot."
The Rt Hon Patrick Jenkin MP, Hansard, 3 December 1975, at col. 1687.

"Sadly, all...attempts to secure justice for the Burmah shareholders have proved entirely in vain...but if a Government is determined to remain deaf to appeals on behalf of disadvantaged citizens, there is not very much that an Opposition can do except to sustain protest, as we have been doing."
The Rt Hon Sir Geoffrey Howe QC MP for Surrey East (now Chancellor of the Exchequer) - letter of 7 August 1975 to Mr Ralph Howell MP for North Norfolk.

"I and my colleagues will certainly do what we can...we shall certainly keep at the matter on behalf of those affected."
The Rt Hon David Howell MP for Guildford (now Secretary of State for Energy) - letter of 5 August 1975 to constituent Mr V G Clarke.

"...we have challenged the Government on their intentions and good faith vis-a-vis the BP shares...I can assure you that the Conservative Party will continue to press the Government over this disgraceful issue."
Mr Keith Speed RD MP for Ashford (now Parliamentary Under Secretary of State for Defence) - letter of 31 October 1975 to constituent Mr F G Barnes.

"...if a Government is intransigent and deaf to appeals on behalf of disadvantaged groups, there is not very much that an Opposition can do except protest."
The Rt Hon Patrick Jenkin MP - letter of 25 July 1975 to the Rt Hon Edward Heath MBE MP for Bexley, Sidcup.

"I quite agree with you that the Government is treating Burmah Oil Shareholders in a particularly shabby way."
Mr Kenneth Baker MP for St Marylebone - letter of 8 August 1975 to constituent Mr I J Fields.

"You may assure your constituent that I and my team will continue to keep the whole disgraceful issue closely in view."
Mr Patrick McNair-Wilson MP for New Forest (Opposition Front Bench Spokesman on Energy 1974/76) - letter of 12 November 1975 to the Rt Hon Sir Ian Gilmour, Bart. MP for Chesham and Amersham (now Lord Privy Seal)

"...if a Government is determined to remain deaf to appeals on behalf of disadvantaged citizens, there is not very much that an Opposition can do except to sustain their protest as we have been doing."
The Rt Hon Michael Heseltine MP for Henley (now Secretary of State for the Environment) - letter of 19 January 1976 to constituent Mr Stanley Davis.

"The Conservative Party as a whole is doing what it can to help in this very worrying matter. Thank you for taking the trouble to write."
The Rt Hon Maurice Macmillan MP for Farnham - letter of 4 May 1976 to constituent Mr B Lasseter.

In Government

"...The Government would not consider it proper to intervene between the Parties...the Crown is not and never has been in any capacity a party to the main action."
The Rt Hon Sir Geoffrey Howe QC MP - letter of 8 May 1980 to Sir Raymond Gower MP for Barry Division of Glamorganshire.

"...it would be quite wrong for me to comment...."
The Rt Hon David Howell MP - letter of 17 August 1979 to BSAG.

"But a lot of people also work hard to try to keep the party of their choice in power, which is the best form of insurance against the injustices of socialism."
Mr Cranley Onslow MP for Woking - letter of 19 July 1980 to constituent Mr J P C Hartley.

"Frankly I regret that promises were made in opposition."
Mr Matthew Parris MP for West Derbyshire - letter of 8 July 1980 to constituent Mr Robert Gray.

"I am afraid that there are no comments I can make on this matter, at least at the moment, but I shall of course bear it closely in mind."
Mr Nicholas Scott MBE MP for Kensington and Chelsea - letter of 16 May 1980 to constituent Mrs C V Lawson.

"I am sure you will appreciate that it is now extremely difficult...for the Government to intervene...."
Mr Keith Speed RD MP - letter of 18 July 1980 to constituent Mrs A B Pimbton.

"I do not think that it would be right for me to comment further...."
The Rt Hon Patrick Jenkin MP - letter of 27 June 1980 to constituent Mr G A Luton.

"...I would however have thought it an essential part of doing what is just, to bear in mind...that the tax payer who voted for the 1974 Government has a right to consideration as well."
Mr Nicholas Baker MP for North Dorset - letter of 2 July 1980 to BSAG.

"...there is collective responsibility. This means that, whatever my views were before, I cannot express different views from those of the Treasury."
Sir Ian Gilmour, Bart. MP - letter of 16 June 1980 to constituent Mr A R Wylie

"...there is, I fear, little that I can do to help."
The Rt Hon Maurice Macmillan MP - letter of 31 July 1980 to BSAG.

Facing Facts and Talking Straight

At the 50th Annual Women's Conservative Conference held recently at the Royal Festival Hall, the Prime Minister said:-
"In the Conservative Party we are proud of our reputation for straight talk and for facing facts."

In the House of Commons on 17 June 1980 the Chancellor of the Exchequer said:-
"the Government does not consider it proper to intervene in the litigation between Burmah and the Bank of England."

However, in this case intervention would not be improper since:-
(i) **as a matter of Law**, under the Bank of England Act, 1946, the Treasury (which owns the whole of the stock of the Bank) has clear rights to intervene; and
(ii) **as a matter of fact**, the Treasury does intervene in the affairs of the Bank of England. Indeed litigation would never have been necessary if the Treasury had not forbidden the Bank to carry out the "rescue" of Burmah in its own way, viz, with a profit-sharing arrangement with Burmah on the eventual disposal of the BP Stock.

This Conservative Government should either live up to its principles and right this glaring injustice without further delay or stop claiming a "reputation for straight talk and for facing facts".

Burmah

The Burmah Shareholders Action Group 71 Burlington Arcade Piccadilly London W1V 9AF

Source: *The Times,* 7 October 1980

Burmah also felt that the price it received for its BP holding underestimated the value of the shares. On the day the second rescue package was announced, BP shares were traded at £2.68. Moreover, many investment professionals believed that a strategic stake in a quoted company could be sold at a premium above the ruling market price. In fact in mid-January 1975, both Gulf Oil and the Shah of Iran were potential buyers of the BP shares at a price higher than that paid by the Bank; but negotiations could not be concluded sufficiently fast, and on 21 January, the talks had been terminated.

A final, if rather bizarre, aspect of the affair relates to a statement by the Deputy Governor of the Bank of England at the 22 January 1975 rescue negotiations. He went on record as saying that the price of £2.30 per share was fair in the light of the share price 'high' of £2.56 for 1974 shown in the *Financial Times* editions of January 21 and 22. This price was incorrect because of a printing error, and the true high for that year was in fact £5.90

In May 1979, Margaret Thatcher led the Conservative Party to an overwhelming victory in the General Election. Her husband, Dennis, was with Burmah (though not on the main board) at the time of the financial crisis, and had been a director of Burmah Oil Trading. Her colleagues included several Cabinet Members who had gone on record with comments favourable to Burmah shareholders. But in government, the Action Group's supporters seemed to have changed their tune.

The Action Group resumed its campaign, asking Prime Minister Thatcher to 'overcome any personal embarrassment and instruct her Cabinet to settle the Burmah affair with honour and without delay'. They wrote to all 150 000 shareholders, lobbied politicians, published newspaper adverts (Exhibit 13) and used various other channels of communication. The group even sent a recorded speech to every Member of Parliament, urging the government to return the Bank of England's one-fifth holding in BP to Burmah.

Two years after the Conservatives took office, Burmah's High Court action against the Bank of England commenced. The *Financial Times* noted that, unless there was an out-of-court settlement, the case might drag on for several years. Indeed, the initial hearing was expected to last for up to 2 months. Both sides were evidently willing to take the action through the Appeals Court, and if necessary, to fight the case all the way through to the House of Lords.

In mid-1981, Burmah's 144 million shares were trading at around £1.40 each. The company was claiming the return of 310 million BP shares (after a 4-for-1 stock split), currently worth £1200 million plus accrued income, less the original purchase price of £179 million. On the first day of the hearing (2 June 1981), the London *Standard* reported a remark to Burmah's Counsel by the judge Mr Justice Walton: 'You are trying to push back the frontiers of the law in this case.'

CASE STUDIES

Case Questions

Students and case teachers differ in their views on whether case studies should be accompanied by suggested questions. Purists argue that case studies should simply be descriptions of situations which companies and their managements find themselves in. To pose specific questions is artificial, in the sense that real-life problems do not come complete with a list of questions. Purists maintain that, frequently, the most important question is to 'Decide what the problem is'. To ask more is to impose too much structure, and to lead the student too much.

Purists should read no further, for they have reached the end of the book. Others should read on, since this section contains a suggested list of questions for each of the case studies. You may find these questions interesting and useful.

PART A: INVESTMENT APPRAISAL

1. United Metal

(a) Critically evaluate the arguments used by the purchasing and production managers. Which (if either) is correct?
(b) What are the important issues in this situation, and which factors should (and should not) be included in the financial analysis?
(c) What should United Metal do? Back up your recommendation with a financial appraisal.
(d) What are the risks of following your recommended action? What alternatives might United Metal consider?

2. Lee Valley Water Company

(a) Develop a set of guidelines which Lee Valley Water Company's customers could use to appraise the financial attractiveness of installing a water meter.
(b) How many households would benefit from switching to domestic metering?

(c) What proportion of households might have taken this option in, say, 20 years' time? What impact would this have on the company's revenues?

(d) What other policy options could the water industry pursue? For example, should it consider compulsory changes in the methods used for charging for water usage?

3. Dane Carter International

(a) Comment critically on the way Dane Carter International have evaluated the Egyptian pharmaceutical containers project.

(b) What is the net present value of this project?

(c) What assumptions have you made regarding utilization rates in order to evaluate this proposal?

(d) Comment on Dane Carter's method of charging for existing machine capacity. Should the company base its investment decisions on average or on marginal costs of capacity?

(e) How might Jonathan Long improve Dane Carter's project appraisal and post-audit systems?

4. Guinness Hop Farms

(a) What methodology would you use to decide whether and when to replant a particular hop garden?

(b) Illustrate your methodology by analysing when the 'Plough' garden should be replanted. (If it helps, start off by assuming that hop prices stay constant in real terms.) What assumptions have you made, and to what factors is your analysis most sensitive? How do/would the assumed changes in real prices affect your analysis?

(c) From your analysis of the 'Plough' garden, what can you say (qualitatively) about the case for replanting the other gardens?

(d) How might this decision be influenced by short-term profit and loss and funding considerations? Should it be? If you were Bob Porter, would you let this influence you?

5. Bloomsbury Health Authority

(a) What were the options facing Bloomsbury Health Authority? And what, in broad brush terms, were the anticipated consequences of each?

(b) What were the relevant capital costs and revenue savings from the major options? What are your best estimates of the cash flows involved? (Where you are forced to make guesstimates, specify clearly what additional information you require, and how in practice you would obtain it.) What are the key underlying assumptions?

(c) What level of confidence would you place on each of the cash flow estimates you have given above, and why? How meaningful is the sensitivity analysis presented in Exhibit 7, and what improvements would you suggest?

(d) In a public sector health care setting of this kind, how should future revenue savings be traded off against current capital costs? For example, is it appropriate to base the discount rate on the current real interest rate? Should it include a risk premium to compensate for the uncertainties inherent in the project? Is it anyway appropriate to use the NPV rule to compare the different options?

(e) What are the implications of each of the options for 'service levels' from the perspective of (i) local mothers, (ii) mothers from outside the area, (iii) the obstetricians, (iv) the nurses, (v) Bloomsbury Health Authority, and (vi) the North-east Thames Regional Health Authority?

(f) What implicit valuations appear to be placed on standards of care? Medical training? Consumer choice? How important are these factors, and how might they be valued?

(g) What criteria were important to/used by the different parties to the decision, and why? Were these in conflict, and if so, how were they, and how should they have been, reconciled?

(h) What do *you* feel should be the correct decision? How would you present and sell this to the various interested parties and to the Region?

PART B: COST OF CAPITAL AND PERFORMANCE MEASUREMENT

6. Norcros

(a) What rate of return do Norcros' shareholders require?

(b) Should Norcros' debt ratio be reflected in the hurdle rates they apply to new investments?

(c) Should Norcros use the same hurdle rate for all of its capital projects? How could they determine specific rates of return for major capital projects in each division, and what should these rates be?

(d) How would these required rates of return tie in with Norcros' existing method of charging for the use of assets in measuring the performance of its divisions? Were the two systems (capital budgeting and divisional performance measurement) consistent?

(e) Should the existing system of charging for the use of assets be modified to accommodate different target rates in each division, and how could this be achieved? If divisions failed to meet the target rates set for them, would this necessarily be indicative of poor performance?

(f) What alternative methods are used by other companies to evaluate divisional performance? Which approach do you favour, and why?

(g) What do you think Norcros' senior management mean when they say they 'recognize' the danger of applying purely financial criteria and taking a short term view in judging new projects? Are financial criteria short-term oriented?

7. Chandler Group

(a) Gareth Deacon considers that the Aluminium Division is unfairly treated, because most of its plant has already been depreciated. Does he have a case?
(b) Is it appropriate to omit inventory holding gains from inflation-adjusted profits, even if the gains exceed the cost of holding the inventory?
(c) Is increased use of debt finance desirable, so as to maximize Chandler's inflation-adjusted profits?
(d) Overall, will CCA measures of earnings (as calculated by Chandler) 'provide a measure of earnings that corresponds more closely . . . with the economic reality of the business? What reservations do you have?
(e) How useful do you think CCA accounting numbers are likely to prove in (i) comparing the profitability of different divisions, and (ii) allocating capital funds between different divisions. What alternative or supplementary measures/systems would you recommend for these two purposes?
(f) Prepare a critique of Christine Dennison's financial planning model (as described in Exhibits 4–7). How useful will it be for 'indicating what rate of growth is sustainable and the policy measures consistent with it'?
(g) What should Christine Dennison do now?

8. British Airports Authority

(a) Is the required rate of return ('cost of capital') for public enterprises the same (in principle) as for private?
(b) What is (should be) the relationship between cost of capital, financial targets, and the Secretary of State's efficiency targets?
(c) What is the cost of capital for BAA?
(d) What is the relationship between accounting returns and cost of capital?
(e) Should BAA's traffic charges be based on long-run marginal costs, and how would you know if they were not?
(f) If BAA needs retained profits to finance expansion, does this justify higher prices?
(g) Can Heathrow be looked at in isolation from the rest of the South-east system, and can traffic revenues and costs be separated from commercial revenues and costs?
(h) Prepare the 'case for the prosecution'. In other words, as the airlines, what repayment do you feel you are entitled to, and why?

(i) Prepare the 'case for the defence'. Thus, as BAA, explain why your prices are justifiable and reasonable, and why no repayment should be made.

(j) What is your own view about the question (and magnitude) of repayments by BAA to the airlines? Justify your position.

Note: This case may be conducted as a debate, or role-playing court case, with some participants placed in the role of the prosecution (the airlines), and others in the role of the defendant (BAA).

PART C: COMPANY VALUATION

9. Bula Mines (A)

(a) What are your estimates of the cash flows from the mine? (Use O'Neill's forecast revenues, as you would require the price of ore in order to come up with your own figures.)

(b) Consider the following questions about the cash flows you have estimated:
(i) Do they include or exclude financing costs, and why? For example, what about the sums payable to Pat Wright? And what about future interest payments?
(ii) What are the differences between 'operating expenses', as disclosed by published accounts, and Bechtel's 'operating cost' estimates? Why are these figures so different (Exhibit 3)?
(iii) Can zinc (or other commodity) prices be expected to 'rise rapidly' over the near future?
(iv) What forecast have you made of inflation rates? Is it strictly necessary to make such a forecast when projecting cash flows, and if so, why?

(c) How risky is this mining project? Use your judgement on risk to estimate a ballpark discount rate.

(d) Use your previous response as a basis for calculating the value of the mine. What, then, should the government's payments for the mine be set at?

(e) What are the major assumptions regarding revenues, costs, timing and discount rates which lie behind your valuation? Discuss the realism of these assumptions, and the sensitivity of your valuation to changes in the assumptions.

10. London European Airways

(a) Estimate pretax cash flows for London European Airways (LEA) for the first 10 years of operations, making reasonable assumptions where necessary. (Assume the aircraft is purchased outright rather than through hire purchase.)

(b) Calculate the company's tax liability in each year (see Exhibit 9).

(c) Choose a suitable discount rate and calculate the net present value of the company's net cash flows.

(d) Have you worked in real or nominal terms? Why? What impact has your choice of method had on your results?

(e) Which of LEA's forecasts and assumptions are most critical? Which seem most questionable?

(f) How might we take account of competitors' reactions within your financial analysis? What implications would competitive reaction have for the project's NPV?

(g) How might the horizon value of the company be estimated, as at the end of the 10 year period? What impact does your estimate have on the NPV of the project?

(h) How would your view of the project differ if it was to be undertaken by a large established airline rather than by a start-up operation.

(i) How many shares should be offered to the public and at what price?

(j) How much do *you* think LEA is worth?

(k) Once LEA is floated, what do you think are the major business uncertainties which it will face? What contingency planning would you recommend?

11. Hesketh Motorcycles

(a) What range of retail prices is appropriate for the V1000 Sports Tourer? At low/middling/high retail prices, what levels of sales do you predict?

(b) Given your assumptions about price and volume, what levels of earnings and cash flows do you envisage from the V1000 Sports Tourer? How sensitive are your projected figures to cost overruns and other adverse factors?

(c) Value the V1000 Sports Tourer project on the basis of (i) pro forma earnings when production is 'on stream', and (ii) discounted future cash flows. Comment on the key assumptions you have to make.

(d) What value would you place on the company (Hesketh Motorcycles) as distinct from the project (the V1000)?

(e) What capital reconstruction would you recommend *prior* to the proposed flotation? What issue terms do you visualize as appropriate? In particular, what proportion of Hesketh Motorcycles should be retained by Tristar, and how many shares should be offered at what price?

PART D: ACQUISITION AND DIVESTMENT

12. Thorn-EMI (A)

(a) What were the causes of EMI's financially distressed condition in 1979?

(b) What options were open to EMI prior to the bid by Thorn? How serious was its financial position?

(c) Evaluate the commercial logic underlying Thorn's bid.

(d) What was the value of EMI to its shareholders? To Thorn? To other potential bidders?

(e) What options were open to EMI once the bid had been made? What should EMI's board do?

13. Hanson Trust

(a) What synergies are there in the proposed Hanson Trust/Imperial Group, Imperial/United Biscuits and United Biscuits/Imperial mergers? Is United Biscuits in a better position to buy Imperial than vice versa?

(b) Does the market think that synergy will be derived from the proposed mergers?

(c) What value does Imperial have as an acquisition candidate? What is the maximum amount Hanson should offer for Imperial? What should be its initial offer and its subsequent negotiating strategy?

(d) Do Imperial shareholders receive a fair stake in the initial and revised Hanson/Imperial and in the initial and revised United Biscuits/Imperial mergers? Who are the winners and losers in each of the alternative deals?

(e) Compare Imperial's share price to the values of the successive offers and suggest possible interpretations for the differences. In your opinion, what would happen to the price if either/both bids were withdrawn?

(f) Estimate the value of the Hanson 8 per cent convertible loan stock 2004/9 and of the Hanson 10 per cent convertible loan stock 2007/2012, for the days on which the offers were first made.

(g) Should Hanson's cash alternatives be underwritten? What are the arguments for and against underwriting such an offer?

(h) In whose interests were Morgan Grenfell's purchases, on its own account, of Imperial shares? What is *your* attitude to transactions of this kind?

(i) Which offer should Imperial shareholders have accepted?

(j) Recommend a contingency plan for Hanson if it is (i) successful, (ii) unsuccessful in acquiring Imperial.

(k) Recommend contingency plans for United Biscuits.

14. Anglian Canners

(a) As Amalgamated Food Products considering the possible sale of Anglian Canners, assess the minimum price which you would be prepared to accept. Base your price (at least initially) on the forecasts given in the exhibits to the case.

(b) What modifications (if any) do you feel should be made to these cash flow forecasts? Are they, for example, consistent with Anglian's historical track record? How would you set about verifying these figures?

(c) How sensitive is your estimate of Anglian's value to the various assumptions you have made?

(d) Under what circumstances might Amalgamated receive more than the minimum price (estimated in question (a)) for Anglian?

(e) What strategies could the management of Anglian adopt to increase the value of the business.

(f) How should Anglian be financed if it were sold off as a stand-alone company?

PART E: FINANCING DECISIONS

15. Commercial Union Assurance

(a) Should (can) companies make rights issues in a bear market? Could other companies have raised money in September 1974 or was the fund-raising ability restricted to a privileged few (see *Investors Chronicle* 27 September 1974 and *The Economist* 29 September 1974)?

(b) Did Commercial Union need the money? If you think so, explain why. What other options were open, and was a rights issue the best alternative?

(c) How did the market react to the news of the issue? Was this rational behaviour, or was it prima facie evidence of a market inefficiency? What will happen to the share price around the issue date?

(d) What was the cost of the new money to Commercial Union? If your answer differs from the views expressed in the financial press, explain why.

(e) In what way did the terms of the issue matter? Was the issue a real bargain to shareholders (*Evening Standard* 24 September 1974) or was there some 'unfairness to shareholders' (*Financial Times* 25 September 1974)? How does this reflect on the rights issue method? Would a placing at 60p have been fairer?

(f) Was the subunderwriting fee a fair one? If the issue had been subunderwritten at a higher price, was there a risk of a 'major disservice' to existing shareholders (*Financial Times* 28 September 1974), and if so, why? If the issue had been one for onc at 30p (see *Financial Times* 25 September 1974) how much would have been 'left to chance'?

16. British Telecom

(a) What impact will the privatization of British Telecom (BT) have on the cash flows to the government, and on the PSBR. In your view, who is likely to gain (or lose) from the privatization, and why? Should BT therefore be privatized?

(b) Who would lose and who would gain from a 'write-off' of (i) the pension fund liability, and (ii) National Loans Fund debt? Comment on the government's arguments, and on their net present value calculations.

(c) In your judgement, what level of gearing, and structure of debt would maximize the stock market valuation of BT and why? Explain which factors you have taken into account in reaching this judgement, and the importance you have attached to each.

(d) As an adviser to the government, what level of gearing would you recommend for BT and why?

(e) Similarly, as an adviser to BT, what level of gearing would you recommend and why? Would your advice differ if you were asked the same question say 2 years after privatization?

(f) Were the preference shares a good idea? If so, from whose perspective, and why?

(g) Assuming that BT agree to 'RPI-3' and to the proposed capital structure, what dividend policy should the company adopt, and why?

(h) What valuation methods are available for deciding on the worth of BT's shares. Which approach do you favour and why? What do you estimate BT to be worth?

(i) Looking ahead, devise a marketing plan for BT's shares, and suggest a set of issue terms. To what extent can good marketing alter the price the government will receive?

17. Williams (Hot Stampers) (A)

(a) Was Caversham Holdings' buyout offer sensible from Caversham's perspective? Was it a good deal for David White?

(b) What amount and type of financing was ideally required for Williams (Hot Stampers)?

(c) As a banker, evaluate Williams (Hot Stampers) as a lending proposition. How much would you lend them, and on what conditions and terms? Would your answer differ depending on whether you were Caversham Holdings' bank or the other bank?

(d) As David White, what kind of offer from the banks would be acceptable? What would be the 'minimal' package required to make the spin-off viable? How would you present your case to the banks?

PART F: VALUATION OF CORPORATE LIABILITIES

18. Redland

(a) What is the 'cost of debt' and 'cost of equity' for Redland? Critically appraise the views on this expressed in the case.

(b) Comment on Redland's gearing and debt policy (that is, on its capital structure; the split between fixed and floating rate borrowings; and on the currency profile of its debt.)

(c) At what price should Redland issue the zero coupon bond? What assumptions (if any) have you made about the likely characteristics of the bondholders?

19. Oasis Lines

(a) As a lessor, calculate the breakeven terms at which the lease is just profitable to you. Estimate how this breakeven point would change with (i) differing interest rates, and (ii) leases of different maturities. What tenders would you submit to the shipping companies?

(b) As Oasis Lines, calculate the breakeven terms at which the lease is just profitable to you. Estimate how this breakeven point would change with (i) differing interest rates and (ii) leases of differing maturities. What tender would you be prepared to accept from the leasing companies?

(c) Within what range of terms is the deal likely to be struck? What factors will influence where the deal falls within this band? Under what circumstances (if any) might a deal be undertaken outside of this range?

Note: This case is frequently conducted as a financial negotiating exercise, with some participants placed in the role of lessors, and some in the role of the shipping companies.

20. ICL

(a) What alternative actions did ICL have open to them in March 1981? What options did the British government have? In your view, was the government right to (i) support ICL, (ii) in this particular way?

(b) Critique the arguments put forward by the various analysts and commentators about the value of the guarantee. In your view, what, in principle, was the cost of the guarantee, and who benefited from it?

(c) Once the guarantee had been given and the £200 million drawn down, what do you estimate as the probability of the guarantee being called?

(d) Use option theory to value the guarantee, assuming that the banks' unsecured loan is the most junior of claims before shareholders, that is, the money is repaid only if all other liabilities are discharged in full. (To do this, first assess the value and volatility of ICL's equity, and hence of its assets, prior to the guarantee. Then assess the value and volatility of the assets after the guarantee has been given and the £200 million drawn down. Finally, value the banks' claim on ICL.)

(e) How would your answer to (d) change had the banks' claim ranked equally with other unsecured creditors? Do you think your estimate of the cost of the guarantee is a good estimate? How accurate is it? Which of your assumptions or simplifications seem most questionable? How would you improve or check your estimate?

21. National Westminster Bank

(a) What value would you have placed on the warrants in January 1970? Compare your conclusions with Mr Bailey's interpretation of market expectations and with Mr Bailey's own judgement (see Exhibit 3).

(b) Why should a company issue warrants? Which types of companies are likely to find issuing warrants relatively attractive? Why not just issue convertibles?

(c) What is the economic cost to National Westminster Bank's shareholders of granting the share options? What are the arguments for and against such an incentive scheme?

(d) Evaluate the terms of the rights issue (see Exhibit 4). Was subunderwriting provided at a fair fee? Should NatWest have dispensed with subunderwriting?

PART G: INTERNATIONAL FINANCE

22. Svenska Neuhaus

(a) Analyse all of the alternative options open to Svenska Neuhaus with regard to its foreign exchange exposure.

(b) What course of action would you advise? Justify your recommendation.

(c) Ericson has just received a newsletter on the Swedish economy giving the latest external deficit figures. The trade account had improved dramatically over the last year. Would you have any reservations about any of the hedging strategies, given this information? Explain.

23. Hallgarten Wines

(a) Comment on Peter Hallgarten's approach to managing the exchange risks and other international financial risks encountered by Hallgarten Wines.

(b) For what purposes might an exchange rate forecast be helpful to Hallgarten? What characteristics should Hallgarten look for in a forecasting service?

(c) Recommend how best to measure the firm's exchange rate exposure.

(d) Specify an operational financial strategy for Hallgarten Wines.

(e) How might Hallgarten Wines use currency futures or options as part of their financial strategy?

(f) How frequently should Peter Hallgarten revise his price list?

24. Cadbury Schweppes

(a) Through its US dollar commercial paper and a series of swaps, Cadbury Schweppes (CS) 'has effectively been able to borrow fixed rate sterling at rates showing appreciable savings over more conventional alternatives'. How, why, and are there any snags?

(b) Critically appraise CS' rationale for obtaining a US quotation.

(c) Compare and contrast the 1981 rights issue with the 1984 ADR issue. Did CS really 'save $12 million' by 'issuing equity in the US rather than in its domestic market'? Which issue was the more expensive, and why?

(d) Comment on CS' financial targets and policies, including the cost of capital figure. Were these various targets mutually consistent? Do you regard it as a good idea (i) to have such a set of policies? (ii) to publishing them?

(e) Comment on CS' gearing and debt policy (that is, on its gearing target, its actual borrowings, its split between fixed and floating rate borrowings, and on the maturity structure and currency profile of its debt). If you are critical of CS, suggest and justify an alternative policy.

(f) What is your view on CS' approach to the management of foreign exchange exposure? What are they trying to hedge, and why? What alternative approach, if any, would you advocate?

(g) Did the rise in the dollar mean that 'action was required . . . with some urgency' in early 1985? What alternative courses of action were available? Critique the arguments used for and against each. Was the convertible issue the best solution?

(h) Assuming the convertible bonds are issued at par, what can you say (quantitatively if possible) about (i) the implicit price that is being paid for the option, (ii) the decision to convert or not after 5 years, (iii) the probability of conversion, (iv) the volatility that should be used to value the option.

(i) Explain qualitatively how you would expect the value of the convertible to depend upon (i) the long term US interest rate, (ii) the dollar/pound exchange rate, (iii) the sterling price of CS equity, (iv) the coupon differential compared with straight bonds, (v) the conversion premium, (vi) the length of the grace period, (vii) the maturity of the bonds, (viii) the terms of the call provision.

(j) One motivation for the issue was to hedge dollar exposure. Explain how the issuance of a convertible rather than straight debt affects the extent of this hedging.

(k) Given the terms of the issue, at what price should the convertible bonds be sold? Comment briefly on Martin Bralsford's valuation procedure.

(l) What would you say were the key qualities required of a corporate treasurer? What kind of background and training would you see as appropriate?

PART H: FINANCIAL PLANNING

25. Precision Engineering (A)

(a) Critique Precision Engineering's (PE) short-term budgets and plans as prepared for the Industrial and Commercial Finance Corporation (ICFC) presentation. Do you regard these as being 'extremely conservative'?

(b) For PE's internal purposes, what systems would you recommend for cash budgeting and short-term financial planning?

(c) What are the benefits and risks arising from PE's relationship with the Davy Corporation? Should it be part of PE's future strategy to seek involvement in Davy's non-metal activities?

(d) Evaluate PE's future plans and strategy. Does PE have a long term future?

(e) What type of financing should PE be seeking? Explain why.

(f) Could PE present a better case to ICFC? If so, how?

(g) As ICFC, would you be prepared to back PE with £250 000? If so, what form would the financing take, and what would be the terms and conditions?

(h) What contingency plans should PE's directors have in case ICFC turns them down?

(i) When the turnaround specialists bought PE for £1 from Nostra Holdings in April 1982, did they get a bargain? What do you think PE's shares were worth at that time? What do you think they were worth 7 months later in November 1982, at the time of the approach to ICFC?

26. Wallis Fashion Group

(a) What were the critical factors influencing Wallis Fashion Group's choice of dividend policy? How did these factors work through to dividend decisions? Compare your interpretation of Wallis's dividend policy with the policies of other quoted companies.

(b) 'It was no surprise that doubling the dividend (in July 1978) led to a doubling of the share price within a few days. After all, the company was paying shareholders more income than they previously received, and this increase had not been discounted by the stock market.' How would you respond to this argument favouring high dividends?

(c) Quite apart from the immediate decisions to be made by the Wallis directors, the board would be helped by having a long-term policy for dividends. What are the arguments for having an above, equal to, or below average yield, relative to comparable companies within the industry? Distinguish between those arguments which apply to listed companies in general and those which relate specifically to Wallis Fashion Group.

(d) Evaluate the recent financial management of Wallis Fashion Group, especially its control of working capital and profit margins.

(e) By preparing a pro forma statement of sources and uses of funds, judge the ability of the company to find the cash to meet its dividend commitments.

(f) What alternatives does Wallis Fashion Group face for its dividend payment for the financial year ending 31 January 1979? What are the arguments for and against each of these alternatives?

(g) As a security analyst, how would you interpret the alternative signals which Wallis' dividend decision might convey to the market? As an investment manager, how would your research efforts have been directed at the time of the case (July 1979?)

(h) As a corporate finance specialist, what advice would you offer the company?

(i) Assume you are a lending officer in a bank which has provided finance to Wallis Fashion Group. What are you going to do now?

27. Burmah Oil

(a) What were the strategic alternatives open to Burmah in 1962? Which option would you personally have advocated, and why?

(b) Evaluate Burmah's debt policy in the context of its BP and Shell holdings as originally advocated in 1962, and as subsequently implemented. How did Burmah's debt policy influence its corporate development?

(c) In what way was BP and Shell's dividend policy relevant to Burmah?

(d) Evaluate the strategy behind Burmah's programme of both internal expansion and acquisitions during the period 1962–1972. One motive for Burmah's acquisition programme was to 'increase the spread and reduce the intensity of risk' by entering new areas of business. Comment.

(e) What is the economic justification which would support the Burmah board's preoccupation with vertical integration of the company? Specifically evaluate the stated rationale and economic logic of integrating forwards into retail distribution (Halfords), and integrating backwards into oil tankers.

(f) How carefully had Burmah done its strategic financial planning? What more might the company have done? Was Burmah just unlucky in 1974, or was its demise the result of inadequate long-term financial planning?

(g) Was Burmah facing bankruptcy in early 1975? If not, why couldn't Burmah have turned to its shareholders for help? Comment on Burmah's financing strategy.

(h) Was the sale of BP shares unfair to Burmah's shareholders? If so, in what way? Does the Burmah Shareholders Action Group have a case?

(i) Suggest and comment on alternative methods for deciding on a purchase price for the BP shares?